Solutions Manual and Supplementary Materials for

Econometric Analysis of Cross Section and Panel Data

Solutions Manual and Supplementary Materials for ***Econometric Analysis of Cross Section and Panel Data***

Jeffrey M. Wooldridge

The MIT Press
Cambridge, Massachusetts
London, England

This book was set in Courier by the author and was printed and bound in the United States of America.

ISBN: 0-262-23233-2

10 9 8 7 6 5 4

CONTENTS

PREFACE

This manual contains the solutions to many of the problems in the book *Econometric Analysis of Cross Section and Panel Data*, by Jeffrey M. Wooldridge, MIT Press, 2002. In addition to solutions to the odd-numbered exercises, I have included solutions to some of the more interesting even-numbered exercises. Also included are several "bonus questions," along with answers, that were either excluded because of space constraints or because they have occurred to me since the text was published.

The empirical examples are solved using various versions of Stata, from 4.0 through 7.0. Because it is helpful to see the computer output of a widely used econometrics package, I have included Stata output rather than type tables. In some cases, my calculations are more tedious than necessary if one uses features appearing in more recent versions of Stata.

In writing these solutions, I have tried to provide, in addition to the algebra, discussions about why a particular problem is interesting, why I solved the problem the way I did, or which conclusions would change if we varied some assumptions.

For instructors adopting the text for a course, I can provide pdf or postscript files containing answers to all of the questions. I would appreciate learning about mistakes to any of the problem solutions, preferably by email at wooldri1@msu.edu.

Jeffrey M. Wooldridge
Michigan State University

SOLUTIONS TO CHAPTER 2 PROBLEMS

2.1. a. $\dfrac{\partial E(y|x_1,x_2)}{\partial x_1} = \beta_1 + \beta_4 x_2$ and $\dfrac{\partial E(y|x_1,x_2)}{\partial x_2} = \beta_2 + 2\beta_3 x_2 + \beta_4 x_1$.

b. By definition, $E(u|x_1,x_2) = 0$. Because x_2^2 and x_1x_2 are just functions of (x_1,x_2), it does not matter whether we also condition on them: $E(u|x_1,x_2,x_2^2,x_1x_2) = 0$.

c. All we can say about $Var(u|x_1,x_2)$ is that it is nonnegative for all x_1 and x_2: $E(u|x_1,x_2) = 0$ in no way restricts $Var(u|x_1,x_2)$.

2.3. a. $y = \beta_0 + \beta_1 x_1 + \beta_2 x_2 + \beta_3 x_1 x_2 + u$, where u has a zero mean given x_1 and x_2: $E(u|x_1,x_2) = 0$. We can say nothing further about u.

b. $\partial E(y|x_1,x_2)/\partial x_1 = \beta_1 + \beta_3 x_2$. Because $E(x_2) = 0$, $\beta_1 = E[\partial E(y|x_1,x_2)/\partial x_1]$. Similarly, $\beta_2 = E[\partial E(y|x_1,x_2)/\partial x_2]$.

c. If x_1 and x_2 are independent with zero mean then $E(x_1x_2) = E(x_1)E(x_2) = 0$. Further, the covariance between x_1x_2 and x_1 is $E(x_1x_2\cdot x_1) = E(x_1^2 x_2) = E(x_1^2)E(x_2)$ (by independence) $= 0$. A similar argument shows that the covariance between x_1x_2 and x_2 is zero. But then the linear projection of x_1x_2 onto $(1,x_1,x_2)$ is identically zero. Now just use the law of iterated projections (Property LP.5 in Appendix 2A):

$$\begin{aligned} L(y|1,x_1,x_2) &= L(\beta_0 + \beta_1 x_1 + \beta_2 x_2 + \beta_3 x_1 x_2 | 1,x_1,x_2) \\ &= \beta_0 + \beta_1 x_1 + \beta_2 x_2 + \beta_3 L(x_1x_2|1,x_1,x_2) \\ &= \beta_0 + \beta_1 x_1 + \beta_2 x_2. \end{aligned}$$

d. Equation (2.47) is more useful because it allows us to compute the partial effects of x_1 and x_2 at *any* values of x_1 and x_2. Under the assumptions we have made, the linear projection in (2.48) does have as its slope coefficients on x_1 and x_2 the partial effects at the population average values of x_1 and x_2 -- zero in both cases -- but it does not allow us to obtain the partial effects at any other values of x_1 and x_2. Incidentally, the main conclusions of this problem go through if we allow x_1 and x_2 to have any population means.

2.5. By definition, $\mathrm{Var}(u_1|\mathbf{x},\mathbf{z}) = \mathrm{Var}(y|\mathbf{x},\mathbf{z})$ and $\mathrm{Var}(u_2|\mathbf{x}) = \mathrm{Var}(y|\mathbf{x})$. By assumption, these are constant and necessarily equal to $\sigma_1^2 \equiv \mathrm{Var}(u_1)$ and $\sigma_2^2 \equiv \mathrm{Var}(u_2)$, respectively. But then Property CV.4 implies that $\sigma_2^2 \geq \sigma_1^2$. This simple conclusion means that, when error variances are constant, the error variance falls as more explanatory variables are conditioned on.

2.7. Write the equation in error form as

$$y = g(\mathbf{x}) + \mathbf{z}\boldsymbol{\beta} + u, \ \mathrm{E}(u|\mathbf{x},\mathbf{z}) = 0.$$

Take the expected value of this equation conditional only on $\mathbf{x}$:

$$\mathrm{E}(y|\mathbf{x}) = g(\mathbf{x}) + [\mathrm{E}(\mathbf{z}|\mathbf{x})]\boldsymbol{\beta},$$

and subtract this from the first equation to get

$$y - \mathrm{E}(y|\mathbf{x}) = [\mathbf{z} - \mathrm{E}(\mathbf{z}|\mathbf{x})]\boldsymbol{\beta} + u$$

or $\tilde{y} = \tilde{\mathbf{z}}\boldsymbol{\beta} + u$. Because $\tilde{\mathbf{z}}$ is a function of $(\mathbf{x},\mathbf{z})$, $\mathrm{E}(u|\tilde{\mathbf{z}}) = 0$ (since $\mathrm{E}(u|\mathbf{x},\mathbf{z}) = 0$), and so $\mathrm{E}(\tilde{y}|\tilde{\mathbf{z}}) = \tilde{\mathbf{z}}\boldsymbol{\beta}$. This basic result is fundamental in the literature on estimating *partial linear models*. First, one estimates $\mathrm{E}(y|\mathbf{x})$ and $\mathrm{E}(\mathbf{z}|\mathbf{x})$ using very flexible methods, typically, so-called *nonparametric methods*. Then, after obtaining residuals of the form $\tilde{y}_i \equiv y_i - \hat{\mathrm{E}}(y_i|\mathbf{x}_i)$ and $\tilde{\mathbf{z}}_i \equiv \mathbf{z}_i$ - - $\hat{\mathrm{E}}(\mathbf{z}_i|\mathbf{x}_i)$, $\boldsymbol{\beta}$ is estimated from an OLS regression $\tilde{y}_i$ on $\tilde{\mathbf{z}}_i$, $i = 1,\ldots,N$. Under general conditions, this kind of nonparametric partialling-out procedure leads to a $\sqrt{N}$-consistent, asymptotically normal estimator of $\boldsymbol{\beta}$. See Robinson (1988) and Powell (1994).

SOLUTIONS TO CHAPTER 3 PROBLEMS

3.1. To prove Lemma 3.1, we must show that for all $\varepsilon > 0$, there exists $b_\varepsilon < \infty$ and an integer N_ε such that $P[|x_N| \geq b_\varepsilon] < \varepsilon$, all $N \geq N_\varepsilon$. We use the following fact: since $x_N \overset{p}{\rightarrow} a$, for any $\varepsilon > 0$ there exists an integer N_ε such that $P[|x_N - a| > 1] < \varepsilon$ for all $N \geq N_\varepsilon$. [The existence of N_ε is implied by Definition 3.3(1).] But $|x_N| = |x_N - a + a| \leq |x_N - a| + |a|$ (by the triangle inequality), and so $|x_N| - |a| \leq |x_N - a|$. It follows that $P[|x_N| - |a| > 1] \leq P[|x_N - a| > 1]$. Therefore, in Definition 3.3(3) we can take $b_\varepsilon \equiv |a| + 1$ (irrespective of the value of ε) and then the existence of N_ε follows from Definition 3.3(1).

3.3. This follows immediately from Lemma 3.1 because $\mathbf{g}(\mathbf{x}_N) \overset{p}{\rightarrow} \mathbf{g}(\mathbf{c})$.

3.5. a. Since $\text{Var}(\bar{y}_N) = \sigma^2/N$, $\text{Var}[\sqrt{N}(\bar{y}_N - \mu)] = N(\sigma^2/N) = \sigma^2$.

b. By the CLT, $\sqrt{N}(\bar{y}_N - \mu) \overset{a}{\sim} \text{Normal}(0,\sigma^2)$, and so $\text{Avar}[\sqrt{N}(\bar{y}_N - \mu)] = \sigma^2$.

c. We Obtain $\text{Avar}(\bar{y}_N)$ by dividing $\text{Avar}[\sqrt{N}(\bar{y}_N - \mu)]$ by N. Therefore, $\text{Avar}(\bar{y}_N) = \sigma^2/N$. As expected, this coincides with the actual variance of $\bar{y}_N$.

d. The asymptotic standard deviation of $\bar{y}_N$ is the square root of its asymptotic variance, or $\sigma/\sqrt{N}$.

e. To obtain the asymptotic standard error of $\bar{y}_N$, we need a consistent estimator of σ. Typically, the unbiased estimator of σ^2 is used: $\hat{\sigma}^2 = (N - 1)^{-1}\sum_{i=1}^{N}(y_i - \bar{y}_N)^2$, and then $\hat{\sigma}$ is the positive square root. The asymptotic standard error of $\bar{y}_N$ is simply $\hat{\sigma}/\sqrt{N}$.

3.7. a. For $\theta > 0$ the natural logarithim is a continuous function, and so $\text{plim}[\log(\hat{\theta})] = \log[\text{plim}(\hat{\theta})] = \log(\theta) = \gamma$.

b. We use the delta method to find $\text{Avar}[\sqrt{N}(\hat{\gamma} - \gamma)]$. In the scalar case, if $\hat{\gamma} = g(\hat{\theta})$ then $\text{Avar}[\sqrt{N}(\hat{\gamma} - \gamma)] = [dg(\theta)/d\theta]^2\text{Avar}[\sqrt{N}(\hat{\theta} - \theta)]$. When $g(\theta) = \log(\theta)$ -- which is, of course, continuously differentiable -- $\text{Avar}[\sqrt{N}(\hat{\gamma} - \gamma)] = (1/\theta)^2\text{Avar}[\sqrt{N}(\hat{\theta} - \theta)]$.

c. In the scalar case, the asymptotic standard error of $\hat{\gamma}$ is generally $|dg(\hat{\theta})/d\theta|\cdot\text{se}(\hat{\theta})$. Therefore, for $g(\theta) = \log(\theta)$, $\text{se}(\hat{\gamma}) = \text{se}(\hat{\theta})/\hat{\theta}$. When $\hat{\theta} = 4$ and $\text{se}(\hat{\theta}) = 2$, $\hat{\gamma} = \log(4) \approx 1.39$ and $\text{se}(\hat{\gamma}) = 1/2$.

d. The asymptotic t statistic for testing H_0: $\theta = 1$ is $(\hat{\theta} - 1)/\text{se}(\hat{\theta}) = 3/2 = 1.5$.

e. Because $\gamma = \log(\theta)$, the null of interest can also be stated as H_0: $\gamma = 0$. The t statistic based on $\hat{\gamma}$ is about $1.39/(.5) = 2.78$. This leads to a very strong rejection of H_0, whereas the t statistic based on $\hat{\theta}$ is, at best, marginally significant. The lesson is that, using the Wald test, we can change the outcome of hypotheses tests by using nonlinear transformations.

3.9. By the delta method,

$$\text{Avar}[\sqrt{N}(\hat{\boldsymbol{\gamma}} - \boldsymbol{\gamma})] = \mathbf{G}(\boldsymbol{\theta})\mathbf{V}_1\mathbf{G}(\boldsymbol{\theta})', \quad \text{Avar}[\sqrt{N}(\tilde{\boldsymbol{\gamma}} - \boldsymbol{\gamma})] = \mathbf{G}(\boldsymbol{\theta})\mathbf{V}_2\mathbf{G}(\boldsymbol{\theta})',$$

where $\mathbf{G}(\boldsymbol{\theta}) = \nabla_\theta \mathbf{g}(\boldsymbol{\theta})$ is $Q \times P$. Therefore,

$$\text{Avar}[\sqrt{N}(\tilde{\boldsymbol{\gamma}} - \boldsymbol{\gamma})] - \text{Avar}[\sqrt{N}(\hat{\boldsymbol{\gamma}} - \boldsymbol{\gamma})] = \mathbf{G}(\boldsymbol{\theta})(\mathbf{V}_2 - \mathbf{V}_1)\mathbf{G}(\boldsymbol{\theta})'.$$

By assumption, $\mathbf{V}_2 - \mathbf{V}_1$ is positive semi-definite, and therefore $\mathbf{G}(\boldsymbol{\theta})(\mathbf{V}_2 - \mathbf{V}_1)\mathbf{G}(\boldsymbol{\theta})'$ is p.s.d. This completes the proof.

SOLUTIONS TO CHAPTER 4 PROBLEMS

4.1. a. Exponentiating equation (4.49) gives

$$\begin{aligned} wage &= \exp(\beta_0 + \beta_1 married + \beta_2 educ + \mathbf{z}\boldsymbol{\gamma} + u) \\ &= \exp(u)\exp(\beta_0 + \beta_1 married + \beta_2 educ + \mathbf{z}\boldsymbol{\gamma}). \end{aligned}$$

Therefore,

$$\mathrm{E}(wage|\mathbf{x}) = \mathrm{E}[\exp(u)|\mathbf{x}]\exp(\beta_0 + \beta_1 married + \beta_2 educ + \mathbf{z}\boldsymbol{\gamma}),$$

where $\mathbf{x}$ denotes all explanatory variables. Now, if u and $\mathbf{x}$ are independent then $\mathrm{E}[\exp(u)|\mathbf{x}] = \mathrm{E}[\exp(u)] = \delta_0$, say. Therefore

$$\mathrm{E}(wage|\mathbf{x}) = \delta_0\exp(\beta_0 + \beta_1 married + \beta_2 educ + \mathbf{z}\boldsymbol{\gamma}).$$

Now, finding the proportionate difference in this expectation at $married = 1$ and $married = 0$ (with all else equal) gives $\exp(\beta_1) - 1$; all other factors cancel out. Thus, the percentage difference is $100\cdot[\exp(\beta_1) - 1]$.

b. Since $\theta_1 = 100\cdot[\exp(\beta_1) - 1] = g(\beta_1)$, we need the derivative of g with respect to β_1: $dg/d\beta_1 = 100\cdot\exp(\beta_1)$. The asymptotic standard error of $\hat{\theta}_1$ using the delta method is obtained as the absolute value of $d\hat{g}/d\beta_1$ times $\mathrm{se}(\hat{\beta}_1)$:

$$\mathrm{se}(\hat{\theta}_1) = [100\cdot\exp(\hat{\beta}_1)]\cdot\mathrm{se}(\hat{\beta}_1).$$

c. We can evaluate the conditional expectation in part (a) at two levels of education, say $educ_0$ and $educ_1$, all else fixed. The proportionate change in expected wage from $educ_0$ to $educ_1$ is

$$\begin{aligned} &[\exp(\beta_2 educ_1) - \exp(\beta_2 educ_0)]/\exp(\beta_2 educ_0) \\ &\quad = \exp[\beta_2(educ_1 - educ_0)] - 1 = \exp(\beta_2\Delta educ) - 1. \end{aligned}$$

Using the same arguments in part (b), $\hat{\theta}_2 = 100\cdot[\exp(\hat{\beta}_2\Delta educ) - 1]$ and

$$\mathrm{se}(\hat{\theta}_2) = 100\cdot|\Delta educ|\exp(\hat{\beta}_2\Delta educ)\mathrm{se}(\hat{\beta}_2)$$

d. For the estimated version of equation (4.29), $\hat{\beta}_1 = .199$, $\mathrm{se}(\hat{\beta}_1) =$

.039, $\hat{\beta}_2$ = .065, se($\hat{\beta}_2$) = .006. Therefore, $\hat{\theta}_1$ = 22.01 and se($\hat{\theta}_1$) = 4.76. For $\hat{\theta}_2$ we set $\Delta educ$ = 4. Then $\hat{\theta}_2$ = 29.7 and se($\hat{\theta}_2$) = 3.11.

4.3. a. Not in general. The conditional variance can always be written as $\mathrm{Var}(u|\mathbf{x}) = \mathrm{E}(u^2|\mathbf{x}) - [\mathrm{E}(u|\mathbf{x})]^2$; if $\mathrm{E}(u|\mathbf{x}) \neq 0$, then $\mathrm{E}(u^2|\mathbf{x}) \neq \mathrm{Var}(u|\mathbf{x})$.

b. It could be that $\mathrm{E}(\mathbf{x}'u) = \mathbf{0}$, in which case OLS is consistent, and $\mathrm{Var}(u|\mathbf{x})$ is constant. But, generally, the usual standard errors would not be valid unless $\mathrm{E}(u|\mathbf{x}) = 0$.

4.5. Write equation (4.50) as $\mathrm{E}(y|\mathbf{w}) = \mathbf{w}\boldsymbol{\delta}$, where $\mathbf{w} = (\mathbf{x}, z)$. Since $\mathrm{Var}(y|\mathbf{w}) = \sigma^2$, it follows by Theorem 4.2 that Avar $\sqrt{N}(\hat{\boldsymbol{\delta}} - \boldsymbol{\delta})$ is $\sigma^2[\mathrm{E}(\mathbf{w}'\mathbf{w})]^{-1}$, where $\hat{\boldsymbol{\delta}} = (\hat{\boldsymbol{\beta}}', \hat{\gamma})'$. Importantly, because $\mathrm{E}(\mathbf{x}'z) = \mathbf{0}$, $\mathrm{E}(\mathbf{w}'\mathbf{w})$ is block diagonal, with upper block $\mathrm{E}(\mathbf{x}'\mathbf{x})$ and lower block $\mathrm{E}(z^2)$. Inverting $\mathrm{E}(\mathbf{w}'\mathbf{w})$ and focusing on the upper $K \times K$ block gives

$$\text{Avar } \sqrt{N}(\hat{\boldsymbol{\beta}} - \boldsymbol{\beta}) = \sigma^2[\mathrm{E}(\mathbf{x}'\mathbf{x})]^{-1}.$$

Next, we need to find Avar $\sqrt{N}(\tilde{\boldsymbol{\beta}} - \boldsymbol{\beta})$. It is helpful to write $y = \mathbf{x}\boldsymbol{\beta} + v$ where $v = \gamma z + u$ and $u \equiv y - \mathrm{E}(y|\mathbf{x}, z)$. Because $\mathrm{E}(\mathbf{x}'z) = \mathbf{0}$ and $\mathrm{E}(\mathbf{x}'u) = \mathbf{0}$, $\mathrm{E}(\mathbf{x}'v) = \mathbf{0}$. Further, $\mathrm{E}(v^2|\mathbf{x}) = \gamma^2\mathrm{E}(z^2|\mathbf{x}) + \mathrm{E}(u^2|\mathbf{x}) + 2\gamma\mathrm{E}(zu|\mathbf{x}) = \gamma^2\mathrm{E}(z^2|\mathbf{x}) + \sigma^2$, where we use $\mathrm{E}(zu|\mathbf{x},z) = z\mathrm{E}(u|\mathbf{x},z) = 0$ and $\mathrm{E}(u^2|\mathbf{x},z) = \mathrm{Var}(y|\mathbf{x},z) = \sigma^2$. Unless $\mathrm{E}(z^2|\mathbf{x})$ is constant, the equation $y = \mathbf{x}\boldsymbol{\beta} + v$ generally violates the homoskedasticity assumption OLS.3. So, without further assumptions,

$$\text{Avar } \sqrt{N}(\tilde{\boldsymbol{\beta}} - \boldsymbol{\beta}) = [\mathrm{E}(\mathbf{x}'\mathbf{x})]^{-1}\mathrm{E}(v^2\mathbf{x}'\mathbf{x})[\mathrm{E}(\mathbf{x}'\mathbf{x})]^{-1}.$$

Now we can show Avar $\sqrt{N}(\tilde{\boldsymbol{\beta}} - \boldsymbol{\beta})$ - Avar $\sqrt{N}(\hat{\boldsymbol{\beta}} - \boldsymbol{\beta})$ is positive semi-definite by writing

$$\text{Avar } \sqrt{N}(\tilde{\boldsymbol{\beta}} - \boldsymbol{\beta}) - \text{Avar } \sqrt{N}(\hat{\boldsymbol{\beta}} - \boldsymbol{\beta})$$

$$= [\mathrm{E}(\mathbf{x}'\mathbf{x})]^{-1}\mathrm{E}(v^2\mathbf{x}'\mathbf{x})[\mathrm{E}(\mathbf{x}'\mathbf{x})]^{-1} - \sigma^2[\mathrm{E}(\mathbf{x}'\mathbf{x})]^{-1}$$

$$= [\mathrm{E}(\mathbf{x}'\mathbf{x})]^{-1}\mathrm{E}(v^2\mathbf{x}'\mathbf{x})[\mathrm{E}(\mathbf{x}'\mathbf{x})]^{-1} - \sigma^2[\mathrm{E}(\mathbf{x}'\mathbf{x})]^{-1}\mathrm{E}(\mathbf{x}'\mathbf{x})[\mathrm{E}(\mathbf{x}'\mathbf{x})]^{-1}$$

$$= [\mathrm{E}(\mathbf{x}'\mathbf{x})]^{-1}[\mathrm{E}(v^2\mathbf{x}'\mathbf{x}) - \sigma^2\mathrm{E}(\mathbf{x}'\mathbf{x})][\mathrm{E}(\mathbf{x}'\mathbf{x})]^{-1}.$$

Because $[\mathrm{E}(\mathbf{x}'\mathbf{x})]^{-1}$ is positive definite, it suffices to show that $\mathrm{E}(v^2\mathbf{x}'\mathbf{x}) - \sigma^2\mathrm{E}(\mathbf{x}'\mathbf{x})$ is p.s.d. To this end, let $h(\mathbf{x}) \equiv \mathrm{E}(z^2|\mathbf{x})$. Then by the law of iterated expectations, $\mathrm{E}(v^2\mathbf{x}'\mathbf{x}) = \mathrm{E}[\mathrm{E}(v^2|\mathbf{x})\mathbf{x}'\mathbf{x}] = \gamma^2\mathrm{E}[h(\mathbf{x})\mathbf{x}'\mathbf{x}] + \sigma^2\mathrm{E}(\mathbf{x}'\mathbf{x})$. Therefore, $\mathrm{E}(v^2\mathbf{x}'\mathbf{x}) - \sigma^2\mathrm{E}(\mathbf{x}'\mathbf{x}) = \gamma^2\mathrm{E}[h(\mathbf{x})\mathbf{x}'\mathbf{x}]$, which, when $\gamma \neq 0$, is actually a positive definite matrix except by fluke. In particular, if $\mathrm{E}(z^2|\mathbf{x}) = \mathrm{E}(z^2) = \eta^2 > 0$ (in which case $y = \mathbf{x}\boldsymbol{\beta} + v$ satisfies the homoskedasticity assumption OLS.3), $\mathrm{E}(v^2\mathbf{x}'\mathbf{x}) - \sigma^2\mathrm{E}(\mathbf{x}'\mathbf{x}) = \gamma^2\eta^2\mathrm{E}(\mathbf{x}'\mathbf{x})$, which is positive definite.

4.7. a. One important omitted factor in u is family income: students that come from wealthier families tend to do better in school, other things equal. Family income and PC ownership are positively correlated because the probability of owning a PC increases with family income. Another factor in u is quality of high school. This may also be correlated with *PC*: a student who had more exposure with computers in high school may be more likely to own a computer.

b. $\hat{\beta}_3$ is *likely* to have an upward bias because of the positive correlation between u and *PC*, but it is not clear-cut because of the other explanatory variables in the equation. If we write the linear projection

$$u = \delta_0 + \delta_1 hsGPA + \delta_2 SAT + \delta_3 PC + r$$

then the bias is upward if δ_3 is greater than zero. This measures the partial correlation between u (say, family income) and *PC*, and it is likely to be positive.

c. If data on family income can be collected then it can be included in the equation. If family income is not available sometimes level of parents' education is. Another possibility is to use average house value in each student's home zip code, as zip code is often part of school records. Proxies for high school quality might be faculty-student ratios, expenditure per student, average teacher salary, and so on.

4.9. a. Just subtract $\log(y_{-1})$ from both sides:

$$\Delta\log(y) = \beta_0 + \mathbf{x}\boldsymbol{\beta} + (\alpha_1 - 1)\log(y_{-1}) + u.$$

Clearly, the intercept and slope estimates on $\mathbf{x}$ will be the same. The coefficient on $\log(y_{-1})$ changes.

b. For simplicity, let $w = \log(y)$, $w_{-1} = \log(y_{-1})$. Then the population slope coefficient in a simple regression is always $\alpha_1 = \mathrm{Cov}(w_{-1},w)/\mathrm{Var}(w_{-1})$. But, by assumption, $\mathrm{Var}(w) = \mathrm{Var}(w_{-1})$, so we can write $\alpha_1 = \mathrm{Cov}(w_{-1},w)/(\sigma_{w_{-1}}\sigma_w)$, where $\sigma_{w_{-1}} = \mathrm{sd}(w_{-1})$ and $\sigma_w = \mathrm{sd}(w)$. But $\mathrm{Corr}(w_{-1},w) = \mathrm{Cov}(w_{-1},w)/(\sigma_{w_{-1}}\sigma_w)$, and since a correlation coefficient is always between -1 and 1, the result follows.

4.11. Here is some Stata output obtained to answer this question:

```
. reg lwage exper tenure married south urban black educ iq kww

  Source |       SS       df       MS                  Number of obs =     935
---------+------------------------------               F(  9,   925) =   37.28
   Model |  44.0967944     9  4.89964382               Prob > F      =  0.0000
Residual |  121.559489   925  .131415664               R-squared     =  0.2662
---------+------------------------------               Adj R-squared =  0.2591
   Total |  165.656283   934  .177362188               Root MSE      =  .36251

------------------------------------------------------------------------------
   lwage |      Coef.   Std. Err.       t     P>|t|       [95% Conf. Interval]
---------+--------------------------------------------------------------------
   exper |   .0127522   .0032308      3.947   0.000       .0064117    .0190927
  tenure |   .0109248   .0024457      4.467   0.000        .006125    .0157246
 married |   .1921449   .0389094      4.938   0.000       .1157839    .2685059
   south |  -.0820295   .0262222     -3.128   0.002      -.1334913   -.0305676
   urban |   .1758226   .0269095      6.534   0.000       .1230118    .2286334
```

```
       black |  -.1303995   .0399014     -3.268   0.001      -.2087073   -.0520917
        educ |   .0498375    .007262      6.863   0.000       .0355856    .0640893
          iq |   .0031183   .0010128      3.079   0.002       .0011306    .0051059
         kww |    .003826   .0018521      2.066   0.039       .0001911    .0074608
       _cons |   5.175644    .127776     40.506   0.000       4.924879    5.426408
------------------------------------------------------------------------------

. test iq kww

 ( 1)  iq = 0.0
 ( 2)  kww = 0.0

       F(  2,   925) =    8.59
            Prob > F =    0.0002
```

a. The estimated return to education using both *IQ* and *KWW* as proxies for ability is about 5%. When we used no proxy the estimated return was about 6.5%, and with only *IQ* as a proxy it was about 5.4%. Thus, we have an even lower estimated return to education, but it is still practically nontrivial and statistically very significant.

b. We can see from the t statistics that these variables are going to be jointly significant. The F test verifies this, with p-value = .0002.

c. The wage differential between nonblacks and blacks does not disappear. Blacks are estimated to earn about 13% less than nonblacks, holding all other factors fixed.

4.13. a. Using the 90 counties for 1987 gives the following Stata output:

```
. reg lcrmrte lprbarr lprbconv lprbpris lavgsen if d87

      Source |       SS       df       MS              Number of obs =      90
-------------+------------------------------           F(  4,    85) =   15.15
       Model |  11.1549601     4  2.78874002           Prob > F      =  0.0000
    Residual |  15.6447379    85   .18405574           R-squared     =  0.4162
-------------+------------------------------           Adj R-squared =  0.3888
       Total |   26.799698    89  .301120202           Root MSE      =  .42902

------------------------------------------------------------------------------
     lcrmrte |      Coef.   Std. Err.       t     P>|t|       [95% Conf. Interval]
-------------+----------------------------------------------------------------
```

lprbarr	-.7239696	.1153163	-6.28	0.000	-.9532493	-.4946899
lprbconv	-.4725112	.0831078	-5.69	0.000	-.6377519	-.3072706
lprbpris	.1596698	.2064441	0.77	0.441	-.2507964	.570136
lavgsen	.0764213	.1634732	0.47	0.641	-.2486073	.4014499
_cons	-4.867922	.4315307	-11.28	0.000	-5.725921	-4.009923

Because of the log-log functional form, all coefficients are elasticities. The elasticities of crime with respect to the arrest and conviction probabilities are the sign we expect, and both are practically and statistically significant. The elasticities with respect to the probability of serving a prison term and the average sentence length are positive but are statistically insignificant.

b. To add the previous year's crime rate we first generate the lag:

```
. gen lcrmr_1 = lcrmrte[_n-1] if d87
(540 missing values generated)

. reg lcrmrte lprbarr lprbconv lprbpris lavgsen lcrmr_1 if d87
```

Source	SS	df	MS
Model	23.3549731	5	4.67099462
Residual	3.4447249	84	.04100863
Total	26.799698	89	.301120202

Number of obs	90
F(5, 84)	113.90
Prob > F	0.0000
R-squared	0.8715
Adj R-squared	0.8638
Root MSE	.20251

lcrmrte	Coef.	Std. Err.	t	P>|t|	[95% Conf.	Interval]
lprbarr	-.1850424	.0627624	-2.95	0.004	-.3098523	-.0602325
lprbconv	-.0386768	.0465999	-0.83	0.409	-.1313457	.0539921
lprbpris	-.1266874	.0988505	-1.28	0.204	-.3232625	.0698876
lavgsen	-.1520228	.0782915	-1.94	0.056	-.3077141	.0036684
lcrmr_1	.7798129	.0452114	17.25	0.000	.6899051	.8697208
_cons	-.7666256	.3130986	-2.45	0.016	-1.389257	-.1439946

There are some notable changes in the coefficients on the original variables. The elasticities with respect to *prbarr* and *prbconv* are much smaller now, but still have signs predicted by a deterrent-effect story. The conviction probability is no longer statistically significant. Adding the lagged crime rate changes the signs of the elasticities with respect to *prbpris* and *avgsen*, and the latter is almost statistically significant at the 5% level against a two-sided alternative (*p*-value = .056). Not surprisingly, the elasticity with respect to the lagged crime rate is large and very statistically significant. (The elasticity is also statistically different from unity.)

c. Adding the logs of the nine wage variables gives the following:

```
. reg lcrmrte lprbarr lprbconv lprbpris lavgsen lcrmr_1 lwcon-lwloc if d87

      Source |       SS       df       MS              Number of obs =      90
-------------+------------------------------           F( 14,    75) =   43.81
       Model |  23.8798774    14  1.70570553           Prob > F      =  0.0000
    Residual |  2.91982063    75  .038930942           R-squared     =  0.8911
-------------+------------------------------           Adj R-squared =  0.8707
       Total |   26.799698    89  .301120202           Root MSE      =  .19731

------------------------------------------------------------------------------
     lcrmrte |      Coef.   Std. Err.       t     P>|t|      [95% Conf. Interval]
-------------+----------------------------------------------------------------
     lprbarr |  -.1725122   .0659533     -2.62    0.011     -.3038978   -.0411265
    lprbconv |  -.0683639    .049728     -1.37    0.173     -.1674273    .0306994
    lprbpris |  -.2155553   .1024014     -2.11    0.039     -.4195493   -.0115614
     lavgsen |  -.1960546   .0844647     -2.32    0.023      -.364317   -.0277923
     lcrmr_1 |   .7453414   .0530331     14.05    0.000      .6396942    .8509887
       lwcon |  -.2850008   .1775178     -1.61    0.113     -.6386344    .0686327
       lwtuc |   .0641312    .134327      0.48    0.634     -.2034619    .3317244
       lwtrd |    .253707   .2317449      1.09    0.277     -.2079524    .7153665
       lwfir |  -.0835258   .1964974     -0.43    0.672     -.4749687    .3079171
       lwser |   .1127542   .0847427      1.33    0.187     -.0560619    .2815703
       lwmfg |   .0987371   .1186099      0.83    0.408     -.1375459    .3350201
       lwfed |   .3361278   .2453134      1.37    0.175     -.1525615    .8248172
       lwsta |   .0395089   .2072112      0.19    0.849     -.3732769    .4522947
       lwloc |  -.0369855   .3291546     -0.11    0.911     -.6926951     .618724
       _cons |  -3.792525   1.957472     -1.94    0.056     -7.692009    .1069592
------------------------------------------------------------------------------

. testparm lwcon-lwloc

 ( 1)  lwcon = 0.0
 ( 2)  lwtuc = 0.0
 ( 3)  lwtrd = 0.0
 ( 4)  lwfir = 0.0
 ( 5)  lwser = 0.0
```

```
( 6)  lwmfg = 0.0
( 7)  lwfed = 0.0
( 8)  lwsta = 0.0
( 9)  lwloc = 0.0

      F(  9,    75) =    1.50
           Prob > F =    0.1643
```

The nine wage variables are jointly insignificant even at the 15% level. Plus, the elasticities are not consistently positive or negative. The two largest elasticities -- which also have the largest absolute t statistics -- have the opposite sign. These are with respect to the wage in construction (-.285) and the wage for federal employees (.336).

d. Using the "robust" option in Stata, which is appended to the "reg" command, gives the heteroskedasiticity-robust F statistic as $F = 2.19$ and p-value = .032. (This F statistic is the heteroskedasticity-robust Wald statistic divided by the number of restrictions being tested, nine in this example. The division by the number of restrictions turns the asymptotic chi-square statistic into one that roughly has an F distribution.)

4.15. a. Because each x_j has finite second moment, $\text{Var}(\mathbf{x}\boldsymbol{\beta}) < \infty$. Since $\text{Var}(u) < \infty$, $\text{Cov}(\mathbf{x}\boldsymbol{\beta},u)$ is well-defined. But each x_j is uncorrelated with u, so $\text{Cov}(\mathbf{x}\boldsymbol{\beta},u) = 0$. Therefore, $\text{Var}(y) = \text{Var}(\mathbf{x}\boldsymbol{\beta}) + \text{Var}(u)$, or $\sigma_y^2 = \text{Var}(\mathbf{x}\boldsymbol{\beta}) + \sigma_u^2$.

b. This is nonsense when we view the $\mathbf{x}_i$ as random draws along with y_i. The statement "$\text{Var}(u_i) = \sigma^2 = \text{Var}(y_i)$ for all i" assumes that the regressors are nonrandom (or $\boldsymbol{\beta} = \mathbf{0}$, which is not a very interesting case). This is another example of how the assumption of nonrandom regressors can lead to counterintuitive conclusions. Suppose that an element of the error term, say z, which is uncorrelated with each x_j, suddenly becomes observed. When we add z to the regressor list, the error changes, and so does the error variance.

(It gets smaller.) In the vast majority of economic applications, it makes no sense to think we have access to the entire set of factors that one would ever want to control for, so we should allow for error variances to change across different models for the same response variable.

c. Write $R^2 = 1 - \text{SSR/SST} = 1 - (\text{SSR}/N)/(\text{SST}/N)$. Therefore, $\text{plim}(R^2) = 1 - \text{plim}[(\text{SSR}/N)/(\text{SST}/N)] = 1 - [\text{plim}(\text{SSR}/N)]/[\text{plim}(\text{SST}/N)] = 1 - \sigma_u^2/\sigma_y^2 = \rho^2$, where we use the fact that SSR/N is a consistent estimator of σ_u^2 and SST/N is a consistent estimator of σ_y^2.

d. The derivation in part (c) assumed nothing about $\text{Var}(u|\mathbf{x})$. The population R-squared depends on only the *unconditional* variances of u and y. Therefore, regardless of the nature of heteroskedasticity in $\text{Var}(u|\mathbf{x})$, the usual R-squared consistently estimates the population R-squared. Neither R-squared nor the adjusted R-squared has desirable finite-sample properties, such as unbiasedness, so the only analysis we can do in any generality involves asymptotics. The statement in the problem is simply wrong.

SOLUTIONS TO CHAPTER 5 PROBLEMS

5.1. Define $\mathbf{x}_1 \equiv (\mathbf{z}_1, y_2)$ and $x_2 \equiv \hat{v}_2$, and let $\hat{\boldsymbol{\beta}} \equiv (\hat{\boldsymbol{\beta}}_1', \hat{\rho}_1)'$ be OLS estimator from (5.52), where $\hat{\boldsymbol{\beta}}_1 = (\hat{\boldsymbol{\delta}}_1', \hat{\alpha}_1)'$. Using the hint, $\hat{\boldsymbol{\beta}}_1$ can also be obtained by partitioned regression:

(i) Regress $\mathbf{x}_1$ onto $\hat{v}_2$ and save the residuals, say $\ddot{\mathbf{x}}_1$.

(ii) Regress y_1 onto $\ddot{\mathbf{x}}_1$.

But when we regress $\mathbf{z}_1$ onto $\hat{v}_2$, the residuals are just $\mathbf{z}_1$ since $\hat{v}_2$ is orthogonal in sample to $\mathbf{z}$. (More precisely, $\sum_{i=1}^{N} \mathbf{z}_{i1}'\hat{v}_{i2} = \mathbf{0}$.) Further, because we can write $y_2 = \hat{y}_2 + \hat{v}_2$, where $\hat{y}_2$ and $\hat{v}_2$ are orthogonal in sample, the residuals from regressing y_2 onto $\hat{v}_2$ are simply the first stage fitted values, $\hat{y}_2$. In other words, $\ddot{\mathbf{x}}_1 = (\mathbf{z}_1, \hat{y}_2)$. But the 2SLS estimator of $\boldsymbol{\beta}_1$ is obtained exactly from the OLS regression y_1 on $\mathbf{z}_1$, $\hat{y}_2$.

5.3. a. There may be unobserved health factors correlated with smoking behavior that affect infant birth weight. For example, women who smoke during pregnancy may, on average, drink more coffee or alcohol, or eat less nutritious meals.

b. Basic economics says that *packs* should be negatively correlated with cigarette price, although the correlation might be small (especially because price is aggregated at the state level). At first glance it seems that cigarette price should be exogenous in equation (5.54), but we must be a little careful. One component of cigarette price is the state tax on cigarettes. States that have lower taxes on cigarettes may also have lower quality of health care, on average. Quality of health care is in u, and so maybe cigarette price fails the exogeneity requirement for an IV.

c. OLS is followed by 2SLS (IV, in this case):

```
. reg lbwght male parity lfaminc packs

  Source |       SS       df       MS                  Number of obs =    1388
---------+------------------------------               F(  4,  1383) =   12.55
   Model |  1.76664363     4  .441660908               Prob > F      =  0.0000
Residual |    48.65369  1383  .035179819               R-squared     =  0.0350
---------+------------------------------               Adj R-squared =  0.0322
   Total |  50.4203336  1387  .036352079               Root MSE      =  .18756

------------------------------------------------------------------------------
  lbwght |      Coef.   Std. Err.       t     P>|t|       [95% Conf. Interval]
---------+--------------------------------------------------------------------
    male |   .0262407   .0100894      2.601   0.009       .0064486    .0460328
  parity |   .0147292   .0056646      2.600   0.009       .0036171    .0258414
 lfaminc |   .0180498   .0055837      3.233   0.001       .0070964    .0290032
   packs |  -.0837281   .0171209     -4.890   0.000      -.1173139   -.0501423
   _cons |   4.675618   .0218813    213.681   0.000       4.632694    4.718542
------------------------------------------------------------------------------

. reg lbwght male parity lfaminc packs (male parity lfaminc cigprice)
                                                                      (2SLS)
  Source |       SS       df       MS                  Number of obs =    1388
---------+------------------------------               F(  4,  1383) =    2.39
   Model | -91.3500269     4 -22.8375067               Prob > F      =  0.0490
Residual |  141.770361  1383  .102509299               R-squared     =       .
---------+------------------------------               Adj R-squared =       .
   Total |  50.4203336  1387  .036352079               Root MSE      =  .32017

------------------------------------------------------------------------------
  lbwght |      Coef.   Std. Err.       t     P>|t|       [95% Conf. Interval]
---------+--------------------------------------------------------------------
   packs |   .7971063   1.086275      0.734   0.463      -1.333819    2.928031
    male |   .0298205    .017779      1.677   0.094      -.0050562    .0646972
  parity |  -.0012391   .0219322     -0.056   0.955       -.044263    .0417848
 lfaminc |    .063646   .0570128      1.116   0.264      -.0481949    .1754869
   _cons |   4.467861   .2588289     17.262   0.000       3.960122    4.975601
------------------------------------------------------------------------------
```

(Note: Stata automatically shifts endogenous explanatory variables to the beginning of the list when it reports coefficients, standard errors, and so on.) The difference between OLS and IV in the estimated effect of *packs* on *bwght* is huge. With the OLS estimate, one more pack of cigarettes is estimated to reduce *bwght* by about 8.4%, and is statistically significant.

The IV estimate has the opposite sign, is huge in magnitude, and is not statistically significant. The sign and size of the smoking effect are not realistic.

d. We can see the problem with IV by estimating the reduced form for *packs*:

```
. reg packs male parity lfaminc cigprice

  Source |       SS       df       MS                  Number of obs =    1388
---------+------------------------------               F(  4,  1383) =   10.86
   Model |  3.76705108     4  .94176277                Prob > F      =  0.0000
Residual |  119.929078  1383  .086716615               R-squared     =  0.0305
---------+------------------------------               Adj R-squared =  0.0276
   Total |  123.696129  1387  .089182501               Root MSE      =  .29448

------------------------------------------------------------------------------
   packs |      Coef.   Std. Err.       t     P>|t|       [95% Conf. Interval]
---------+--------------------------------------------------------------------
    male |  -.0047261   .0158539     -0.298   0.766      -.0358264    .0263742
  parity |   .0181491   .0088802      2.044   0.041       .0007291    .0355692
 lfaminc |  -.0526374   .0086991     -6.051   0.000      -.0697023   -.0355724
cigprice |    .000777   .0007763      1.001   0.317      -.0007459    .0022999
   _cons |   .1374075   .1040005      1.321   0.187      -.0666084    .3414234
------------------------------------------------------------------------------
```

The reduced form estimates show that *cigprice* does not significantly affect *packs*; in fact, the coefficient on *cigprice* is not the sign we expect. Thus, *cigprice* fails as an IV for *packs* because *cigprice* is not partially correlated with *packs* (with a sensible sign for the correlation). This is separate from the problem that *cigprice* may not truly be exogenous in the birth weight equation.

5.5. Under the null hypothesis that q and $\mathbf{z}_2$ are uncorrelated, $\mathbf{z}_1$ and $\mathbf{z}_2$ are exogenous in (5.55) because each is uncorrelated with u_1. Unfortunately, y_2 is correlated with u_1, and so the regression of y_1 on $\mathbf{z}_1$, y_2, $\mathbf{z}_2$ does not produce a consistent estimator of $\mathbf{0}$ on $\mathbf{z}_2$ even when $\mathrm{E}(\mathbf{z}_2'q) = \mathbf{0}$. We could find that $\hat{\boldsymbol{\psi}}_1$ from this regression is statistically different from zero even when q and $\mathbf{z}_2$ are uncorrelated -- in which case we would incorrectly conclude that $\mathbf{z}_2$ is not a valid IV candidate. Or, we might fail to reject H_0: $\boldsymbol{\psi}_1 = \mathbf{0}$ when $\mathbf{z}_2$ and q are correlated -- in which case we incorrectly conclude that the elements in $\mathbf{z}_2$ are valid as instruments.

The point of this exercise is that one cannot simply add instrumental variable candidates in the structural equation and then test for significance of these variables using OLS. This is the sense in which identification cannot be tested. With a single endogenous variable, we must take a stand that at least one element of $\mathbf{z}_2$ is uncorrelated with q.

5.7. a. If we plug $q = (1/\delta_1)q_1 - (1/\delta_1)a_1$ into equation (5.45) we get

$$y = \beta_0 + \beta_1 x_1 + \ldots + \beta_K x_K + \eta_1 q_1 + v - \eta_1 a_1, \tag{5.56}$$

where $\eta_1 \equiv (1/\delta_1)$. Now, since the z_h are redundant in (5.45), they are uncorrelated with the structural error, v (by definition of redundancy). Further, we have assumed that the z_h are uncorrelated with a_1. Since each x_j is also uncorrelated with $v - \eta_1 a_1$, we can estimate (5.56) by 2SLS using instruments $(1, x_1, \ldots, x_K, z_1, z_2, \ldots, z_M)$ to get consistent of the β_j and η_1.

Given all of the zero correlation assumptions, what we need for identification is that at least one of the z_h appears in the reduced form for q_1. More formally, in the linear projection

$$q_1 = \pi_0 + \pi_1 x_1 + \ldots + \pi_K x_K + \pi_{K+1} z_1 + \ldots + \pi_{K+M} z_M + r_1,$$

at least one of π_{K+1}, ..., π_{K+M} must be different from zero.

b. We need family background variables to be redundant in the log(*wage*) equation once ability (and other factors, such as *educ* and *exper*), have been controlled for. The idea here is that family background may influence ability but should have no partial effect on log(*wage*) once ability has been accounted for. For the rank condition to hold, we need family background variables to be correlated with the indicator, q_1, say *IQ*, once the x_j have been netted out. This is likely to be true if we think that family background and ability are (partially) correlated.

c. Applying the procedure to the data set in NLS80.RAW gives the following results:

```
. reg lwage exper tenure educ married south urban black iq (exper tenure educ
married south urban black meduc feduc sibs)

Instrumental variables (2SLS) regression

      Source |       SS       df       MS              Number of obs =     722
-------------+------------------------------           F(  8,   713) =   25.81
       Model |  19.6029198     8  2.45036497           Prob > F      =  0.0000
    Residual |  107.208996   713  .150363248           R-squared     =  0.1546
-------------+------------------------------           Adj R-squared =  0.1451
       Total |  126.811916   721  .175883378           Root MSE      =  .38777

------------------------------------------------------------------------------
       lwage |      Coef.   Std. Err.      t    P>|t|     [95% Conf. Interval]
-------------+----------------------------------------------------------------
          iq |   .0154368   .0077077     2.00   0.046     .0003044    .0305692
      tenure |   .0076754   .0030956     2.48   0.013     .0015979    .0137529
        educ |   .0161809   .0261982     0.62   0.537     -.035254    .0676158
     married |   .1901012   .0467592     4.07   0.000     .0982991    .2819033
       south |   -.047992   .0367425    -1.31   0.192    -.1201284    .0241444
       urban |   .1869376   .0327986     5.70   0.000     .1225442    .2513311
       black |   .0400269   .1138678     0.35   0.725    -.1835294    .2635832
       exper |   .0162185   .0040076     4.05   0.000     .0083503    .0240867
       _cons |   4.471616    .468913     9.54   0.000        3.551    5.392231
------------------------------------------------------------------------------

. reg lwage exper tenure educ married south urban black kww (exper tenure educ
married south urban black meduc feduc sibs)

Instrumental variables (2SLS) regression

      Source |       SS       df       MS              Number of obs =     722
-------------+------------------------------           F(  8,   713) =   25.70
       Model |   19.820304     8    2.477538           Prob > F      =  0.0000
    Residual |  106.991612   713  .150058361           R-squared     =  0.1563
-------------+------------------------------           Adj R-squared =  0.1468
       Total |  126.811916   721  .175883378           Root MSE      =  .38737
```

lwage	Coef.	Std. Err.	t	P>|t|	[95% Conf.	Interval]
kww	.0249441	.0150576	1.66	0.098	-.0046184	.0545067
tenure	.0051145	.0037739	1.36	0.176	-.0022947	.0125238
educ	.0260808	.0255051	1.02	0.307	-.0239933	.0761549
married	.1605273	.0529759	3.03	0.003	.0565198	.2645347
south	-.091887	.0322147	-2.85	0.004	-.1551341	-.0286399
urban	.1484003	.0411598	3.61	0.000	.0675914	.2292093
black	-.0424452	.0893695	-0.47	0.635	-.2179041	.1330137
exper	.0068682	.0067471	1.02	0.309	-.0063783	.0201147
_cons	5.217818	.1627592	32.06	0.000	4.898273	5.537362

Even though there are 935 men in the sample, only 722 are used for the estimation, because data are missing on *meduc* and *feduc*. What we could do is define binary indicators for whether the corresponding variable is missing, set the missing values to zero, and then use the binary indicators as instruments along with *meduc*, *feduc*, and *sibs*. This would allow us to use all 935 observations.

The return to education is estimated to be small and insignificant whether *IQ* or *KWW* used is used as the indicator. This could be because family background variables do not satisfy the appropriate redundancy condition, or they might be correlated with a_1. (In both first-stage regressions, the F statistic for joint significance of *meduc*, *feduc*, and *sibs* have p-values below .002, so it seems the family background variables are sufficiently partially correlated with the ability indicators.)

5.9. Define $\theta_4 = \beta_4 - \beta_3$, so that $\beta_4 = \beta_3 + \theta_4$. Plugging this expression into the equation and rearranging gives

$$\log(wage) = \beta_0 + \beta_1 exper + \beta_2 exper^2 + \beta_3(twoyr + fouryr) + \theta_4 fouryr + u$$

$$= \beta_0 + \beta_1 exper + \beta_2 exper^2 + \beta_3\ totcoll + \theta_4 fouryr + u,$$

where *totcoll* = *twoyr* + *fouryr*. Now, just estimate the latter equation by 2SLS using *exper*, $exper^2$, *dist2yr* and *dist4yr* as the full set of instruments. We can use the t statistic on $\hat{\theta}_4$ to test H_0: $\theta_4 = 0$ against H_1: $\theta_4 > 0$.

5.11. Following the hint, let y_2^0 be the linear projection of y_2 on $\mathbf{z}_2$, let a_2 be the projection error, and assume that $\boldsymbol{\lambda}_2$ is known. (The results on generated regressors in Section 6.1.1 show that the argument carries over to the case when $\boldsymbol{\lambda}_2$ is estimated.) Plugging in $y_2 = y_2^0 + a_2$ gives

$$y_1 = \mathbf{z}_1\boldsymbol{\delta}_1 + \alpha_1 y_2^0 + \alpha_1 a_2 + u_1.$$

Effectively, we regress y_1 on $\mathbf{z}_1$, y_2^0. The key consistency condition is that each explanatory is orthogonal to the composite error, $\alpha_1 a_2 + u_1$. By assumption, $E(\mathbf{z}'u_1) = \mathbf{0}$. Further, $E(y_2^0 a_2) = 0$ by construction. The problem is that $E(\mathbf{z}_1'a_2) \neq \mathbf{0}$ necessarily because $\mathbf{z}_1$ was not included in the linear projection for y_2. Therefore, OLS will be inconsistent for all parameters in general. Contrast this with 2SLS when y_2^* is the projection on $\mathbf{z}_1$ and $\mathbf{z}_2$: $y_2 = y_2^* + r_2 = \mathbf{z}\boldsymbol{\pi}_2 + r_2$, where $E(\mathbf{z}'r_2) = \mathbf{0}$. The second step regression (assuming that $\boldsymbol{\pi}_2$ is known) is essentially

$$y_1 = \mathbf{z}_1\boldsymbol{\delta}_1 + \alpha_1 y_2^* + \alpha_1 r_2 + u_1.$$

Now, r_2 is uncorrelated with $\mathbf{z}$, and so $E(\mathbf{z}_1'r_2) = \mathbf{0}$ and $E(y_2^* r_2) = 0$. The lesson is that one must be very careful if manually carrying out 2SLS by explicitly doing the first- and second-stage regressions.

5.13. a. In a simple regression model with a single IV, the IV estimate of the slope can be written as $\hat{\beta}_1 = \left(\sum_{i=1}^{N}(z_i - \bar{z})(y_i - \bar{y})\right)/\left(\sum_{i=1}^{N}(z_i - \bar{z})(x_i - \bar{x})\right) = \left(\sum_{i=1}^{N} z_i(y_i - \bar{y})\right)/\left(\sum_{i=1}^{N} z_i(x_i - \bar{x})\right)$. Now the numerator can be written as

$$\sum_{i=1}^{N} z_i(y_i - \bar{y}) = \sum_{i=1}^{N} z_i y_i - \left(\sum_{i=1}^{N} z_i\right)\bar{y} = N_1\bar{y}_1 - N_1\bar{y} = N_1(\bar{y}_1 - \bar{y}).$$

where $N_1 = \sum_{i=1}^{N} z_i$ is the number of observations in the sample with $z_i = 1$ and $\bar{y}_1$ is the average of the y_i over the observations with $z_i = 1$. Next, write $\bar{y}$ as a weighted average: $\bar{y} = (N_0/N)\bar{y}_0 + (N_1/N)\bar{y}_1$, where the notation should be clear. Straightforward algebra shows that $\bar{y}_1 - \bar{y} = [(N - N_1)/N]\bar{y}_1 - (N_0/N)\bar{y}_0 = (N_0/N)(\bar{y}_1 - \bar{y}_0)$. So the numerator of the IV estimate is $(N_0N_1/N)(\bar{y}_1 - \bar{y}_0)$. The same argument shows that the denominator is $(N_0N_1/N)(\bar{x}_1 - \bar{x}_0)$. Taking the ratio proves the result.

b. If x is also binary -- representing some "treatment" -- $\bar{x}_1$ is the fraction of observations receiving treatment when $z_i = 1$ and $\bar{x}_0$ is the fraction receiving treatment when $z_i = 0$. So, suppose $x_i = 1$ if person i participates in a job training program, and let $z_i = 1$ if person i is eligible for participation in the program. Then $\bar{x}_1$ is the fraction of people participating in the program out of those made eligibile, and $\bar{x}_0$ is the fraction of people participating who are not eligible. (When eligibility is necessary for participation, $\bar{x}_0 = 0$.) Generally, $\bar{x}_1 - \bar{x}_0$ is the difference in participation rates when $z = 1$ and $z = 0$. So the difference in the mean response between the $z = 1$ and $z = 0$ groups gets divided by the difference in participation rates across the two groups.

5.15. In $L(\mathbf{x}|\mathbf{z}) = \mathbf{z}\mathbf{\Pi}$, we can write $\mathbf{\Pi} = \begin{pmatrix} \mathbf{\Pi}_{11} & \mathbf{0} \\ \mathbf{\Pi}_{12} & \mathbf{I}_{K_2} \end{pmatrix}$, where $\mathbf{I}_{K_2}$ is the K_2 x K_2 identity matrix, $\mathbf{0}$ is the L_1 x K_2 zero matrix, $\mathbf{\Pi}_{11}$ is L_1 x K_1, and $\mathbf{\Pi}_{12}$ is K_2 x K_1. As in Problem 5.12, the rank condition holds if and only if rank($\mathbf{\Pi}$) = K.

a. If for some x_j, the vector $\mathbf{z}_1$ does not appear in $L(x_j|\mathbf{z})$, then $\mathbf{\Pi}_{11}$ has a column which is entirely zeros. But then that column of $\mathbf{\Pi}$ can be written as a linear combination of the last K_2 elements of $\mathbf{\Pi}$, which means rank($\mathbf{\Pi}$) < K.

Therefore, a necessary condition for the rank condition is that no columns of $\mathbf{\Pi}_{11}$ be exactly zero, which means that at least one z_h must appear in the reduced form of each x_j, $j = 1,\ldots,K_1$.

b. Suppose $K_1 = 2$ and $L_1 = 2$, where z_1 appears in the reduced form form both x_1 and x_2, but z_2 appears in neither reduced form. Then the 2 x 2 matrix $\mathbf{\Pi}_{11}$ has zeros in its second row, which means that the second row of $\mathbf{\Pi}$ is all zeros. It cannot have rank K, in that case. Intuitively, while we began with two instruments, only one of them turned out to be partially correlated with x_1 and x_2.

c. Without loss of generality, we assume that z_j appears in the reduced form for x_j; we can simply reorder the elements of $\mathbf{z}_1$ to ensure this is the case. Then $\mathbf{\Pi}_{11}$ is a K_1 x K_1 diagonal matrix with nonzero diagonal elements. Looking at $\mathbf{\Pi} = \begin{pmatrix} \mathbf{\Pi}_{11} & \mathbf{0} \\ \mathbf{\Pi}_{12} & \mathbf{I}_{K_2} \end{pmatrix}$, we see that if $\mathbf{\Pi}_{11}$ is diagonal with all nonzero diagonals then $\mathbf{\Pi}$ is lower triangular with all nonzero diagonal elements. Therefore, rank $\mathbf{\Pi} = K$.

SOLUTIONS TO CHAPTER 6 PROBLEMS

6.1. a. Here is abbreviated Stata output for testing the null hypothesis that *educ* is exogenous:

```
. qui reg educ nearc4 nearc2 exper expersq black south smsa reg661-reg668
smsa66

. predict v2hat, resid

. reg lwage educ exper expersq black south smsa reg661-reg668 smsa66 v2hat
```

lwage	Coef.	Std. Err.	t	P>|t|	[95% Conf.	Interval]
educ	.1570594	.0482814	3.253	0.001	.0623912	.2517275
exper	.1188149	.0209423	5.673	0.000	.0777521	.1598776
expersq	-.0023565	.0003191	-7.384	0.000	-.0029822	-.0017308
black	-.1232778	.0478882	-2.574	0.010	-.2171749	-.0293807
south	-.1431945	.0261202	-5.482	0.000	-.1944098	-.0919791
smsa	.100753	.0289435	3.481	0.000	.0440018	.1575042
reg661	-.102976	.0398738	-2.583	0.010	-.1811588	-.0247932
reg662	-.0002286	.0310325	-0.007	0.994	-.0610759	.0606186
reg663	.0469556	.0299809	1.566	0.117	-.0118296	.1057408
reg664	-.0554084	.0359807	-1.540	0.124	-.1259578	.0151411
reg665	.0515041	.0436804	1.179	0.238	-.0341426	.1371509
reg666	.0699968	.0489487	1.430	0.153	-.0259797	.1659733
reg667	.0390596	.0456842	0.855	0.393	-.050516	.1286352
reg668	-.1980371	.0482417	-4.105	0.000	-.2926273	-.1034468
smsa66	.0150626	.0205106	0.734	0.463	.0251538	.0552789
v2hat	-.0828005	.0484086	-1.710	0.087	-.177718	.0121169
_cons	3.339687	.821434	4.066	0.000	1.729054	4.950319

The *t* statistic on $\hat{v}_2$ is -1.71, which is not significant at the 5% level against a two-sided alternative. The negative correlation between u_1 and *educ* is essentially the same finding that the 2SLS estimated return to education is larger than the OLS estimate. In any case, I would call this marginal evidence that *educ* is endogenous. (Depending on the application or purpose of a study, the same researcher may take *t* = -1.71 as evidence for or against endogeneity.)

b. To test the single overidentifying restiction we obtain the 2SLS residuals:

```
. qui reg lwage educ exper expersq black south smsa reg661-reg668 smsa66
(nearc4 nearc2 exper expersq black south smsa reg661-reg668 smsa66)

. predict uhat1, resid
```

Now, we regress the 2SLS residuals on all exogenous variables:

```
. reg uhat1 exper expersq black south smsa reg661-reg668 smsa66 nearc4 nearc2

  Source |       SS       df       MS                  Number of obs =    3010
---------+------------------------------               F( 16,  2993) =    0.08
   Model |  .203922832    16  .012745177               Prob > F      =  1.0000
Residual |  491.568721  2993  .164239466               R-squared     =  0.0004
---------+------------------------------               Adj R-squared = -0.0049
   Total |  491.772644  3009  .163433913               Root MSE      =  .40526
```

The test statistic is the sample size times the *R*-squared from this regression:

```
. di 3010*.0004
1.204

. di chiprob(1,1.2)
.27332168
```

The *p*-value, obtained from a χ_1^2 distribution, is about .273, so the instruments pass the overidentification test.

6.3. a. We need prices to satisfy two requirements. First, *calories* and *protein* must be partially correlated with prices of food. While this is easy to test for each by estimating the two reduced forms, the rank condition could still be violated (although see Problem 15.5c). In addition, we must also assume prices are exogenous in the productivity equation. Ideally, prices vary because of things like transportation costs that are not systematically related to regional variations in individual productivity. A potential problem is that prices reflect food quality and that features of the food other than calories and protein appear in the disturbance u_1.

b. Since there are two endogenous explanatory variables we need at least two prices.

c. We would first estimate the two reduced forms for *calories* and *protein* by regressing each on a constant, *exper*, $exper^2$, *educ*, and the *M* prices, p_1, ..., p_M. We obtain the residuals, $\hat{v}_{21}$ and $\hat{v}_{22}$. Then we would run the regression log(*produc*) on 1, *exper*, $exper^2$, *educ*, $\hat{v}_{21}$, $\hat{v}_{22}$ and do a joint significance test on $\hat{v}_{21}$ and $\hat{v}_{22}$. We could use a standard *F* test or use a heteroskedasticity-robust test.

6.5. a. For simplicity, absorb the intercept in $\mathbf{x}$, so $y = \mathbf{x}\boldsymbol{\beta} + u$, $\mathrm{E}(u|\mathbf{x}) = 0$, $\mathrm{Var}(u|\mathbf{x}) = \sigma^2$. In these tests, $\hat{\sigma}^2$ is implictly SSR/N -- there is no degrees of freedom adjustment. (In any case, the df adjustment makes no difference asymptotically.) So $\hat{u}_i^2 - \hat{\sigma}^2$ has a zero sample average, which means that

$$N^{-1/2}\sum_{i=1}^{N}(\mathbf{h}_i - \boldsymbol{\mu}_h)'(\hat{u}_i^2 - \hat{\sigma}^2) = N^{-1/2}\sum_{i=1}^{N}\mathbf{h}_i'(\hat{u}_i^2 - \hat{\sigma}^2).$$

Next, $N^{-1/2}\sum_{i=1}^{N}(\mathbf{h}_i - \boldsymbol{\mu}_h)' = O_p(1)$ by the central limit theorem and $\hat{\sigma}^2 - \sigma^2 = o_p(1)$. So $N^{-1/2}\sum_{i=1}^{N}(\mathbf{h}_i - \boldsymbol{\mu}_h)'(\hat{\sigma}^2 - \sigma^2) = O_p(1)\cdot o_p(1) = o_p(1)$. Therefore, so far we have

$$N^{-1/2}\sum_{i=1}^{N}\mathbf{h}_i'(\hat{u}_i^2 - \hat{\sigma}^2) = N^{-1/2}\sum_{i=1}^{N}(\mathbf{h}_i - \boldsymbol{\mu}_h)'(\hat{u}_i^2 - \sigma^2) + o_p(1).$$

We are done with this part if we show $N^{-1/2}\sum_{i=1}^{N}(\mathbf{h}_i - \boldsymbol{\mu}_h)'\hat{u}_i^2 = N^{-1/2}\sum_{i=1}^{N}(\mathbf{h}_i - \boldsymbol{\mu}_h)'u_i^2 + o_p(1)$. Now, as in Problem 4.4, we can write $\hat{u}_i^2 = u_i^2 - 2u_i\mathbf{x}_i(\hat{\boldsymbol{\beta}} - \boldsymbol{\beta}) + [\mathbf{x}_i(\hat{\boldsymbol{\beta}} - \boldsymbol{\beta})]^2$, so

$$\begin{aligned} N^{-1/2}\sum_{i=1}^{N}(\mathbf{h}_i - \boldsymbol{\mu}_h)'\hat{u}_i^2 &= N^{-1/2}\sum_{i=1}^{N}(\mathbf{h}_i - \boldsymbol{\mu}_h)'u_i^2 \\ &\quad - 2\left(N^{-1/2}\sum_{i=1}^{N}u_i(\mathbf{h}_i - \boldsymbol{\mu}_h)'\mathbf{x}_i\right)(\hat{\boldsymbol{\beta}} - \boldsymbol{\beta}) \qquad (6.40) \\ &\quad + \left(N^{-1/2}\sum_{i=1}^{N}(\mathbf{h}_i - \boldsymbol{\mu}_h)'(\mathbf{x}_i \otimes \mathbf{x}_i)\right)\{\mathrm{vec}[(\hat{\boldsymbol{\beta}} - \boldsymbol{\beta})(\hat{\boldsymbol{\beta}} - \boldsymbol{\beta})']\}, \end{aligned}$$

where the expression for the third term follows from $[\mathbf{x}_i(\hat{\beta} - \beta)]^2 = \mathbf{x}_i(\hat{\beta} - \beta)(\hat{\beta} - \beta)'\mathbf{x}_i' = (\mathbf{x}_i \otimes \mathbf{x}_i)\text{vec}[(\hat{\beta} - \beta)(\hat{\beta} - \beta)']$. Dropping the "-2" the second term can be written as $\left(N^{-1}\sum_{i=1}^{N} u_i(\mathbf{h}_i - \boldsymbol{\mu}_h)'\mathbf{x}_i\right)\sqrt{N}(\hat{\beta} - \beta) = o_p(1)\cdot O_p(1)$ because $\sqrt{N}(\hat{\beta} - \beta) = O_p(1)$ and, under $E(u_i|\mathbf{x}_i) = 0$, $E[u_i(\mathbf{h}_i - \boldsymbol{\mu}_h)'\mathbf{x}_i] = \mathbf{0}$; the law of large numbers implies that the sample average is $o_p(1)$. The third term can be written as $N^{-1/2}\left(N^{-1}\sum_{i=1}^{N}(\mathbf{h}_i - \boldsymbol{\mu}_h)'(\mathbf{x}_i \otimes \mathbf{x}_i)\right)\{\text{vec}[\sqrt{N}(\hat{\beta} - \beta)\sqrt{N}(\hat{\beta} - \beta)']\} = N^{-1/2}\cdot O_p(1)\cdot O_p(1)$, where we again use the fact that sample averages are $O_p(1)$ by the law of large numbers and $\text{vec}[\sqrt{N}(\hat{\beta} - \beta)\sqrt{N}(\hat{\beta} - \beta)'] = O_p(1)$. We have shown that the last two terms in (6.40) are $o_p(1)$, which proves part (a).

b. By part (a), the asymptotic variance of $N^{-1/2}\sum_{i=1}^{N}\mathbf{h}_i'(\hat{u}_i^2 - \hat{\sigma}^2)$ is $\text{Var}[(\mathbf{h}_i - \boldsymbol{\mu}_h)'(u_i^2 - \sigma^2)] = E[(u_i^2 - \sigma^2)^2(\mathbf{h}_i - \boldsymbol{\mu}_h)'(\mathbf{h}_i - \boldsymbol{\mu}_h)]$. Now $(u_i^2 - \sigma^2)^2 = u_i^4 - 2u_i^2\sigma^2 + \sigma^4$. Under the null, $E(u_i^2|\mathbf{x}_i) = \text{Var}(u_i|\mathbf{x}_i) = \sigma^2$ [since $E(u_i|\mathbf{x}_i) = 0$ is assumed] and therefore, when we add (6.27), $E[(u_i^2 - \sigma^2)^2|\mathbf{x}_i] = \kappa^2 - \sigma^4 \equiv \eta^2$. A standard iterated expectations argument gives $E[(u_i^2 - \sigma^2)^2(\mathbf{h}_i - \boldsymbol{\mu}_h)'(\mathbf{h}_i - \boldsymbol{\mu}_h)] = E\{E[(u_i^2 - \sigma^2)^2(\mathbf{h}_i - \boldsymbol{\mu}_h)'(\mathbf{h}_i - \boldsymbol{\mu}_h)]|\mathbf{x}_i\} = E\{E[(u_i^2 - \sigma^2)^2|\mathbf{x}_i](\mathbf{h}_i - \boldsymbol{\mu}_h)'(\mathbf{h}_i - \boldsymbol{\mu}_h)\}$ [since $\mathbf{h}_i = \mathbf{h}(\mathbf{x}_i)$] $= \eta^2 E[(\mathbf{h}_i - \boldsymbol{\mu}_h)'(\mathbf{h}_i - \boldsymbol{\mu}_h)]$. This is what we wanted to show. (Whether we do the argument for a random draw *i* or for random variables representing the population is a matter of taste.)

c. From part (b) and Lemma 3.8, the following statistic has an asymptotic χ_Q^2 distribution:

$$\left(N^{-1/2}\sum_{i=1}^{N}(\hat{u}_i^2 - \hat{\sigma}^2)\mathbf{h}_i\right)\{\eta^2 E[(\mathbf{h}_i - \boldsymbol{\mu}_h)'(\mathbf{h}_i - \boldsymbol{\mu}_h)]\}^{-1}\left(N^{-1/2}\sum_{i=1}^{N}\mathbf{h}_i'(\hat{u}_i^2 - \hat{\sigma}^2)\right).$$

Using again the fact that $\sum_{i=1}^{N}(\hat{u}_i^2 - \hat{\sigma}^2) = 0$, we can replace $\mathbf{h}_i$ with $\mathbf{h}_i - \bar{\mathbf{h}}$ in the two vectors forming the quadratic form. Then, again by Lemma 3.8, we can replace the matrix in the quadratic form with a consistent estimator, which is

$$\hat{\eta}^2\left(N^{-1}\sum_{i=1}^{N}(\mathbf{h}_i - \bar{\mathbf{h}})'(\mathbf{h}_i - \bar{\mathbf{h}})\right),$$

where $\hat{\eta}^2 = N^{-1}\sum_{i=1}^{N}(\hat{u}_i^2 - \hat{\sigma}^2)^2$. The computable statistic, after simple algebra, can be written as

$$\left(\sum_{i=1}^{N}(\hat{u}_i^2 - \hat{\sigma}^2)(\mathbf{h}_i - \bar{\mathbf{h}})\right)\left(\sum_{i=1}^{N}(\mathbf{h}_i - \bar{\mathbf{h}})'(\mathbf{h}_i - \bar{\mathbf{h}})\right)^{-1}\left(\sum_{i=1}^{N}(\mathbf{h}_i - \bar{\mathbf{h}})'(\hat{u}_i^2 - \hat{\sigma}^2)\right)/\hat{\eta}^2.$$

Now $\hat{\eta}^2$ is just the total sum of squares in the $\hat{u}_i^2$, divided by N. The numerator of the statistic is simply the explained sum of squares from the regression $\hat{u}_i^2$ on 1, $\mathbf{h}_i$, $i = 1,\ldots,N$. Therefore, the test statistic is N times the usual (centered) R-squared from the regression $\hat{u}_i^2$ on 1, $\mathbf{h}_i$, $i = 1,\ldots,N$, or NR_c^2.

d. Without assumption (6.37) we need to estimate $\mathrm{E}[(u_i^2 - \sigma^2)^2(\mathbf{h}_i - \boldsymbol{\mu}_h)'(\mathbf{h}_i - \boldsymbol{\mu}_h)]$ generally. Hopefully, the approach is by now pretty clear. We replace the population expected value with the sample average and replace any unknown parameters -- $\boldsymbol{\beta}$, σ^2, and $\boldsymbol{\mu}_h$ in this case -- with their consistent estimators (under H_0). So a generally consistent estimator of $\mathrm{Avar}\left(N^{-1/2}\sum_{i=1}^{N}\mathbf{h}_i'(\hat{u}_i^2 - \hat{\sigma}^2)\right)$ is

$$N^{-1}\sum_{i=1}^{N}(\hat{u}_i^2 - \hat{\sigma}^2)^2(\mathbf{h}_i - \bar{\mathbf{h}})'(\mathbf{h}_i - \bar{\mathbf{h}}),$$

and the test statistic robust to heterokurtosis can be written as

$$\left(\sum_{i=1}^{N}(\hat{u}_i^2 - \hat{\sigma}^2)(\mathbf{h}_i - \bar{\mathbf{h}})\right)\left(\sum_{i=1}^{N}(\hat{u}_i^2 - \hat{\sigma}^2)^2(\mathbf{h}_i - \bar{\mathbf{h}})'(\mathbf{h}_i - \bar{\mathbf{h}})\right)^{-1} \cdot\left(\sum_{i=1}^{N}(\mathbf{h}_i - \bar{\mathbf{h}})'(\hat{u}_i^2 - \hat{\sigma}^2)\right),$$

which is easily seen to be the explained sum of squares from the regression of 1 on $(\hat{u}_i^2 - \hat{\sigma}^2)(\mathbf{h}_i - \bar{\mathbf{h}})$, $i = 1,\ldots,N$ (without an intercept). Since the total sum of squares, without demeaning, is $N = (1 + 1 + \ldots + 1)$ (N times), the statistic is equivalent to $N - \mathrm{SSR}_0$, where SSR_0 is the sum of squared residuals.

6.7. a. The simple regression results are

```
. reg lprice ldist if y81

  Source |       SS       df       MS                  Number of obs =     142
---------+------------------------------               F(  1,   140) =   30.79
   Model |  3.86426989     1  3.86426989               Prob > F      =  0.0000
Residual |  17.5730845   140  .125522032               R-squared     =  0.1803
---------+------------------------------               Adj R-squared =  0.1744
   Total |  21.4373543   141  .152037974               Root MSE      =  .35429

------------------------------------------------------------------------------
  lprice |      Coef.   Std. Err.       t     P>|t|       [95% Conf. Interval]
---------+--------------------------------------------------------------------
   ldist |   .3648752   .0657613      5.548   0.000       .2348615    .4948889
   _cons |   8.047158   .6462419     12.452   0.000       6.769503    9.324813
------------------------------------------------------------------------------
```

This regression suggests a strong link between housing price and distance from the incinerator (as distance increases, so does housing price). The elasticity is .365 and the *t* statistic is 5.55. However, this is not a good causal regression: the incinerator may have been put near homes with lower values to begin with. If so, we would expect the positive relationship found in the simple regression even if the new incinerator had no effect on housing prices.

b. The parameter δ_3 should be positive: after the incinerator is built a house should be worth more the farther it is from the incinerator. Here is my Stata session:

```
. gen y81ldist = y81*ldist

. reg lprice y81 ldist y81ldist

  Source |       SS       df       MS                  Number of obs =     321
---------+------------------------------               F(  3,   317) =   69.22
   Model |  24.3172548     3  8.10575159               Prob > F      =  0.0000
Residual |  37.1217306   317  .117103251               R-squared     =  0.3958
---------+------------------------------               Adj R-squared =  0.3901
   Total |  61.4389853   320  .191996829               Root MSE      =   .3422

------------------------------------------------------------------------------
  lprice |      Coef.   Std. Err.       t     P>|t|       [95% Conf. Interval]
```

```
---------+--------------------------------------------------------------------
     y81 |  -.0113101   .8050622     -0.014   0.989       -1.59525    1.57263
   ldist |    .316689   .0515323      6.145   0.000       .2153006   .4180775
y81ldist |   .0481862   .0817929      0.589   0.556      -.1127394   .2091117
   _cons |   8.058468   .5084358     15.850   0.000       7.058133   9.058803
------------------------------------------------------------------------------
```

The coefficient on *ldist* reveals the shortcoming of the regression in part (a). This coefficient measures the relationship between *lprice* and *ldist* in 1978, before the incinerator was even being rumored. The causal effect of the incinerator is supposed to be given by the coefficient on the interaction, *y81ldist*. While the direction of the effect is as expected, it is not especially large, and it is statistically insignificant, anyway. Therefore, at this point, we cannot reject the null hypothesis that building the incinerator had no effect on housing prices.

c. Adding the variables listed in the problem gives

```
. reg lprice y81 ldist y81ldist lintst lintstsq larea lland age agesq rooms
baths

  Source |       SS       df       MS                  Number of obs =     321
---------+------------------------------               F( 11,    309) =  108.04
   Model |  48.7611143    11  4.43282858               Prob > F      =  0.0000
Residual |   12.677871   309  .041028709               R-squared     =  0.7937
---------+------------------------------               Adj R-squared =  0.7863
   Total |  61.4389853   320  .191996829               Root MSE      =  .20256

------------------------------------------------------------------------------
  lprice |      Coef.   Std. Err.       t     P>|t|       [95% Conf. Interval]
---------+--------------------------------------------------------------------
     y81 |   -.229847   .4877198     -0.471   0.638      -1.189519   .7298249
   ldist |   .0866424   .0517205      1.675   0.095      -.0151265   .1884113
y81ldist |   .0617759   .0495705      1.246   0.214      -.0357625   .1593143
  lintst |   .9633332   .3262647      2.953   0.003       .3213518   1.605315
lintstsq |  -.0591504   .0187723     -3.151   0.002       -.096088  -.0222128
   larea |   .3548562   .0512328      6.926   0.000       .2540468   .4556655
   lland |    .109999   .0248165      4.432   0.000       .0611683   .1588297
     age |  -.0073939   .0014108     -5.241   0.000      -.0101699  -.0046178
   agesq |   .0000315   8.69e-06      3.627   0.000       .0000144   .0000486
   rooms |   .0469214   .0171015      2.744   0.006       .0132713   .0805715
   baths |   .0958867    .027479      3.489   0.000        .041817   .1499564
   _cons |   2.305525   1.774032      1.300   0.195      -1.185185   5.796236
------------------------------------------------------------------------------
```

The incinerator effect is now larger (the elasticity is about .062) and the *t* statistic is larger than before, but the interaction is still statistically insignificant. Using these models and this two years of data we must conclude the evidence that housing prices were adversely affected by the new incinerator is somewhat weak.

6.9. a. The Stata results are

```
. reg ldurat afchnge highearn afhigh male married head-construc if ky

      Source |       SS       df       MS                  Number of obs =    5349
-------------+------------------------------               F( 14,  5334) =   16.37
       Model |  358.441793    14  25.6029852               Prob > F      =  0.0000
    Residual |  8341.41206  5334  1.56381928               R-squared     =  0.0412
-------------+------------------------------               Adj R-squared =  0.0387
       Total |  8699.85385  5348  1.62674904               Root MSE      =  1.2505

------------------------------------------------------------------------------
      ldurat |      Coef.   Std. Err.       t     P>|t|      [95% Conf. Interval]
-------------+----------------------------------------------------------------
     afchnge |   .0106274   .0449167      0.24   0.813     -.0774276    .0986824
    highearn |   .1757598   .0517462      3.40   0.001      .0743161    .2772035
      afhigh |   .2308768   .0695248      3.32   0.001      .0945798    .3671738
        male |  -.0979407   .0445498     -2.20   0.028     -.1852766   -.0106049
     married |   .1220995   .0391228      3.12   0.002      .0454027    .1987962
        head |  -.5139003   .1292776     -3.98   0.000     -.7673372   -.2604634
        neck |   .2699126   .1614899      1.67   0.095     -.0466737    .5864988
      upextr |   -.178539   .1011794     -1.76   0.078      -.376892    .0198141
       trunk |   .1264514   .1090163      1.16   0.246     -.0872651     .340168
     lowback |  -.0085967   .1015267     -0.08   0.933     -.2076305    .1904371
     lowextr |  -.1202911   .1023262     -1.18   0.240     -.3208922    .0803101
      occdis |   .2727118    .210769      1.29   0.196     -.1404816    .6859052
       manuf |  -.1606709   .0409038     -3.93   0.000     -.2408591   -.0804827
    construc |   .1101967   .0518063      2.13   0.033      .0086352    .2117581
       _cons |   1.245922   .1061677     11.74   0.000       1.03779    1.454054
------------------------------------------------------------------------------
```

The estimated coefficient on the interaction term is actually higher now, and even more statistically significant than in equation (6.33). Adding the other explanatory variables only slightly increased the standard error on the interaction term.

b. The small *R*-squared, on the order of 4.1%, or 3.9% if we used the adjusted *R*-squared, means that we cannot explain much of the variation in time on workers compensation using the variables included in the regression. This is often the case in the social sciences: it is very difficult to include the multitude of factors that can affect something like *durat*. The low *R*-squared means that making predictions of log(*durat*) would be very difficult given the factors we have included in the regression: the variation in the unobservables pretty much swamps the explained variation. However, the low *R*-squared does not mean we have a biased or consistent estimator of the effect of the policy change. Provided the Kentucky change is a good natural experiment, the OLS estimator is consistent. With over 5,000 observations, we can get a reasonably precise estimate of the effect, although the 95% confidence interval is pretty wide.

c. Using the data for Michigan to estimate the basic model gives

```
. reg ldurat afchnge highearn afhigh if mi

      Source |       SS       df       MS              Number of obs =    1524
-------------+------------------------------           F(  3,  1520) =    6.05
       Model |  34.3850177     3  11.4616726           Prob > F      =  0.0004
    Residual |  2879.96981  1520  1.89471698           R-squared     =  0.0118
-------------+------------------------------           Adj R-squared =  0.0098
       Total |  2914.35483  1523  1.91356194           Root MSE      =  1.3765

------------------------------------------------------------------------------
      ldurat |      Coef.   Std. Err.      t    P>|t|     [95% Conf. Interval]
-------------+----------------------------------------------------------------
     afchnge |   .0973808   .0847879     1.15   0.251    -.0689329    .2636945
    highearn |   .1691388   .1055676     1.60   0.109    -.0379348    .3762124
      afhigh |   .1919906   .1541699     1.25   0.213    -.1104176    .4943988
       _cons |   1.412737   .0567172    24.91   0.000     1.301485    1.523989
------------------------------------------------------------------------------
```

The coefficient on the interaction term, .192, is remarkably similar to that for Kentucky. Because of the many fewer observations, the *t* statistic is insignificant at the 10% level against a one-sided alternative. Asymptotic theory predicts that the standard error for Michigan will be about $(5,626/1,524)^{1/2} \approx 1.92$ larger than that for Kentucky. In fact, the ratio of standard errors is about 2.23. The difference in statistical significance between the KY and MI cases illustrates the importance of a large sample size for this kind of policy analysis.

6.11. The following is Stata output that I will use to answer the first three parts:

```
. reg lwage y85 educ y85educ exper expersq union female y85fem

      Source |       SS       df       MS              Number of obs =    1084
-------------+------------------------------           F(  8,  1075) =   99.80
       Model |  135.992074     8  16.9990092           Prob > F      =  0.0000
    Residual |  183.099094  1075  .170324738           R-squared     =  0.4262
-------------+------------------------------           Adj R-squared =  0.4219
       Total |  319.091167  1083   .29463635           Root MSE      =   .4127

------------------------------------------------------------------------------
       lwage |      Coef.   Std. Err.      t    P>|t|     [95% Conf. Interval]
-------------+----------------------------------------------------------------
         y85 |   .1178062   .1237817     0.95   0.341     -.125075    .3606874
        educ |   .0747209   .0066764    11.19   0.000     .0616206    .0878212
     y85educ |   .0184605   .0093542     1.97   0.049      .000106     .036815
       exper |   .0295843   .0035673     8.29   0.000     .0225846     .036584
     expersq |  -.0003994   .0000775    -5.15   0.000    -.0005516   -.0002473
       union |   .2021319   .0302945     6.67   0.000     .1426888    .2615749
      female |  -.3167086   .0366215    -8.65   0.000    -.3885663    -.244851
      y85fem |    .085052    .051309     1.66   0.098    -.0156251     .185729
       _cons |   .4589329   .0934485     4.91   0.000     .2755707     .642295
------------------------------------------------------------------------------
```

a. The return to another year of education increased by about .0185, or 1.85 percentage points, between 1978 and 1985. The *t* statistic is 1.97, which is marginally significant at the 5% level against a two-sided alternative.

b. The coefficient on *y85fem* is positive and shows that the estimated gender gap declined by about 8.5 percentage points. But the *t* statistic is only significant at about the 10% level against a two-sided alternative. Still, this is suggestive of some closing of wage differentials between men and women at given levels of education and workforce experience.

c. Only the coefficient on *y85* changes if wages are measured in 1978 dollars. In fact, you can check that when 1978 wages are used, the coefficient on *y85* becomes about -.383, which shows a significant fall in real wages for given productivity characteristics and gender over the seven-year period. (But see part e for the proper interpretation of the coefficient.)

d. To answer this question, I just took the squared OLS residuals and regressed those on the year dummy, *y85*. The coefficient is about .042 with a standard error of about .022, which gives a *t* statistic of about 1.91. So there is some evidence that the variance of the unexplained part of log wages (or log real wages) has increased over time.

e. As the equation is written in the problem, the coefficient δ_0 is the growth in nominal wages for a male with no years of education! For a male with 12 years of education, we want $\theta_0 \equiv \delta_0 + 12\delta_1$. A simple way to obtain the standard error of $\hat{\theta}_0 = \hat{\delta}_0 + 12\hat{\delta}_1$ is to replace *y85·educ* with *y85·(educ - 12)*. Simple algebra shows that, in the new model, θ_0 is the coefficient on *educ*. In Stata we have

```
. gen y85educ0 = y85*(educ - 12)

. reg lwage y85 educ y85educ0 exper expersq union female y85fem

      Source |       SS       df       MS              Number of obs =    1084
-------------+------------------------------           F(  8,  1075) =   99.80
       Model |  135.992074     8  16.9990092           Prob > F      =  0.0000
    Residual |  183.099094  1075  .170324738           R-squared     =  0.4262
-------------+------------------------------           Adj R-squared =  0.4219
```

Total	319.091167	1083	.29463635	Root MSE	= .4127

lwage	Coef.	Std. Err.	t	P>|t|	[95% Conf.	Interval]
y85	.3393326	.0340099	9.98	0.000	.2725993	.4060659
educ	.0747209	.0066764	11.19	0.000	.0616206	.0878212
y85educ0	.0184605	.0093542	1.97	0.049	.000106	.036815
exper	.0295843	.0035673	8.29	0.000	.0225846	.036584
expersq	-.0003994	.0000775	-5.15	0.000	-.0005516	-.0002473
union	.2021319	.0302945	6.67	0.000	.1426888	.2615749
female	-.3167086	.0366215	-8.65	0.000	-.3885663	-.244851
y85fem	.085052	.051309	1.66	0.098	-.0156251	.185729
_cons	.4589329	.0934485	4.91	0.000	.2755707	.642295

So the growth in nominal wages for a man with *educ* = 12 is about .339, or 33.9%. [We could use the more accurate estimate, .404, obtained from exp(.339) - 1.] The 95% confidence interval goes from about 27.3 to 40.6.

6.13 (Bonus Question): Let y_1 and y_2 be scalars, and suppose the structural model is

$$y_1 = \mathbf{z}_1\boldsymbol{\delta}_1 + \mathbf{g}(y_2)\boldsymbol{\alpha}_1 + u_1, \quad \mathrm{E}(u_1|\mathbf{z}) = 0,$$

where $\mathbf{g}(\cdot)$ is a $1 \times G_1$ vector of functions of y_2. Assume that y_2 has a linear conditional expectation for a reduced form,

$$y_2 = \mathbf{z}\boldsymbol{\delta}_2 + v_2, \quad \mathrm{E}(v_2|\mathbf{z}) = 0.$$

(Remember, this is much stronger than just specifying a linear projection.) Further, assume that (u_1, v_2) is independent of $\mathbf{z}$.

When might this model apply? To allow nonlinear effects, $\mathbf{g}(\cdot)$ might include y_2 and powers of y_2. Or, y_2 might be a roughly continuous variable but we enter it categorically (as a sequence of dummy variables) in the structural equation.

a. Show that

$$\mathrm{E}(y_1|\mathbf{z}, v_2) = \mathbf{z}_1\boldsymbol{\delta}_1 + \mathbf{g}(y_2)\boldsymbol{\alpha}_1 + \mathrm{E}(u_1|v_2).$$

b. Assume also that $E(u_1|v_2) = \gamma_1 v_2$. Use part a to propose a $\sqrt{N}$-consistent two-step estimator of $(\boldsymbol{\delta}_1, \boldsymbol{\alpha}_1)$.

c. What would be a minimal requirement for identification of $\boldsymbol{\delta}_1$ and $\boldsymbol{\alpha}_1$ to be convincing?

d. What is a more robust way of estimating $\boldsymbol{\delta}_1$ and $\boldsymbol{\alpha}_1$? In particular, suppose you are only willing to assume $E(u_1|\mathbf{z}) = 0$.

Answer:

a. First, y_2 is a function of $(\mathbf{z}, v_2)$, and so, from the structural equation,

$$E(y_1|\mathbf{z}, v_2) = \mathbf{z}_1\boldsymbol{\delta}_1 + \mathbf{g}(y_2)\boldsymbol{\alpha}_1 + E(u_1|\mathbf{z}, v_2)$$

$$= \mathbf{z}_1\boldsymbol{\delta}_1 + \mathbf{g}(y_2)\boldsymbol{\alpha}_1 + E(u_1|v_2)$$

because (u_1, v_2) is independent of $\mathbf{z}$ and so $E(u_1|\mathbf{z}, v_2) = E(u_1|v_2)$.

b. If $E(u_1|v_2) = \gamma_1 v_2$ then, under the previous assumptions,

$$E(y_1|\mathbf{z}, v_2) = \mathbf{z}_1\boldsymbol{\delta}_1 + \mathbf{g}(y_2)\boldsymbol{\alpha}_1 + \gamma_1 v_2.$$

Therefore, in the first step, we would run OLS of y_{i2} on $\mathbf{z}_i$, $i = 1, \ldots, N$, and obtain the OLS residuals, $\hat{v}_{i2}$. In the second step, we would regress y_{i1} on $\mathbf{z}_{i1}$, $\mathbf{g}(y_{i2})$, $\hat{v}_{i2}$, $i = 1, \ldots, N$. By the usual two-step estimation results, all coefficients are $\sqrt{N}$-consistent and asymptotically normal for the corresponding population parameter. Under H_0: $\gamma_1 = 0$, no adjustment is needed to the asymptotic variance, so we can use the usual t statistic on $\hat{v}_{i2}$ as a test of endogeneity. The interesting thing about this method is that, if $G_1 > 1$ we have more than one endogenous explanatory variable -- $g_1(y_1)$, ..., $g_{G_1}(y_2)$ -- but adding a single regressor, $\hat{v}_{i2}$, cleans up the endogeneity. This occurs because all endogenous regressors are a function of y_2, and we have assumed a linear $E(y_2|\mathbf{z})$ (and we have made some other strong assumptions).

As specific examples, the second stage regression might be

$$y_{i1} \text{ on } \mathbf{z}_{i1},\ y_{i2},\ y_{i2}^2,\ y_{i2}^3,\ \hat{v}_{i2},\ i = 1,\ldots,N$$

or

$$y_{i1} \text{ on } \mathbf{z}_{i1},\ 1[a_1 < y_{i2} \le a_2],\ \ldots,\ 1[a_{m-1} < y_{i2} \le a_m],$$
$$1[y_{i2} > a_M],\ \hat{v}_{i2},\ i = 1,\ldots,N.$$

In the latter case, dummies for whether y_{i2} falls into one of the intervals $(-\infty,a_1]$, $(a_1,a_2]$, ..., $(a_{M-1},a_M]$, (a_M,∞) appear in the structural model.

c. We would require at least one element in $\mathbf{z}$, with a nonzero coefficient in $\boldsymbol{\delta}_2$, that is not also in $\mathbf{z}_1$. We know this is needed in the leading case $\mathbf{g}(y_2) = y_2$. If $\mathbf{z} = \mathbf{z}_1$, or $\mathbf{z}_2$ does not appear in $\mathrm{E}(y_2|\mathbf{z})$, then identification would come entirely off of nonlinearities in $\mathbf{g}(y_2)$.

d. We would use traditional 2SLS, where we need at least one IV for each $g_j(y_2)$. Methods for coming up with such IVs are discussed in Section 9.5. Briefly, they will be nonlinear functions of $\mathbf{z}$, which is why $\mathrm{E}(u_1|\mathbf{z}) = 0$ should be assumed. Generally, we add enough nonlinear functions, say $\mathbf{h}(\mathbf{z})$, to the original instrument list $\mathbf{z}$. So, do 2SLS of y_1 on $\mathbf{z}_1$, $\mathbf{g}_2$ using IVs $[\mathbf{z},\mathbf{h}(\mathbf{z})]$. 2SLS will be more robust than the method described in part b because the reduced form for y_2 is not restricted in any way, and we need not assume u_1 is independent of $\mathbf{z}$.

SOLUTIONS TO CHAPTER 7 PROBLEMS

7.1. Write (with probability approaching one)

$$\hat{\boldsymbol{\beta}} = \boldsymbol{\beta} + \left(N^{-1}\sum_{i=1}^{N}\mathbf{X}_i'\mathbf{X}_i\right)^{-1}\left(N^{-1}\sum_{i=1}^{N}\mathbf{X}_i'\mathbf{u}_i\right).$$

From SOLS.2, the weak law of large numbers, and Slutsky's Theorem,

$$\text{plim}\left(N^{-1}\sum_{i=1}^{N}\mathbf{X}_i'\mathbf{X}_i\right)^{-1} = \mathbf{A}^{-1}.$$

Further, under SOLS.1, the WLLN implies that $\text{plim}\left(N^{-1}\sum_{i=1}^{N}\mathbf{X}_i'\mathbf{u}_i\right) = \mathbf{0}$. Thus,

$$\text{plim}\,\hat{\boldsymbol{\beta}} = \boldsymbol{\beta} + \text{plim}\left(N^{-1}\sum_{i=1}^{N}\mathbf{X}_i'\mathbf{X}_i\right)^{-1}\cdot\text{plim}\left(N^{-1}\sum_{i=1}^{N}\mathbf{X}_i'\mathbf{u}_i\right) = \boldsymbol{\beta} + \mathbf{A}^{-1}\cdot\mathbf{0} = \boldsymbol{\beta}. \blacksquare$$

7.3. a. Since OLS equation-by-equation is the same as GLS when $\boldsymbol{\Omega}$ is diagonal, it suffices to show that the GLS estimators for different equations are asymptotically uncorrelated. This follows if the asymptotic variance matrix is block diagonal (see Section 3.5), where the blocking is by the parameter vector for each equation. To establish block diagonality, we use the result from Theorem 7.4: under SGLS.1, SGLS.2, and SGLS.3,

$$\text{Avar}\,\sqrt{N}(\hat{\boldsymbol{\beta}} - \boldsymbol{\beta}) = [\text{E}(\mathbf{X}_i'\boldsymbol{\Omega}^{-1}\mathbf{X}_i)]^{-1}.$$

Now, we can use the special form of $\mathbf{X}_i$ for SUR (see Example 7.1), the fact that $\boldsymbol{\Omega}^{-1}$ is diagonal, and SGLS.3. In the SUR model with diagonal $\boldsymbol{\Omega}$, SGLS.3 implies that $\text{E}(u_{ig}^2\mathbf{x}_{ig}'\mathbf{x}_{ig}) = \sigma_g^2\text{E}(\mathbf{x}_{ig}'\mathbf{x}_{ig})$ for all $g = 1,\ldots,G$, and $\text{E}(u_{ig}u_{ih}\mathbf{x}_{ig}'\mathbf{x}_{ih}) = \text{E}(u_{ig}u_{ih})\text{E}(\mathbf{x}_{ig}'\mathbf{x}_{ih}) = 0$, all $g \neq h$. Therefore, we have

$$\text{E}(\mathbf{X}_i'\boldsymbol{\Omega}^{-1}\mathbf{X}_i) = \begin{pmatrix} \sigma_1^{-2}\text{E}(\mathbf{x}_{i1}'\mathbf{x}_{i1}) & \mathbf{0} & & \mathbf{0} \\ \mathbf{0} & \cdot & & \\ & & \cdot & \mathbf{0} \\ \mathbf{0} & \mathbf{0} & \cdot & \sigma_G^{-2}\text{E}(\mathbf{x}_{iG}'\mathbf{x}_{iG}) \end{pmatrix}.$$

When this matrix is inverted, it is also block diagonal. This shows that the asymptotic variance of what we wanted to show.

b. To test any linear hypothesis, we can either construct the Wald statistic or we can use the weighted sum of squared residuals form of the statistic as in (7.52) or (7.53). For the restricted SSR we must estimate the model with the restriction $\boldsymbol{\beta}_1 = \boldsymbol{\beta}_2$ imposed. See Problem 7.6 for one way to impose general linear restrictions.

c. When $\boldsymbol{\Omega}$ is diagonal in a SUR system, system OLS and GLS are the same. Under SGLS.1 and SGLS.2, GLS and FGLS are asymptotically equivalent (regardless of the structure of $\boldsymbol{\Omega}$) whether or not SGLS.3 holds. But, if $\hat{\boldsymbol{\beta}}_{SOLS} = \hat{\boldsymbol{\beta}}_{GLS}$ and $\sqrt{N}(\hat{\boldsymbol{\beta}}_{FGLS} - \hat{\boldsymbol{\beta}}_{GLS}) = o_p(1)$, then $\sqrt{N}(\hat{\boldsymbol{\beta}}_{SOLS} - \hat{\boldsymbol{\beta}}_{FGLS}) = o_p(1)$. Thus, when $\boldsymbol{\Omega}$ is diagonal, OLS and FGLS are asymptotically equivalent, even if $\hat{\boldsymbol{\Omega}}$ is estimated in an unrestricted fashion and even if the system homoskedasticity assumption SGLS.3 does not hold.

7.5. This is easy with the hint. Note that

$$\left[\hat{\boldsymbol{\Omega}}^{-1} \otimes \left(\sum_{i=1}^{N} \mathbf{x}_i'\mathbf{x}_i\right)\right]^{-1} = \hat{\boldsymbol{\Omega}} \otimes \left(\sum_{i=1}^{N} \mathbf{x}_i'\mathbf{x}_i\right)^{-1}.$$

Therefore,

$$\hat{\boldsymbol{\beta}} = \left[\hat{\boldsymbol{\Omega}} \otimes \left(\sum_{i=1}^{N} \mathbf{x}_i'\mathbf{x}_i\right)^{-1}\right](\hat{\boldsymbol{\Omega}}^{-1} \otimes \mathbf{I}_K)\begin{pmatrix} \sum_{i=1}^{N} \mathbf{x}_i'y_{i1} \\ \vdots \\ \sum_{i=1}^{N} \mathbf{x}_i'y_{iG} \end{pmatrix} = \left[\mathbf{I}_G \otimes \left(\sum_{i=1}^{N} \mathbf{x}_i'\mathbf{x}_i\right)^{-1}\right]\begin{pmatrix} \sum_{i=1}^{N} \mathbf{x}_i'y_{i1} \\ \vdots \\ \sum_{i=1}^{N} \mathbf{x}_i'y_{iG} \end{pmatrix}.$$

Straightforward multiplication shows that the right hand side of the equation is just the vector of stacked $\hat{\hat{\boldsymbol{\beta}}}_g$, $g = 1,\ldots,G$. where $\hat{\hat{\boldsymbol{\beta}}}_g$ is the OLS estimator for equation g. ■

7.7. a. First, the diagonal elements of $\boldsymbol{\Omega}$ are easily found since $E(u_{it}^2) = E[E(u_{it}^2|\mathbf{x}_{it})] = \sigma_t^2$ by iterated expectations. Now, consider $E(u_{it}u_{is})$, and take $s < t$ without loss of generality. Under (7.79), $E(u_{it}|u_{is}) = 0$ since u_{is} is a subset of the conditioning information in (7.80). Applying the law of iterated expectations (LIE) again we have $E(u_{it}u_{is}) = E[E(u_{it}u_{is}|u_{is})] = E[E(u_{it}|u_{is})u_{is})] = 0$.

b. The GLS estimator is

$$\beta^* \equiv \left(\sum_{i=1}^{N} \mathbf{X}_i'\Omega^{-1}\mathbf{X}_i\right)^{-1}\left(\sum_{i=1}^{N} \mathbf{X}_i'\Omega^{-1}\mathbf{y}_i\right)$$

$$= \left(\sum_{i=1}^{N}\sum_{t=1}^{T} \sigma_t^{-2}\mathbf{x}_{it}'\mathbf{x}_{it}\right)^{-1}\left(\sum_{i=1}^{N}\sum_{t=1}^{T} \sigma_t^{-2}\mathbf{x}_{it}'y_{it}\right).$$

c. If, say, $y_{it} = \beta_0 + \beta_1 y_{i,t-1} + u_{it}$, then y_{it} is clearly correlated with u_{it}, which says that $\mathbf{x}_{i,t+1} = y_{it}$ is correlated with u_{it}. Thus, SGLS.1 does not hold. Generally, SGLS.1 holds whenever there is feedback from y_{it} to $\mathbf{x}_{is}$, $s > t$. However, since Ω^{-1} is diagonal, $\mathbf{X}_i'\Omega^{-1}\mathbf{u}_i = \sum_{t=1}^{T} \mathbf{x}_{it}'\sigma_t^{-2}u_{it}$, and so

$$E(\mathbf{X}_i'\Omega^{-1}\mathbf{u}_i) = \sum_{t=1}^{T} \sigma_t^{-2}E(\mathbf{x}_{it}'u_{it}) = \mathbf{0}$$

since $E(\mathbf{x}_{it}'u_{it}) = \mathbf{0}$ under (7.80). Thus, GLS is consistent in this case without SGLS.1.

d. First, since Ω^{-1} is diagonal, $\mathbf{X}_i'\Omega^{-1} = (\sigma_1^{-2}\mathbf{x}_{i1}', \sigma_2^{-2}\mathbf{x}_{i2}', \ldots, \sigma_T^{-2}\mathbf{x}_{iT}')'$, and so

$$E(\mathbf{X}_i'\Omega^{-1}\mathbf{u}_i\mathbf{u}_i'\Omega^{-1}\mathbf{X}_i) = \sum_{t=1}^{T}\sum_{s=1}^{T} \sigma_t^{-2}\sigma_s^{-2}E(u_{it}u_{is}\mathbf{x}_{it}'\mathbf{x}_{is}).$$

First consider the terms for $s \neq t$. Under (7.80), if $s < t$, $E(u_{it}|\mathbf{x}_{it}, u_{is}, \mathbf{x}_{is}) = 0$, and so by the LIE, $E(u_{it}u_{is}\mathbf{x}_{it}'\mathbf{x}_{is}) = \mathbf{0}$, $t \neq s$. Next, for each t,

$$E(u_{it}^2\mathbf{x}_{it}'\mathbf{x}_{it}) = E[E(u_{it}^2\mathbf{x}_{it}'\mathbf{x}_{it}|\mathbf{x}_{it})] = E[E(u_{it}^2|\mathbf{x}_{it})\mathbf{x}_{it}'\mathbf{x}_{it})]$$

$$= E[\sigma_t^2\mathbf{x}_{it}'\mathbf{x}_{it}] = \sigma_t^2E(\mathbf{x}_{it}'\mathbf{x}_{it}), \quad t = 1,2,\ldots,T.$$

It follows that

$$E(\mathbf{X}_i'\Omega^{-1}\mathbf{u}_i\mathbf{u}_i'\Omega^{-1}\mathbf{X}_i) = \sum_{t=1}^{T} \sigma_t^{-2}E(\mathbf{x}_{it}'\mathbf{x}_{it}) = E(\mathbf{X}_i'\Omega^{-1}\mathbf{X}_i).$$

e. First, run pooled regression across all i and t; let $\hat{\hat{u}}_{it}$ denote the pooled OLS residuals. Then, for each t, define

$$\hat{\sigma}_t^2 = N^{-1} \sum_{i=1}^{N} \hat{\hat{u}}_{it}^2$$

(We might replace N with $N - K$ as a degrees-of-freedom adjustment.) Then, by standard arguments, $\hat{\sigma}_t^2 \xrightarrow{p} \sigma_t^2$ as $N \to \infty$.

f. We have verified the assumptions under which standard FGLS statistics have nice properties (although we relaxed SGLS.1). In particular, standard errors obtained from (7.51) are asymptotically valid, and F statistics from (7.53) are valid. Now, if $\hat{\boldsymbol{\Omega}}$ is taken to be the diagonal matrix with $\hat{\sigma}_t^2$ as the tth diagonal, then the FGLS statistics are easily shown to be identical to the statistics obtained by performing pooled OLS on the equation

$$(y_{it}/\hat{\sigma}_t) = (\mathbf{x}_{it}/\hat{\sigma}_t)\boldsymbol{\beta} + error_{it}, \quad t = 1,2,\ldots,T, \quad i = 1,\ldots,N.$$

We can obtain valid standard errors, t statistics, and F statistics from this weighted least squares analysis. For F testing, note that the $\hat{\sigma}_t^2$ should be obtained from the pooled OLS residuals for the unrestricted model.

g. If $\sigma_t^2 = \sigma^2$ for all $t = 1,\ldots,T$, inference is very easy. FGLS reduces to pooled OLS. Thus, we can use the standard errors and test statistics reported by a standard OLS regression pooled across i and t.

7.9. The Stata session follows. I first test for serial correlation before computing the fully robust standard errors:

```
. reg lscrap d89 grant grant_1 lscrap_1 if year != 1987

  Source |       SS       df       MS                  Number of obs =     108
---------+------------------------------               F(  4,   103) =  153.67
   Model |  186.376973     4  46.5942432               Prob > F      =  0.0000
Residual |  31.2296502   103  .303200488               R-squared     =  0.8565
---------+------------------------------               Adj R-squared =  0.8509
   Total |  217.606623   107  2.03370676               Root MSE      =  .55064
```

```
------------------------------------------------------------------------------
      lscrap |      Coef.   Std. Err.       t     P>|t|       [95% Conf. Interval]
-------------+----------------------------------------------------------------
         d89 |  -.1153893   .1199127     -0.962   0.338      -.3532078    .1224292
       grant |  -.1723924   .1257443     -1.371   0.173      -.4217765    .0769918
     grant_1 |  -.1073226   .1610378     -0.666   0.507       -.426703    .2120579
    lscrap_1 |   .8808216   .0357963     24.606   0.000        .809828    .9518152
       _cons |  -.0371354   .0883283     -0.420   0.675      -.2123137     .138043
------------------------------------------------------------------------------
```

The estimated effect of *grant*, and its lag, are now the expected sign, but neither is strongly statistically significant. The variable *grant* would be if we use a 10% significance level and a one-sided test. The results are certainly different from when we omit the lag of log(*scrap*).

Now test for AR(1) serial correlation:

```
. predict uhat, resid
(363 missing values generated)

. gen uhat_1 = uhat[_n-1] if d89
(417 missing values generated)

. reg lscrap grant grant_1 lscrap_1 uhat_1 if d89

  Source |       SS       df       MS                  Number of obs =      54
---------+------------------------------               F(  4,    49) =   73.47
   Model |  94.4746525     4  23.6186631               Prob > F      =  0.0000
Residual |  15.7530202    49  .321490208               R-squared     =  0.8571
---------+------------------------------               Adj R-squared =  0.8454
   Total |  110.227673    53  2.07976741               Root MSE      =    .567

------------------------------------------------------------------------------
  lscrap |      Coef.   Std. Err.       t     P>|t|       [95% Conf. Interval]
---------+--------------------------------------------------------------------
   grant |   .0165089    .215732      0.077   0.939      -.4170208    .4500385
 grant_1 |  -.0276544   .1746251     -0.158   0.875      -.3785767    .3232679
lscrap_1 |   .9204706   .0571831     16.097   0.000       .8055569    1.035384
  uhat_1 |   .2790328   .1576739      1.770   0.083      -.0378247    .5958904
   _cons |   -.232525   .1146314     -2.028   0.048      -.4628854   -.0021646
------------------------------------------------------------------------------

. reg lscrap d89 grant grant_1 lscrap_1 if year != 1987, robust cluster(fcode)

Regression with robust standard errors                 Number of obs =     108
                                                       F(  4,    53) =   77.24
                                                       Prob > F      =  0.0000
```

```
                                                   R-squared      =  0.8565
Number of clusters (fcode) = 54                    Root MSE       =  .55064

------------------------------------------------------------------------------
             |               Robust
      lscrap |      Coef.   Std. Err.       t     P>|t|      [95% Conf. Interval]
-------------+----------------------------------------------------------------
         d89 |  -.1153893    .1145118     -1.01   0.318     -.3450708    .1142922
       grant |  -.1723924    .1188807     -1.45   0.153     -.4108369    .0660522
     grant_1 |  -.1073226    .1790052     -0.60   0.551     -.4663616    .2517165
    lscrap_1 |   .8808216    .0645344     13.65   0.000      .7513821    1.010261
       _cons |  -.0371354    .0893147     -0.42   0.679      -.216278    .1420073
------------------------------------------------------------------------------
```

The robust standard errors for *grant* and $grant_{-1}$ are actually smaller than the usual ones, making both more statistically significant. However, *grant* and $grant_{-1}$ are jointly insignificant:

```
. test grant grant_1

 ( 1)  grant = 0.0
 ( 2)  grant_1 = 0.0

       F(  2,    53) =    1.14
            Prob > F =    0.3266
```

7.11. a. The following Stata output should be self-explanatory. There is strong evidence of positive serial correlation in the static model, and the fully robust standard errors are much larger than the nonrobust ones.

```
. reg lcrmrte lprbarr lprbconv lprbpris lavgsen lpolpc d82-d87

  Source |       SS       df       MS                  Number of obs =     630
---------+------------------------------               F( 11,   618) =   74.49
   Model |  117.644669    11  10.6949699               Prob > F      =  0.0000
Residual |   88.735673   618  .143585231               R-squared     =  0.5700
---------+------------------------------               Adj R-squared =  0.5624
   Total |  206.380342   629  .328108652               Root MSE      =  .37893

------------------------------------------------------------------------------
 lcrmrte |      Coef.   Std. Err.       t     P>|t|       [95% Conf. Interval]
---------+--------------------------------------------------------------------
 lprbarr |  -.7195033   .0367657    -19.570   0.000      -.7917042   -.6473024
lprbconv |  -.5456589   .0263683    -20.694   0.000      -.5974413   -.4938765
```

```
   lprbpris |   .2475521    .0672268      3.682   0.000       .1155314    .3795728
    lavgsen |  -.0867575    .0579205     -1.498   0.135      -.2005023    .0269872
     lpolpc |   .3659886    .0300252     12.189   0.000       .3070248    .4249525
        d82 |   .0051371     .057931      0.089   0.929      -.1086284    .1189026
        d83 |   -.043503    .0576243     -0.755   0.451      -.1566662    .0696601
        d84 |  -.1087542     .057923     -1.878   0.061       -.222504    .0049957
        d85 |  -.0780454    .0583244     -1.338   0.181      -.1925835    .0364927
        d86 |  -.0420791    .0578218     -0.728   0.467        -.15563    .0714718
        d87 |  -.0270426     .056899     -0.475   0.635      -.1387815    .0846963
      _cons |  -2.082293    .2516253     -8.275   0.000      -2.576438   -1.588149
------------------------------------------------------------------------------

. predict uhat, resid

. gen uhat_1 = uhat[_n-1] if year > 81
(90 missing values generated)

. reg uhat uhat_1

  Source |       SS       df       MS                  Number of obs =     540
---------+------------------------------               F(  1,   538) =  831.46
   Model |  46.6680407     1  46.6680407               Prob > F      =  0.0000
Residual |  30.1968286   538  .056127934               R-squared     =  0.6071
---------+------------------------------               Adj R-squared =  0.6064
   Total |  76.8648693   539  .142606437               Root MSE      =  .23691

------------------------------------------------------------------------------
    uhat |      Coef.   Std. Err.       t     P>|t|       [95% Conf. Interval]
---------+--------------------------------------------------------------------
  uhat_1 |   .7918085     .02746     28.835   0.000       .7378666    .8457504
   _cons |   1.74e-10   .0101951      0.000   1.000      -.0200271    .0200271
------------------------------------------------------------------------------
```

Because of the strong serial correlation, I obtain the fully robust standard errors:

```
. reg lcrmrte lprbarr lprbconv lprbpris lavgsen lpolpc d82-d87, robust
cluster(county)

Regression with robust standard errors                 Number of obs =     630
                                                       F( 11,    89) =   37.19
                                                       Prob > F      =  0.0000
                                                       R-squared     =  0.5700
Number of clusters (county) = 90                       Root MSE      =  .37893

------------------------------------------------------------------------------
             |               Robust
     lcrmrte |      Coef.   Std. Err.      t     P>|t|      [95% Conf. Interval]
-------------+----------------------------------------------------------------
```

```
    lprbarr |  -.7195033   .1095979     -6.56   0.000      -.9372719   -.5017347
   lprbconv |  -.5456589   .0704368     -7.75   0.000      -.6856152   -.4057025
   lprbpris |   .2475521   .1088453      2.27   0.025       .0312787    .4638255
    lavgsen |  -.0867575   .1130321     -0.77   0.445      -.3113499    .1378348
     lpolpc |   .3659886    .121078      3.02   0.003       .1254092    .6065681
        d82 |   .0051371   .0367296      0.14   0.889      -.0678438    .0781181
        d83 |   -.043503    .033643     -1.29   0.199      -.1103509    .0233448
        d84 |  -.1087542   .0391758     -2.78   0.007      -.1865956   -.0309127
        d85 |  -.0780454   .0385625     -2.02   0.046      -.1546683   -.0014224
        d86 |  -.0420791   .0428788     -0.98   0.329      -.1272783    .0431201
        d87 |  -.0270426   .0381447     -0.71   0.480      -.1028353    .0487502
      _cons |  -2.082293   .8647054     -2.41   0.018      -3.800445   -.3641423
------------------------------------------------------------------------------

. drop uhat uhat_1
```

b. We lose the first year, 1981, when we add the lag of log(*crmrte*):

```
. gen lcrmrt_1 = lcrmrte[_n-1] if year > 81
(90 missing values generated)

. reg lcrmrte lprbarr lprbconv lprbpris lavgsen lpolpc d83-d87 lcrmrt_1

  Source |       SS       df       MS                  Number of obs =     540
---------+------------------------------               F( 11,   528) =  464.68
   Model |  163.287174    11  14.8442885               Prob > F      =  0.0000
Residual |  16.8670945   528  .031945255               R-squared     =  0.9064
---------+------------------------------               Adj R-squared =  0.9044
   Total |  180.154268   539  .334237975               Root MSE      =  .17873

------------------------------------------------------------------------------
 lcrmrte |      Coef.   Std. Err.       t     P>|t|       [95% Conf. Interval]
---------+--------------------------------------------------------------------
 lprbarr |  -.1668349   .0229405     -7.273   0.000      -.2119007   -.1217691
lprbconv |  -.1285118   .0165096     -7.784   0.000      -.1609444   -.0960793
lprbpris |  -.0107492   .0345003     -0.312   0.755       -.078524    .0570255
 lavgsen |  -.1152298    .030387     -3.792   0.000       -.174924   -.0555355
  lpolpc |    .101492   .0164261      6.179   0.000       .0692234    .1337606
     d83 |  -.0649438   .0267299     -2.430   0.015      -.1174537   -.0124338
     d84 |  -.0536882   .0267623     -2.006   0.045      -.1062619   -.0011145
     d85 |  -.0085982   .0268172     -0.321   0.749      -.0612797    .0440833
     d86 |   .0420159    .026896      1.562   0.119      -.0108203    .0948522
     d87 |   .0671272   .0271816      2.470   0.014       .0137298    .1205245
lcrmrt_1 |   .8263047   .0190806     43.306   0.000       .7888214    .8637879
   _cons |  -.0304828   .1324195     -0.230   0.818      -.2906166     .229651
------------------------------------------------------------------------------
```

Not surprisingly, the lagged crime rate is very significant. Further, including it makes all other coefficients much smaller in magnitude. The variable log(*prbpris*) now has a negative sign, although it is insignificant. We still get a positive relationship between size of police force and crime rate, however.

c. There is no evidence of serial correlation in the model with a lagged dependent variable:

```
. predict uhat, resid
(90 missing values generated)

. gen uhat_1 = uhat[_n-1] if year > 82
(180 missing values generated)

. reg lcrmrte lprbarr lprbconv lprbpris lavgsen lpolpc d84-d87 lcrmrt_1 uhat_1
```

From this regression the coefficient on $uhat_{-1}$ is only -.059 with t statistic -.986, which means that there is little evidence of serial correlation (especially since $\hat{\rho}$ is practically small). Thus, I will not correct the standard errors.

d. None of the log(*wage*) variables is statistically significant, and the magnitudes are pretty small in all cases:

```
. reg lcrmrte lprbarr lprbconv lprbpris lavgsen lpolpc d83-d87 lcrmrt_1 lwcon-
lwloc

  Source |       SS       df       MS              Number of obs =     540
---------+------------------------------           F( 20,   519) =  255.32
   Model |  163.533423    20  8.17667116           Prob > F      =  0.0000
Residual |  16.6208452   519   .03202475           R-squared     =  0.9077
---------+------------------------------           Adj R-squared =  0.9042
   Total |  180.154268   539  .334237975           Root MSE      =  .17895

------------------------------------------------------------------------------
 lcrmrte |      Coef.   Std. Err.       t     P>|t|       [95% Conf. Interval]
---------+--------------------------------------------------------------------
 lprbarr |  -.1746053   .0238458     -7.322   0.000      -.2214516   -.1277591
lprbconv |  -.1337714   .0169096     -7.911   0.000       -.166991   -.1005518
lprbpris |  -.0195318   .0352873     -0.554   0.580      -.0888553    .0497918
 lavgsen |  -.1108926   .0311719     -3.557   0.000      -.1721313    -.049654
  lpolpc |   .1050704   .0172627      6.087   0.000        .071157    .1389838
     d83 |  -.0729231   .0286922     -2.542   0.011      -.1292903   -.0165559
     d84 |  -.0652494   .0287165     -2.272   0.023      -.1216644   -.0088345
```

d85	-.0258059	.0326156	-0.791	0.429	-.0898807	.038269
d86	.0263763	.0371746	0.710	0.478	-.0466549	.0994076
d87	.0465632	.0418004	1.114	0.266	-.0355555	.1286819
lcrmrt_1	.8087768	.0208067	38.871	0.000	.767901	.8496525
lwcon	-.0283133	.0392516	-0.721	0.471	-.1054249	.0487983
lwtuc	-.0034567	.0223995	-0.154	0.877	-.0474615	.0405482
lwtrd	.0121236	.0439875	0.276	0.783	-.0742918	.098539
lwfir	.0296003	.0318995	0.928	0.354	-.0330676	.0922683
lwser	.012903	.0221872	0.582	0.561	-.0306847	.0564908
lwmfg	-.0409046	.0389325	-1.051	0.294	-.1173893	.0355801
lwfed	.1070534	.0798526	1.341	0.181	-.0498207	.2639275
lwsta	-.0903894	.0660699	-1.368	0.172	-.2201867	.039408
lwloc	.0961124	.1003172	0.958	0.338	-.1009652	.29319
_cons	-.6438061	.6335887	-1.016	0.310	-1.88852	.6009076

```
------------------------------------------------------------------------------

. test lwcon lwtuc lwtrd lwfir lwser lwmfg lwfed lwsta lwloc

 ( 1)  lwcon = 0.0
 ( 2)  lwtuc = 0.0
 ( 3)  lwtrd = 0.0
 ( 4)  lwfir = 0.0
 ( 5)  lwser = 0.0
 ( 6)  lwmfg = 0.0
 ( 7)  lwfed = 0.0
 ( 8)  lwsta = 0.0
 ( 9)  lwloc = 0.0

       F(  9,   519) =    0.85
            Prob > F =    0.5663
```

7.13 (Bonus Question): Consider the standard linear system

$$\mathbf{y}_i = \mathbf{X}_i\boldsymbol{\beta} + \mathbf{u}_i, \ \mathrm{E}(\mathbf{X}_i \otimes \mathbf{u}_i) = \mathbf{0}$$

$$\mathrm{E}(\mathbf{u}_i\mathbf{u}_i' | \mathbf{X}_i) = \mathrm{E}(\mathbf{u}_i\mathbf{u}_i') = \boldsymbol{\Omega},$$

where $\boldsymbol{\Omega}$ is a positive definite $G \times G$ matrix. Under these assumptions, any feasible GLS estimator, $\hat{\boldsymbol{\beta}}$, that uses a consistent estimator $\hat{\boldsymbol{\Omega}}$ of $\boldsymbol{\Omega}$, is consistent and $\sqrt{N}$-asymptotically normal for $\boldsymbol{\beta}$. Plus,

$$\mathrm{Avar}[\sqrt{N}(\hat{\boldsymbol{\beta}} - \boldsymbol{\beta})] = [\mathrm{E}(\mathbf{X}_i'\Omega^{-1}\mathbf{X}_i)]^{-1}.$$

Now, let $\hat{\hat{\boldsymbol{\beta}}}$ be a feasible GLS estimator using a positive definite variance matrix estimator $\hat{\boldsymbol{\Lambda}} \overset{p}{\to} \boldsymbol{\Lambda} \neq \boldsymbol{\Omega}$. For example, in a system context we might incorrectly assume that all covariances in $\boldsymbol{\Omega}$ are zero. In a panel data context, we might assume an AR(1) structure for the error term when $\mathbf{\Omega}$ is a more general form.

a. Show that $\hat{\hat{\boldsymbol{\beta}}}$ is consistent for $\boldsymbol{\beta}$ under standard assumptions.

b. Find Avar$[\sqrt{N}(\hat{\hat{\boldsymbol{\beta}}} - \boldsymbol{\beta})]$.

c. How would you consistently estimate Avar$[\sqrt{N}(\hat{\hat{\boldsymbol{\beta}}} - \boldsymbol{\beta})]$ if you are willing to assume system homoskedasticity -- $E(\mathbf{u}_i\mathbf{u}_i'|\mathbf{X}_i) = E(\mathbf{u}_i\mathbf{u}_i')$ -- but not necessarily $\mathbf{\Lambda} = \mathbf{\Omega}$?

d. Show that FGLS with a consistent estimator of $\mathbf{\Omega}$ is always as efficient as FGLS with an inconsistent estimator of $\mathbf{\Lambda}$.

Answer:

a. This follows from the standard expansion for any FGLS estimator, a rank condition, and the law of large numbers:

$$\hat{\hat{\boldsymbol{\beta}}} = \left(\sum_{i=1}^{N}\mathbf{X}_i'\hat{\mathbf{\Lambda}}^{-1}\mathbf{X}_i\right)^{-1}\left(\sum_{i=1}^{N}\mathbf{X}_i'\hat{\mathbf{\Lambda}}^{-1}\mathbf{y}_i\right) =$$
$$= \boldsymbol{\beta} + \left(N^{-1}\sum_{i=1}^{N}\mathbf{X}_i'\hat{\mathbf{\Lambda}}^{-1}\mathbf{X}_i\right)^{-1}\left(N^{-1}\sum_{i=1}^{N}\mathbf{X}_i'\hat{\mathbf{\Lambda}}^{-1}\mathbf{u}_i\right).$$

Since $\hat{\mathbf{\Lambda}}^{-1} \xrightarrow{p} \mathbf{\Lambda}^{-1}$, standard arguments give

$$\left(N^{-1}\sum_{i=1}^{N}\mathbf{X}_i'\hat{\mathbf{\Lambda}}^{-1}\mathbf{X}_i\right)^{-1} \xrightarrow{p} [E(\mathbf{X}_i'\mathbf{\Lambda}^{-1}\mathbf{X}_i)]^{-1},$$
$$N^{-1}\sum_{i=1}^{N}\mathbf{X}_i'\hat{\mathbf{\Lambda}}^{-1}\mathbf{u}_i \xrightarrow{p} E(\mathbf{X}_i'\mathbf{\Lambda}^{-1}\mathbf{u}_i) = \mathbf{0},$$

where $E(\mathbf{X}_i'\mathbf{\Lambda}^{-1}\mathbf{u}_i) = \mathbf{0}$ follows by $E(\mathbf{X}_i \otimes \mathbf{u}_i) = \mathbf{0}$.

b. From part a and the usual manipulations we can write

$$\sqrt{N}(\hat{\hat{\boldsymbol{\beta}}} - \boldsymbol{\beta}) = \left(N^{-1}\sum_{i=1}^{N}\mathbf{X}_i'\hat{\mathbf{\Lambda}}^{-1}\mathbf{X}_i\right)^{-1}\left(N^{-1/2}\sum_{i=1}^{N}\mathbf{X}_i'\hat{\mathbf{\Lambda}}^{-1}\mathbf{u}_i\right)$$
$$= [E(\mathbf{X}_i'\mathbf{\Lambda}^{-1}\mathbf{X}_i)]^{-1}\left(N^{-1/2}\sum_{i=1}^{N}\mathbf{X}_i'\mathbf{\Lambda}^{-1}\mathbf{u}_i\right) + o_p(1).$$

Therefore,

$$\text{Avar}[\sqrt{N}(\hat{\hat{\boldsymbol{\beta}}} - \boldsymbol{\beta})] = [E(\mathbf{X}_i'\mathbf{\Lambda}^{-1}\mathbf{X}_i)]^{-1}E(\mathbf{X}_i'\mathbf{\Lambda}^{-1}\mathbf{u}_i\mathbf{u}_i'\mathbf{\Lambda}^{-1}\mathbf{X}_i)[E(\mathbf{X}_i'\mathbf{\Lambda}^{-1}\mathbf{X}_i)]^{-1}.$$

Now, under the system homoskedasticity assumption $E(\mathbf{u}_i\mathbf{u}_i'|\mathbf{X}_i) = \mathbf{\Omega}$, the usual iterated expectations argument gives

$$E[\mathbf{X}_i'\Lambda^{-1}\mathbf{u}_i\mathbf{u}_i'\Lambda^{-1}\mathbf{X}_i] = E(\mathbf{X}_i'\Lambda^{-1}\Omega\Lambda^{-1}\mathbf{X}_i).$$

So,

$$\text{Avar}[\sqrt{N}(\hat{\hat{\boldsymbol{\beta}}} - \boldsymbol{\beta})] = [E(\mathbf{X}_i'\Lambda^{-1}\mathbf{X}_i)]^{-1}E(\mathbf{X}_i'\Lambda^{-1}\Omega\Lambda^{-1}\mathbf{X}_i)[E(\mathbf{X}_i'\Lambda^{-1}\mathbf{X}_i)]^{-1}.$$

c. We need to estimate Ω consistently. Let $\hat{\hat{\mathbf{u}}}_i = \mathbf{y}_i - \mathbf{X}_i\hat{\hat{\boldsymbol{\beta}}}$ be the residuals from the incorrect FGLS estimation. Then a consistent estimator of Ω is $\hat{\hat{\Omega}} = N^{-1}\sum_{i=1}^{N}\hat{\hat{\mathbf{u}}}_i\hat{\hat{\mathbf{u}}}_i'$. So a consistent estimator that uses system homoskedasticity is

$$\left(N^{-1}\sum_{i=1}^{N}\mathbf{X}_i'\hat{\Lambda}^{-1}\mathbf{X}_i\right)^{-1}\left(N^{-1/2}\sum_{i=1}^{N}\mathbf{X}_i'\hat{\Lambda}^{-1}\hat{\hat{\Omega}}\hat{\Lambda}^{-1}\mathbf{X}_i\right)\left(N^{-1}\sum_{i=1}^{N}\mathbf{X}_i'\hat{\Lambda}^{-1}\mathbf{X}_i\right)^{-1}$$

d. We have to compare the asymptotic variance from part b with the usual FGLS asymptotic variance. To show the difference is positive semi-definite, it suffices to show

$$E(\mathbf{X}_i'\Omega^{-1}\mathbf{X}_i) - E(\mathbf{X}_i'\Lambda^{-1}\mathbf{X}_i)[E(\mathbf{X}_i'\Lambda^{-1}\Omega\Lambda^{-1}\mathbf{X}_i)]^{-1}E(\mathbf{X}_i'\Lambda^{-1}\mathbf{X}_i)$$

is positive semi-definite. Define $\mathbf{Z}_i \equiv \Omega^{-1/2}\mathbf{X}_i$ and $\mathbf{W}_i \equiv \Omega^{1/2}\Lambda^{-1}\mathbf{X}_i$. Then the difference above can be written as $E(\mathbf{Z}_i'\mathbf{Z}_i) - E(\mathbf{Z}_i'\mathbf{W}_i)[E(\mathbf{W}_i'\mathbf{W}_i)]^{-1}E(\mathbf{W}_i'\mathbf{Z}_i)$, which is easily seen to be $E(\mathbf{R}_i'\mathbf{R}_i)$, where $\mathbf{R}_i$ is the $G \times K$ matrix of population residuals from the regression of $\mathbf{Z}_i$ on $\mathbf{W}_i$: $\mathbf{R}_i = \mathbf{Z}_i - \mathbf{W}_i\Pi$, $\Pi = [E(\mathbf{W}_i'\mathbf{W}_i)]^{-1}E(\mathbf{W}_i'\mathbf{Z}_i)$. Naturally, $E(\mathbf{R}_i'\mathbf{R}_i)$ is at least positive semi-definite.

SOLUTIONS TO CHAPTER 8 PROBLEMS

8.1. Letting $Q(\mathbf{b})$ denote the objective function in (8.23), it follows from multivariable calculus that

$$\frac{\partial Q(\mathbf{b})'}{\partial \mathbf{b}} = -2\left(\sum_{i=1}^{N} \mathbf{Z}_i'\mathbf{X}_i\right)'\hat{\mathbf{W}}\left(\sum_{i=1}^{N} \mathbf{Z}_i'(\mathbf{y}_i - \mathbf{X}_i\mathbf{b})\right).$$

Evaluating the derivative at the solution $\hat{\boldsymbol{\beta}}$ gives

$$\left(\sum_{i=1}^{N} \mathbf{Z}_i'\mathbf{X}_i\right)'\hat{\mathbf{W}}\left(\sum_{i=1}^{N} \mathbf{Z}_i'(\mathbf{y}_i - \mathbf{X}_i\hat{\boldsymbol{\beta}})\right) = \mathbf{0}.$$

In terms of full data matrices, we can write, after simple algebra,

$$(\mathbf{X}'\mathbf{Z}\hat{\mathbf{W}}\mathbf{Z}'\mathbf{X})\hat{\boldsymbol{\beta}} = (\mathbf{X}'\mathbf{Z}\hat{\mathbf{W}}\mathbf{Z}'\mathbf{Y}).$$

Solving for $\hat{\boldsymbol{\beta}}$ gives (8.24).

8.3. First, we can always write $\mathbf{x}$ as its linear projection plus an error: $\mathbf{x} = \mathbf{x}^* + \mathbf{e}$, where $\mathbf{x}^* = \mathbf{z}\boldsymbol{\Pi}$ and $E(\mathbf{z}'\mathbf{e}) = \mathbf{0}$. Therefore, $E(\mathbf{z}'\mathbf{x}) = E(\mathbf{z}'\mathbf{x}^*)$, which verifies the first part of the hint. To verify the second step, let $\mathbf{h} \equiv \mathbf{h}(\mathbf{z})$, and write the linear projection as

$$L(\mathbf{y}|\mathbf{z},\mathbf{h}) = \mathbf{z}\boldsymbol{\Pi}_1 + \mathbf{h}\boldsymbol{\Pi}_2,$$

where $\boldsymbol{\Pi}_1$ is $M \times K$ and $\boldsymbol{\Pi}_2$ is $Q \times K$. Then we must show that $\boldsymbol{\Pi}_2 = \mathbf{0}$. But, from the two-step projection theorem (see Property LP.7 in Chapter 2),

$$\boldsymbol{\Pi}_2 = [E(\mathbf{s}'\mathbf{s})]^{-1}E(\mathbf{s}'\mathbf{r}), \text{ where } \mathbf{s} \equiv \mathbf{h} - L(\mathbf{h}|\mathbf{z}) \text{ and } \mathbf{r} \equiv \mathbf{x} - L(\mathbf{x}|\mathbf{z}).$$

Now, by the assumption that $E(\mathbf{x}|\mathbf{z}) = L(\mathbf{x}|\mathbf{z})$, $\mathbf{r}$ is also equal to $\mathbf{x} - E(\mathbf{x}|\mathbf{z})$. Therefore, $E(\mathbf{r}|\mathbf{z}) = \mathbf{0}$, and so $\mathbf{r}$ is uncorrelated with all functions of $\mathbf{z}$. But $\mathbf{s}$ is simply a function of $\mathbf{z}$ since $\mathbf{h} \equiv \mathbf{h}(\mathbf{z})$. Therefore, $E(\mathbf{s}'\mathbf{r}) = \mathbf{0}$, and this shows that $\boldsymbol{\Pi}_2 = \mathbf{0}$.

8.5. This follows directly from the hint. Straightforward matrix algebra shows that $(\mathbf{C}'\boldsymbol{\Lambda}^{-1}\mathbf{C}) - (\mathbf{C}'\mathbf{W}\mathbf{C})(\mathbf{C}'\mathbf{W}\boldsymbol{\Lambda}\mathbf{W}\mathbf{C})^{-1}(\mathbf{C}'\mathbf{W}\mathbf{C})$ can be written as

$$\mathbf{C}'\boldsymbol{\Lambda}^{-1/2}[\mathbf{I}_L - \mathbf{D}(\mathbf{D}'\mathbf{D})^{-1}\mathbf{D}']\boldsymbol{\Lambda}^{-1/2}\mathbf{C},$$

where $\mathbf{D} \equiv \boldsymbol{\Lambda}^{1/2}\mathbf{W}\mathbf{C}$. Since this is a matrix quadratic form in the $L \times L$ symmetric, idempotent matrix $\mathbf{I}_L - \mathbf{D}(\mathbf{D}'\mathbf{D})^{-1}\mathbf{D}'$, it is necessarily itself positive semi-definite.

8.7. When $\hat{\boldsymbol{\Omega}}$ is diagonal and $\mathbf{Z}_i$ has the form in (8.15), $\sum_{i=1}^{N} \mathbf{Z}_i'\hat{\boldsymbol{\Omega}}\mathbf{Z}_i = \mathbf{Z}'(\mathbf{I}_N \otimes \hat{\boldsymbol{\Omega}})\mathbf{Z}$ is a block diagonal matrix with g^{th} block $\hat{\sigma}_g^2\left(\sum_{i=1}^{N} \mathbf{z}_{ig}'\mathbf{z}_{ig}\right) \equiv \hat{\sigma}_g^2\mathbf{Z}_g'\mathbf{Z}_g$, where $\mathbf{Z}_g$ denotes the $N \times L_g$ matrix of instruments for the gth equation. Further, $\mathbf{Z}'\mathbf{X}$ is block diagonal with g^{th} block $\mathbf{Z}_g'\mathbf{X}_g$. Using these facts, it is now straightforward to show that the 3SLS estimator consists of $[\mathbf{X}_g'\mathbf{Z}_g(\mathbf{Z}_g'\mathbf{Z}_g)^{-1}\mathbf{Z}_g'\mathbf{X}_g]^{-1}\mathbf{X}_g'\mathbf{Z}_g(\mathbf{Z}_g'\mathbf{Z}_g)^{-1}\mathbf{Z}_g'\mathbf{Y}_g$ stacked from $g = 1,\ldots,G$. This is just the system 2SLS estimator or, equivalently, 2SLS equation-by-equation.

8.8. a. With $\mathbf{Z}_i = (\mathbf{z}_{i1}',\mathbf{z}_{i2}',\ldots,\mathbf{z}_{iT}')'$ and $\mathbf{X}_i = (\mathbf{x}_{i1}',\mathbf{x}_{i2}',\ldots,\mathbf{x}_{iT}')'$,

$$\mathbf{Z}_i'\mathbf{Z}_i = \sum_{t=1}^{T} \mathbf{z}_{it}'\mathbf{z}_{it},\quad \mathbf{Z}_i'\mathbf{X}_i = \sum_{t=1}^{T} \mathbf{z}_{it}'\mathbf{x}_{it},\ \text{and}\ \mathbf{Z}_i'\mathbf{y}_i = \sum_{t=1}^{T} \mathbf{z}_{it}'y_{it}.$$

Summing over all i gives

$$\mathbf{Z}'\mathbf{Z} = \sum_{i=1}^{N}\sum_{t=1}^{T} \mathbf{z}_{it}'\mathbf{z}_{it},\quad \mathbf{Z}'\mathbf{X} = \sum_{i=1}^{N}\sum_{t=1}^{T} \mathbf{z}_{it}'\mathbf{x}_{it},\ \text{and}\ \mathbf{Z}'\mathbf{Y} = \sum_{i=1}^{N}\sum_{t=1}^{T} \mathbf{z}_{it}'y_{it}.$$

b. $\text{rank}\ \mathrm{E}\left(\sum_{t=1}^{T} \mathbf{z}_{it}'\mathbf{x}_{it}\right) = K.$

c. Let $\hat{\mathbf{u}}_i$ be the T x 1 vector of pooled 2SLS residuals, $\hat{\mathbf{u}}_i = \mathbf{y}_i - \mathbf{X}_i\hat{\boldsymbol{\beta}}$. Then we just use (8.27) with $\hat{\mathbf{W}} = (\mathbf{Z}'\mathbf{Z}/N)^{-1}$ and $\hat{\boldsymbol{\Lambda}} = N^{-1}\sum_{i=1}^{N} \mathbf{Z}_i'\hat{\mathbf{u}}_i\hat{\mathbf{u}}_i'\mathbf{Z}_i$, cancelling N everywhere:

$$[(\mathbf{X}'\mathbf{Z})(\mathbf{Z}'\mathbf{Z})^{-1}(\mathbf{Z}'\mathbf{X})]^{-1}(\mathbf{X}'\mathbf{Z})(\mathbf{Z}'\mathbf{Z})^{-1}\left(\sum_{i=1}^{N} \mathbf{Z}_i'\hat{\mathbf{u}}_i\hat{\mathbf{u}}_i'\mathbf{Z}_i\right) \qquad (8.58)$$

$$\cdot(\mathbf{Z}'\mathbf{Z}^{-1})(\mathbf{Z}'\mathbf{X})[(\mathbf{X}'\mathbf{Z})(\mathbf{Z}'\mathbf{Z})^{-1}(\mathbf{Z}'\mathbf{X})]^{-1}.$$

d. Using reasoning almost identical to Problem 7.7, (8.56) implies that, for $s < t$,

$$\begin{aligned} E(u_{it}u_{is}\mathbf{z}_{it}'\mathbf{z}_{is}) &= E[E(u_{it}u_{is}\mathbf{z}_{it}'\mathbf{z}_{is}|\mathbf{z}_{it},u_{is},\mathbf{z}_{is})] \\ &= E[E(u_{it}|\mathbf{z}_{it},u_{is},\mathbf{z}_{is})u_{is}\mathbf{z}_{it}'\mathbf{z}_{is}] \\ &= E[0\cdot u_{is}\mathbf{z}_{it}'\mathbf{z}_{is}] = \mathbf{0} \end{aligned}$$

because $E(u_{it}|\mathbf{z}_{it},u_{is},\mathbf{z}_{is}) = 0$ for $s < t$. A similar argument works for $t > s$. So for all $t \neq s$,

$$E(u_{it}u_{is}\mathbf{z}_{it}'\mathbf{z}_{is}) = \mathbf{0}.$$

Similarly, (8.57) and iterated expectations implies that

$$\begin{aligned} E(u_{it}^2\mathbf{z}_{it}'\mathbf{z}_{it}) &= E[E(u_{it}^2\mathbf{z}_{it}'\mathbf{z}_{it}|\mathbf{z}_{it})] \\ &= E[E(u_{it}^2|\mathbf{z}_{it})\mathbf{z}_{it}'\mathbf{z}_{it}] = \sigma^2 E[(\mathbf{z}_{it}'\mathbf{z}_{it}), \quad t = 1,\ldots,T. \end{aligned}$$

Together, these results imply that

$$\mathrm{Var}(\mathbf{Z}_i'\mathbf{u}_i) = \sigma^2\sum_{t=1}^{T} E(\mathbf{z}_{it}'\mathbf{z}_{it}).$$

A consistent estimator of this matrix is $\hat{\sigma}^2(\mathbf{Z}'\mathbf{Z}/N)$, where $\hat{\sigma}^2 = 1/(NT)\sum_{i=1}^{N}\sum_{t=1}^{T}\hat{u}_{it}^2$, by the usual law-of-large-numbers arguments. A degrees-of-freedom adjustment replaces NT with $NT - K$. Replacing $\sum_{i=1}^{N}\mathbf{Z}_i'\hat{\mathbf{u}}_i\hat{\mathbf{u}}_i'\mathbf{Z}_i$ in (8.58) with $\hat{\sigma}^2(\mathbf{Z}'\mathbf{Z})$ [since $\hat{\sigma}^2(\mathbf{Z}'\mathbf{Z}/N)$ can play the role of $\hat{\mathbf{\Lambda}}$ under the maintained assumptions] and cancelling gives the estimated asymptotic variance of $\hat{\boldsymbol{\beta}}$ as

$$\hat{\sigma}^2[(\mathbf{X}'\mathbf{Z})(\mathbf{Z}'\mathbf{Z})^{-1}(\mathbf{Z}'\mathbf{X})]^{-1}.$$

This is exactly the variance estimator that would be computed from the pooled 2SLS estimation. This means that the usual 2SLS standard errors and test statistics are asymptotically valid.

e. If the unconditional variance changes across t, the simplest thing to do is to weight the variables in each time period by $1/\hat{\sigma}_t$, where $\hat{\sigma}_t$ is a consistent estimator of $\sigma_t = \mathrm{sd}(u_{it})$. A consistent estimator of σ_t^2 is

$$\hat{\sigma}_t^2 = N^{-1}\sum_{i=1}^{N}\hat{u}_{it}^2.$$

Now, apply pooled 2SLS to the equation

$$(y_{it}/\hat{\sigma}_t) = (\mathbf{x}_{it}/\hat{\sigma}_t)\boldsymbol{\beta} + error_{it}$$

using instruments $\mathbf{z}_{it}/\hat{\sigma}_t$. The usual statistics from this procedure will be valid. This estimator, which is a special case of a *generalized instrumental variables* (GIV) estimator, turns out to be identical to the GMM estimator that uses weighting matrix $\left(N^{-1}\sum_{i=1}^{N}\sum_{t=1}^{T}\hat{\sigma}_t^2\mathbf{z}_{it}'\mathbf{z}_{it}\right)^{-1}$, which is optimal under the assumptions made. See Im, Ahn, Schmidt, and Wooldridge (1999, Section 2) for discussion of a more general result.

8.9. The optimal instruments are given in Theorem 8.5, with $G = 1$:

$$\mathbf{z}_i^* = [\omega(\mathbf{z}_i)]^{-1}\mathrm{E}(\mathbf{x}_i|\mathbf{z}_i),\ \omega(\mathbf{z}_i) = \mathrm{E}(u_i^2|\mathbf{z}_i).$$

If $\mathrm{E}(u_i^2|\mathbf{z}_i) = \sigma^2$ and $\mathrm{E}(\mathbf{x}_i|\mathbf{z}_i) = \mathbf{z}_i\mathbf{\Pi}$, the the optimal instruments are $\sigma^{-2}\mathbf{z}_i\mathbf{\Pi}$. The constant multiple σ^{-2} clearly has no effect on the optimal IV estimator, so the optimal instruments are $\mathbf{z}_i\mathbf{\Pi}$. These are the optimal IVs underlying 2SLS, except that $\mathbf{\Pi}$ is replaced with its $\sqrt{N}$-consistent OLS estimator. The 2SLS estimator has the same asymptotic variance whether $\mathbf{\Pi}$ or $\hat{\mathbf{\Pi}}$ is used, and so 2SLS is asymptotically efficient.

If $\mathrm{E}(u|\mathbf{x}) = 0$ and $\mathrm{E}(u^2|\mathbf{x}) = \sigma^2$ then the optimal instruments are $\sigma^{-2}\mathrm{E}(\mathbf{x}|\mathbf{x}) = \sigma^{-2}\mathbf{x}$, and this leads to the OLS estimator.

8.11. a. This is a simple application of Theorem 8.5 when $G = 1$. Without the i subscript, $\mathbf{x}_1 = (\mathbf{z}_1, y_2)$ and so $\mathrm{E}(\mathbf{x}_1|\mathbf{z}) = [\mathbf{z}_1, \mathrm{E}(y_2|\mathbf{z})]$. Further, $\mathbf{\Omega}(\mathbf{z}) = \mathrm{Var}(u_1|\mathbf{z}) = \sigma_1^2$. It follows that the optimal instruments are $(1/\sigma_1^2)[\mathbf{z}_1, \mathrm{E}(y_2|\mathbf{z})]$. Dropping the division by σ_1^2 clearly does not affect the optimal instruments.

b. If y_2 is binary then $\mathrm{E}(y_2|\mathbf{z}) = \mathrm{P}(y_2 = 1|\mathbf{z}) = F(\mathbf{z})$, and so the optimal IVs are $[\mathbf{z}_1, F(\mathbf{z})]$.

SOLUTIONS TO CHAPTER 9 PROBLEMS

9.1. a. No. What causal inference could one draw from this? We may be interested in the tradeoff between wages and benefits, but then either of these can be taken as the dependent variable and the analysis would be by OLS. Of course, if we have omitted some important factors or have a measurement error problem, OLS could be inconsistent for estimating the tradeoff. But it is not a simultaneity problem.

b. Yes. We can certainly think of an exogenous change in law enforcement expenditures causing a reduction in crime, and we are certainly interested in such thought experiments. If we could do the appropriate experiment, where expenditures are assigned randomly across cities, then we could estimate the crime equation by OLS. (In fact, we could use a simple regression analysis.) The simultaneous equations model recognizes that cities choose law enforcement expenditures in part on what they expect the crime rate to be. An SEM is a convenient way to allow expenditures to depend on unobservables (to the econometrician) that affect crime.

c. No. These are both choice variables of the firm, and the parameters in a two-equation system modeling one in terms of the other, and vice versa, have no economic meaning. If we want to know how a change in the price of foreign technology affects foreign technology (FT) purchases, why would we want to hold fixed R&D spending? Clearly FT purchases and R&D spending are simultaneously chosen, but we should use a SUR model where neither is an explanatory variable in the other's equation.

d. Yes. We we can certainly be interested in the causal effect of alcohol consumption on productivity, and therefore wage. One's hourly wage is determined by the demand for skills; alcohol consumption is determined by individual behavior.

e. No. These are choice variables by the same household. It makes no sense to think about how exogenous changes in one would affect the other. Further, suppose that we look at the effects of changes in local property tax rates. We would not want to hold fixed family saving and then measure the effect of changing property taxes on housing expenditures. When the property tax changes, a family will generally adjust expenditure in all categories. A SUR system with property tax as an explanatory variable seems to be the appropriate model.

f. No. These are both chosen by the firm, presumably to maximize profits. It makes no sense to hold advertising expenditures fixed while looking at how other variables affect price markup.

9.3. a. We can apply part b of Problem 9.2. First, the only variable excluded from the *support* equation is the variable *mremarr*; since the *support* equation contains one endogenous variable, this equation is identified if and only if $\delta_{21} \neq 0$. This ensures that there is an exogenous variable shifting the mother's reaction function that does not also shift the father's reaction function.

The *visits* equation is identified if and only if at least one of *finc* and *fremarr* actually appears in the *support* equation; that is, we need $\delta_{11} \neq 0$ or $\delta_{13} \neq 0$.

b. Each equation can be estimated by 2SLS using instruments 1, *finc*, *fremarr*, *dist*, *mremarr*.

c. First, obtain the reduced form for *visits*:

$$visits = \pi_{20} + \pi_{21}finc + \pi_{22}fremarr + \pi_{23}dist + \pi_{24}mremarr + v_2.$$

Estimate this equation by OLS, and save the residuals, $\hat{v}_2$. Then, run the OLS regression

$$support \text{ on } 1, visits, finc, fremarr, dist, \hat{v}_2$$

and do a (heteroskedasticity-robust) *t* test that the coefficient on $\hat{v}_2$ is zero. If this test rejects we conclude that *visits* is in fact endogenous in the *support* equation.

d. There is one overidentifying restriction in the *visits* equation, assuming that δ_{11} and δ_{12} are both different from zero. Assuming homoskedasticity of u_2, the easiest way to test the overidentifying restriction is to first estimate the *visits* equation by 2SLS, as in part b. Let $\hat{u}_2$ be the 2SLS residuals. Then, run the auxiliary regression

$$\hat{u}_2 \text{ on } 1, finc, fremarr, dist, mremarr;$$

the sample size times the usual *R*-squared from this regression is distributed asymptotically as χ_1^2 under the null hypothesis that all instruments are exogenous.

A heteroskedasticity-robust test is also easy to obtain. Let $\widehat{support}$ denote the fitted values from the reduced form regression for *support*. Next, regress *finc* (or *fremarr*) on $\widehat{support}$, *mremarr*, *dist*, and save the residuals, say $\hat{r}_1$. Then, run the simple regression (without intercept) of 1 on $\hat{u}_2\hat{r}_1$; N - SSR_0 from this regression is asymptotically χ_1^2 under H_0. (SSR_0 is just the usual sum of squared residuals.)

9.5. a. Let $\boldsymbol{\beta}_1$ denote the 7×1 vector of parameters in the first equation with only the normalization restriction imposed:

$$\boldsymbol{\beta}_1' = (-1, \gamma_{12}, \gamma_{13}, \delta_{11}, \delta_{12}, \delta_{13}, \delta_{14}).$$

The restrictions $\delta_{12} = 0$ and $\delta_{13} + \delta_{14} = 1$ are obtained by choosing

$$\mathbf{R}_1 = \begin{pmatrix} 0 & 0 & 0 & 0 & 1 & 0 & 0 \\ 1 & 0 & 0 & 0 & 0 & 1 & 1 \end{pmatrix}.$$

Because $\mathbf{R}_1$ has two rows, and $G - 1 = 2$, the order condition is satisfied. Now, we need to check the rank condition. Letting $\mathbf{B}$ denote the 7×3 matrix of all structural parameters with only the three normalizations, straightforward matrix multiplication gives

$$\mathbf{R}_1\mathbf{B} = \begin{pmatrix} \delta_{12} & \delta_{22} & \delta_{32} \\ \delta_{13} + \delta_{14} - 1 & \delta_{23} + \delta_{24} - \gamma_{21} & \delta_{33} + \delta_{34} - \gamma_{31} \end{pmatrix}.$$

By definition of the constraints on the first equation, the first column of $\mathbf{R}_1\mathbf{B}$ is zero. Next, we use the constraints in the remainder of the system to get the expression for $\mathbf{R}_1\mathbf{B}$ with all information imposed. But $\gamma_{23} = 0$, $\delta_{22} = 0$, $\delta_{23} = 0$, $\delta_{24} = 0$, $\gamma_{31} = 0$, and $\gamma_{32} = 0$, and so $\mathbf{R}_1\mathbf{B}$ becomes

$$\mathbf{R}_1\mathbf{B} = \begin{pmatrix} 0 & 0 & \delta_{32} \\ 0 & -\gamma_{21} & \delta_{33} + \delta_{34} - \gamma_{31} \end{pmatrix}.$$

Identification requires $\gamma_{21} \neq 0$ and $\delta_{32} \neq 0$.

b. It is easy to see how to estimate the first equation under the given assumptions. Set $\delta_{14} = 1 - \delta_{13}$ and plug this into the equation. After simple algebra we get

$$y_1 - z_4 = \gamma_{12}y_2 + \gamma_{13}y_3 + \delta_{11}z_1 + \delta_{13}(z_3 - z_4) + u_1.$$

This equation can be estimated by 2SLS using instruments (z_1, z_2, z_3, z_4). Note that, if we just count instruments, there are just enough instruments to estimate this equation.

9.6. a. If $\gamma_{13} = 0$ then the two equations constitute a linear SEM. Then, equation (1) is identified if and only if $\delta_{23} \neq 0$ and equation (2) is identified if and only if $\delta_{12} \neq 0$.

b. If we plug the second equation into the first we obtain

$$(1 - \gamma_{12}\gamma_{21} - \gamma_{13}\gamma_{21}z_1)y_1 = (\delta_{10} + \gamma_{12}\delta_{20}) + (\gamma_{12}\delta_{21} + \gamma_{13}\delta_{20} + \delta_{11})z_1$$

$$+ \gamma_{13}\delta_{21}z_1^2 + \delta_{12}z_2 + \gamma_{12}\delta_{23}z_3 + \gamma_{13}\delta_{23}z_1z_3 + u_1 + (\gamma_{12} + \gamma_{13}z_1)u_2.$$

This can be solved for y_1 provided $(1 - \gamma_{12}\gamma_{21} - \gamma_{13}\gamma_{21}z_1) \neq 0$. Given the solution for y_1, we can use the second equation to get y_2. Note that both are nonlinear in z_1 unless $\gamma_{13} = 0$.

c. Since $E(u_1|\mathbf{z}) = E(u_2|\mathbf{z}) = 0$, we can use part b. to get

$$E(y_1|z_1,z_2,z_3) = [(\delta_{10} + \gamma_{12}\delta_{20}) + (\gamma_{12}\delta_{21} + \gamma_{13}\delta_{20} + \delta_{11})z_1$$

$$+ \gamma_{13}\delta_{21}z_1^2 + \delta_{12}z_2 + \gamma_{12}\delta_{23}z_3 + \gamma_{13}\delta_{23}z_1z_3]/(1 - \gamma_{12}\gamma_{21} - \gamma_{13}\gamma_{21}z_1).$$

Again, this is a nonlinear function of the exogenous variables appearing in the system unless $\gamma_{13} = 0$. If $\gamma_{21} = 0$, $E(y_1|z_1,z_2,z_3)$ becomes linear in z_2 and quadratic in z_1 and z_3.

d. If $\gamma_{13} = 0$, we saw in part a that equation (1) is identified. If we include $\gamma_{13}y_2z_1$ in the model, we need at least one instrument for it. But regardless of the value of γ_{13}, the terms z_1^2 and z_1z_3 -- as well as many other nonlinear functions of $\mathbf{z}$ -- are partially correlated with y_2z_1. In other words, the linear projection of y_2z_1 onto 1, z_1, z_2, z_3, z_1^2 and z_1z_3 will -- except by fluke -- depend on at least one of the last two terms. In any case, we can test this using a heteroskedasticity-robust test of two exclusion restrictions. Identification of the second equation is no problem, as z_3 is always available as an IV for y_2. To enhance efficiency when $\gamma_{13} \neq 0$, we could add z_1^2 and z_1z_3 (say) to the instrument list.

e. We could use IVs $(1,z_1,z_2,z_3,z_1^2,z_1z_3)$. A generic command, where IVs are given in parentheses (and an intercept is included by default) is

reg y_1 y_2 y_2z_1 z_1 z_2 (z_1 z_2 z_3 z_1^2 z_1z_3)

Stata, for one, uses this command structure. Other sets of IVs are possible, perhaps even including reciprocals, such as $1/z_1$, or $1/(1 + |z_1|)$ if z_1 can equal zero.

f. We can use the instruments in part e. for *both* equations. Again, other functions (say, involving ratios) could be added with a large sample size.

g. Technically, the parameters in the first equation can be consistently estimated because $E(y_2|\mathbf{z})$ is a nonlinear function of $\mathbf{z}$, and so z_1^2, z_1z_2, and other nonlinear functions would generally be partially correlated with y_2 and y_2z_1. But, if $\gamma_{13} = 0$ also, $E(y_2|\mathbf{z})$ is linear in z_1 and z_2, and additional nonlinear functions are not partially correlated with y_2; thus, there is no instrument for y_2. Since the equation is not identified when $\gamma_{13} = 0$ (and $\delta_{23} = 0$), H_0: $\gamma_{13} = 0$ cannot be tested.

9.7. a. Because *alcohol* and *educ* are endogenous in the first equation, we need at least two elements in $\mathbf{z}_{(2)}$ and/or $\mathbf{z}_{(3)}$ that are not also in $\mathbf{z}_{(1)}$. Ideally, we have at least one such element in $\mathbf{z}_{(2)}$ and at least one such element in $\mathbf{z}_{(3)}$.

b. Let $\mathbf{z}$ denote all nonredundant exogenous variables in the system. Then use these as instruments in a 2SLS analysis.

c. The matrix of instruments for each i is

$$\mathbf{Z}_i = \begin{pmatrix} \mathbf{z}_i & 0 & 0 \\ 0 & (\mathbf{z}_i, educ_i) & \\ 0 & 0 & \mathbf{z}_i \end{pmatrix}.$$

d. $\mathbf{z}_{(3)} = \mathbf{z}$. That is, we should not make any exclusion restrictions in the reduced form for *educ*.

9.8. a. I interact *nearc4* with experience and its quadratic, and the race indicator. Here is my Stata output:

```
. gen nc4exp = nearc4*exper

. gen nc4expsq = nearc4*expersq

. gen nc4blck = nearc4*black

. gen educsq = educ^2

. reg educsq exper expersq black south smsa reg661-reg668 smsa66 nearc4 nc4exp
nc4expsq nc4blck, robust

Regression with robust standard errors                 Number of obs =    3010
                                                       F( 18,  2991) =  233.34
                                                       Prob > F      =  0.0000
                                                       R-squared     =  0.4505
                                                       Root MSE      =  52.172

------------------------------------------------------------------------------
             |               Robust
      educsq |      Coef.   Std. Err.      t    P>|t|     [95% Conf. Interval]
-------------+----------------------------------------------------------------
       exper |  -18.01791   1.229128   -14.66   0.000    -20.42793   -15.60789
     expersq |   .3700966    .058167     6.36   0.000     .2560453    .4841479
       black |  -21.04009   3.569591    -5.89   0.000    -28.03919   -14.04098
       south |  -.5738389   3.973465    -0.14   0.885     -8.36484    7.217162
        smsa |   10.38892   3.036816     3.42   0.001     4.434463    16.34338
      reg661 |  -6.175308   5.574484    -1.11   0.268    -17.10552    4.754903
      reg662 |  -6.092379   4.254714    -1.43   0.152    -14.43484    2.250083
      reg663 |  -6.193772   4.010618    -1.54   0.123    -14.05762    1.670077
      reg664 |  -3.413348   5.069994    -0.67   0.501    -13.35438     6.52768
      reg665 |  -12.31649   5.439968    -2.26   0.024    -22.98295   -1.650031
      reg666 |  -13.27102   5.693005    -2.33   0.020    -24.43362   -2.108421
      reg667 |  -10.83381   5.814901    -1.86   0.063    -22.23542    .5678007
      reg668 |   8.427749   6.627727     1.27   0.204    -4.567616    21.42311
      smsa66 |  -.4621454   3.058084    -0.15   0.880    -6.458307    5.534016
      nearc4 |  -12.25914   7.012394    -1.75   0.081    -26.00874    1.490464
      nc4exp |   4.192304    1.55785     2.69   0.007     1.137738     7.24687
    nc4expsq |  -.1623635   .0753242    -2.16   0.031     -.310056    -.014671
     nc4blck |  -4.789202   4.247869    -1.13   0.260    -13.11824    3.539839
       _cons |    307.212   6.617862    46.42   0.000     294.2359     320.188
------------------------------------------------------------------------------

. test nc4exp nc4expsq nc4blck

 ( 1)  nc4exp = 0.0
```

```
( 2)  nc4expsq = 0.0
( 3)  nc4blck = 0.0

      F(  3,  2991) =    3.72
           Prob > F =    0.0110
```

```
. reg lwage educ educsq exper expersq black south smsa reg661-reg668 smsa66
(exper expersq black south smsa reg661-reg668 smsa66 nearc4 nc4exp nc4expsq
nc4blck)
```

Instrumental variables (2SLS) regression

Source	SS	df	MS
Model	116.731381	16	7.29571132
Residual	475.910264	2993	.159007773
Total	592.641645	3009	.196956346

Number of obs	3010
F(16, 2993)	45.92
Prob > F	0.0000
R-squared	0.1970
Adj R-squared	0.1927
Root MSE	.39876

lwage	Coef.	Std. Err.	t	P>|t|	[95% Conf.	Interval]
educ	.3161298	.1457578	2.17	0.030	.0303342	.6019254
educsq	-.0066592	.0058401	-1.14	0.254	-.0181103	.0047918
exper	.0840117	.0361077	2.33	0.020	.0132132	.1548101
expersq	-.0007825	.0014221	-0.55	0.582	-.0035709	.0020058
black	-.1360751	.0455727	-2.99	0.003	-.2254322	-.0467181
south	-.141488	.0279775	-5.06	0.000	-.1963451	-.0866308
smsa	.1072011	.0290324	3.69	0.000	.0502755	.1641267
reg661	-.1098848	.0428194	-2.57	0.010	-.1938432	-.0259264
reg662	.0036271	.0325364	0.11	0.911	-.0601688	.0674231
reg663	.0428246	.0315082	1.36	0.174	-.0189553	.1046045
reg664	-.0639842	.0391843	-1.63	0.103	-.1408151	.0128468
reg665	.0480365	.0445934	1.08	0.281	-.0394003	.1354733
reg666	.0672512	.0498043	1.35	0.177	-.0304028	.1649052
reg667	.0347783	.0471451	0.74	0.461	-.0576617	.1272183
reg668	-.1933844	.0512395	-3.77	0.000	-.2938526	-.0929161
smsa66	.0089666	.0222745	0.40	0.687	-.0347083	.0526414
_cons	2.610889	.9706341	2.69	0.007	.7077117	4.514067

The heteroskedasticity-robust *F* test from the first regression shows that the interaction terms are partially correlated with $educ^2$. Thus, as long as we think *nearc4* is exogenous, we can use these additional instruments in 2SLS. The 2SLS estimates of the log(*wage*) equation with a quadratic in *educ* are given above. The quadratic term is not statistically significant at even the 20% level against a two-sided alternative, and so we would probably omit it in the final analysis.

b. If $E(u_1|\mathbf{z}) = 0$, as we would typically assume, than any function of $\mathbf{z}$ is uncorrelated with u_1, including interactions of the form $black\cdot z_j$ for any exogenous variable z_j. Such interactions are likely to be correlated with $black\cdot educ$ if z_j is correlated with *educ*.

9.11. a. Since z_2 and z_3 are both omitted from the first equation, we just need $\delta_{22} \neq 0$ or $\delta_{23} \neq 0$ (or both, of course). The second equation is identified if and only if $\delta_{11} \neq 0$.

b. After substitution and straightforward algebra, it can be seen that $\pi_{11} = \delta_{11}/(1 - \gamma_{12}\gamma_{21})$.

c. We can estimate the system by 3SLS; for the second equation, this is identical to 2SLS since it is just identified. Or, we could just use 2SLS on each equation. Given $\hat{\delta}_{11}$, $\hat{\gamma}_{12}$, and $\hat{\gamma}_{21}$, we would form $\hat{\pi}_{11} = \hat{\delta}_{11}/(1 - \hat{\gamma}_{12}\hat{\gamma}_{21})$.

d. Whether we estimate the parameters by 2SLS or 3SLS, we will generally inconsistently estimate δ_{11} and γ_{12}. (Since we are estimating the second equation by 2SLS, we will still consistently estimate γ_{21} provided we have not misspecified this equation.) So our estimate of $\pi_{11} = \partial E(y_2|\mathbf{z})/\partial z_1$ will be inconsistent in any case.

e. We can just estimate the reduced form $E(y_2|z_1,z_2,z_3)$ by ordinary least squares.

f. Consistency of OLS for π_{11} does not hinge on the validity of the exclusion restrictions in the structural model, whereas using an SEM does. Of course, if the SEM is correctly specified, we obtain a more efficient estimator of the reduced form parameters by imposing the restrictions in estimating π_{11}.

9.12. a. Generally, $E(y_2^2|\mathbf{z}) = Var(y_2|\mathbf{z}) + [E(y_2|\mathbf{z})]^2$; when $\gamma_{13} = 0$ and u_1 and u_2 are homoskedastic, $Var(y_2|\mathbf{z})$ is constant, say τ_2^2. (This is easily seen from the reduced form for y_2.) So $E(y_2^2|\mathbf{z}) = \tau_2^2 + (\pi_{20} + \mathbf{z}\boldsymbol{\pi}_2)^2$.

b. We do not really need to use part a; in fact, it turns out to be a red herring for this problem. Since $\gamma_{13} = 0$, $E(y_1|\mathbf{z}) = \delta_{10} + \gamma_{12}E(y_2|\mathbf{z}) + \mathbf{z}_1\boldsymbol{\delta}_1 + E(u_1|\mathbf{z}) = \delta_{10} + \gamma_{12}E(y_2|\mathbf{z}) + \mathbf{z}_1\boldsymbol{\delta}_1$.

c. When $\gamma_{13} = 0$, *any* nonlinear function of $\mathbf{z}$, including $(\pi_{20} + \mathbf{z}\boldsymbol{\pi}_2)^2$, has zero coefficient in $E(y_1|\mathbf{z}) = \delta_{10} + \gamma_{12}(\pi_{20} + \mathbf{z}\boldsymbol{\pi}_2) + \mathbf{z}_1\boldsymbol{\delta}_1$. Plus, if $\gamma_{13} = 0$, then the parameters π_{20} and $\boldsymbol{\pi}_2$ are consistently estimated from the first stage regression y_{i2} on 1, $\mathbf{z}_i$, $i = 1,\ldots,N$. Therefore, the regression y_{i1} on 1, $(\hat{\pi}_{20} + \mathbf{z}_i\hat{\boldsymbol{\pi}}_2)$, $(\hat{\pi}_{20} + \mathbf{z}_i\hat{\boldsymbol{\pi}}_2)^2$, $\mathbf{z}_{i1}$, $i = 1,\ldots,N$ consistently estimates δ_{10}, γ_{12}, 0, and $\boldsymbol{\delta}_1$, respectively. But this is just the regression y_{i1} on 1, $\hat{y}_{i2}$, $(\hat{y}_{i2})^2$, $\mathbf{z}_{i1}$, $i = 1,\ldots,N$.

d. Since $E(u_1|\mathbf{z}) = 0$ and $Var(u_1|\mathbf{z}) = \sigma_1^2$, we can immediately apply Theorem 8.5 to conclude that the optimal IVs for estimating the first equation are $[1,E(y_2|\mathbf{z}),E(y_2^2|\mathbf{z}),\mathbf{z}_1]/\sigma_1^2$, and we can drop the division by σ_1^2. But, if $\gamma_{13} = 0$, then $E(y_2|\mathbf{z})$ is linear in $\mathbf{z}$ and, from part a, $E(y_2^2|\mathbf{z}) = \tau_2^2 + [E(y_2|\mathbf{z})]^2$. So the optimal IVs are a linear combination of $\{1,E(y_2|\mathbf{z}),[E(y_2|\mathbf{z})]^2\}$, which means they are a linear combination of $\{1,\mathbf{z},[E(y_2|\mathbf{z})]^2\}$. We never do worse asymptotically by using more IVs, so we can use $\{1,\mathbf{z},[E(y_2|\mathbf{z})]^2\}$ as an optimal set. Why would we use this larger set instead of $\{1,E(y_2|\mathbf{z}),[E(y_2|\mathbf{z})]^2\}$? For one, the larger set will generally yield overidentifying restrictions. In addition, if $\gamma_{13} \neq 0$, we will generally be better off using more instruments: **z** rather than only $L(y_2|1,\mathbf{z})$.

e. Here is my Stata session:

```
. reg lwage educ age kidslt6 kidsge6 nwifeinc exper expersq

      Source |       SS       df       MS              Number of obs =     428
-------------+------------------------------           F(  7,   420) =   11.78
       Model |  36.6476796     7  5.2353828            Prob > F      =  0.0000
    Residual |  186.679761   420  .444475622           R-squared     =  0.1641
-------------+------------------------------           Adj R-squared =  0.1502
       Total |  223.327441   427  .523015084           Root MSE      =  .66669

------------------------------------------------------------------------------
       lwage |      Coef.   Std. Err.      t    P>|t|     [95% Conf. Interval]
-------------+----------------------------------------------------------------
        educ |   .0998844   .0150975     6.62   0.000      .0702084    .1295604
         age |  -.0035204   .0054145    -0.65   0.516     -.0141633    .0071225
     kidslt6 |  -.0558725   .0886034    -0.63   0.529     -.2300339    .1182889
     kidsge6 |  -.0176484    .027891    -0.63   0.527     -.0724718    .0371749
    nwifeinc |   .0056942   .0033195     1.72   0.087     -.0008307    .0122192
       exper |   .0407097   .0133723     3.04   0.002      .0144249    .0669946
     expersq |  -.0007473   .0004018    -1.86   0.064     -.0015371    .0000424
       _cons |  -.3579972   .3182963    -1.12   0.261     -.9836494    .2676551
------------------------------------------------------------------------------

. predict lwageh
(option xb assumed; fitted values)

. gen lwagehsq = lwageh^2

. gen lwagesq = lwage^2
(325 missing values generated)

. reg hours lwage lwagesq educ age kidslt6 kidsge6 nwifeinc (educ age kidslt6
kidsge6 nwifeinc exper expersq lwagehsq)

Instrumental variables (2SLS) regression

      Source |       SS       df       MS              Number of obs =     428
-------------+------------------------------           F(  7,   420) =    3.48
       Model |  -324605400     7 -46372199.9           Prob > F      =  0.0012
    Residual |   581916420   420  1385515.28           R-squared     =       .
-------------+------------------------------           Adj R-squared =       .
       Total |   257311020   427   602601.92           Root MSE      =  1177.1

------------------------------------------------------------------------------
       hours |      Coef.   Std. Err.      t    P>|t|     [95% Conf. Interval]
-------------+----------------------------------------------------------------
```

lwage	1846.902	600.1593	3.08	0.002	667.2121	3026.592
lwagesq	-373.16	314.6018	-1.19	0.236	-991.5501	245.2301
educ	-103.2347	66.05414	-1.56	0.119	-233.0726	26.60321
age	-9.425115	8.688977	-1.08	0.279	-26.50441	7.654183
kidslt6	-187.0236	163.4171	-1.14	0.253	-508.241	134.1937
kidsge6	-55.70163	51.04568	-1.09	0.276	-156.0385	44.6352
nwifeinc	-7.5979	5.892772	-1.29	0.198	-19.1809	3.985099
_cons	1775.847	743.8091	2.39	0.017	313.7946	3237.899

These estimates are not much different from those reported in Section 9.5.2, where we just added $educ^2$, age^2, and $nwifeinc^2$ to the IV list. In particular, the coefficient on $[\log(wage)]^2$ is still insignificant.

SOLUTIONS TO CHAPTER 10 PROBLEMS

10.1. a. Since investment is likely to be affected by macroeconomic factors, it is important to allow for these by including separate time intercepts; this is done by using T - 1 time period dummies.

b. Putting the unobserved effect c_i in the equation is a simple way to account for time-constant features of a county that affect investment and might also be correlated with the tax variable. Something like "average" county economic climate, which affects investment, could easily be correlated with tax rates because tax rates are, at least to a certain extent, selected by state and local officials. If only a cross section were available, we would have to find an instrument for the tax variable that is uncorrelated with c_i and correlated with the tax rate. This is often a difficult task.

c. Standard investment theories suggest that, ceteris paribus, larger marginal tax rates decrease investment.

d. I would start with a fixed effects analysis to allow arbitrary correlation between all time-varying explanatory variables and c_i. (Actually, doing pooled OLS is a useful initial exercise; these results can be compared with those from an FE analysis). Such an analysis assumes strict exogeneity of $\mathbf{z}_{it}$, tax_{it}, and $disaster_{it}$ in the sense that these are uncorrelated with the errors u_{is} for all t and s.

I have no strong intuition for the likely serial correlation properties of the $\{u_{it}\}$. These might have little serial correlation because we have allowed for c_i, in which case I would use standard fixed effects. However, it seems more likely that the u_{it} are positively autocorrelated, in which case I might use first differencing instead. In either case, I would compute the fully robust standard errors along with the usual ones. Remember, with first-differencing it is easy to test whether the changes Δu_{it} are serially uncorrelated.

e. If tax_{it} and $disaster_{it}$ do not have lagged effects on investment, then the only possible violation of the strict exogeneity assumption is if future values of these variables are correlated with u_{it}. It is safe to say that this is not a worry for the disaster variable: presumably, future natural disasters are not determined by past investment. On the other hand, state officials might look at the levels of past investment in determining future tax policy, especially if there is a target level of tax revenue the officials are are trying to achieve. This could be similar to setting property tax rates: sometimes property tax rates are set depending on recent housing values, since a larger base means a smaller rate can achieve the same amount of revenue. Given that we allow tax_{it} to be correlated with c_i, this might not be much of a problem. But it cannot be ruled out ahead of time.

10.3. a. Let $\bar{\mathbf{x}}_i = (\mathbf{x}_{i1} + \mathbf{x}_{i2})/2$, $\bar{y}_i = (y_{i1} + y_{i2})/2$, $\ddot{\mathbf{x}}_{i1} = \mathbf{x}_{i1} - \bar{\mathbf{x}}_i$, $\ddot{\mathbf{x}}_{i2} = \mathbf{x}_{i2} - \bar{\mathbf{x}}_i$, and similarly for $\ddot{y}_{i1}$ and $\ddot{y}_{i2}$. For $T = 2$ the fixed effects estimator can be written as

$$\hat{\boldsymbol{\beta}}_{FE} = \left(\sum_{i=1}^{N} (\ddot{\mathbf{x}}_{i1}'\ddot{\mathbf{x}}_{i1} + \ddot{\mathbf{x}}_{i2}'\ddot{\mathbf{x}}_{i2})\right)^{-1}\left(\sum_{i=1}^{N} (\ddot{\mathbf{x}}_{i1}'\ddot{y}_{i1} + \ddot{\mathbf{x}}_{i2}'\ddot{y}_{i2})\right).$$

Now, by simple algebra,

$$\ddot{\mathbf{x}}_{i1} = (\mathbf{x}_{i1} - \mathbf{x}_{i2})/2 = -\Delta\mathbf{x}_i/2$$

$$\ddot{\mathbf{x}}_{i2} = (\mathbf{x}_{i2} - \mathbf{x}_{i1})/2 = \Delta\mathbf{x}_i/2$$

$$\ddot{y}_{i1} = (y_{i1} - y_{i2})/2 = -\Delta y_i/2$$

$$\ddot{y}_{i2} = (y_{i2} - y_{i1})/2 = \Delta y_i/2.$$

Therefore,

$$\ddot{\mathbf{x}}_{i1}'\ddot{\mathbf{x}}_{i1} + \ddot{\mathbf{x}}_{i2}'\ddot{\mathbf{x}}_{i2} = \Delta\mathbf{x}_i'\Delta\mathbf{x}_i/4 + \Delta\mathbf{x}_i'\Delta\mathbf{x}_i/4 = \Delta\mathbf{x}_i'\Delta\mathbf{x}_i/2$$

$$\ddot{\mathbf{x}}_{i1}'\ddot{y}_{i1} + \ddot{\mathbf{x}}_{i2}'\ddot{y}_{i2} = \Delta\mathbf{x}_i'\Delta y_i/4 + \Delta\mathbf{x}_i'\Delta y_i/4 = \Delta\mathbf{x}_i'\Delta y_i/2,$$

and so

$$\hat{\boldsymbol{\beta}}_{FE} = \left(\sum_{i=1}^{N}\Delta\mathbf{x}_i'\Delta\mathbf{x}_i/2\right)^{-1}\left(\sum_{i=1}^{N}\Delta\mathbf{x}_i'\Delta y_i/2\right)$$
$$= \left(\sum_{i=1}^{N}\Delta\mathbf{x}_i'\Delta\mathbf{x}_i\right)^{-1}\left(\sum_{i=1}^{N}\Delta\mathbf{x}_i'\Delta y_i\right) = \hat{\boldsymbol{\beta}}_{FD}.$$

b. Let $\hat{u}_{i1} = \ddot{y}_{i1} - \ddot{\mathbf{x}}_{i1}\hat{\boldsymbol{\beta}}_{FE}$ and $\hat{u}_{i2} = \ddot{y}_{i2} - \ddot{\mathbf{x}}_{i2}\hat{\boldsymbol{\beta}}_{FE}$ be the fixed effects residuals for the two time periods for cross section observation i. Since $\hat{\boldsymbol{\beta}}_{FE} = \hat{\boldsymbol{\beta}}_{FD}$, and using the representations in (4.1′), we have

$$\hat{u}_{i1} = -\Delta y_i/2 - (-\Delta\mathbf{x}_i/2)\hat{\boldsymbol{\beta}}_{FD} = -(\Delta y_i - \Delta\mathbf{x}_i\hat{\boldsymbol{\beta}}_{FD})/2 \equiv -\hat{e}_i/2$$
$$\hat{u}_{i2} = \Delta y_i/2 - (\Delta\mathbf{x}_i/2)\hat{\boldsymbol{\beta}}_{FD} = (\Delta y_i - \Delta\mathbf{x}_i\hat{\boldsymbol{\beta}}_{FD})/2 \equiv \hat{e}_i/2,$$

where $\hat{e}_i \equiv \Delta y_i - \Delta\mathbf{x}_i\hat{\boldsymbol{\beta}}_{FD}$ are the first difference residuals, $i = 1,2,\ldots,N$. Therefore,

$$\sum_{i=1}^{N}(\hat{u}_{i1}^2 + \hat{u}_{i2}^2) = (1/2)\sum_{i=1}^{N}\hat{e}_i^2.$$

This shows that the sum of squared residuals from the fixed effects regression is exactly one have the sum of squared residuals from the first difference regression. Since we know the variance estimate for fixed effects is the SSR divided by $N - K$ (when $T = 2$), and the variance estimate for first difference is the SSR divided by $N - K$, the error variance from fixed effects is always half the size as the error variance for first difference estimation, that is, $\hat{\sigma}_u^2 = \hat{\sigma}_e^2/2$ (contrary to what the problem asks you so show). What I wanted you to show is that the variance matrix estimates of $\hat{\boldsymbol{\beta}}_{FE}$ and $\hat{\boldsymbol{\beta}}_{FD}$ are identical. This is easy since the variance matrix estimate for fixed effects is

$$\hat{\sigma}_u^2\left(\sum_{i=1}^{N}(\ddot{\mathbf{x}}_{i1}'\ddot{\mathbf{x}}_{i1} + \ddot{\mathbf{x}}_{i2}'\ddot{\mathbf{x}}_{i2})\right)^{-1} = (\hat{\sigma}_e^2/2)\left(\sum_{i=1}^{N}\Delta\mathbf{x}_i'\Delta\mathbf{x}_i/2\right)^{-1} = \hat{\sigma}_e^2\left(\sum_{i=1}^{N}\Delta\mathbf{x}_i'\Delta\mathbf{x}_i\right)^{-1},$$

which is the variance matrix estimator for first difference. Thus, the standard errors, and in fact all other test statistics (F statistics) will be numerically identical using the two approaches.

10.5. a. Write $\mathbf{v}_i\mathbf{v}_i' = c_i^2\mathbf{j}_T\mathbf{j}_T' + \mathbf{u}_i\mathbf{u}_i' + \mathbf{j}_T(c_i\mathbf{u}_i') + (c_i\mathbf{u}_i)\mathbf{j}_T'$. Under RE.1, $E(\mathbf{u}_i|\mathbf{x}_i,c_i) = \mathbf{0}$, which implies that $E[(c_i\mathbf{u}_i')|\mathbf{x}_i) = \mathbf{0}$ by interated expecations. Under RE.3a, $E(\mathbf{u}_i\mathbf{u}_i'|\mathbf{x}_i,c_i) = \sigma_u^2\mathbf{I}_T$, which implies that $E(\mathbf{u}_i\mathbf{u}_i'|\mathbf{x}_i) = \sigma_u^2\mathbf{I}_T$ (again, by iterated expectations). Therefore,

$$E(\mathbf{v}_i\mathbf{v}_i'|\mathbf{x}_i) = E(c_i^2|\mathbf{x}_i)\mathbf{j}_T\mathbf{j}_T' + E(\mathbf{u}_i\mathbf{u}_i'|\mathbf{x}_i) = h(\mathbf{x}_i)\mathbf{j}_T\mathbf{j}_T' + \sigma_u^2\mathbf{I}_T,$$

where $h(\mathbf{x}_i) \equiv \mathrm{Var}(c_i|\mathbf{x}_i) = E(c_i^2|\mathbf{x}_i)$ (by RE.1b). This shows that the conditional variance matrix of $\mathbf{v}_i$ given $\mathbf{x}_i$ has the same covariance for all $t \neq s$, $h(\mathbf{x}_i)$, and the same variance for all t, $h(\mathbf{x}_i) + \sigma_u^2$. Therefore, while the variances and covariances depend on $\mathbf{x}_i$ in general, they do not depend on time separately.

b. The RE estimator is still consistent and $\sqrt{N}$-asymptotically normal without assumption RE.3b, but the usual random effects variance estimator of $\hat{\boldsymbol{\beta}}_{RE}$ is no longer valid because $E(\mathbf{v}_i\mathbf{v}_i'|\mathbf{x}_i)$ does not have the form (10.30) (because it depends on $\mathbf{x}_i$). The robust variance matrix estimator given in (7.49) should be used in obtaining standard errors or Wald statistics.

10.7. I provide annotated Stata output, and I compute the nonrobust regression-based statistic from equation (10.79). This question was done before Stata would easily compute a robust version based on random effects estimation. See Problem 10.9 for a simpler way to obtain Hausman tests.

```
. * random effects estimation
```

```
. iis id

. tis term

. xtreg trmgpa spring crsgpa frstsem season sat verbmath hsperc hssize black
female, re

                                                 Random-effects GLS regression
sd(u_id)                    = .3718544                Number of obs =      732
sd(e_id_t)                  = .4088283                            n =      366
sd(e_id_t + u_id)           = .5526448                            T =        2

corr(u_id, X)               = 0 (assumed)             R-sq within   =   0.2067
                                                           between  =   0.5390
                                                           overall  =   0.4785

                                                      chi2( 10)     =   512.77
(theta = 0.3862)                                        Prob > chi2 =   0.0000

------------------------------------------------------------------------------
  trmgpa |      Coef.   Std. Err.        z     P>|z|       [95% Conf. Interval]
---------+--------------------------------------------------------------------
  spring |  -.0606536   .0371605    -1.632    0.103      -.1334868    .0121797
  crsgpa |   1.082365   .0930877    11.627    0.000       .8999166    1.264814
 frstsem |   .0029948   .0599542     0.050    0.960      -.1145132    .1205028
  season |  -.0440992   .0392381    -1.124    0.261      -.1210044    .0328061
     sat |   .0017052   .0001771     9.630    0.000       .0013582    .0020523
verbmath |  -.1575199     .16351    -0.963    0.335      -.4779937    .1629538
  hsperc |  -.0084622   .0012426    -6.810    0.000      -.0108977   -.0060268
  hssize |  -.0000775   .0001248    -0.621    0.534       -.000322     .000167
   black |  -.2348189   .0681573    -3.445    0.000      -.3684048   -.1012331
  female |   .3581529   .0612948     5.843    0.000       .2380173    .4782886
   _cons |   -1.73492   .3566599    -4.864    0.000       -2.43396   -1.035879
------------------------------------------------------------------------------

. * fixed effects estimation, with time-varying variables only.

. xtreg trmgpa spring crsgpa frstsem season, fe

                                             Fixed-effects (within) regression
sd(u_id)                    =   .679133               Number of obs =      732
sd(e_id_t)                  = .4088283                            n =      366
sd(e_id_t + u_id)           =   .792693                           T =        2

corr(u_id, Xb)              =   -0.0893               R-sq within   =   0.2069
                                                           between  =   0.0333
                                                           overall  =   0.0613

                                                      F(   4,   362) =   23.61
                                                           Prob > F =   0.0000

------------------------------------------------------------------------------
```

```
  trmgpa |      Coef.   Std. Err.       t     P>|t|       [95% Conf. Interval]
---------+--------------------------------------------------------------------
  spring |  -.0657817   .0391404     -1.681   0.094      -.1427528    .0111895
  crsgpa |   1.140688   .1186538      9.614   0.000       .9073506    1.374025
 frstsem |   .0128523   .0688364      0.187   0.852      -.1225172    .1482218
  season |  -.0566454   .0414748     -1.366   0.173      -.1382072    .0249165
   _cons |  -.7708056   .3305004     -2.332   0.020      -1.420747   -.1208637
------------------------------------------------------------------------------
      id |          F(365,362) =      5.399   0.000          (366 categories)

. * Obtaining the regression-based Hausman test is a bit tedious.  First,
compute the time-averages for all of the time-varying variables:

. egen atrmgpa = mean(trmgpa), by(id)

. egen aspring = mean(spring), by(id)

. egen acrsgpa = mean(crsgpa), by(id)

. egen afrstsem = mean(frstsem), by(id)

. egen aseason = mean(season), by(id)

. * Now obtain GLS transformations for both time-constant and
. * time-varying variables.  Note that lamdahat = .386.

. di 1 - .386
.614

. gen bone = .614

. gen bsat = .614*sat

. gen bvrbmth = .614*verbmath

. gen bhsperc = .614*hsperc

. gen bhssize = .614*hssize

. gen bblack = .614*black

. gen bfemale = .614*female

. gen btrmgpa = trmgpa - .386*atrmgpa

. gen bspring = spring - .386*aspring

. gen bcrsgpa = crsgpa - .386*acrsgpa

. gen bfrstsem = frstsem - .386*afrstsem

. gen bseason = season - .386*aseason
```

```
. * Check to make sure that pooled OLS on transformed data is random
. * effects.

. reg btrmgpa bone bspring bcrsgpa bfrstsem bseason bsat bvrbmth bhsperc
bhssize bblack bfemale, nocons

  Source |       SS       df       MS                  Number of obs =     732
---------+------------------------------               F( 11,   721) =  862.67
   Model |  1584.10163    11  144.009239               Prob > F      =  0.0000
Residual |  120.359125   721    .1669336               R-squared     =  0.9294
---------+------------------------------               Adj R-squared =  0.9283
   Total |  1704.46076   732   2.3284983               Root MSE      =  .40858

------------------------------------------------------------------------------
 btrmgpa |      Coef.   Std. Err.       t     P>|t|       [95% Conf. Interval]
---------+--------------------------------------------------------------------
    bone |  -1.734843   .3566396     -4.864   0.000      -2.435019   -1.034666
 bspring |   -.060651   .0371666     -1.632   0.103      -.1336187    .0123167
 bcrsgpa |   1.082336   .0930923     11.626   0.000       .8995719    1.265101
bfrstsem |   .0029868   .0599604      0.050   0.960       -.114731    .1207046
 bseason |  -.0440905   .0392441     -1.123   0.262      -.1211368    .0329558
    bsat |   .0017052    .000177      9.632   0.000       .0013577    .0020528
 bvrbmth |  -.1575166   .1634784     -0.964   0.336      -.4784672     .163434
 bhsperc |  -.0084622   .0012424     -6.811   0.000      -.0109013   -.0060231
 bhssize |  -.0000775   .0001247     -0.621   0.535      -.0003224    .0001674
  bblack |  -.2348204   .0681441     -3.446   0.000      -.3686049   -.1010359
 bfemale |   .3581524   .0612839      5.844   0.000       .2378363    .4784686
------------------------------------------------------------------------------

. * These are the RE estimates, subject to rounding error.

. * Now add the time averages of the variables that change across i and t
. * to perform the Hausman test:

. reg btrmgpa bone bspring bcrsgpa bfrstsem bseason bsat bvrbmth bhsperc
bhssize bblack bfemale acrsgpa afrstsem aseason, nocons

  Source |       SS       df       MS                  Number of obs =     732
---------+------------------------------               F( 14,   718) =  676.85
   Model |  1584.40773    14  113.171981               Prob > F      =  0.0000
Residual |  120.053023   718  .167204767               R-squared     =  0.9296
---------+------------------------------               Adj R-squared =  0.9282
   Total |  1704.46076   732   2.3284983               Root MSE      =  .40891

------------------------------------------------------------------------------
 btrmgpa |      Coef.   Std. Err.       t     P>|t|       [95% Conf. Interval]
---------+--------------------------------------------------------------------
    bone |  -1.423761   .5182286     -2.747   0.006      -2.441186   -.4063367
 bspring |  -.0657817   .0391479     -1.680   0.093      -.1426398    .0110764
 bcrsgpa |   1.140688   .1186766      9.612   0.000       .9076934    1.373683
bfrstsem |   .0128523   .0688496      0.187   0.852      -.1223184     .148023
```

```
     bseason |  -.0566454    .0414828     -1.366   0.173     -.1380874    .0247967
        bsat |   .0016681    .0001804      9.247   0.000      .001314     .0020223
     bvrbmth |  -.1316462    .1654425     -0.796   0.426     -.4564551    .1931626
     bhsperc |  -.0084655    .0012551     -6.745   0.000     -.0109296   -.0060013
     bhssize |  -.0000783    .0001249     -0.627   0.531     -.0003236     .000167
      bblack |  -.2447934    .0685972     -3.569   0.000     -.3794684   -.1101184
     bfemale |   .3357016    .0711669      4.717   0.000      .1959815    .4754216
     acrsgpa |  -.1142992    .1234835     -0.926   0.355     -.3567312    .1281327
    afrstsem |  -.0480418    .0896965     -0.536   0.592     -.2241405    .1280569
     aseason |   .0763206    .0794119      0.961   0.337     -.0795867    .2322278
------------------------------------------------------------------------------

. test acrsgpa afrstsem aseason

 ( 1)  acrsgpa = 0.0
 ( 2)  afrstsem = 0.0
 ( 3)  aseason = 0.0

       F(  3,   718) =    0.61
            Prob > F =    0.6085

. * Thus, we fail to reject the random effects assumptions even at very large
. * significance levels.
```

For comparison, the usual form of the Hausman test gives p-value = .770, based on a χ_4^2 distribution, using Stata 7.0. As it turns out, the degrees-of-freedom should only be three, because there is a singularity caused by the introduction of *spring*, which is just a time dummy. It would have been easy to make the regression-based test robust to any violation of RE.3: add "robust cluster(id)" to the regression command.

10.9. a. One simple way to compute a Hausman test is to just add the time averages of all explanatory variables, excluding the dummy variables, and then estimate the equation by random effects. I should have done a better job of spelling this out in the text. In other words, write

$$y_{it} = \mathbf{x}_{it}\boldsymbol{\beta} + \bar{\mathbf{w}}_i\boldsymbol{\xi} + r_{it}, \ t = 1,\ldots,T,$$

where $\mathbf{x}_{it}$ includes an overall intercept along with time dummies, as well as $\mathbf{w}_{it}$, the covariates that change across i and t. We can estimate this equation by random effects and test H_0: $\xi = 0$. Conveniently, we can use this formulation to compute a test that is fully robust to violations of RE.3. The Stata session follows. The "xtgee" command is needed to obtain the robust test. (The generalized estimating equation approach in the linear random effects context is iterated random effects estimation. In the example here, it iterates only once.)

```
. xtreg lcrmrte lprbarr lprbconv lprbpris lavgsen lpolpc d82-d87, fe

Fixed-effects (within) regression               Number of obs      =       630
Group variable (i) : county                     Number of groups   =        90

R-sq:  within  = 0.4342                         Obs per group: min =         7
       between = 0.4066                                        avg =       7.0
       overall = 0.4042                                        max =         7

                                                F(11,529)          =     36.91
corr(u_i, Xb)  = 0.2068                         Prob > F           =    0.0000

------------------------------------------------------------------------------
     lcrmrte |      Coef.   Std. Err.       t     P>|t|     [95% Conf. Interval]
-------------+----------------------------------------------------------------
     lprbarr |  -.3597944   .0324192   -11.10   0.000    -.4234806   -.2961083
    lprbconv |  -.2858733   .0212173   -13.47   0.000    -.3275538   -.2441928
    lprbpris |  -.1827812   .0324611    -5.63   0.000    -.2465496   -.1190127
     lavgsen |  -.0044879   .0264471    -0.17   0.865    -.0564421    .0474663
      lpolpc |   .4241142   .0263661    16.09   0.000     .3723191    .4759093
         d82 |   .0125802   .0215416     0.58   0.559    -.0297373    .0548977
         d83 |  -.0792813   .0213399    -3.72   0.000    -.1212027   -.0373598
         d84 |  -.1177281   .0216145    -5.45   0.000    -.1601888   -.0752673
         d85 |  -.1119561   .0218459    -5.12   0.000    -.1548715   -.0690407
         d86 |  -.0818268   .0214266    -3.82   0.000    -.1239185   -.0397352
         d87 |  -.0404704   .0210392    -1.92   0.055    -.0818011    .0008602
       _cons |  -1.604135   .1685739    -9.52   0.000    -1.935292   -1.272979
-------------+----------------------------------------------------------------
     sigma_u |  .43487416
     sigma_e |  .13871215
         rho |  .90765322   (fraction of variance due to u_i)
------------------------------------------------------------------------------
F test that all u_i=0:     F(89, 529) =    45.87            Prob > F = 0.0000

. xtreg lcrmrte lprbarr lprbconv lprbpris lavgsen lpolpc d82-d87, re

Random-effects GLS regression                   Number of obs      =       630
Group variable (i) : county                     Number of groups   =        90
```

```
R-sq:  within  = 0.4287                         Obs per group: min =         7
       between = 0.4533                                        avg =       7.0
       overall = 0.4454                                        max =         7

Random effects u_i ~ Gaussian                   Wald chi2(11)      =    459.17
corr(u_i, X)       = 0 (assumed)                Prob > chi2        =    0.0000

------------------------------------------------------------------------------
     lcrmrte |      Coef.   Std. Err.      z    P>|z|     [95% Conf. Interval]
-------------+----------------------------------------------------------------
     lprbarr |  -.4252097   .0318705   -13.34   0.000    -.4876748   -.3627447
    lprbconv |  -.3271464   .0209708   -15.60   0.000    -.3682485   -.2860443
    lprbpris |  -.1793507   .0339945    -5.28   0.000    -.2459788   -.1127226
     lavgsen |  -.0083696   .0279544    -0.30   0.765    -.0631592    .0464201
      lpolpc |   .4294148   .0261488    16.42   0.000      .378164    .4806655
         d82 |   .0137442    .022943     0.60   0.549    -.0312232    .0587117
         d83 |   -.075388   .0227367    -3.32   0.001    -.1199511   -.0308249
         d84 |  -.1130975   .0230083    -4.92   0.000     -.158193    -.068002
         d85 |  -.1057261   .0232488    -4.55   0.000    -.1512928   -.0601593
         d86 |  -.0795307   .0228326    -3.48   0.000    -.1242817   -.0347796
         d87 |  -.0424581   .0223994    -1.90   0.058    -.0863601     .001444
       _cons |  -1.672632   .1749952    -9.56   0.000    -2.015617   -1.329648
-------------+----------------------------------------------------------------
     sigma_u |  .30032934
     sigma_e |  .13871215
         rho |  .82418424   (fraction of variance due to u_i)
------------------------------------------------------------------------------

. xthausman

Hausman specification test

                ---- Coefficients ----
             |      Fixed       Random
     lcrmrte |    Effects      Effects       Difference
-------------+-----------------------------------------
     lprbarr |  -.3597944    -.4252097         .0654153
    lprbconv |  -.2858733    -.3271464         .0412731
    lprbpris |  -.1827812    -.1793507        -.0034305
     lavgsen |  -.0044879    -.0083696         .0038816
      lpolpc |   .4241142     .4294148        -.0053005
         d82 |   .0125802     .0137442         -.001164
         d83 |  -.0792813     -.075388        -.0038933
         d84 |  -.1177281    -.1130975        -.0046306
         d85 |  -.1119561    -.1057261          -.00623
         d86 |  -.0818268    -.0795307        -.0022962
         d87 |  -.0404704    -.0424581         .0019876

    Test:  Ho:  difference in coefficients not systematic

                 chi2( 11) = (b-B)'[S^(-1)](b-B), S = (S_fe - S_re)
```

```
                     =    121.31
               Prob>chi2 =      0.0000

. * This version of the Hausman test reports too many degrees-of-freedom.
. * It turns out that there are degeneracies in the asymptotic variance
. * of the Hausman statistic.  This problem is easily overcome by only
. * testing the coefficients on the non-year dummies.  To do this, we
. * compute the time averages for the explanatory variables, excluding
. * the time dummies.

. egen lprbata = mean(lprbarr), by(county)

. egen lprbcta = mean(lprbconv), by(county)

. egen lprbpta = mean(lprbpris), by(county)

. egen lavgta = mean(lavgsen), by(county)

. egen lpolta = mean(lpolpc), by(county)

. xtreg lcrmrte lprbarr lprbconv lprbpris lavgsen lpolpc d82-d87 lprbata-
lpolta, re

Random-effects GLS regression                   Number of obs      =       630
Group variable (i) : county                     Number of groups   =        90

R-sq:  within  = 0.4342                         Obs per group: min =         7
       between = 0.7099                                        avg =       7.0
       overall = 0.6859                                        max =         7

Random effects u_i ~ Gaussian                   Wald chi2(16)      =    611.57
corr(u_i, X)       = 0 (assumed)                Prob > chi2        =    0.0000

------------------------------------------------------------------------------
     lcrmrte |      Coef.   Std. Err.       z     P>|z|     [95% Conf. Interval]
-------------+----------------------------------------------------------------
     lprbarr |  -.3597944   .0324192   -11.10   0.000    -.4233349    -.296254
    lprbconv |  -.2858733   .0212173   -13.47   0.000    -.3274584   -.2442881
    lprbpris |  -.1827812   .0324611    -5.63   0.000    -.2464037   -.1191586
     lavgsen |  -.0044879   .0264471    -0.17   0.865    -.0563232    .0473474
      lpolpc |   .4241142   .0263661    16.09   0.000     .3724376    .4757908
         d82 |   .0125802   .0215416     0.58   0.559    -.0296405    .0548009
         d83 |  -.0792813   .0213399    -3.72   0.000    -.1211068   -.0374557
         d84 |  -.1177281   .0216145    -5.45   0.000    -.1600917   -.0753645
         d85 |  -.1119561   .0218459    -5.12   0.000    -.1547734   -.0691389
         d86 |  -.0818268   .0214266    -3.82   0.000    -.1238222   -.0398315
         d87 |  -.0404704   .0210392    -1.92   0.054    -.0817065    .0007657
     lprbata |  -.4530581   .0980908    -4.62   0.000    -.6453126   -.2608036
     lprbcta |  -.3061992    .073276    -4.18   0.000    -.4498175   -.1625808
     lprbpta |   1.343451   .2397992     5.60   0.000     .8734534    1.813449
      lavgta |   -.126782    .210188    -0.60   0.546    -.5387428    .2851789
      lpolta |  -.0794158   .0763314    -1.04   0.298    -.2290227     .070191
```

```
       _cons |  -1.455678   .7064912    -2.06   0.039    -2.840375   -.0709804
-------------+----------------------------------------------------------------
     sigma_u |  .30032934
     sigma_e |  .13871215
         rho |  .82418424   (fraction of variance due to u_i)
------------------------------------------------------------------------------

. testparm lprbata-lpolta

 ( 1)  lprbata = 0.0
 ( 2)  lprbcta = 0.0
 ( 3)  lprbpta = 0.0
 ( 4)  lavgta = 0.0
 ( 5)  lpolta = 0.0

           chi2(  5) =   89.57
         Prob > chi2 =    0.0000

. * This is a strong statistical rejection that the plims of fixed effects
. * and random effects are the same.  Note that the estimates on the
. * original variables are simply the fixed effects estimates, including
. * those on the time dummies.

. * The above test maintains RE.3 in addition to RE.1.  The following gives
. * a test that works without RE.3:

. xtgee lcrmrte lprbarr lprbconv lprbpris lavgsen lpolpc d82-d87 lprbata-
lpolta, corr(excha) robust

Iteration 1: tolerance = 6.134e-08

GEE population-averaged model                   Number of obs      =       630
Group variable:                     county      Number of groups   =        90
Link:                             identity      Obs per group: min =         7
Family:                           Gaussian                     avg =       7.0
Correlation:                  exchangeable                     max =         7
                                                Wald chi2(16)      =    401.23
Scale parameter:                  .1029064      Prob > chi2        =    0.0000

                             (standard errors adjusted for clustering on county)
------------------------------------------------------------------------------
             |             Semi-robust
     lcrmrte |      Coef.   Std. Err.      z    P>|z|     [95% Conf. Interval]
-------------+----------------------------------------------------------------
     lprbarr |  -.3597944   .0589455    -6.10   0.000    -.4753255   -.2442633
    lprbconv |  -.2858733   .0510695    -5.60   0.000    -.3859677   -.1857789
    lprbpris |  -.1827812   .0448835    -4.07   0.000    -.2707511   -.0948112
     lavgsen |  -.0044879    .033057    -0.14   0.892    -.0692785    .0603027
      lpolpc |   .4241142   .0841595     5.04   0.000     .2591647    .5890638
         d82 |   .0125802    .015866     0.79   0.428    -.0185167    .0436771
         d83 |  -.0792813   .0193921    -4.09   0.000    -.1172891   -.0412734
         d84 |  -.1177281   .0215211    -5.47   0.000    -.1599087   -.0755474
```

```
         d85 |  -.1119561    .025433    -4.40   0.000    -.1618038   -.0621084
         d86 |  -.0818268   .0234201    -3.49   0.000    -.1277294   -.0359242
         d87 |  -.0404704   .0239642    -1.69   0.091    -.0874394    .0064985
     lprbata |  -.4530581   .1072689    -4.22   0.000    -.6633013   -.2428149
     lprbcta |  -.3061992   .0986122    -3.11   0.002    -.4994755   -.1129229
     lprbpta |   1.343451   .2902148     4.63   0.000     .7746406    1.912262
      lavgta |   -.126782   .2587182    -0.49   0.624    -.6338604    .3802965
      lpolta |  -.0794158   .0955707    -0.83   0.406    -.2667309    .1078992
       _cons |  -1.455678   .8395033    -1.73   0.083    -3.101074    .1897186
------------------------------------------------------------------------------

. testparm lprbata-lpolta

 ( 1)  lprbata = 0.0
 ( 2)  lprbcta = 0.0
 ( 3)  lprbpta = 0.0
 ( 4)  lavgta = 0.0
 ( 5)  lpolta = 0.0

           chi2(  5) =   62.11
         Prob > chi2 =    0.0000

. * Perhaps not surprisingly, the robust statistic is smaller, but the
. * statistical rejection is still very strong.
```

b. Fixed effects estimation with the nine wage variables gives:

```
. xtreg lcrmrte lprbarr lprbconv lprbpris lavgsen lpolpc lwcon-lwloc d82-d87,
fe

Fixed-effects (within) regression               Number of obs      =       630
Group variable (i) : county                     Number of groups   =        90

R-sq:  within  = 0.4575                         Obs per group: min =         7
       between = 0.2518                                        avg =       7.0
       overall = 0.2687                                        max =         7

                                                F(20,520)          =     21.92
corr(u_i, Xb)  = 0.0804                         Prob > F           =    0.0000

------------------------------------------------------------------------------
     lcrmrte |      Coef.   Std. Err.       t     P>|t|     [95% Conf. Interval]
-------------+----------------------------------------------------------------
     lprbarr |  -.3563515   .0321591   -11.08   0.000    -.4195292   -.2931738
    lprbconv |  -.2859539   .0210513   -13.58   0.000    -.3273099   -.2445979
    lprbpris |  -.1751355   .0323403    -5.42   0.000    -.2386693   -.1116017
     lavgsen |  -.0028739   .0262108    -0.11   0.913     -.054366    .0486181
      lpolpc |      .4229   .0263942    16.02   0.000     .3710476    .4747524
       lwcon |  -.0345448   .0391616    -0.88   0.378    -.1114792    .0423896
       lwtuc |   .0459747    .019034     2.42   0.016     .0085817    .0833677
       lwtrd |  -.0201766   .0406073    -0.50   0.619    -.0999511    .0595979
```

```
       lwfir |  -.0035445    .028333    -0.13   0.900    -.0592058    .0521168
       lwser |   .0101264   .0191915     0.53   0.598     -.027576    .0478289
       lwmfg |  -.3005691   .1094068    -2.75   0.006    -.5155028   -.0856354
       lwfed |  -.3331226    .176448    -1.89   0.060    -.6797612     .013516
       lwsta |   .0215209   .1130648     0.19   0.849    -.2005991    .2436409
       lwloc |   .1810215   .1180643     1.53   0.126    -.0509202    .4129632
         d82 |   .0188915   .0251244     0.75   0.452    -.0304662    .0682492
         d83 |   -.055286   .0330287    -1.67   0.095    -.1201721    .0096001
         d84 |  -.0615162   .0410805    -1.50   0.135    -.1422204    .0191879
         d85 |  -.0397115   .0561635    -0.71   0.480    -.1500468    .0706237
         d86 |  -.0001133   .0680124    -0.00   0.999    -.1337262    .1334996
         d87 |   .0537042   .0798953     0.67   0.502    -.1032531    .2106615
       _cons |   .8931726   1.424067     0.63   0.531    -1.904459    3.690805
-------------+----------------------------------------------------------------
     sigma_u |  .47756823
     sigma_e |  .13700505
         rho |  .92395784   (fraction of variance due to u_i)
------------------------------------------------------------------------------
F test that all u_i=0:     F(89, 520) =    39.12             Prob > F = 0.0000

. testparm lwcon-lwloc

 ( 1)  lwcon = 0.0
 ( 2)  lwtuc = 0.0
 ( 3)  lwtrd = 0.0
 ( 4)  lwfir = 0.0
 ( 5)  lwser = 0.0
 ( 6)  lwmfg = 0.0
 ( 7)  lwfed = 0.0
 ( 8)  lwsta = 0.0
 ( 9)  lwloc = 0.0

       F(  9,   520) =    2.47
            Prob > F =    0.0090

. * Jointly, the wage variables are significant (using the version of the
. * test that maintains FE.3), but the signs in some cases are hard to
. * interpret.
```

c. First, we need to compute the changes in log wages. Then, we just used pooled OLS.

```
. sort county year

. gen clwcon = lwcon - lwcon[_n-1] if year > 81
(90 missing values generated)

. gen clwtuc = lwtuc - lwtuc[_n-1] if year > 81
(90 missing values generated)
```

```
. gen clwtrd = lwtrd - lwtrd[_n-1] if year > 81
(90 missing values generated)

. gen clwfir = lwfir - lwfir[_n-1] if year > 81
(90 missing values generated)

. gen clwser = lwser - lwser[_n-1] if year > 81
(90 missing values generated)

. gen clwmfg = lwmfg - lwmfg[_n-1] if year > 81
(90 missing values generated)

. gen clwfed = lwfed - lwfed[_n-1] if year > 81
(90 missing values generated)

. gen clwsta = lwsta - lwsta[_n-1] if year > 81
(90 missing values generated)

. gen clwloc = lwloc - lwloc[_n-1] if year > 81
(90 missing values generated)

. reg clcrmrte clprbarr clprbcon clprbpri clavgsen clpolpc clwcon-clwloc d83-
d87

      Source |       SS       df       MS              Number of obs =     540
-------------+------------------------------           F( 19,   520) =   21.90
       Model |  9.86742162    19  .51933798           Prob > F      =  0.0000
    Residual |  12.3293822   520  .02371035           R-squared     =  0.4445
-------------+------------------------------           Adj R-squared =  0.4242
       Total |  22.1968038   539  .041181454           Root MSE      =  .15398

------------------------------------------------------------------------------
    clcrmrte |      Coef.   Std. Err.      t    P>|t|     [95% Conf. Interval]
-------------+----------------------------------------------------------------
    clprbarr |  -.3230993   .0300195   -10.76   0.000    -.3820737   -.2641248
    clprbcon |  -.2402885   .0182474   -13.17   0.000    -.2761362   -.2044407
    clprbpri |  -.1693859     .02617    -6.47   0.000    -.2207978    -.117974
    clavgsen |  -.0156167   .0224126    -0.70   0.486    -.0596469    .0284136
     clpolpc |   .3977221    .026987    14.74   0.000     .3447051     .450739
      clwcon |  -.0442368   .0304142    -1.45   0.146    -.1039865     .015513
      clwtuc |   .0253997   .0142093     1.79   0.074     -.002515    .0533144
      clwtrd |  -.0290309   .0307907    -0.94   0.346    -.0895203    .0314586
      clwfir |    .009122   .0212318     0.43   0.668    -.0325886    .0508326
      clwser |   .0219549   .0144342     1.52   0.129    -.0064016    .0503113
      clwmfg |  -.1402482   .1019317    -1.38   0.169    -.3404967    .0600003
      clwfed |   .0174221   .1716065     0.10   0.919     -.319705    .3545493
      clwsta |  -.0517891   .0957109    -0.54   0.589    -.2398166    .1362385
      clwloc |  -.0305153   .1021028    -0.30   0.765    -.2310999    .1700694
         d83 |  -.1108653   .0268105    -4.14   0.000    -.1635355   -.0581951
         d84 |  -.0374103    .024533    -1.52   0.128    -.0856063    .0107856
         d85 |  -.0005856    .024078    -0.02   0.981    -.0478877    .0467164
```

```
         d86 |   .0314757   .0245099     1.28   0.200    -.0166749    .0796262
         d87 |   .0388632   .0247819     1.57   0.117    -.0098218    .0875482
       _cons |   .0198522   .0206974     0.96   0.338    -.0208086     .060513
------------------------------------------------------------------------------

. * There are no notable differences between the FE and FD estimates, or
. * their standard errors.
```

d. The following set of commands tests the differenced errors for serial correlation:

```
. predict ehat, resid
(90 missing values generated)

. gen ehat_1 = ehat[_n-1] if year > 82
(180 missing values generated)

. reg ehat ehat_1

      Source |       SS       df       MS              Number of obs =     450
-------------+------------------------------           F(  1,   448) =   21.29
       Model |  .490534556     1  .490534556           Prob > F      =  0.0000
    Residual |  10.3219221   448  .023040005           R-squared     =  0.0454
-------------+------------------------------           Adj R-squared =  0.0432
       Total |  10.8124566   449  .024081195           Root MSE      =  .15179

------------------------------------------------------------------------------
        ehat |      Coef.   Std. Err.      t    P>|t|     [95% Conf. Interval]
-------------+----------------------------------------------------------------
      ehat_1 |   -.222258   .0481686    -4.61   0.000    -.3169225   -.1275936
       _cons |   5.97e-10   .0071554     0.00   1.000    -.0140624    .0140624
------------------------------------------------------------------------------

. * There is evidence of negative serial correlation, which suggests that the
. * idiosyncratic errors in levels may follow a stable AR(1) process.
```

10.11. a. The key coefficient is β_1. Since AFDC participation gives women access to better nutrition and prenatal care, we hope that AFDC participation causes the percent of low-weight births to fall. This only makes sense, of course, when we think about holding economic variables fixed, and controlling for quality of other kinds of health care. My expectation was that β_2 would be negative: more physicians means relatively fewer low-weight births. The variable *bedspc* is another proxy for health-care availibility, and we expect $\beta_3 < 0$. Higher per capita income should lead to lower *lowbrth* ($\beta_4 < 0$). The effect of population on a per capita variable is ambiguous, especially since it is not a density measure.

b. The Stata output follows. Both the usual and fully robust standard errors are computed. The standard errors robust to serial correlation (and heteroskedasticity) are, as expected, somewhat larger. (If you test for AR(1) serial correlation in the composite error, v_{it}, it is very strong. In fact, the estimated AR(1) coefficient is slightly above one.) Only the per capita income variable is statistically significant. The estimate implies that a 10 percent rise in per capita income is associated with a .25 percentage point fall in the percent of low-weight births.

```
. reg lowbrth d90 afdcprc lphypc lbedspc lpcinc lpopul

      Source |       SS       df       MS              Number of obs =     100
-------------+------------------------------           F(  6,    93) =    5.19
       Model |  33.7710894     6  5.6285149            Prob > F      =  0.0001
    Residual |  100.834005    93  1.08423661           R-squared     =  0.2509
-------------+------------------------------           Adj R-squared =  0.2026
       Total |  134.605095    99  1.35964742           Root MSE      =  1.0413

------------------------------------------------------------------------------
     lowbrth |      Coef.   Std. Err.      t    P>|t|     [95% Conf. Interval]
-------------+----------------------------------------------------------------
         d90 |   .5797136   .2761244     2.10   0.038      .0313853    1.128042
     afdcprc |   .0955932   .0921802     1.04   0.302     -.0874584    .2786448
      lphypc |   .3080648     .71546     0.43   0.668     -1.112697    1.728827
     lbedspc |   .2790041   .5130275     0.54   0.588     -.7397668    1.297775
      lpcinc |  -2.494685   .9783021    -2.55   0.012     -4.437399   -.5519712
      lpopul |    .739284   .7023191     1.05   0.295     -.6553825    2.133951
       _cons |   26.57786   7.158022     3.71   0.000      12.36344    40.79227
------------------------------------------------------------------------------

. reg lowbrth d90 afdcprc lphypc lbedspc lpcinc lpopul, robust cluster(state)

Regression with robust standard errors                 Number of obs =     100
                                                       F(  6,    49) =    4.73
                                                       Prob > F      =  0.0007
```

```
                                                     R-squared     =  0.2509
Number of clusters (state) = 50                      Root MSE      =  1.0413

------------------------------------------------------------------------------
             |               Robust
    lowbrth  |      Coef.   Std. Err.      t    P>|t|     [95% Conf. Interval]
-------------+----------------------------------------------------------------
        d90  |   .5797136   .2214303     2.62   0.012     .1347327    1.024694
   afdcprc   |   .0955932   .1199883     0.80   0.429    -.1455324    .3367188
     lphypc  |   .3080648   .9063342     0.34   0.735    -1.513282    2.129411
    lbedspc  |   .2790041   .7853754     0.36   0.724    -1.299267    1.857275
     lpcinc  |  -2.494685   1.203901    -2.07   0.044    -4.914014   -.0753567
     lpopul  |    .739284   .9041915     0.82   0.418    -1.077757    2.556325
      _cons  |   26.57786    9.29106     2.86   0.006     7.906773    45.24894
------------------------------------------------------------------------------
```

c. The FD (equivalently, FE) estimates are give below. The heteroskedasticity-robust standard error for the AFDC variable is actually smaller. In any case, removing the state unobserved effect changes the sign on the AFDC participation variable, and it is marginally significant. Oddly, physicians-per-capita now has a positive, significant effect on percent of low-weight births. The hospital beds-per-capita variable has the expected negative effect.

```
. reg clowbrth cafdcprc clphypc clbedspc clpcinc clpopul

     Source  |       SS       df       MS              Number of obs =      50
-------------+------------------------------           F(  5,     44) =    2.53
      Model  |  .861531934     5  .172306387           Prob > F      =  0.0428
   Residual  |  3.00026764    44  .068187901           R-squared     =  0.2231
-------------+------------------------------           Adj R-squared =  0.1348
      Total  |  3.86179958    49  .078812236           Root MSE      =  .26113

------------------------------------------------------------------------------
   clowbrth  |      Coef.   Std. Err.      t    P>|t|     [95% Conf. Interval]
-------------+----------------------------------------------------------------
   cafdcprc  |  -.1760763   .0903733    -1.95   0.058    -.3582116     .006059
    clphypc  |   5.894509   2.816689     2.09   0.042     .2178453    11.57117
   clbedspc  |  -1.576195   .8852111    -1.78   0.082     -3.36022    .2078308
    clpcinc  |  -.8455268   1.356773    -0.62   0.536    -3.579924     1.88887
    clpopul  |   3.441116   2.872175     1.20   0.237    -2.347372    9.229604
      _cons  |   .1060158   .3090664     0.34   0.733    -.5168667    .7288983
------------------------------------------------------------------------------
```

d. Adding a quadratic in *afdcprc* yields, not surprisingly, a diminishing impact of AFDC participation. The turning point in the quadratic is at about *afdcprc* = 6.3, and only four states have AFDC participation rates about 6.3 percent. So, the largest effect is at low AFDC participation rates, but the effect is negative until *afdcprc* = 6.3. This seems reasonable. However, the quadratic is not statistically significant at the usual levels.

```
. reg clowbrth cafdcprc cafdcpsq clphypc clbedspc clpcinc clpopul

      Source |       SS       df       MS              Number of obs =      50
-------------+------------------------------           F(  6,    43) =    2.39
       Model |  .964889165     6  .160814861           Prob > F      =  0.0444
    Residual |  2.89691041    43   .06737001           R-squared     =  0.2499
-------------+------------------------------           Adj R-squared =  0.1452
       Total |  3.86179958    49  .078812236           Root MSE      =  .25956

------------------------------------------------------------------------------
    clowbrth |      Coef.   Std. Err.       t     P>|t|     [95% Conf. Interval]
-------------+----------------------------------------------------------------
    cafdcprc |  -.5035049   .2791959    -1.80   0.078     -1.066557    .0595472
    cafdcpsq |   .0396094   .0319788     1.24   0.222     -.0248819    .1041008
     clphypc |   6.620885   2.860505     2.31   0.025      .8521271    12.38964
    clbedspc |  -1.407963   .8903074    -1.58   0.121     -3.203439    .3875124
     clpcinc |  -.9987865   1.354276    -0.74   0.465     -3.729945    1.732372
     clpopul |   4.429026   2.964218     1.49   0.142      -1.54889    10.40694
       _cons |   .1245915   .3075731     0.41   0.687     -.4956887    .7448718
------------------------------------------------------------------------------

. di .504/(2*.040)
6.3

. sum afdcprc if d90

    Variable |     Obs        Mean    Std. Dev.       Min        Max
-------------+-----------------------------------------------------
     afdcprc |      50    4.162976    1.317277   1.688183   7.358795

. count if d90 & afdcprc > 6.3
    4
```

10.12. a. Even if c_i is uncorrelated with $\mathbf{x}_{it}$ for all t, the usual OLS standard errors do not account for the serial correlation in $v_{it} = c_i + u_{it}$.

You can see that the robust standard errors are substantially larger than the usual ones, in some cases more than double.

```
. reg lwage educ black hisp exper expersq married union d81-d87, robust
cluster(nr)

Regression with robust standard errors                 Number of obs =    4360
                                                       F( 14,    544) =   47.10
                                                       Prob > F      =  0.0000
                                                       R-squared     =  0.1893
Number of clusters (nr) = 545                          Root MSE      =  .48033

------------------------------------------------------------------------------
             |               Robust
       lwage |      Coef.   Std. Err.      t    P>|t|     [95% Conf. Interval]
-------------+----------------------------------------------------------------
        educ |   .0913498   .0110822     8.24   0.000     .0695807    .1131189
       black |  -.1392342   .0505238    -2.76   0.006    -.2384798   -.0399887
        hisp |   .0160195   .0390781     0.41   0.682     -.060743     .092782
       exper |   .0672345   .0195958     3.43   0.001     .0287417    .1057273
     expersq |  -.0024117   .0010252    -2.35   0.019    -.0044255   -.0003979
     married |   .1082529    .026034     4.16   0.000     .0571135    .1593924
       union |   .1824613   .0274435     6.65   0.000     .1285531    .2363695
         d81 |     .05832    .028228     2.07   0.039     .0028707    .1137693
         d82 |   .0627744   .0369735     1.70   0.090    -.0098538    .1354027
         d83 |   .0620117    .046248     1.34   0.181    -.0288348    .1528583
         d84 |   .0904672    .057988     1.56   0.119    -.0234406     .204375
         d85 |   .1092463   .0668474     1.63   0.103    -.0220644     .240557
         d86 |   .1419596   .0762348     1.86   0.063     -.007791    .2917102
         d87 |   .1738334   .0852056     2.04   0.042     .0064612    .3412057
       _cons |   .0920558   .1609365     0.57   0.568    -.2240773    .4081888
------------------------------------------------------------------------------

. reg lwage educ black hisp exper expersq married union d81-d87

      Source |       SS       df       MS              Number of obs =    4360
-------------+------------------------------           F( 14,  4345) =   72.46
       Model |  234.048277    14  16.7177341           Prob > F      =  0.0000
    Residual |  1002.48136  4345  .230720682           R-squared     =  0.1893
-------------+------------------------------           Adj R-squared =  0.1867
       Total |  1236.52964  4359  .283672779           Root MSE      =  .48033

------------------------------------------------------------------------------
       lwage |      Coef.   Std. Err.      t    P>|t|     [95% Conf. Interval]
-------------+----------------------------------------------------------------
        educ |   .0913498   .0052374    17.44   0.000     .0810819    .1016177
       black |  -.1392342   .0235796    -5.90   0.000    -.1854622   -.0930062
        hisp |   .0160195   .0207971     0.77   0.441    -.0247535    .0567925
       exper |   .0672345   .0136948     4.91   0.000     .0403856    .0940834
```

```
     expersq |  -.0024117     .00082    -2.94   0.003    -.0040192   -.0008042
     married |   .1082529   .0156894     6.90   0.000     .0774937    .1390122
       union |   .1824613   .0171568    10.63   0.000     .1488253    .2160973
         d81 |     .05832   .0303536     1.92   0.055    -.0011886    .1178286
         d82 |   .0627744   .0332141     1.89   0.059    -.0023421    .1278909
         d83 |   .0620117   .0366601     1.69   0.091    -.0098608    .1338843
         d84 |   .0904672   .0400907     2.26   0.024      .011869    .1690654
         d85 |   .1092463   .0433525     2.52   0.012     .0242533    .1942393
         d86 |   .1419596    .046423     3.06   0.002     .0509469    .2329723
         d87 |   .1738334    .049433     3.52   0.000     .0769194    .2707474
       _cons |   .0920558   .0782701     1.18   0.240    -.0613935    .2455051
------------------------------------------------------------------------------
```

b. The random effects estimates on the time-constant variables are similar to the pooled OLS estimates. The effect of experience is initially large for the random effects estimates. The key difference is that the marriage and union premiums are notably lower for random effects. The random effects marriage premium is about 6.4%, while the pooled OLS estimate is about 10.8%. For union status, the random effects estimate is 10.6% compared with a pooled OLS estimate of 18.2%.

```
. xtreg lwage educ black hisp exper expersq married union d81-d87, re

Random-effects GLS regression                   Number of obs      =      4360
Group variable (i) : nr                         Number of groups   =       545

R-sq:  within  = 0.1799                         Obs per group: min =         8
       between = 0.1860                                        avg =       8.0
       overall = 0.1830                                        max =         8

Random effects u_i ~ Gaussian                   Wald chi2(14)      =    957.77
corr(u_i, X)       = 0 (assumed)                Prob > chi2        =    0.0000

------------------------------------------------------------------------------
       lwage |      Coef.   Std. Err.       z     P>|z|     [95% Conf. Interval]
-------------+----------------------------------------------------------------
        educ |   .0918763   .0106597     8.62   0.000     .0709836    .1127689
       black |  -.1393767   .0477228    -2.92   0.003    -.2329117   -.0458417
        hisp |   .0217317   .0426063     0.51   0.610    -.0617751    .1052385
       exper |   .1057545   .0153668     6.88   0.000     .0756361    .1358729
     expersq |  -.0047239   .0006895    -6.85   0.000    -.0060753   -.0033726
     married |    .063986   .0167742     3.81   0.000     .0311091    .0968629
       union |   .1061344   .0178539     5.94   0.000     .0711415    .1411273
         d81 |    .040462   .0246946     1.64   0.101    -.0079385    .0888626
```

```
         d82 |   .0309212   .0323416     0.96   0.339    -.0324672    .0943096
         d83 |   .0202806    .041582     0.49   0.626    -.0612186    .1017798
         d84 |   .0431187   .0513163     0.84   0.401    -.0574595    .1436969
         d85 |   .0578155   .0612323     0.94   0.345    -.0621977    .1778286
         d86 |   .0919476   .0712293     1.29   0.197    -.0476592    .2315544
         d87 |   .1349289   .0813135     1.66   0.097    -.0244427    .2943005
       _cons |   .0235864   .1506683     0.16   0.876     -.271718    .3188907
-------------+----------------------------------------------------------------
     sigma_u |  .32460315
     sigma_e |  .35099001
         rho |  .46100216   (fraction of variance due to u_i)
------------------------------------------------------------------------------
```

c. The variable $exper_{it}$ is redundant because everyone in the sample works every year, so $exper_{i,t+1} = exper_{it}$, $t = 1,\ldots,7$, for all i. The effects of the initial levels of experience, $exper_{i1}$, cannot be distinguished from c_i. Then, because each experience variable follows the same linear time trend, the effects cannot be separated from the aggregate time effects.

The following are the fixed effects estimates. The marriage and union premiums fall even more, although both are still statistically significant and economically relevant.

```
. xtreg lwage expersq married union d81-d87, fe

Fixed-effects (within) regression               Number of obs      =      4360
Group variable (i) : nr                         Number of groups   =       545

R-sq:  within  = 0.1806                         Obs per group: min =         8
       between = 0.0286                                        avg =       8.0
       overall = 0.0888                                        max =         8

                                                F(10,3805)         =     83.85
corr(u_i, Xb)  = -0.1222                        Prob > F           =    0.0000

------------------------------------------------------------------------------
       lwage |      Coef.   Std. Err.       t    P>|t|     [95% Conf. Interval]
-------------+----------------------------------------------------------------
     expersq |  -.0051855   .0007044    -7.36   0.000    -.0065666   -.0038044
     married |   .0466804   .0183104     2.55   0.011     .0107811    .0825796
       union |   .0800019   .0193103     4.14   0.000     .0421423    .1178614
         d81 |   .1511912   .0219489     6.89   0.000     .1081584     .194224
         d82 |   .2529709   .0244185    10.36   0.000     .2050963    .3008454
         d83 |   .3544437   .0292419    12.12   0.000     .2971125    .4117749
```

```
         d84 |   .4901148   .0362266    13.53   0.000     .4190894    .5611402
         d85 |   .6174823   .0452435    13.65   0.000     .5287784    .7061861
         d86 |   .7654966   .0561277    13.64   0.000     .6554532    .8755399
         d87 |   .9250249   .0687731    13.45   0.000     .7901893    1.059861
       _cons |   1.426019   .0183415    77.75   0.000     1.390058    1.461979
-------------+----------------------------------------------------------------
     sigma_u |  .39176195
     sigma_e |  .35099001
         rho |  .55472817   (fraction of variance due to u_i)
------------------------------------------------------------------------------
F test that all u_i=0:     F(544, 3805) =     9.16           Prob > F = 0.0000
```

d. The following Stata session adds the year dummy-education interaction terms:

```
. gen d81educ = d81*educ

. gen d82educ = d82*educ

. gen d83educ = d83*educ

. gen d84educ = d84*educ

. gen d85educ = d85*educ

. gen d86educ = d86*educ

. gen d87educ = d87*educ

. xtreg lwage expersq married union d81-d87 d81educ-d87educ, fe

Fixed-effects (within) regression               Number of obs      =      4360
Group variable (i) : nr                         Number of groups   =       545

R-sq:  within  = 0.1814                         Obs per group: min =         8
       between = 0.0211                                        avg =       8.0
       overall = 0.0784                                        max =         8

                                                F(17,3798)         =     49.49
corr(u_i, Xb)  = -0.1732                        Prob > F           =    0.0000

------------------------------------------------------------------------------
       lwage |      Coef.   Std. Err.      t    P>|t|     [95% Conf. Interval]
-------------+----------------------------------------------------------------
     expersq |  -.0060437   .0008633    -7.00   0.000    -.0077362   -.0043512
     married |   .0474337   .0183277     2.59   0.010     .0115006    .0833667
       union |   .0789759   .0193328     4.09   0.000     .0410722    .1168796
         d81 |   .0984201    .145999     0.67   0.500    -.1878239    .3846641
         d82 |   .2472016   .1493785     1.65   0.098    -.0456682    .5400714
```

```
         d83 |    .408813   .1557146     2.63   0.009     .1035207    .7141053
         d84 |   .6399247   .1652396     3.87   0.000     .3159578    .9638916
         d85 |   .7729397   .1779911     4.34   0.000     .4239723    1.121907
         d86 |   .9699322   .1941747     5.00   0.000     .5892354    1.350629
         d87 |   1.188777   .2135856     5.57   0.000     .7700231     1.60753
     d81educ |   .0049906    .012222     0.41   0.683    -.0189718     .028953
     d82educ |    .001651   .0123304     0.13   0.893    -.0225239    .0258259
     d83educ |  -.0026621   .0125098    -0.21   0.831    -.0271887    .0218644
     d84educ |  -.0098257   .0127593    -0.77   0.441    -.0348414      .01519
     d85educ |  -.0092145   .0130721    -0.70   0.481    -.0348436    .0164146
     d86educ |  -.0121382   .0134419    -0.90   0.367    -.0384922    .0142159
     d87educ |  -.0157892    .013868    -1.14   0.255    -.0429785    .0114002
       _cons |   1.436283   .0192766    74.51   0.000     1.398489    1.474076
-------------+----------------------------------------------------------------
     sigma_u |  .39876325
     sigma_e |   .3511451
         rho |  .56324361   (fraction of variance due to u_i)
------------------------------------------------------------------------------
F test that all u_i=0:     F(544, 3798) =     8.25           Prob > F = 0.0000

. testparm d81educ-d87educ

 ( 1)  d81educ = 0.0
 ( 2)  d82educ = 0.0
 ( 3)  d83educ = 0.0
 ( 4)  d84educ = 0.0
 ( 5)  d85educ = 0.0
 ( 6)  d86educ = 0.0
 ( 7)  d87educ = 0.0

       F(  7,  3798) =    0.52
            Prob > F =    0.8202
```

There is no evidence that the return to education has changed over time for the population represented by these men.

e. First, I created the lead variable, and then included it in an FE estimation. As you can see, *unionp1* is statistically significant, and its coefficient is not small. This means that $union_{it}$ fails the strict exogeneity assumption, and we might have to use an IV approach described in Chapter 11.

```
. gen unionp1 = union[_n+1] if year < 1987
(545 missing values generated)

. xtreg lwage expersq married union unionp1 d81-d86, fe
```

```
Fixed-effects (within) regression               Number of obs      =      3815
Group variable (i) : nr                         Number of groups   =       545

R-sq:  within  = 0.1474                         Obs per group: min =         7
       between = 0.0305                                        avg =       7.0
       overall = 0.0744                                        max =         7

                                                F(10,3260)         =     56.34
corr(u_i, Xb)  = -0.1262                        Prob > F           =    0.0000

------------------------------------------------------------------------------
       lwage |      Coef.   Std. Err.       t     P>|t|     [95% Conf. Interval]
-------------+----------------------------------------------------------------
     expersq |  -.0054448   .0008771     -6.21   0.000     -.0071646   -.003725
     married |   .0448778   .0208817      2.15   0.032      .0039353   .0858203
       union |   .0763554   .0217672      3.51   0.000      .0336766   .1190342
    unionp1 |   .0497356   .0223618      2.22   0.026       .005891   .0935802
         d81 |   .1528275   .0226526      6.75   0.000      .1084128   .1972422
         d82 |   .2576486    .026211      9.83   0.000      .2062568   .3090403
         d83 |   .3618296   .0328716     11.01   0.000      .2973786   .4262806
         d84 |   .5023642   .0422128     11.90   0.000      .4195979   .5851305
         d85 |   .6342402   .0539623     11.75   0.000      .5284368   .7400435
         d86 |   .7841312   .0679011     11.55   0.000      .6509981   .9172642
       _cons |   1.417924   .0204562     69.32   0.000      1.377815   1.458032
-------------+----------------------------------------------------------------
     sigma_u |  .39716048
     sigma_e |  .35740734
         rho |   .5525375   (fraction of variance due to u_i)
------------------------------------------------------------------------------
F test that all u_i=0:     F(544, 3260) =     7.93          Prob > F = 0.0000
```

10.13. The short answer is: Yes, we can justify this procedure with fixed T as $N \to \infty$. In particular, it produces a $\sqrt{N}$-consistent, asymptotically normal estimator of $\boldsymbol{\beta}$. Therefore, "fixed effects weighted least squares," where the weights are known functions of exogenous variables (including $\mathbf{x}_i$ and possible other covariates that do not appear in the conditional mean), is another case where "estimating" the fixed effects leads to an estimator of $\boldsymbol{\beta}$ with good properties. (As usual with fixed T, there is no sense in which we can estimate the c_i consistently.) Verifying this claim takes much more work, but it is mostly just algebra.

First, in the sum of squared residuals, we can "concentrate" the a_i out by finding $\hat{a}_i(\mathbf{b})$ as a function of $(\mathbf{x}_i, \mathbf{y}_i)$ and $\mathbf{b}$, substituting back into the sum of squared residuals, and then minimizing with respect to $\mathbf{b}$ only. Straightforward algebra gives the first order conditions for each i as

$$\sum_{t=1}^{T} (y_{it} - \hat{a}_i - \mathbf{x}_{it}\mathbf{b})/h_{it} = 0,$$

which gives

$$\hat{a}_i(\mathbf{b}) = w_i\left(\sum_{t=1}^{T} y_{it}/h_{it}\right) - w_i\left(\sum_{t=1}^{T} \mathbf{x}_{it}/h_{it}\right)\mathbf{b}$$
$$\equiv \bar{y}_i^w - \bar{\mathbf{x}}_i^w\mathbf{b},$$

where $w_i \equiv 1/\left(\sum_{t=1}^{T} (1/h_{it})\right) > 0$ and $\bar{y}_i^w \equiv w_i\left(\sum_{t=1}^{T} y_{it}/h_{it}\right)$, and a similar definition holds for $\bar{\mathbf{x}}_i^w$. Note that $\bar{y}_i^w$ and $\bar{\mathbf{x}}_i^w$ are simply weighted averages. If h_{it} equals the same constant for all t, $\bar{y}_i^w$ and $\bar{\mathbf{x}}_i^w$ are the usual time averages.

Now we can plug each $\hat{a}_i(\mathbf{b})$ into the SSR to get the problem solved by $\hat{\boldsymbol{\beta}}$:

$$\min_{\mathbf{b}\in\mathbb{R}^K} \sum_{i=1}^{N}\sum_{t=1}^{T} [(y_{it} - \bar{y}_i^w) - (\mathbf{x}_{it} - \bar{\mathbf{x}}_i^w)\mathbf{b}]^2/h_{it}.$$

But this is just a pooled weighted least squares regression of $(y_{it} - \bar{y}_i^w)$ on $(\mathbf{x}_{it} - \bar{\mathbf{x}}_i^w)$ with weights $1/h_{it}$. Equivalently, define $\tilde{y}_{it} \equiv (y_{it} - \bar{y}_i^w)/\sqrt{h_{it}}$, $\tilde{\mathbf{x}}_{it} \equiv (\mathbf{x}_{it} - \bar{\mathbf{x}}_i^w)/\sqrt{h_{it}}$, all $t = 1,...,T$, $i = 1,...,N$. Then $\hat{\boldsymbol{\beta}}$ can be expressed in usual pooled OLS form:

$$\hat{\boldsymbol{\beta}} = \left(\sum_{i=1}^{N}\sum_{t=1}^{T} \tilde{\mathbf{x}}_{it}'\tilde{\mathbf{x}}_{it}\right)^{-1}\left(\sum_{i=1}^{N}\sum_{t=1}^{T} \tilde{\mathbf{x}}_{it}'\tilde{y}_{it}\right). \quad (10.82)$$

Note carefully how the initial y_{it} are weighted by $1/h_{it}$ to obtain $\bar{y}_i^w$, but where the usual $1/\sqrt{h_{it}}$ weighting shows up in the sum of squared residuals on the time-demeaned data (where the demeaming is a weighted average). Given (10.82), we can study the asymptotic ($N \to \infty$) properties of $\hat{\boldsymbol{\beta}}$. First, it is easy to show that $\bar{y}_i^w = \bar{\mathbf{x}}_i^w\boldsymbol{\beta} + c_i + \bar{u}_i^w$, where $\bar{u}_i^w \equiv w_i\left(\sum_{t=1}^{T} u_{it}/h_{it}\right)$. Subtracting this equation from $y_{it} = \mathbf{x}_{it}\boldsymbol{\beta} + c_i + u_{it}$ for all t gives $\tilde{y}_{it} = \tilde{\mathbf{x}}_{it}\boldsymbol{\beta} + \tilde{u}_{it}$, where $\tilde{u}_{it} \equiv (u_{it} - \bar{u}_i^w)/\sqrt{h_{it}}$. When we plug this in for $\tilde{y}_{it}$ in (10.82) and divide by N in the appropriate places we get

$$\hat{\boldsymbol{\beta}} = \boldsymbol{\beta} + \left(N^{-1}\sum_{i=1}^{N}\sum_{t=1}^{T}\tilde{\mathbf{x}}_{it}'\tilde{\mathbf{x}}_{it}\right)^{-1}\left(N^{-1}\sum_{i=1}^{N}\sum_{t=1}^{T}\tilde{\mathbf{x}}_{it}'\tilde{u}_{it}\right).$$

Straightforward algebra shows that $\sum_{t=1}^{T}\tilde{\mathbf{x}}_{it}'\tilde{u}_{it} = \sum_{t=1}^{T}\tilde{\mathbf{x}}_{it}'u_{it}/\sqrt{h_{it}}$, $i = 1,\ldots,N$, and so we have the convenient expression

$$\hat{\boldsymbol{\beta}} = \boldsymbol{\beta} + \left(N^{-1}\sum_{i=1}^{N}\sum_{t=1}^{T}\tilde{\mathbf{x}}_{it}'\tilde{\mathbf{x}}_{it}\right)^{-1}\left(N^{-1}\sum_{i=1}^{N}\sum_{t=1}^{T}\tilde{\mathbf{x}}_{it}'u_{it}/\sqrt{h_{it}}\right). \qquad (10.83)$$

From (10.83) we can immediately read off the consistency of $\hat{\boldsymbol{\beta}}$. Why? We assumed that $E(u_{it}|\mathbf{x}_i,\mathbf{h}_i,c_i) = 0$, which means u_{it} is uncorrelated with any function of $(\mathbf{x}_i,\mathbf{h}_i)$, including $\tilde{\mathbf{x}}_{it}$. So $E(\tilde{\mathbf{x}}_{it}'u_{it}) = \mathbf{0}$, $t = 1,\ldots,T$. As long as we assume $\text{rank}\left(\sum_{t=1}^{T}E(\tilde{\mathbf{x}}_{it}'\tilde{\mathbf{x}}_{it})\right) = K$, we can use the usual proof to show $\text{plim}(\hat{\boldsymbol{\beta}}) = \boldsymbol{\beta}$. (We can even show that $E(\hat{\boldsymbol{\beta}}|\mathbf{X},\mathbf{H}) = \boldsymbol{\beta}$.)

It is also clear from (10.83) that $\hat{\boldsymbol{\beta}}$ is $\sqrt{N}$-asymptotically normal under mild assumptions. The asymptotic variance is generally

$$\text{Avar}\,\sqrt{N}(\hat{\boldsymbol{\beta}} - \boldsymbol{\beta}) = \mathbf{A}^{-1}\mathbf{B}\mathbf{A}^{-1},$$

where

$$\mathbf{A} \equiv \sum_{t=1}^{T}E(\tilde{\mathbf{x}}_{it}'\tilde{\mathbf{x}}_{it}) \text{ and } \mathbf{B} \equiv \text{Var}\left(\sum_{t=1}^{T}\tilde{\mathbf{x}}_{it}'u_{it}/\sqrt{h_{it}}\right).$$

If we assume that $\text{Cov}(u_{it},u_{is}|\mathbf{x}_i,\mathbf{h}_i,c_i) = 0$, $t \neq s$, in addition to the variance assumption $\text{Var}(u_{it}|\mathbf{x}_i,\mathbf{h}_i,c_i) = \sigma_u^2 h_{it}$, then it is easily shown that $\mathbf{B} = \sigma_u^2\mathbf{A}$, and so $\sqrt{N}(\hat{\boldsymbol{\beta}} - \boldsymbol{\beta}) = \sigma_u^2\mathbf{A}^{-1}$.

The same subtleties that arise in estimating σ_u^2 for the usual fixed effects estimator crop up here as well. Assume the zero conditional covariance assumption and correct variance specification in the previous paragraph. Then, note that the residuals from the pooled OLS regression

$$\tilde{y}_{it} \text{ on } \tilde{\mathbf{x}}_{it},\ t = 1,\ldots,T,\ i = 1,\ldots,N, \qquad (10.84)$$

say $\hat{r}_{it}$, are estimating $\tilde{u}_{it} = (u_{it} - \bar{u}_i^w)/\sqrt{h_{it}}$ (in the sense that we obtain $\hat{r}_{it}$ from $\tilde{u}_{it}$ by replacing $\boldsymbol{\beta}$ with $\hat{\boldsymbol{\beta}}$). Now $E(\tilde{u}_{it}^2) = E[(u_{it}^2/h_{it})] - 2E[(u_{it}\bar{u}_i^w)/h_{it}]$

$+ \mathrm{E}[(\bar{u}_i^w)^2/h_{it}] = \sigma_u^2 - 2\sigma_u^2\mathrm{E}[(w_i/h_{it})] + \sigma_u^2\mathrm{E}[(w_i/h_{it})]$, where the law of iterated expectations is applied several times, and $\mathrm{E}[(\bar{u}_i^w)^2|\mathbf{x}_i,\mathbf{h}_i] = \sigma_u^2 w_i$ has been used. Therefore, $\mathrm{E}(\tilde{u}_{it}^2) = \sigma_u^2[1 - \mathrm{E}(w_i/h_{it})]$, $t = 1,\ldots,T$, and so

$$\sum_{t=1}^{T}\mathrm{E}(\tilde{u}_{it}^2) = \sigma_u^2\{T - \mathrm{E}[w_i\cdot\textstyle\sum_{t=1}^{T}(1/h_{it})]\} = \sigma_u^2(T - 1).$$

This contains the usual result for the within transformation as a special case. A consistent estimator of σ_u^2 is SSR/$[N(T - 1) - K]$, where SSR is the usual sum of squared residuals from (10.84), and the subtraction of K is optional. The estimator of $\mathrm{Avar}(\hat{\boldsymbol{\beta}})$ is then

$$\hat{\sigma}_u^2\left(\sum_{i=1}^{N}\sum_{t=1}^{T}\tilde{\mathbf{x}}_{it}'\tilde{\mathbf{x}}_{it}\right)^{-1}.$$

If we want to allow serial correlation in the $\{u_{it}\}$, or allow $\mathrm{Var}(u_{it}|\mathbf{x}_i,\mathbf{h}_i,c_i) \neq \sigma_u^2 h_{it}$, then we can just apply the robust formula for the pooled OLS regression (10.84).

10.15. (Bonus Question): Consider a standard unobserved effects model but where we explicitly separate out aggregate time effects, say $\mathbf{z}_t$, a $1 \times M$ vector, $M \leq T - 1$. Therefore, the model is

$$y_{it} = \alpha + \mathbf{z}_t\boldsymbol{\gamma} + \mathbf{x}_{it}\boldsymbol{\beta} + c_i + u_{it},\ t = 1,\ldots,T,$$

where $\mathbf{x}_{it}$ is the $1 \times K$ vector of explanatory variables that vary across individual and time. Because the $\mathbf{z}_t$ do not change across individual, we take them to be nonrandom. For example, $\mathbf{z}_t$ can contain year dummy variables or polynomials in time. Since we have included an overall intercept in the model we can assume $\mathrm{E}(c_i) = 0$. Let $\lambda = 1 - \{1/[1 + T(\sigma_c^2/\sigma_u^2)\}^{1/2}$ be the usual quasi-time-demeaning parameter for random effects estimation. In what follows, we take λ as known because that does not affect the asymptotic distribution results.

a. Show that we can write the quasi-time-demeaned equation for random effects estimation as

$$y_{it} - \lambda\bar{y}_i = \mu + (\mathbf{z}_t - \bar{\mathbf{z}})\boldsymbol{\gamma} + (\mathbf{x}_{it} - \lambda\bar{\mathbf{x}}_i) + (v_{it} - \lambda\bar{v}_i),$$

where $\mu = (1 - \lambda)\alpha + (1 - \lambda)\bar{\mathbf{z}}\boldsymbol{\gamma}$ and $v_{it} = c_i + u_{it}$, and $\bar{\mathbf{z}} = T^{-1}\sum_{t=1}^{T}\mathbf{z}_t$ is nonrandom.

b. To simplify the algebra -- without changing the substance of the findings -- assume that $\mu = 0$, and that we exclude an intercept. Write $\mathbf{g}_{it} = (\mathbf{z}_t - \bar{\mathbf{z}},\mathbf{x}_{it} - \lambda\bar{\mathbf{x}}_i)$ and $\boldsymbol{\delta}' = (\boldsymbol{\gamma}',\boldsymbol{\beta}')'$. We will study the asymptotic distribution of the pooled OLS estimator $y_{it} - \lambda\bar{y}_i$ on $\mathbf{g}_{it}$, $t = 1,\ldots,T$; $i = 1,\ldots,N$. Show that under RE.1 and RE.2,

$$\sqrt{N}(\hat{\boldsymbol{\delta}}_{RE} - \boldsymbol{\delta}) = \mathbf{A}_1^{-1}\left(N^{-1/2}\sum_{i=1}^{N}\sum_{t=1}^{T}\mathbf{g}_{it}'(v_{it} - \lambda\bar{v}_i)\right) + o_p(1),$$

where $\mathbf{A}_1 \equiv \sum_{t=1}^{T}\mathrm{E}(\mathbf{g}_{it}'\mathbf{g}_{it})$. Further, verify that for any i,

$$\sum_{t=1}^{T}(\mathbf{z}_t - \bar{\mathbf{z}})(v_{it} - \lambda\bar{v}_i) = \sum_{t=1}^{T}(\mathbf{z}_t - \bar{\mathbf{z}})u_{it}.$$

c. Show that under FE.1 and FE.2,

$$\sqrt{N}(\hat{\boldsymbol{\delta}}_{FE} - \boldsymbol{\delta}) = \mathbf{A}_2^{-1}\left(N^{-1/2}\sum_{i=1}^{N}\sum_{t=1}^{T}\mathbf{h}_{it}'u_{it}\right) + o_p(1),$$

where $\mathbf{h}_{it} \equiv (\mathbf{z}_t - \bar{\mathbf{z}},\mathbf{x}_{it} - \bar{\mathbf{x}}_i)$ and $\mathbf{A}_2 \equiv \sum_{t=1}^{T}\mathrm{E}(\mathbf{h}_{it}'\mathbf{h}_{it})$.

d. Under RE.1, RE.2, and FE.2, show that $\mathbf{A}_1\sqrt{N}(\hat{\boldsymbol{\delta}}_{RE} - \boldsymbol{\delta}) - \mathbf{A}_2\sqrt{N}(\hat{\boldsymbol{\delta}}_{FE} - \boldsymbol{\delta})$ has an asymptotic variance of rank K rather than $M + K$.

e. What implications does part d have for a Hausman test that compares fixed effects and random effects, when the model contains aggregate time variables of any sort? Does it matter whether or not we also assume RE.3?

Answer:

a. The usual quasi-time-demeaned equation can be written as

$$y_{it} - \lambda\bar{y}_i = (1 - \lambda)\alpha + (\mathbf{z}_t - \lambda\bar{\mathbf{z}})\boldsymbol{\gamma} + (\mathbf{x}_{it} - \lambda\bar{\mathbf{x}}_i) + (v_{it} - \lambda\bar{v}_i)$$

$$= [(1 - \lambda)\alpha + (1 - \lambda)\bar{\mathbf{z}}\boldsymbol{\gamma}] + (\mathbf{z}_t - \bar{\mathbf{z}})\boldsymbol{\gamma}$$

$$+ (\mathbf{x}_{it} - \lambda\bar{\mathbf{x}}_i) + (v_{it} - \lambda\bar{v}_i),$$

which is what we wanted to show.

b. The first part is just the usual linear representation of a pooled OLS estimator laid out in Chapter 7. It also follows from the discussion of random effects in Section 10.7.2. For the second part,

$$\begin{aligned}\sum_{t=1}^{T}(\mathbf{z}_t - \bar{\mathbf{z}})(v_{it} - \lambda\bar{v}_i) &= \sum_{t=1}^{T}(\mathbf{z}_t - \bar{\mathbf{z}})(1 - \lambda)c_i - \sum_{t=1}^{T}(\mathbf{z}_t - \bar{\mathbf{z}})\lambda\bar{u}_i \\ &\quad + \sum_{t=1}^{T}(\mathbf{z}_t - \bar{\mathbf{z}})u_{it} \\ &= [(1 - \lambda)c_i]\sum_{t=1}^{T}(\mathbf{z}_t - \bar{\mathbf{z}}) - (\lambda\bar{u}_i)\sum_{t=1}^{T}(\mathbf{z}_t - \bar{\mathbf{z}}) + \sum_{t=1}^{T}(\mathbf{z}_t - \bar{\mathbf{z}})u_{it} \\ &= \sum_{t=1}^{T}(\mathbf{z}_t - \bar{\mathbf{z}})u_{it}\end{aligned}$$

since $\sum_{t=1}^{T}(\mathbf{z}_t - \bar{\mathbf{z}}) = \mathbf{0}$.

c. There is really nothing to do here. This is just the usual first-order representation of the fixed effects estimator, which follows from the general pooled OLS results.

d. From part b we can write

$$\begin{aligned}\mathbf{A}_1\sqrt{N}(\hat{\boldsymbol{\delta}}_{RE} - \boldsymbol{\delta}) &= \left(N^{-1/2}\sum_{i=1}^{N}\sum_{t=1}^{T}\mathbf{g}_{it}'(v_{it} - \lambda\bar{v}_i)\right) + o_p(1) \\ &\equiv \left(N^{-1/2}\sum_{i=1}^{N}\sum_{t=1}^{T}\mathbf{r}_{it}\right) + o_p(1)\end{aligned}$$

where $\mathbf{r}_{it} = [(\mathbf{z}_t - \bar{\mathbf{z}})u_{it}, (\mathbf{x}_{it} - \lambda\bar{\mathbf{x}}_i)(v_{it} - \lambda\bar{v}_i)]'$. From part c we can write

$$\begin{aligned}\mathbf{A}_2\sqrt{N}(\hat{\boldsymbol{\delta}}_{FE} - \boldsymbol{\delta}) &= \left(N^{-1/2}\sum_{i=1}^{N}\sum_{t=1}^{T}\mathbf{h}_{it}'u_{it}\right) + o_p(1) \\ &\equiv \left(N^{-1/2}\sum_{i=1}^{N}\sum_{t=1}^{T}\mathbf{s}_{it}\right) + o_p(1),\end{aligned}$$

where $\mathbf{s}_{it} \equiv [(\mathbf{z}_t - \bar{\mathbf{z}})u_{it}, (\mathbf{x}_{it} - \bar{\mathbf{x}}_i)u_{it}]'$. But the first M elements of $\mathbf{r}_{it}$ and $\mathbf{s}_{it}$ are identical, which implies that

$$\begin{aligned}&\mathbf{A}_1\sqrt{N}(\hat{\boldsymbol{\delta}}_{RE} - \boldsymbol{\delta}) - \mathbf{A}_2\sqrt{N}(\hat{\boldsymbol{\delta}}_{FE} - \boldsymbol{\delta}) \\ &\quad = N^{-1/2}\sum_{i=1}^{N}\sum_{t=1}^{T}\begin{pmatrix}\mathbf{0} \\ (\mathbf{x}_{it} - \lambda\bar{\mathbf{x}}_i)'e_{it} - (\mathbf{x}_{it} - \bar{\mathbf{x}}_i)'u_{it}\end{pmatrix} + o_p(1),\end{aligned}$$

where "**0**" is $M \times 1$. The second part of the vector is $K \times 1$, and satisfies the central limit theorem. Under standard rank assumptions, it would have variance matrix with rank K.

e. If there were no $\mathbf{x}_{it}$, part d would imply that the limiting distribution of the difference between RE and FE is degenerate. In other words, we cannot compute the Hausman test comparing the FE and RE estimators if the only time-varying covariates are aggregates. (In fact, the FE and FE estimates are numerically identical in this case.) More generally, the variance-covariance matrix of the difference has rank K, not $M + K$ (whether or not we assume RE.3 under H_0). A properly computed Hausman test will have only K degrees-of-freedom, not $M + K$, as is often resported by econometrics packages. The regression-based test described in Problem 10.9 makes the degeneracies obvious, and it is easily made robust in Stata using the "xtgee" command.

SOLUTIONS TO CHAPTER 11 PROBLEMS

11.1. a. It is important to remember that, any time we put a variable in a regression model (whether we are using cross section or panel data), we are controlling for the effects of that variable on the dependent variable. The whole point of regression analysis is that it allows the explanatory variables to be correlated while estimating ceteris paribus effects. Thus, the inclusion of $y_{i,t-1}$ in the equation allows $prog_{it}$ to be correlated with $y_{i,t-1}$, and also recognizes that, due to inertia, y_{it} is often strongly related to $y_{i,t-1}$.

An assumption that implies pooled OLS is consistent is

$$E(u_{it}|\mathbf{z}_i,\mathbf{x}_{it},y_{i,t-1},prog_{it}) = 0, \text{ all } t,$$

which is implied by but is weaker than dynamic completeness. Without additional assumptions, the pooled OLS standard errors and test statistics need to be adjusted for heteroskedasticity and serial correlation (although the later will not be present under dynamic completeness).

b. As we discussed in Section 7.8.2, this statement is incorrect. Provided our interest is in $E(y_{it}|\mathbf{z}_i,\mathbf{x}_{it},y_{i,t-1},prog_{it})$, we do not care about serial correlation in the implied errors, nor does serial correlation cause inconsistency in the OLS estimators.

c. Such a model is the standard unobserved effects model:

$$y_{it} = \mathbf{x}_{it}\boldsymbol{\beta} + \delta_1 prog_{it} + c_i + u_{it}, \quad t=1,2,\ldots,T.$$

We would probably assume that $(\mathbf{x}_{it},prog_{it})$ is strictly exogenous; the weakest form of strict exogeneity is that $(\mathbf{x}_{it},prog_{it})$ is uncorrelated with u_{is} for all t and s. Then we could estimate the equation by fixed effects or first differencing. If the u_{it} are serially uncorrelated, FE is preferred. We could also do a GLS analysis after the fixed effects or first-differencing transformations, but we should have a large N.

d. A model that incorporates features from parts a and c is

$$y_{it} = \mathbf{x}_{it}\boldsymbol{\beta} + \delta_1 prog_{it} + \rho_1 y_{i,t-1} + c_i + u_{it}, \quad t = 1,\ldots,T.$$

Now, program participation can depend on unobserved city heterogeneity as well as on lagged y_{it} (we assume that y_{i0} is observed). Fixed effects and first-differencing are both inconsistent as $N \to \infty$ with fixed T.

Assuming that $\mathrm{E}(u_{it}|\mathbf{x}_i,\mathbf{prog}_i,y_{i,t-1},y_{i,t-2},\ldots,y_{i0}) = 0$, a consistent procedure is obtained by first differencing, to get

$$y_{it} = \Delta\mathbf{x}_{it}\boldsymbol{\beta} + \delta_1\Delta prog_{it} + \rho_1\Delta y_{i,t-1} + \Delta u_{it}, \quad t=2,\ldots,T.$$

At time t and $\Delta\mathbf{x}_{it}$, $\Delta prog_{it}$ can be used as there own instruments, along with $y_{i,t-j}$ for $j \geq 2$. Either pooled 2SLS or a GMM procedure can be used. Under strict exogeneity, past and future values of $\mathbf{x}_{it}$ can also be used as instruments.

11.3. Writing $y_{it} = \beta x_{it} + c_i + u_{it} - \beta r_{it}$, the fixed effects estimator $\hat{\beta}_{FE}$ can be written as

$$\beta + \left(N^{-1}\sum_{i=1}^{N}\sum_{t=1}^{T}(x_{it} - \bar{x}_i)\right)^2\left(N^{-1}\sum_{i=1}^{N}\sum_{t=1}^{T}(x_{it} - \bar{x}_i)(u_{it} - \bar{u}_i - \beta(r_{it} - \bar{r}_i)\right).$$

Now, $x_{it} - \bar{x}_i = (x_{it}^* - \bar{x}_i^*) + (r_{it} - \bar{r}_i)$. Then, because $\mathrm{E}(r_{it}|\mathbf{x}_i^*,c_i) = 0$ for all t, $(x_{it}^* - \bar{x}_i^*)$ and $(r_{it} - \bar{r}_i)$ are uncorrelated, and so

$$\mathrm{Var}(x_{it} - \bar{x}_i) = \mathrm{Var}(x_{it}^* - \bar{x}_i^*) + \mathrm{Var}(r_{it} - \bar{r}_i), \text{ all } t.$$

Similarly, under (11.30), $(x_{it} - \bar{x}_i)$ and $(u_{it} - \bar{u}_i)$ are uncorrelated for all t. Now $\mathrm{E}[(x_{it} - \bar{x}_i)(r_{it} - \bar{r}_i)] = \mathrm{E}[\{(x_{it}^* - \bar{x}_i^*) + (r_{it} - \bar{r}_i)\}(r_{it} - \bar{r}_i)] = \mathrm{Var}(r_{it} - \bar{r}_i)$. By the law of large numbers and the assumption of constant variances across t,

$$N^{-1}\sum_{i=1}^{N}\sum_{t=1}^{T}(x_{it} - \bar{x}_i) \xrightarrow{p} \sum_{t=1}^{T}\mathrm{Var}(x_{it} - \bar{x}_i) = T[\mathrm{Var}(x_{it}^{*} - \bar{x}_i^{*}) + \mathrm{Var}(r_{it} - \bar{r}_i)]$$

and

$$N^{-1}\sum_{i=1}^{N}\sum_{t=1}^{T}(x_{it} - \bar{x}_i)(u_{it} - \bar{u}_i - \beta(r_{it} - \bar{r}_i) \xrightarrow{p} -T\beta\mathrm{Var}(r_{it} - \bar{r}_i).$$

Therefore,

$$\begin{aligned}\mathrm{plim}\ \hat{\beta}_{FE} &= \beta - \beta\left(\frac{\mathrm{Var}(r_{it} - \bar{r}_i)}{[\mathrm{Var}(x_{it}^{*} - \bar{x}_i^{*}) + \mathrm{Var}(r_{it} - \bar{r}_i)]}\right) \\ &= \beta\left(1 - \frac{\mathrm{Var}(r_{it} - \bar{r}_i)}{[\mathrm{Var}(x_{it}^{*} - \bar{x}_i^{*}) + \mathrm{Var}(r_{it} - \bar{r}_i)]}\right).\end{aligned}$$

11.5. a. $\mathrm{E}(\mathbf{v}_i|\mathbf{z}_i,\mathbf{x}_i) = \mathbf{Z}_i[\mathrm{E}(\mathbf{a}_i|\mathbf{z}_i,\mathbf{x}_i) - \alpha] + \mathrm{E}(\mathbf{u}_i|\mathbf{z}_i,\mathbf{x}_i) = \mathbf{Z}_i(\alpha - \alpha) + \mathbf{0} = \mathbf{0}$. Next, $\mathrm{Var}(\mathbf{v}_i|\mathbf{z}_i,\mathbf{x}_i) = \mathbf{Z}_i\mathrm{Var}(\mathbf{a}_i|\mathbf{z}_i,\mathbf{x}_i)\mathbf{Z}_i' + \mathrm{Var}(\mathbf{u}_i|\mathbf{z}_i,\mathbf{x}_i) + \mathrm{Cov}(\mathbf{a}_i,\mathbf{u}_i|\mathbf{z}_i,\mathbf{x}_i) + \mathrm{Cov}(\mathbf{u}_i,\mathbf{a}_i|\mathbf{z}_i,\mathbf{x}_i) = \mathbf{Z}_i\mathrm{Var}(\mathbf{a}_i|\mathbf{z}_i,\mathbf{x}_i)\mathbf{Z}_i' + \mathrm{Var}(\mathbf{u}_i|\mathbf{z}_i,\mathbf{x}_i)$ because $\mathbf{a}_i$ and $\mathbf{u}_i$ are uncorrelated, conditional on $(\mathbf{z}_i,\mathbf{x}_i)$, by FE.1′ and the usual iterated expectations argument. Therefore, $\mathrm{Var}(\mathbf{v}_i|\mathbf{z}_i,\mathbf{x}_i) = \mathbf{Z}_i\mathbf{\Lambda}\mathbf{Z}_i' + \sigma_u^2\mathbf{I}_T$ under the assumptions given, which shows that the conditional variance depends on $\mathbf{z}_i$. Unlike in the standard random effects model, there is conditional heteroskedasticity.

b. If we use the usual RE analysis, we are applying FGLS to the equation $\mathbf{y}_i = \mathbf{Z}_i\alpha + \mathbf{X}_i\beta + \mathbf{v}_i$, where $\mathbf{v}_i = \mathbf{Z}_i(\mathbf{a}_i - \alpha) + \mathbf{u}_i$. From part a, we know that $\mathrm{E}(\mathbf{v}_i|\mathbf{x}_i,\mathbf{z}_i) = \mathbf{0}$, and so the usual RE estimator is consistent (as $N \rightarrow \infty$ for fixed T) and $\sqrt{N}$-asymptotically normal, provided the rank condition, Assumption RE.2, holds. (Remember, a feasible GLS analysis with any $\hat{\mathbf{\Omega}}$ will be consistent provided $\hat{\mathbf{\Omega}}$ converges in probability to a nonsingular matrix as $N \rightarrow \infty$. It need not be the case that $\mathrm{Var}(\mathbf{v}_i|\mathbf{x}_i,\mathbf{z}_i) = \mathrm{plim}(\hat{\mathbf{\Omega}})$, or even that $\mathrm{Var}(\mathbf{v}_i) = \mathrm{plim}(\hat{\mathbf{\Omega}})$.

From part a, we know that $\mathrm{Var}(\mathbf{v}_i|\mathbf{x}_i,\mathbf{z}_i)$ depends on $\mathbf{z}_i$ unless we restrict almost all elements of $\mathbf{\Lambda}$ to be zero (all but those corresponding to the constant in $\mathbf{z}_{it}$). Therefore, the usual random effects inference -- that is, based on the usual RE variance matrix estimator -- will be invalid.

c. We can easily make the RE analysis fully robust to an arbitrary $\mathrm{Var}(\mathbf{v}_i|\mathbf{x}_i,\mathbf{z}_i)$, as in equation (7.49). Naturally, we expand the set of explanatory variables to $(\mathbf{z}_{it},\mathbf{x}_{it})$, and we estimate $\boldsymbol{\alpha}$ along with $\boldsymbol{\beta}$.

11.7. When $\boldsymbol{\lambda}_t = \boldsymbol{\lambda}/T$ for all t, we can rearrange (11.60) to get

$$y_{it} = \mathbf{x}_{it}\boldsymbol{\beta} + \bar{\mathbf{x}}_i\boldsymbol{\lambda} + v_{it},\quad t = 1,2,\ldots,T.$$

Let $\hat{\boldsymbol{\beta}}$ (along with $\hat{\boldsymbol{\lambda}}$) denote the pooled OLS estimator from this equation. By standard results on partitioned regression [for example, Davidson and MacKinnon (1993, Section 1.4)], $\hat{\boldsymbol{\beta}}$ can be obtained by the following two-step procedure:

(i) Regress $\mathbf{x}_{it}$ on $\bar{\mathbf{x}}_i$ across all t and i, and save the $1 \times K$ vectors of residuals, say $\hat{\mathbf{r}}_{it}$, $t = 1,\ldots,T$, $i = 1,\ldots,N$.

(ii) Regress y_{it} on $\hat{\mathbf{r}}_{it}$ across all t and i. The OLS vector on $\hat{\mathbf{r}}_{it}$ is $\hat{\boldsymbol{\beta}}$. We want to show that $\hat{\boldsymbol{\beta}}$ is the FE estimator. Given that the FE estimator can be obtained by pooled OLS of y_{it} on $(\mathbf{x}_{it} - \bar{\mathbf{x}}_i)$, it suffices to show that $\hat{\mathbf{r}}_{it} = \mathbf{x}_{it} - \bar{\mathbf{x}}_i$ for all t and i. But

$$\hat{\mathbf{r}}_{it} = \mathbf{x}_{it} - \bar{\mathbf{x}}_i\left(\sum_{i=1}^{N}\sum_{t=1}^{T}\bar{\mathbf{x}}_i'\bar{\mathbf{x}}_i\right)^{-1}\left(\sum_{i=1}^{N}\sum_{t=1}^{T}\bar{\mathbf{x}}_i'\mathbf{x}_{it}\right)$$

and $\sum_{i=1}^{N}\sum_{t=1}^{T}\bar{\mathbf{x}}_i'\mathbf{x}_{it} = \sum_{i=1}^{N}\bar{\mathbf{x}}_i'\sum_{t=1}^{T}\mathbf{x}_{it} = \sum_{i=1}^{N}T\bar{\mathbf{x}}_i'\bar{\mathbf{x}}_i = \sum_{i=1}^{N}\sum_{t=1}^{T}\bar{\mathbf{x}}_i'\bar{\mathbf{x}}_i$, and so $\hat{\mathbf{r}}_{it} = \mathbf{x}_{it} - \bar{\mathbf{x}}_i\mathbf{I}_K = \mathbf{x}_{it} - \bar{\mathbf{x}}_i$. This completes the proof.

11.9. a. We can apply Problem 8.8.b, as we are applying pooled 2SLS to the time-demeaned equation: $\mathrm{rank}\left(\sum_{t=1}^{T}\mathrm{E}(\ddot{\mathbf{z}}_{it}'\ddot{\mathbf{x}}_{it})\right) = K$. This clearly fails if $\mathbf{x}_{it}$ contains any time-constant explanatory variables (across all i, as usual). The condition $\mathrm{rank}\left(\sum_{t=1}^{T}\mathrm{E}(\ddot{\mathbf{z}}_{it}'\ddot{\mathbf{z}}_{it})\right) = L$ is also needed, and this rules out time-constant instruments. But if the rank condition holds, we can always redefine $\mathbf{z}_{it}$ so that $\sum_{t=1}^{T} E(\ddot{\mathbf{z}}_{it}'\ddot{\mathbf{z}}_{it})$ has full rank.

b. We can apply the results on GMM estimation in Chapter 8. In particular, in equation (8.25), take $\mathbf{C} = E(\ddot{\mathbf{Z}}_i'\ddot{\mathbf{X}}_i)$, $\mathbf{W} = [E(\ddot{\mathbf{Z}}_i'\ddot{\mathbf{Z}}_i)]^{-1}$, and $\mathbf{\Lambda} = E(\ddot{\mathbf{Z}}_i'\ddot{\mathbf{u}}_i\ddot{\mathbf{u}}_i'\ddot{\mathbf{Z}}_i)$. A key point is that $\ddot{\mathbf{Z}}_i'\ddot{\mathbf{u}}_i = (\mathbf{Q}_T\mathbf{Z}_i)'(\mathbf{Q}_T\mathbf{u}_i) = \mathbf{Z}_i'\mathbf{Q}_T\mathbf{u}_i = \ddot{\mathbf{Z}}_i'\mathbf{u}_i$, where $\mathbf{Q}_T$ is the T x T time-demeaning matrix defined in Chapter 10. Under (11.80), $E(\mathbf{u}_i\mathbf{u}_i'|\ddot{\mathbf{Z}}_i) = \sigma_u^2\mathbf{I}_T$ (by the usual iterated expectations argument), and so $\mathbf{\Lambda} = E(\ddot{\mathbf{Z}}_i'\mathbf{u}_i\mathbf{u}_i'\ddot{\mathbf{Z}}_i) = \sigma_u^2 E(\ddot{\mathbf{Z}}_i'\ddot{\mathbf{Z}}_i)$. If we plug these choices of $\mathbf{C}$, $\mathbf{W}$, and $\mathbf{\Lambda}$ into (8.25) and simplify, we obtain

$$\text{Avar } \sqrt{N}(\hat{\boldsymbol{\beta}} - \boldsymbol{\beta}) = \sigma_u^2\{E(\ddot{\mathbf{X}}_i'\ddot{\mathbf{Z}}_i)[E(\ddot{\mathbf{Z}}_i'\ddot{\mathbf{Z}}_i)]^{-1}E(\ddot{\mathbf{Z}}_i'\ddot{\mathbf{X}}_i)\}^{-1}.$$

c. The argument is very similar to the case of the fixed effects estimator. First, $\sum_{t=1}^{T} E(\ddot{u}_{it}^2) = (T - 1)\sigma_u^2$, just as before. If $\hat{u}_{it} = \ddot{y}_{it} - \ddot{\mathbf{x}}_{it}\hat{\boldsymbol{\beta}}$ are the pooled 2SLS residuals applied to the time-demeaned data, then $[N(T - 1)]^{-1}\sum_{i=1}^{N}\sum_{t=1}^{T}\hat{u}_{it}^2$ is a consistent estimator of σ_u^2. Typically, $N(T - 1)$ would be replaced by $N(T - 1) - K$ as a degrees of freedom adjustment.

d. From Problem 5.1 (which is purely algebraic, and so applies immediately to pooled 2SLS), the 2SLS estimator of all parameters in (11.81), including $\boldsymbol{\beta}$, can be obtained as follows: first run the regression $\mathbf{x}_{it}$ on $d1_i$, ..., dN_i, $\mathbf{z}_{it}$ across all t and i, and obtain the residuals, say $\hat{\mathbf{r}}_{it}$; second, obtain $\hat{c}_1$, ..., $\hat{c}_N$, $\hat{\boldsymbol{\beta}}$ from the pooled regression y_{it} on $d1_i$, ..., dN_i, $\mathbf{x}_{it}$, $\hat{\mathbf{r}}_{it}$. Now, by algebra of partial regression, $\hat{\boldsymbol{\beta}}$ and the coefficient on $\hat{\mathbf{r}}_{it}$, say $\hat{\boldsymbol{\delta}}$, from this last regression can be obtained by first partialling out the dummy variables, $d1_i$, ..., dN_i. As we know from Chapter 10, this partialling out is equivalent to time demeaning all variables. Therefore, $\hat{\boldsymbol{\beta}}$ and $\hat{\boldsymbol{\delta}}$ can be obtained from the pooled regression $\ddot{y}_{it}$ on $\ddot{\mathbf{x}}_{it}$, $\hat{\mathbf{r}}_{it}$, where we use the fact that the time average of $\hat{\mathbf{r}}_{it}$ for each i is identically zero.

Now consider the 2SLS estimator of $\boldsymbol{\beta}$ from (11.79). This is equivalent to first regressing $\ddot{\mathbf{x}}_{it}$ on $\ddot{\mathbf{z}}_{it}$ and saving the residuals, say $\hat{\mathbf{s}}_{it}$, and then running the OLS regression $\ddot{y}_{it}$ on $\ddot{\mathbf{x}}_{it}$, $\hat{\mathbf{s}}_{it}$. But, again by partial regression and the fact that regressing on $d1_i$, ..., dN_i results in time demeaning, $\hat{\mathbf{s}}_{it} = \hat{\mathbf{r}}_{it}$ for all i and t. This proves that the 2SLS estimates of $\boldsymbol{\beta}$ from (11.79) and (11.81) are identical. (If some elements of $\mathbf{x}_{it}$ are included in $\mathbf{z}_{it}$, as would usually be the case, some entries in $\hat{\mathbf{r}}_{it}$ are identically zero for all t and i. But we can simply drop those without changing any other steps in the argument.)

e. First, by writing down the first order condition for the 2SLS estimates from (11.81) (with dn_i as their own instruments, and $\hat{\mathbf{x}}_{it}$ as the IVs for $\mathbf{x}_{it}$), it is easy to show that $\hat{c}_i = \bar{y}_i - \bar{\mathbf{x}}_i\hat{\boldsymbol{\beta}}$, where $\hat{\boldsymbol{\beta}}$ is the IV estimator from (11.81) (and also (11.79)). Therefore, the 2SLS residuals from (11.81) are computed as $y_{it} - (\bar{y}_i - \bar{\mathbf{x}}_i\hat{\boldsymbol{\beta}}) - \mathbf{x}_{it}\hat{\boldsymbol{\beta}} = (y_{it} - \bar{y}_i) - (\mathbf{x}_{it} - \bar{\mathbf{x}}_i)\hat{\boldsymbol{\beta}} = \ddot{y}_{it} - \ddot{\mathbf{x}}_{it}\hat{\boldsymbol{\beta}}$, which are exactly the 2SLS residuals from (11.79). Because the N dummy variables are explicitly included in (11.81), the degrees of freedom in estimating σ_u^2 from part c are properly calculated.

f. The general, messy estimator in equation (8.27) should be used, where $\mathbf{X}$ and $\mathbf{Z}$ are replaced with $\ddot{\mathbf{X}}$ and $\ddot{\mathbf{Z}}$, $\hat{\mathbf{W}} = (\ddot{\mathbf{Z}}'\ddot{\mathbf{Z}}/N)^{-1}$, $\hat{\mathbf{u}}_i = \ddot{\mathbf{y}}_i - \ddot{\mathbf{X}}_i\hat{\boldsymbol{\beta}}$, and $\hat{\boldsymbol{\Lambda}} = \left(N^{-1}\sum_{i=1}^{N}\ddot{\mathbf{Z}}_i'\hat{\mathbf{u}}_i\hat{\mathbf{u}}_i'\ddot{\mathbf{Z}}_i\right)$.

g. The 2SLS procedure is inconsistent as $N \rightarrow \infty$ with fixed T, as is any IV method that uses time-demeaning to eliminate the unobserved effect. This is because the time-demeaned IVs will generally be correlated with some elements of $\mathbf{u}_i$ (usually, all elements).

11.10. Let $\tilde{\mathbf{a}}_i$, $i = 1,\ldots,N$, $\tilde{\boldsymbol{\beta}}$ be the OLS estimates from the pooled OLS regression (11.82). By partial regression, $\tilde{\boldsymbol{\beta}}$ can be obtained by first regressing y_{it} on $d1_i\mathbf{z}_{it}$, $d2_i\mathbf{z}_{it}$, ..., $dN_i\mathbf{z}_{it}$ and obtaining the residuals, $\ddot{y}_{it}$, and likewise for $\ddot{\mathbf{x}}_{it}$. Then, we regress $\ddot{y}_{it}$ on $\ddot{\mathbf{x}}_{it}$, $t = 1,\ldots,T$, $i = 1,\ldots,N$. But regressing on $d1_i\mathbf{z}_{it}$, $d2_i\mathbf{z}_{it}$, ..., $dN_i\mathbf{z}_{it}$ across all t and i is the same as regressing on $\mathbf{z}_{it}$, $t = 1,\ldots,T$, for each cross section observation, i. So, $\ddot{y}_{it} = y_{it} - \mathbf{z}_{it}[(\mathbf{Z}_i'\mathbf{Z}_i)^{-1}\mathbf{Z}_i'\mathbf{y}_i]$ and $\ddot{\mathbf{y}}_i = \mathbf{M}_i\mathbf{y}_i$, where $\mathbf{M}_i = \mathbf{I}_T - \mathbf{Z}_i[(\mathbf{Z}_i'\mathbf{Z}_i)^{-1}\mathbf{Z}_i'$. A similar expression holds for $\ddot{\mathbf{x}}_{it}$. We have shown that regression (11.82) is identical to the pooled OLS regression $\ddot{y}_{it}$ on $\ddot{\mathbf{x}}_{it}$, $t = 1,\ldots,T$, $i = 1,\ldots,N$. The residuals from the two regressions are exactly the same by the two-step projection result. The regression in (11.82) results in $NT - NJ - K = N(T - J) - K$ degrees of freedom, which is exactly what we need in (11.48).

11.11. Differencing twice and using the resulting cross section is easily done in Stata. Alternatively, I can used fixed effects on the first differences:

```
. gen cclscrap = clscrap - clscrap[_n-1] if d89
(417 missing values generated)

. gen ccgrnt = cgrant - cgrant[_n-1] if d89
(314 missing values generated)

. gen ccgrnt_1 = cgrant_1 - cgrant_1[_n-1] if d89
(314 missing values generated)

. reg cclscrap ccgrnt ccgrnt_1

  Source |       SS       df       MS                  Number of obs =      54
---------+------------------------------               F(  2,    51) =    0.97
   Model |  .958448372     2  .479224186               Prob > F      =  0.3868
Residual |  25.2535328    51   .49516731               R-squared     =  0.0366
---------+------------------------------               Adj R-squared = -0.0012
   Total |  26.2119812    53  .494565682               Root MSE      =  .70368
```

```
------------------------------------------------------------------------------
cclscrap |      Coef.   Std. Err.       t     P>|t|       [95% Conf. Interval]
---------+--------------------------------------------------------------------
  ccgrnt |   .1564748   .2632934      0.594   0.555      -.3721087    .6850584
ccgrnt_1 |   .6099015   .6343411      0.961   0.341      -.6635913    1.883394
   _cons |  -.2377384   .1407363     -1.689   0.097      -.5202783    .0448014
------------------------------------------------------------------------------


. xtreg clscrap d89 cgrant cgrant_1, fe

                                                Fixed-effects (within) regression
sd(u_fcode)                 =    .509567                 Number of obs =      108
sd(e_fcode_t)               =   .4975778                             n =       54
sd(e_fcode_t + u_fcode)     =   .7122094                             T =        2

corr(u_fcode, Xb)           =    -0.4011                 R-sq within   =   0.0577
                                                              between  =   0.0476
                                                              overall  =   0.0050

                                                         F(   3,    51) =     1.04
                                                              Prob > F =   0.3826

------------------------------------------------------------------------------
 clscrap |      Coef.   Std. Err.       t     P>|t|       [95% Conf. Interval]
---------+--------------------------------------------------------------------
     d89 |  -.2377385   .1407362     -1.689   0.097      -.5202783    .0448014
  cgrant |   .1564748   .2632934      0.594   0.555      -.3721087    .6850584
cgrant_1 |   .6099016   .6343411      0.961   0.341      -.6635913    1.883394
   _cons |  -.2240491    .114748     -1.953   0.056      -.4544153    .0063171
------------------------------------------------------------------------------
   fcode |          F(53,51) =        1.674   0.033           (54 categories)
```

The estimates from the random growth model are pretty bad -- the estimates on the grant variables are of the wrong sign -- and they are very imprecise. The joint *F* test for the 53 different intercepts is significant at the 5% level, so it is hard to know what to make of this. It does cast doubt on the standard unobserved effects model without a random growth term.

11.13. a. The following Stata output estimates the reduced form for $\Delta\log(pris)$ and tests joint significance of *final1* and *final2*, and also tests equality of the coefficients on *final1* and *final2*. The latter is actually not very interesting. Technically, because we do not reject, we could reduce our instrument to *final1* + *final2*, but we could always look ex post for restrictions on the parameters in a reduced form.

```
. reg gpris final1 final2 gpolpc gincpc cunem cblack cmetro cag0_14 cag15_17
cag18_24 cag25_34 y81-y93

      Source |       SS       df       MS              Number of obs =     714
-------------+------------------------------           F( 24,   689) =    5.15
       Model |  .481041472    24  .020043395           Prob > F      =  0.0000
    Residual |  2.68006631   689  .003889791           R-squared     =  0.1522
-------------+------------------------------           Adj R-squared =  0.1226
       Total |  3.16110778   713  .004433531           Root MSE      =  .06237

------------------------------------------------------------------------------
       gpris |      Coef.   Std. Err.      t    P>|t|       [95% Conf. Interval]
-------------+----------------------------------------------------------------
      final1 |   -.077488   .0259556    -2.99   0.003      -.1284496   -.0265265
      final2 |  -.0529558   .0184078    -2.88   0.004      -.0890979   -.0168136
      gpolpc |  -.0286921   .0440058    -0.65   0.515      -.1150937    .0577094
      gincpc |   .2095521   .1313169     1.60   0.111      -.0482772    .4673815
       cunem |   .1616595   .3111688     0.52   0.604      -.4492934    .7726124
      cblack |  -.0044763   .0262118    -0.17   0.864       -.055941    .0469883
      cmetro |  -1.418389   .7860435    -1.80   0.072      -2.961717    .1249392
     cag0_14 |   2.617307   1.582611     1.65   0.099      -.4900125    5.724627
    cag15_17 |  -1.608738   3.755564    -0.43   0.669      -8.982461    5.764986
    cag18_24 |   .9533678   1.731188     0.55   0.582      -2.445669    4.352405
    cag25_34 |  -1.031684   1.763248    -0.59   0.559      -4.493667      2.4303
         y81 |   .0124113    .013763     0.90   0.367      -.0146111    .0394337
         y82 |   .0773503   .0156924     4.93   0.000       .0465396     .108161
         y83 |   .0767785   .0153929     4.99   0.000       .0465559    .1070011
         y84 |   .0289763   .0176504     1.64   0.101      -.0056787    .0636314
         y85 |   .0279051   .0164176     1.70   0.090      -.0043295    .0601397
         y86 |   .0541489   .0179305     3.02   0.003        .018944    .0893539
         y87 |   .0312716   .0171317     1.83   0.068       -.002365    .0649082
         y88 |    .019245   .0170725     1.13   0.260      -.0142754    .0527654
         y89 |   .0184651   .0172867     1.07   0.286      -.0154759     .052406
         y90 |   .0635926   .0165775     3.84   0.000       .0310442    .0961411
         y91 |   .0263719   .0168913     1.56   0.119      -.0067927    .0595366
         y92 |   .0190481   .0179372     1.06   0.289      -.0161701    .0542663
         y93 |   .0134109   .0189757     0.71   0.480      -.0238461     .050668
       _cons |   .0272013   .0170478     1.60   0.111      -.0062705    .0606731
------------------------------------------------------------------------------

. test final1 final2

 ( 1)  final1 = 0.0
 ( 2)  final2 = 0.0
```

```
       F(  2,   689) =    8.56
            Prob > F =    0.0002


. test final1 = final2

 ( 1)  final1 - final2 = 0.0

       F(  1,   689) =    0.60
            Prob > F =    0.4401
```

Jointly, *final1* and *final2* are pretty significant. Next, test for serial correlation in $a_{it} \equiv \Delta v_{it}$:

```
. predict ahat, resid

. gen ahat_1 = ahat[_n-1] if year > 80
(51 missing values generated)

. reg ahat ahat_1

      Source |       SS       df       MS              Number of obs =     663
-------------+------------------------------           F(  1,   661) =   14.33
       Model |  .051681199     1  .051681199           Prob > F      =  0.0002
    Residual |  2.38322468   661  .003605484           R-squared     =  0.0212
-------------+------------------------------           Adj R-squared =  0.0197
       Total |  2.43490588   662  .003678106           Root MSE      =  .06005

------------------------------------------------------------------------------
        ahat |      Coef.   Std. Err.       t     P>|t|     [95% Conf. Interval]
-------------+----------------------------------------------------------------
      ahat_1 |   .1426247   .0376713      3.79   0.000      .0686549    .2165945
       _cons |   4.24e-11    .002332      0.00   1.000      -.004579     .004579
------------------------------------------------------------------------------
```

There is strong evidence of positive serial correlation, although the estimated size of the AR(1) coefficient is not especially large. Still, a fully robust variance matrix should be used for the joint significance test of *final1* and *final2*. (However, it turns out that these two IVs are even more significant when the robust variance matrix is used.)

b. First, we do pooled 2SLS to obtain the 2SLS residuals, $\hat{e}_{it}$. Then we add the lagged residual to the equation, and use it as its own IV:

```
. reg gcriv gpris gpolpc gincpc cunem cblack cmetro cag0_14 cag15_17 cag18_24
cag25_34 y81-y91 (final1 final2 gpolpc gincpc cunem cblack cmetro cag0_14
cag15_17 cag18_24 cag25_34 y81-y91)

Instrumental variables (2SLS) regression

      Source |       SS       df       MS              Number of obs =     714
-------------+------------------------------           F( 21,   692) =    6.73
       Model | -.639452237    21 -.030450107           Prob > F      =  0.0000
    Residual |  6.23095906   692  .009004276           R-squared     =       .
-------------+------------------------------           Adj R-squared =       .
       Total |  5.59150682   713  .007842226           Root MSE      =  .09489

------------------------------------------------------------------------------
       gcriv |      Coef.   Std. Err.      t    P>|t|     [95% Conf. Interval]
-------------+----------------------------------------------------------------
       gpris |  -1.017724   .3640963    -2.80   0.005     -1.73259   -.3028583
      gpolpc |    .034514   .0670342     0.51   0.607    -.0971008    .1661288
      gincpc |   .8804841   .2023009     4.35   0.000      .483287    1.277681
       cunem |   .4043515   .4306021     0.94   0.348    -.4410918    1.249795
      cblack |   -.016093   .0398597    -0.40   0.687    -.0943535    .0621675
      cmetro |  -.6341352   1.293964    -0.49   0.624    -3.174702    1.906432
     cag0_14 |   3.436976   2.621361     1.31   0.190      -1.7098    8.583751
    cag15_17 |    4.67406   5.591208     0.84   0.403    -6.303706    15.65183
    cag18_24 |   2.898237   2.604161     1.11   0.266    -2.214767     8.01124
    cag25_34 |   1.158599   2.458384     0.47   0.638    -3.668188    5.985386
         y81 |  -.0599461   .0209435    -2.86   0.004    -.1010666   -.0188256
         y82 |   .0173948   .0342413     0.51   0.612    -.0498346    .0846241
         y83 |   .0117646   .0317449     0.37   0.711    -.0505634    .0740926
         y84 |  -.0030135   .0215164    -0.14   0.889    -.0452588    .0392318
         y85 |   .0196991   .0196581     1.00   0.317    -.0188976    .0582958
         y86 |    .074723   .0256253     2.92   0.004     .0244103    .1250357
         y87 |  -.0123046   .0196877    -0.62   0.532    -.0509593    .0263502
         y88 |   .0371433   .0191951     1.94   0.053    -.0005443    .0748308
         y89 |   .0277369   .0205669     1.35   0.178    -.0126441    .0681179
         y90 |   .1257373    .025475     4.94   0.000     .0757197    .1757549
         y91 |   .0431782   .0169334     2.55   0.011     .0099311    .0764253
       _cons |   .0307815   .0218654     1.41   0.160     -.012149    .0737119
------------------------------------------------------------------------------

. predict ehat, resid

. gen ehat_1 = ehat[_n-1] if year > 80
(51 missing values generated)
```

```
. reg gcriv ehat_1 gpris gpolpc gincpc cunem cblack cmetro cag0_14 cag15_17
cag18_24 cag25_34 y81-y91 (ehat_1 final1 final2 gpolpc gincpc cunem cblack
cmetro cag0_14 cag15_17 cag18_24 cag25_34 y81-y91)

Instrumental variables (2SLS) regression

      Source |       SS       df       MS              Number of obs =     663
-------------+------------------------------           F( 22,   640) =    5.38
       Model | -.815771104    22 -.037080505           Prob > F      =  0.0000
    Residual |  5.90415463   640  .009225242           R-squared     =       .
-------------+------------------------------           Adj R-squared =       .
       Total |  5.08838353   662   .00768638           Root MSE      =  .09605

------------------------------------------------------------------------------
       gcriv |      Coef.   Std. Err.       t     P>|t|       [95% Conf. Interval]
-------------+----------------------------------------------------------------
       gpris |  -1.083743   .4066275     -2.67   0.008     -1.882228   -.2852575
      ehat_1 |   .0758421   .0454607      1.67   0.096      -.013428    .1651122
      gpolpc |   .0161487   .0718857      0.22   0.822     -.1250116    .1573091
      gincpc |   .7799592   .2383162      3.27   0.001      .3119831    1.247935
       cunem |   .2774521   .4951121      0.56   0.575     -.6947883    1.249693
      cblack |  -.0098112   .0424186     -0.23   0.817     -.0931078    .0734853
      cmetro |    -.53858   1.357447     -0.40   0.692     -3.204169    2.127009
     cag0_14 |   3.188324   3.029703      1.05   0.293     -2.761036    9.137683
    cag15_17 |   .2937978   6.086153      0.05   0.962     -11.65744    12.24504
    cag18_24 |   2.920399   2.808588      1.04   0.299     -2.594763     8.43556
    cag25_34 |   2.535425   2.796121      0.91   0.365     -2.955255    8.026105
         y81 |  -.0844017   .0320334     -2.63   0.009      -.147305   -.0214984
         y82 |   .0018088   .0387641      0.05   0.963     -.0743115     .077929
         y83 |   -.005779   .0346923     -0.17   0.868     -.0739035    .0623456
         y84 |  -.0169376   .0236783     -0.72   0.475     -.0634342    .0295589
         y85 |    .009244   .0219791      0.42   0.674      -.033916    .0524039
         y86 |   .0685768   .0271351      2.53   0.012      .0152922    .1218614
         y87 |  -.0261797   .0212959     -1.23   0.219      -.067998    .0156386
         y88 |   .0209943   .0215837      0.97   0.331     -.0213891    .0633777
         y89 |   .0120815   .0233517      0.52   0.605     -.0337737    .0579366
         y90 |    .120643   .0268328      4.50   0.000      .0679521    .1733339
         y91 |   .0366637   .0183029      2.00   0.046      .0007226    .0726047
       _cons |   .0484156   .0259236      1.87   0.062       -.00249    .0993212
------------------------------------------------------------------------------
```

There is only marginal evidence of positive serial correlation, and it is pratically small, anyway ($\hat{\rho}$ = .076).

c. Adding a fixed effect to the original model changes very little. In this example, there seems to be little need for a random growth model. The estimated prison effect becomes a little smaller in magnitude, -.959:

```
. xtivreg gcriv  gpolpc gincpc cunem cblack cmetro cag0_14 cag15_17 cag18_24
cag25_34 y81-y91 (gpris = final1 final2 gpolpc gincpc cunem cblack cmetro
cag0_14 cag15_17 cag18_24 cag25_34 y81-y91), fe

Fixed-effects (within) IV regression          Number of obs      =       714
Group variable: state                         Number of groups   =        51

R-sq:  within  =      .                       Obs per group: min =        14
       between = 0.0001                                      avg =      14.0
       overall = 0.1299                                      max =        14

                                              Wald chi2(21)      =    179.72
corr(u_i, Xb)  = -0.2523                      Prob > chi2        =    0.0000

------------------------------------------------------------------------------
       gcriv |      Coef.   Std. Err.      z    P>|z|     [95% Conf. Interval]
-------------+----------------------------------------------------------------
       gpris |  -.9592837    .392784    -2.44   0.015    -1.729126   -.1894412
      gpolpc |   .0444715   .0662122     0.67   0.502     -.085302     .174245
      gincpc |   1.028326      .2076     4.95   0.000     .6214376    1.435215
       cunem |   .6600077   .4309158     1.53   0.126    -.1845717    1.504587
      cblack |   .0707593   .1493523     0.47   0.636    -.2219658    .3634843
      cmetro |   3.204919   4.567142     0.70   0.483    -5.746516    12.15635
     cag0_14 |   1.142691   2.737224     0.42   0.676     -4.22217    6.507552
    cag15_17 |   1.381084   6.238813     0.22   0.825    -10.84677    13.60893
    cag18_24 |   1.183823   2.770876     0.43   0.669    -4.246995    6.614641
    cag25_34 |  -2.050005   2.959179    -0.69   0.488    -7.849888    3.749879
         y81 |  -.0589748   .0225154    -2.62   0.009    -.1031042   -.0148453
         y82 |   .0036388   .0355185     0.10   0.918    -.0659762    .0732538
         y83 |   .0083887   .0337724     0.25   0.804     -.057804    .0745814
         y84 |  -.0014582   .0216725    -0.07   0.946    -.0439354     .041019
         y85 |    .022499   .0197169     1.14   0.254    -.0161454    .0611435
         y86 |    .076121   .0259716     2.93   0.003     .0252176    .1270245
         y87 |  -.0119665   .0197591    -0.61   0.545    -.0506935    .0267605
         y88 |   .0334972   .0195912     1.71   0.087    -.0049008    .0718951
         y89 |   .0191959   .0213518     0.90   0.369    -.0226528    .0610446
         y90 |   .1163255   .0260638     4.46   0.000     .0652413    .1674097
         y91 |   .0384424   .0166514     2.31   0.021     .0058062    .0710786
       _cons |   .0010018    .023068     0.04   0.965    -.0442106    .0462143
-------------+----------------------------------------------------------------
     sigma_u |  .03035725
     sigma_e |  .09235021
         rho |  .09751858   (fraction of variance due to u_i)
------------------------------------------------------------------------------
F  test that all u_i=0:     F(50,642) =     0.70             Prob > F    = 0.9434
------------------------------------------------------------------------------
Instrumented:   gpris
Instruments:    gpolpc gincpc cunem cblack cmetro cag0_14 cag15_17 cag18_24
                cag25_34 y81 y82 y83 y84 y85 y86 y87 y88 y89 y90 y91 final1
                final2
```

d. When we use the property crime rate, the estimate elasticity with respect to prison size is substantially smaller, but still negative and marginally significant:

```
. reg gcrip gpris gpolpc gincpc cunem cblack cmetro cag0_14 cag15_17 cag18_24
cag25_34 y81-y91 (final1 final2 gpolpc gincpc cunem cblack cmetro cag0_14
cag15_17 cag18_24 cag25_34 y81-y91)

Instrumental variables (2SLS) regression

      Source |       SS       df       MS              Number of obs =     714
-------------+------------------------------           F( 21,   692) =   19.51
       Model |  .87282473    21  .041563082           Prob > F      =  0.0000
    Residual | 1.74793481   692  .002525917           R-squared     =  0.3330
-------------+------------------------------           Adj R-squared =  0.3128
       Total | 2.62075954   713   .00367568           Root MSE      =  .05026

------------------------------------------------------------------------------
       gcrip |      Coef.   Std. Err.      t    P>|t|     [95% Conf. Interval]
-------------+----------------------------------------------------------------
       gpris |  -.3827585   .1928419    -1.98   0.048     -.761384   -.004133
      gpolpc |   .0174542   .0355044     0.49   0.623     -.052255   .0871634
      gincpc |    .173374   .1071477     1.62   0.106    -.0369997   .3837476
       cunem |   1.326544   .2280664     5.82   0.000     .8787585   1.774329
      cblack |  -.0497733   .0211115    -2.36   0.019    -.0912236   -.008323
      cmetro |   .2054547   .6853421     0.30   0.764    -1.140145   1.551054
     cag0_14 |   1.661992   1.388392     1.20   0.232    -1.063974   4.387957
    cag15_17 |   1.373138   2.961357     0.46   0.643    -4.441185   7.187461
    cag18_24 |   3.475112   1.379282     2.52   0.012     .7670337   6.183191
    cag25_34 |   6.504132   1.302072     5.00   0.000     3.947646   9.060617
         y81 |  -.0621681   .0110927    -5.60   0.000    -.0839474  -.0403888
         y82 |  -.0553792   .0181358    -3.05   0.002    -.0909869  -.0197715
         y83 |  -.0593311   .0168136    -3.53   0.000    -.0923428  -.0263194
         y84 |  -.0194953   .0113961    -1.71   0.088    -.0418703   .0028797
         y85 |   .0293698   .0104118     2.82   0.005     .0089272   .0498123
         y86 |   .0505646   .0135723     3.73   0.000     .0239167   .0772125
         y87 |   .0350292   .0104275     3.36   0.001     .0145558   .0555025
         y88 |   .0186913   .0101666     1.84   0.066    -.0012697   .0386524
         y89 |   .0234738   .0108932     2.15   0.032     .0020862   .0448614
         y90 |    .041789   .0134927     3.10   0.002     .0152974   .0682805
         y91 |   .0216405   .0089687     2.41   0.016     .0040313   .0392497
       _cons |   .0238751   .0115809     2.06   0.040     .0011372    .046613
------------------------------------------------------------------------------
```

The test for serial correlation yields a coefficient on $\hat{e}_{i,t-1}$ of -.034 (t = -.82), and so we conclude that serial correlation is not an issue.

11.15. a. We would have to assume that $grant_{it}$ is uncorrelated with the idiosyncratic errors, u_{is}, for all t and s. One way to think of this is that while grant designation may depend on c_i, it is not related to idiosyncratic fluctuations. Further, the grants have an effect on scrap rates only through their effects on job training.

b. The following simple regression shows that $\Delta hrsemp_{it}$ and $\Delta grant_{it}$ are highly positively correlated, as expected:

```
. reg chrsemp cgrant if d88

      Source |       SS       df       MS              Number of obs =     125
-------------+------------------------------           F(  1,   123) =   79.37
       Model |  18117.5987     1  18117.5987           Prob > F      =  0.0000
    Residual |  28077.3319   123  228.270991           R-squared     =  0.3922
-------------+------------------------------           Adj R-squared =  0.3873
       Total |  46194.9306   124  372.539763           Root MSE      =  15.109

------------------------------------------------------------------------------
     chrsemp |      Coef.   Std. Err.       t     P>|t|       [95% Conf. Interval]
-------------+----------------------------------------------------------------
      cgrant |   27.87793   3.129216      8.91   0.000      21.68384    34.07202
       _cons |   .5093234   1.558337      0.33   0.744      -2.57531    3.593956
------------------------------------------------------------------------------
```

Unfortunately, this is on a bigger sample than we can use to estimate the scrap rate equation, because the scrap rate is missing for so many firms. Restricted to that sample, we get:

```
. reg chrsemp cgrant if d88 & clscrap ~= .

      Source |       SS       df       MS              Number of obs =      45
-------------+------------------------------           F(  1,    43) =   22.23
       Model |  6316.65458     1  6316.65458           Prob > F      =  0.0000
    Residual |  12217.3517    43  284.124457           R-squared     =  0.3408
```

```
-------------+------------------------------           Adj R-squared =  0.3255
       Total |  18534.0062    44  421.227414           Root MSE      =  16.856

------------------------------------------------------------------------------
     chrsemp |      Coef.   Std. Err.      t    P>|t|     [95% Conf. Interval]
-------------+----------------------------------------------------------------
      cgrant |   24.43691   5.182712     4.72   0.000     13.98498    34.88885
       _cons |   1.580598   3.185483     0.50   0.622     -4.84354    8.004737
------------------------------------------------------------------------------
```

So there is still a pretty strong relationship.

c. The IV estimate is:

```
. reg clscrap chrsemp (cgrant) if d88

Instrumental variables (2SLS) regression

      Source |       SS       df       MS              Number of obs =      45
-------------+------------------------------           F(  1,    43) =    3.20
       Model |  .274951237     1  .274951237           Prob > F      =  0.0808
    Residual |  17.0148885    43  .395695081           R-squared     =  0.0159
-------------+------------------------------           Adj R-squared = -0.0070
       Total |  17.2898397    44  .392950903           Root MSE      =  .62904

------------------------------------------------------------------------------
     clscrap |      Coef.   Std. Err.      t    P>|t|     [95% Conf. Interval]
-------------+----------------------------------------------------------------
     chrsemp |  -.0141532   .0079147    -1.79   0.081    -.0301148    .0018084
       _cons |  -.0326684   .1269512    -0.26   0.798    -.2886898     .223353
------------------------------------------------------------------------------
```

The estimate says that 10 more hours training per employee would lower the average scrap rate by about 14.2 percent, which is a pretty large effect. It is marginally significant (for IV with 45 observations).

d. The OLS estimates is only about -.0076 -- about half of the IV estimate -- with t = -1.68.

e. Any effect pretty much disappears using two years of differences (even though you can verify the rank condition easily holds):

```
. reg clscrap chrsemp d89 (cgrant d89)
```

Instrumental variables (2SLS) regression

Source	SS	df	MS
Model	.538688387	2	.269344194
Residual	33.2077492	88	.377360787
Total	33.7464376	90	.374960418

Number of obs	=	91	
F(2, 88)	=	0.90	
Prob > F	=	0.4087	
R-squared	=	0.0160	
Adj R-squared	=	-0.0064	
Root MSE	=	.6143	

clscrap	Coef.	Std. Err.	t	P>|t|	[95% Conf.	Interval]
chrsemp	-.0028567	.0030577	-0.93	0.353	-.0089332	.0032198
d89	-.1387379	.1296916	-1.07	0.288	-.3964728	.1189969
_cons	-.1548094	.0973592	-1.59	0.115	-.3482902	.0386715

11.17. To obtain (11.55), we use (11.54) and the representation $\sqrt{N}(\hat{\boldsymbol{\beta}}_{FE} - \boldsymbol{\beta}) = \mathbf{A}^{-1}(N^{-1/2}\sum_{i=1}^{N}\ddot{\mathbf{X}}_i'\mathbf{u}_i) + o_p(1)$. Simple algebra and standard properties of $O_p(1)$ and $o_p(1)$ give

$$\begin{aligned}\sqrt{N}(\hat{\boldsymbol{\alpha}} - \boldsymbol{\alpha}) &= N^{-1/2}\sum_{i=1}^{N}[(\mathbf{Z}_i'\mathbf{Z}_i)^{-1}\mathbf{Z}_i'(\mathbf{y}_i - \mathbf{X}_i\boldsymbol{\beta}) - \boldsymbol{\alpha}] \\ &\quad - \left(N^{-1}\sum_{i=1}^{N}(\mathbf{Z}_i'\mathbf{Z}_i)^{-1}\mathbf{Z}_i'\mathbf{X}_i\right)\sqrt{N}(\hat{\boldsymbol{\beta}}_{FE} - \boldsymbol{\beta}) \\ &= N^{-1/2}\sum_{i=1}^{N}(\mathbf{s}_i - \boldsymbol{\alpha}) - \mathbf{C}\mathbf{A}^{-1}N^{-1/2}\sum_{i=1}^{N}\ddot{\mathbf{X}}_i'\mathbf{u}_i + o_p(1)\end{aligned}$$

where $\mathbf{C} \equiv E[(\mathbf{Z}_i'\mathbf{Z}_i)^{-1}\mathbf{Z}_i'\mathbf{X}_i]$ and $\mathbf{s}_i \equiv (\mathbf{Z}_i'\mathbf{Z}_i)^{-1}\mathbf{Z}_i'(\mathbf{y}_i - \mathbf{X}_i\boldsymbol{\beta})$. By definition, $E(\mathbf{s}_i) = \boldsymbol{\alpha}$. By combining terms in the sum we have

$$\sqrt{N}(\hat{\boldsymbol{\alpha}} - \boldsymbol{\alpha}) = N^{-1/2}\sum_{i=1}^{N}[(\mathbf{s}_i - \boldsymbol{\alpha}) - \mathbf{C}\mathbf{A}^{-1}\ddot{\mathbf{X}}_i'\mathbf{u}_i] + o_p(1),$$

which implies by the central limit theorem and the asymptotic equivalence lemma that $\sqrt{N}(\hat{\boldsymbol{\alpha}} - \boldsymbol{\alpha})$ is asymptotically normal with zero mean and variance $E(\mathbf{r}_i\mathbf{r}_i')$, where $\mathbf{r}_i \equiv (\mathbf{s}_i - \boldsymbol{\alpha}) - \mathbf{C}\mathbf{A}^{-1}\ddot{\mathbf{X}}_i'\mathbf{u}_i$. If we replace $\boldsymbol{\alpha}$, $\mathbf{C}$, $\mathbf{A}$, and $\boldsymbol{\beta}$ with their consistent estimators, we get exactly (11.55), since the $\hat{\mathbf{u}}_i$ are the FE residuals.

11.18. (Bonus Question): Consider a linear panel data model with individual-specific slopes as well as an individual-specific intercept, of the kind covered in Section 11.2.2.

$$y_{it} = \mathbf{x}_{it}\mathbf{b}_i + c_i + u_{it}$$

$$\mathrm{E}(u_{it}|\mathbf{x}_{i1},\ldots,\mathbf{x}_{iT},\mathbf{b}_i,c_i) = 0,\ t = 1,\ldots,T,$$

where $\mathbf{x}_{it}$ is $1 \times K$ and $\mathbf{b}_i$ is $K \times 1$. We are interested in estimating the average slope effects, $\boldsymbol{\beta} \equiv \mathrm{E}(\mathbf{b}_i)$. Make the standard rank assumption, rank $\mathrm{E}(\ddot{\mathbf{X}}_i'\ddot{\mathbf{X}}_i) = K$, where $\ddot{\mathbf{X}}_i$ is just the usual $T \times K$ matrix of time-demeaned $\mathbf{x}_{it}$.

a. Let $\mathbf{d}_i \equiv \mathbf{b}_i - \boldsymbol{\beta}$, and write the time-demeaned equation in terms of $\ddot{y}_{it}$, $\ddot{\mathbf{x}}_{it}$, $\ddot{u}_{it}$, $\boldsymbol{\beta}$, and $\mathbf{d}_i$.

b. Show that the usual within estimator, $\hat{\boldsymbol{\beta}}$, is consistent for $\boldsymbol{\beta}$ under the additional assumptions

$$\mathrm{E}(\mathbf{b}_i|\ddot{\mathbf{x}}_{it}) = \mathrm{E}(\mathbf{b}_i) = \boldsymbol{\beta},\ t = 1,\ldots,T.$$

c. Explain why $\mathrm{E}(\mathbf{b}_i|\ddot{\mathbf{x}}_{it}) = \mathrm{E}(\mathbf{b}_i)$ allows $\mathbf{b}_i$ to be correlated with the time average, $\bar{\mathbf{x}}_i$, thereby allowing the unobserved slopes to be correlated with observed characteristics.

d. If we make the assumption $\mathrm{E}(\mathbf{u}_i\mathbf{u}_i'|\mathbf{x}_i,\mathbf{b}_i,c_i) = \sigma_u^2\mathbf{I}_T$ -- so that the idiosyncratic errors are serially uncorrelated conditional on observed and unobserved variances -- is there any need to use a serial-correlation-robust estimator of the variance-covariance matrix for the within estimator?

e. Do we get consistency of the within estimator if we simply assume $\mathbf{b}_i$ and $\ddot{\mathbf{x}}_{it}$ are uncorrelated, $t = 1,\ldots,T$?

Answer:

a. By direct substitution,

$$y_{it} = \mathbf{x}_{it}\mathbf{b}_i + c_i + u_{it} = \mathbf{x}_{it}(\boldsymbol{\beta} + \mathbf{d}_i) + c_i + u_{it}$$

$$= \mathbf{x}_{it}\boldsymbol{\beta} + \mathbf{x}_{it}\mathbf{d}_i + c_i + u_{it}.$$

The time-averaged equation is $\bar{y}_i = \bar{\mathbf{x}}_i\boldsymbol{\beta} + \bar{\mathbf{x}}_i\mathbf{d}_i + c_i + \bar{u}_i$, and so the time-demeaned equation for each t is

$$\ddot{y}_{it} = \ddot{\mathbf{x}}_{it}\boldsymbol{\beta} + \ddot{\mathbf{x}}_{it}\mathbf{d}_i + \ddot{u}_{it}.$$

Note that c_i has been eliminated by the time-demeaning, as usual.

b. The within estimator is just the pooled OLS estimator on the time-demeaned data, $\ddot{y}_{it}$ on $\ddot{\mathbf{x}}_{it}$, $t = 1,\ldots,T$, $i = 1,\ldots,N$. Letting $\ddot{v}_{it} \equiv \ddot{\mathbf{x}}_{it}\mathbf{d}_i + \ddot{u}_{it}$ we have

$$\hat{\boldsymbol{\beta}} = \left(\sum_{i=1}^{N}\sum_{t=1}^{T}\ddot{\mathbf{x}}_{it}'\ddot{\mathbf{x}}_{it}\right)^{-1}\left(\sum_{i=1}^{N}\sum_{t=1}^{T}\ddot{\mathbf{x}}_{it}'\ddot{y}_{it}\right)$$
$$= \boldsymbol{\beta} + \left(N^{-1}\sum_{i=1}^{N}\sum_{t=1}^{T}\ddot{\mathbf{x}}_{it}'\ddot{\mathbf{x}}_{it}\right)^{-1}\left(N^{-1}\sum_{i=1}^{N}\sum_{t=1}^{T}\ddot{\mathbf{x}}_{it}'\ddot{v}_{it}\right).$$

In fact, we know from Section 7.8 that the key condition for consistency of pooled OLS, applied to the current context, is

$$\mathrm{E}(\ddot{\mathbf{x}}_{it}'\ddot{v}_{it}) = \mathbf{0},\ t = 1,\ldots,T.$$

But $\mathrm{E}(\ddot{\mathbf{x}}_{it}'\ddot{v}_{it}) = \mathrm{E}(\ddot{\mathbf{x}}_{it}'\ddot{\mathbf{x}}_{it}\mathbf{d}_i) + \mathrm{E}(\ddot{\mathbf{x}}_{it}'\ddot{u}_{it}) = \mathrm{E}(\ddot{\mathbf{x}}_{it}'\ddot{\mathbf{x}}_{it}\mathbf{d}_i)$ since $\mathrm{E}(\ddot{u}_{it}|\ddot{\mathbf{x}}_{it}) = 0$ under the maintained strict exogeneity assumption. Further, $\mathrm{E}(\mathbf{b}_i|\ddot{\mathbf{x}}_{it}) = \mathrm{E}(\mathbf{b}_i)$ is the same as $\mathrm{E}(\mathbf{d}_i|\ddot{\mathbf{x}}_{it}) = \mathbf{0}$, and so iterated expectations gives $\mathrm{E}(\ddot{\mathbf{x}}_{it}'\ddot{\mathbf{x}}_{it}\mathbf{d}_i) = \mathbf{0}$. It follows that, under the rank condition given earlier, the usual within (fixed effects) estimator is consistent with T fixed and $N \to \infty$.

c. The assumption $\mathrm{E}(\mathbf{b}_i|\ddot{\mathbf{x}}_{it}) = \mathrm{E}(\mathbf{b}_i)$ means that $\mathbf{b}_i$ is conditionally mean independent of the deviations about the average, $\ddot{\mathbf{x}}_{it}$, and says nothing directly about possible correlation between $\mathbf{b}_i$ and $\bar{\mathbf{x}}_i$. As just one example, suppose that $\mathbf{x}_{it} = \mathbf{m}_i + \mathbf{r}_{it}$, $t = 1,\ldots,T$, where $\mathbf{b}_i$ is independent of the idiosyncratic shocks, $\{\mathbf{r}_{i1},\ldots,\mathbf{r}_{iT}\}$, but may be correlated with the vector of unobserved effects, $\mathbf{m}_i$. Then $\ddot{\mathbf{x}}_{it}$ depends on $\{\mathbf{r}_{i1},\ldots,\mathbf{r}_{iT}\}$ but not on $\mathbf{m}_i$. That the usual within estimator is consistent for the average effect in a "random coefficients" model, under the assumption that $\mathbf{b}_i$ is mean independent from the deviations $\ddot{\mathbf{x}}_{it}$, is a nice robustness result.

d. Yes. Even though the idiosyncratic errors $\{u_{it}\}$ are conditionally serially uncorrelated, the term $\ddot{\mathbf{x}}_{it}\mathbf{d}_i$ generally induces serial correlation that cannot be accounted for by the usual within variance matrix estimator. In particular, for $s \neq t$, $E(\ddot{\mathbf{x}}_{is}\mathbf{d}_i\mathbf{d}_i'\ddot{\mathbf{x}}_{it}') \neq \mathbf{0}$. Even if we assume $E(\mathbf{d}_i\mathbf{d}_i'|\mathbf{x}_i) = E(\mathbf{d}_i\mathbf{d}_i'|\mathbf{x}_i) \equiv \boldsymbol{\Lambda}$, $E(\ddot{\mathbf{x}}_{is}\mathbf{d}_i\mathbf{d}_i'\ddot{\mathbf{x}}_{it}'|\mathbf{x}_i) = \ddot{\mathbf{x}}_{is}\boldsymbol{\Lambda}\ddot{\mathbf{x}}_{it}'$. Also, there will be heteroskedasticity, conditional on $\mathbf{x}_i$, in the composite error $\ddot{\mathbf{x}}_{it}\mathbf{d}_i + \ddot{u}_{it}$.

e. No. Zero correlation is the same as $E(\ddot{\mathbf{x}}_{it}'\mathbf{d}_i) = \mathbf{0}$, $t = 1,\ldots,T$, which is not sufficient for $E(\ddot{\mathbf{x}}_{it}'\ddot{\mathbf{x}}_{it}\mathbf{d}_i) = \mathbf{0}$.

SOLUTIONS TO CHAPTER 12 PROBLEMS

12.1. Take the conditional expectation of equation (12.4) with respect to **x**, and use $E(u|\mathbf{x}) = 0$:

$$\begin{aligned} E\{[y - m(\mathbf{x},\boldsymbol{\theta})]^2|\mathbf{x}\} &= E(u^2|\mathbf{x}) + 2[m(\mathbf{x},\boldsymbol{\theta}_o) - m(\mathbf{x},\boldsymbol{\theta})]E(u|\mathbf{x}) \\ &\quad + E\{[m(\mathbf{x},\boldsymbol{\theta}_o) - m(\mathbf{x},\boldsymbol{\theta})]^2|\mathbf{x}\} \\ &= E(u^2|\mathbf{x}) + 0 + [m(\mathbf{x},\boldsymbol{\theta}_o) - m(\mathbf{x},\boldsymbol{\theta})]^2 \\ &= E(u^2|\mathbf{x}) + [m(\mathbf{x},\boldsymbol{\theta}_o) - m(\mathbf{x},\boldsymbol{\theta})]^2. \end{aligned}$$

The first term does not depend on $\boldsymbol{\theta}$ and the second term is clearly minimized at $\boldsymbol{\theta} = \boldsymbol{\theta}_o$ for any **x**. Therefore, the parameters of a correctly specified conditional mean function minimize the squared error conditional on any value of **x**. Usually, there would be multiple solutions for a particular **x** -- for example, in the linear case $m(\mathbf{x},\boldsymbol{\theta}) = \mathbf{x}\boldsymbol{\theta}$, any $\boldsymbol{\theta}$ such that $\mathbf{x}(\boldsymbol{\theta}_o - \boldsymbol{\theta}) = 0$ sets $m(\mathbf{x},\boldsymbol{\theta}_o) - m(\mathbf{x},\boldsymbol{\theta})$ to zero. Uniqueness of $\boldsymbol{\theta}_o$ as a minimizer holds only after we integrate out **x** to obtain $E\{[y - m(\mathbf{x},\boldsymbol{\theta})]^2\}$.

12.2. a. Since $u = y - E(y|\mathbf{x})$, $Var(y|\mathbf{x}) = Var(u|\mathbf{x}) = E(u^2|\mathbf{x})$ since $E(u|\mathbf{x}) = 0$. So $E(u^2|\mathbf{x}) = \exp(\alpha_o + \mathbf{x}\boldsymbol{\gamma}_o)$.

b. If we knew the $u_i = y_i - m(\mathbf{x}_i,\boldsymbol{\theta}_o)$, then we could do a nonlinear regression of u_i^2 on $\exp(\alpha + \mathbf{x}\boldsymbol{\gamma})$ and just use the asymptotic theory for nonlinear regression. The NLS estimators of α and $\boldsymbol{\gamma}$ would then solve

$$\min_{\alpha,\boldsymbol{\gamma}} \sum_{i=1}^{N} [u_i^2 - \exp(\alpha + \mathbf{x}_i\boldsymbol{\gamma})]^2.$$

The problem is that $\boldsymbol{\theta}_o$ is unknown. When we replace $\boldsymbol{\theta}_o$ with its NLS estimator, $\hat{\boldsymbol{\theta}}$ -- that is we replace u_i^2 with $\hat{u}_i^2$, the squared NLS residuals -- we are solving the problem

$$\min_{\alpha,\boldsymbol{\gamma}} \sum_{i=1}^{N} \{[y_i - m(\mathbf{x}_i,\hat{\boldsymbol{\theta}})]^2 - \exp(\alpha + \mathbf{x}_i\boldsymbol{\gamma})\}^2.$$

This objective function has the form of a two-step M-estimator in Section 12.4. Since $\hat{\boldsymbol{\theta}}$ is generally consistent for $\boldsymbol{\theta}_o$, the two-step M-estimator is generally consistent for α_o and $\boldsymbol{\gamma}_o$ (under weak regularity and identification conditions). In fact, $\sqrt{N}$-consistency of $\hat{\alpha}$ and $\hat{\boldsymbol{\gamma}}$ holds very generally.

c. We now estimate $\boldsymbol{\theta}_o$ by solving

$$\min_{\boldsymbol{\theta}} \sum_{i=1}^{N} [y_i - m(\mathbf{x}_i,\boldsymbol{\theta})]^2/\exp(\hat{\alpha} + \mathbf{x}_i\hat{\boldsymbol{\gamma}}),$$

where $\hat{\alpha}$ and $\hat{\boldsymbol{\gamma}}$ are from part b. The general theory of WNLS under WNLS.1 to WNLS.3 can be applied.

d. Using the definition of v, write $u^2 = \exp(\alpha_o + \mathbf{x}\boldsymbol{\gamma}_o)v^2$. Taking logs gives $\log(u^2) = \alpha_o + \mathbf{x}\boldsymbol{\gamma}_o + \log(v^2)$. Now, if v is independent of $\mathbf{x}$, so is $\log(v^2)$. Therefore, $\mathrm{E}[\log(u^2)|\mathbf{x}] = \alpha_o + \mathbf{x}\boldsymbol{\gamma}_o + \mathrm{E}[\log(v^2)|\mathbf{x}] = \alpha_o + \mathbf{x}\boldsymbol{\gamma}_o + \kappa_o$, where $\kappa_o \equiv \mathrm{E}[\log(v^2)]$. So, if we could observe the u_i, and OLS regression of $\log(u_i^2)$ on 1, $\mathbf{x}_i$ would be consistent for $(\alpha_o + \kappa_o)$, $\boldsymbol{\gamma}_o$; in fact, it would be unbiased. By two-step estimation theory, consistency still holds if u_i is replaced with $\hat{u}_i$, by essentially the same argument in part b. So, if $m(\mathbf{x},\boldsymbol{\theta})$ is linear in $\boldsymbol{\theta}$, we can carry out a weighted NLS procedure without ever doing nonlinear estimation.

e. If we have misspecified the variance function -- or, for example, we use the approach in part d but v is not independent of $\mathbf{x}$ -- then we should use a fully robust variance-covariance matrix. It looks just like (12.52) except that $\hat{u}_i$ and $\nabla_\theta \hat{m}_i$ are each multiplied by $\exp[-(\hat{\alpha} + \mathbf{x}_i\hat{\boldsymbol{\gamma}})/2]$ or just $\exp(-\mathbf{x}_i\hat{\boldsymbol{\gamma}}/2)$.

12.3. a. The approximate elasticity is $\partial\log[\hat{E}(y|\mathbf{z})]/\partial\log(z_1) = \partial[\hat{\theta}_1 + \hat{\theta}_2\log(z_1) + \hat{\theta}_3 z_2]/\partial\log(z_1) = \hat{\theta}_2$.

b. This is approximated by $100\cdot\partial\log[\hat{E}(y|\mathbf{z})]/\partial z_2 = 100\cdot\hat{\theta}_3$.

c. Since $\partial\hat{E}(y|\mathbf{z})/\partial z_2 = \exp[\hat{\theta}_1 + \hat{\theta}_2\log(z_1) + \hat{\theta}_3 z_2 + \hat{\theta}_4 z_2^2]\cdot(\hat{\theta}_3 + 2\hat{\theta}_4 z_2)$, the turning point is $z_2^* = \hat{\theta}_3/(-2\hat{\theta}_4)$.

d. Since $\nabla_\theta m(\mathbf{x},\boldsymbol{\theta}) = \exp(\mathbf{x}_1\boldsymbol{\theta}_1 + \mathbf{x}_2\boldsymbol{\theta}_2)\mathbf{x}$, the gradient of the mean function evaluated under the null is $\nabla_\theta\tilde{m}_i = \exp(\mathbf{x}_{i1}\tilde{\boldsymbol{\theta}}_1)\mathbf{x}_i \equiv \tilde{m}_i\mathbf{x}_i$, where $\tilde{\boldsymbol{\theta}}_1$ is the restricted NLS estimator. From (12.72), we can compute the usual LM statistic as NR_u^2 from the regression $\tilde{u}_i$ on $\tilde{m}_i\mathbf{x}_{i1}$, $\tilde{m}_i\mathbf{x}_{i2}$, $i = 1,\ldots,N$, where $\tilde{u}_i = y_i - \tilde{m}_i$. For the robust test, we first regress $\tilde{m}_i\mathbf{x}_{i2}$ on $\tilde{m}_i\mathbf{x}_{i1}$ and obtain the $1 \times K_2$ residuals, $\tilde{\mathbf{r}}_i$. Then we compute the statistic as in regression (12.75).

12.4. a. Write the objective function as $(1/2)\sum_{i=1}^{N}[y_i - m(\mathbf{x}_i,\boldsymbol{\theta})]^2/h(\mathbf{x}_i,\hat{\boldsymbol{\gamma}})$. The objective function, for any value of $\boldsymbol{\gamma}$, is $q(\mathbf{w}_i,\boldsymbol{\theta};\boldsymbol{\gamma}) = (1/2)[y_i - m(\mathbf{x}_i,\boldsymbol{\theta})]^2/h(\mathbf{x}_i,\boldsymbol{\gamma})$. Taking the gradient with respect to $\boldsymbol{\theta}$ gives $\nabla_\theta q(\mathbf{w}_i,\boldsymbol{\theta};\boldsymbol{\gamma}) = -\nabla_\theta m(\mathbf{x}_i,\boldsymbol{\theta})[y_i - m(\mathbf{x}_i,\boldsymbol{\theta})]/h(\mathbf{x}_i,\boldsymbol{\gamma}) = -\nabla_\theta m(\mathbf{x}_i,\boldsymbol{\theta})u_i(\boldsymbol{\theta})/h(\mathbf{x}_i,\boldsymbol{\gamma})$. Taking the transpose gives us the score for any $\boldsymbol{\theta}$ and any $\boldsymbol{\gamma}$.

b. This follows because, under WNLS.1, $u_i \equiv u_i(\boldsymbol{\theta}_o)$ has a zero mean given $\mathbf{x}_i$:

$$E[\mathbf{s}_i(\boldsymbol{\theta}_o;\boldsymbol{\gamma})|\mathbf{x}_i] = -\nabla_\theta m(\mathbf{x}_i,\boldsymbol{\theta}_o)'E(u_i|\mathbf{x}_i)/h(\mathbf{x}_i,\boldsymbol{\gamma}) = \mathbf{0};$$

the value of $\boldsymbol{\gamma}$ plays no role.

c. First, the Jacobian of $\mathbf{s}_i(\boldsymbol{\theta}_o;\boldsymbol{\gamma})$ with respect to $\boldsymbol{\gamma}$ is $\nabla_\gamma\mathbf{s}_i(\boldsymbol{\theta}_o;\boldsymbol{\gamma}) = \nabla_\theta m(\mathbf{x}_i,\boldsymbol{\theta}_o)'u_i\nabla_\gamma h(\mathbf{x}_i,\boldsymbol{\gamma})/[h(\mathbf{x}_i,\boldsymbol{\gamma})]^2$. Everything but u_i is a function only of $\mathbf{x}_i$, so

$$E[\nabla_\gamma\mathbf{s}_i(\boldsymbol{\theta}_o;\boldsymbol{\gamma})|\mathbf{x}_i] = \nabla_\theta m(\mathbf{x}_i,\boldsymbol{\theta}_o)'E(u_i|\mathbf{x}_i)\nabla_\gamma h(\mathbf{x}_i,\boldsymbol{\gamma})/[h(\mathbf{x}_i,\boldsymbol{\gamma})]^2 = \mathbf{0}.$$

It follows by the LIE that the unconditional expectation is zero, too. In other words, we have shown that the key condition (12.37) holds (whether or not WNLS.3 holds).

d. We would use the analog of equation (12.52):

$$\widehat{\text{Avar}}(\hat{\boldsymbol{\theta}}) = \left(\sum_{i=1}^{N} \nabla_\theta \check{m}_i' \nabla_\theta \check{m}_i\right)^{-1} \left(\sum_{i=1}^{N} \check{u}_i^2 \nabla_\theta \check{m}_i' \nabla_\theta \check{m}_i\right) \left(\sum_{i=1}^{N} \nabla_\theta \check{m}_i' \nabla_\theta \check{m}_i\right)^{-1},$$

where $\check{u}_i \equiv \hat{u}_i/\hat{h}_i^{1/2}$ and $\nabla_\theta \check{m}_i \equiv \nabla_\theta \hat{m}_i/\hat{h}_i^{1/2}$.

12.5. We need the gradient of $m(\mathbf{x}_i,\boldsymbol{\theta})$ evaluated under the null hypothesis. By the chain rule, $\nabla_\beta m(\mathbf{x},\boldsymbol{\theta}) = g[\mathbf{x}\boldsymbol{\beta} + \delta_1(\mathbf{x}\boldsymbol{\beta})^2 + \delta_2(\mathbf{x}\boldsymbol{\beta})^3]\cdot[\mathbf{x} + 2\delta_1(\mathbf{x}\boldsymbol{\beta})^2 + 3\delta_2(\mathbf{x}\boldsymbol{\beta})^2]$, $\nabla_\delta m(\mathbf{x},\boldsymbol{\theta}) = g[\mathbf{x}\boldsymbol{\beta} + \delta_1(\mathbf{x}\boldsymbol{\beta})^2 + \delta_2(\mathbf{x}\boldsymbol{\beta})^3]\cdot[(\mathbf{x}\boldsymbol{\beta})^2,(\mathbf{x}\boldsymbol{\beta})^3]$. Let $\tilde{\boldsymbol{\beta}}$ denote the NLS estimator with $\delta_1 = \delta_2 = 0$ imposed. Then $\nabla_\beta m(\mathbf{x}_i,\tilde{\boldsymbol{\theta}}) = g(\mathbf{x}_i\tilde{\boldsymbol{\beta}})\mathbf{x}_i$ and $\nabla_\delta m(\mathbf{x}_i,\tilde{\boldsymbol{\theta}}) = g(\mathbf{x}_i\tilde{\boldsymbol{\beta}})[(\mathbf{x}_i\tilde{\boldsymbol{\beta}})^2,(\mathbf{x}_i\tilde{\boldsymbol{\beta}})^3]$. Therefore, the usual LM statistic can be obtained as NR_u^2 from the regression $\tilde{u}_i$ on $\tilde{g}_i\mathbf{x}_i$, $\tilde{g}_i\cdot(\mathbf{x}_i\tilde{\boldsymbol{\beta}})^2$, $\tilde{g}_i\cdot(\mathbf{x}_i\tilde{\boldsymbol{\beta}})^3$, where $\tilde{g}_i \equiv g(\mathbf{x}_i\tilde{\boldsymbol{\beta}})$. If $G(\cdot)$ is the identity function, $g(\cdot) \equiv 1$, and we get RESET.

12.7. a. For each i and g, define $u_{ig} \equiv y_{ig} - m(\mathbf{x}_{ig},\boldsymbol{\theta}_o)$, so that $\text{E}(u_{ig}|\mathbf{x}_i) = 0$, $g = 1,\ldots,G$. Further, let $\mathbf{u}_i$ be the $G \times 1$ vector containing the u_{ig}. Then $\text{E}(\mathbf{u}_i\mathbf{u}_i'|\mathbf{x}_i) = \text{E}(\mathbf{u}_i\mathbf{u}_i') = \boldsymbol{\Omega}_o$. Let $\hat{\hat{\mathbf{u}}}_i$ be the vector of nonlinear least squares residuals. That is, do NLS for each g, and collect the residuals. Then, by standard arguments, a consistent estimator of $\boldsymbol{\Omega}_o$ is

$$\hat{\boldsymbol{\Omega}} \equiv N^{-1}\sum_{i=1}^{N} \hat{\hat{\mathbf{u}}}_i\hat{\hat{\mathbf{u}}}_i'$$

because each NLS estimator, $\hat{\hat{\boldsymbol{\theta}}}_g$ is consistent for $\boldsymbol{\theta}_{og}$ as $N \to \infty$.

b. This part involves several steps, and I will sketch how each one goes. First, let $\boldsymbol{\gamma}$ be the vector of distinct elements of $\boldsymbol{\Omega}$ -- the nuisance parameters in the context of two-step M-estimation. Then, the score for observation i is

$$\mathbf{s}(\mathbf{w}_i,\boldsymbol{\theta};\boldsymbol{\gamma}) = -\nabla_\theta \mathbf{m}(\mathbf{x}_i,\boldsymbol{\theta})'\boldsymbol{\Omega}^{-1}\mathbf{u}_i(\boldsymbol{\theta})$$

where, hopefully, the notation is clear. With this definition, we can verify condition (12.37), even though the actual derivatives are complicated. Each element of $\mathbf{s}(\mathbf{w}_i,\boldsymbol{\theta};\boldsymbol{\gamma})$ is a linear combination of $\mathbf{u}_i(\boldsymbol{\theta})$. So $\nabla_\gamma s_j(\mathbf{w}_i,\boldsymbol{\theta}_o;\boldsymbol{\gamma})$ is a linear combination of $\mathbf{u}_i(\boldsymbol{\theta}_o) \equiv \mathbf{u}_i$, where the linear combination is a function of $(\mathbf{x}_i,\boldsymbol{\theta}_o,\boldsymbol{\gamma})$. Since $\mathrm{E}(\mathbf{u}_i|\mathbf{x}_i) = \mathbf{0}$, $\mathrm{E}[\nabla_\gamma s_j(\mathbf{w}_i,\boldsymbol{\theta}_o;\boldsymbol{\gamma})|\mathbf{x}_i] = \mathbf{0}$, and so its unconditional expectation is zero, too. This shows that we do not have to adjust for the first-stage estimation of $\boldsymbol{\Omega}_o$. Alternatively, one can verify the hint directly, which has the same consequence.

Next, we derive $\mathbf{B}_o \equiv \mathrm{E}[\mathbf{s}_i(\boldsymbol{\theta}_o;\boldsymbol{\gamma}_o)\mathbf{s}_i(\boldsymbol{\theta}_o;\boldsymbol{\gamma}_o)']$:

$$\begin{aligned}
\mathrm{E}[\mathbf{s}_i(\boldsymbol{\theta}_o;\boldsymbol{\gamma}_o)\mathbf{s}_i(\boldsymbol{\theta}_o;\boldsymbol{\gamma}_o)'] &= \mathrm{E}[\nabla_\theta \mathbf{m}_i(\boldsymbol{\theta}_o)'\boldsymbol{\Omega}_o^{-1}\mathbf{u}_i\mathbf{u}_i'\boldsymbol{\Omega}_o^{-1}\nabla_\theta \mathbf{m}_i(\boldsymbol{\theta}_o)] \\
&= \mathrm{E}\{\mathrm{E}[\nabla_\theta \mathbf{m}_i(\boldsymbol{\theta}_o)'\boldsymbol{\Omega}_o^{-1}\mathbf{u}_i\mathbf{u}_i'\boldsymbol{\Omega}_o^{-1}\nabla_\theta \mathbf{m}_i(\boldsymbol{\theta}_o)|\mathbf{x}_i]\} \\
&= \mathrm{E}[\nabla_\theta \mathbf{m}_i(\boldsymbol{\theta}_o)'\boldsymbol{\Omega}_o^{-1}\mathrm{E}(\mathbf{u}_i\mathbf{u}_i'|\mathbf{x}_i)\boldsymbol{\Omega}_o^{-1}\nabla_\theta \mathbf{m}_i(\boldsymbol{\theta}_o)] \\
&= \mathrm{E}[\nabla_\theta \mathbf{m}_i(\boldsymbol{\theta}_o)'\boldsymbol{\Omega}_o^{-1}\boldsymbol{\Omega}_o\boldsymbol{\Omega}_o^{-1}\nabla_\theta \mathbf{m}_i(\boldsymbol{\theta}_o)] = \mathrm{E}[\nabla_\theta \mathbf{m}_i(\boldsymbol{\theta}_o)'\boldsymbol{\Omega}_o^{-1}\nabla_\theta \mathbf{m}_i(\boldsymbol{\theta}_o)].
\end{aligned}$$

Next, we have to derive $\mathbf{A}_o \equiv \mathrm{E}[\mathbf{H}_i(\boldsymbol{\theta}_o;\boldsymbol{\gamma}_o)]$, and show that $\mathbf{B}_o = \mathbf{A}_o$. The Hessian itself is complicated, but its expected value is not. The Jacobian of $\mathbf{s}_i(\boldsymbol{\theta};\boldsymbol{\gamma})$ with respect to $\boldsymbol{\theta}$ can be written

$$\mathbf{H}_i(\boldsymbol{\theta};\boldsymbol{\gamma}) = \nabla_\theta \mathbf{m}(\mathbf{x}_i,\boldsymbol{\theta})'\boldsymbol{\Omega}^{-1}\nabla_\theta \mathbf{m}(\mathbf{x}_i,\boldsymbol{\theta}) + [\mathbf{I}_P \otimes \mathbf{u}_i(\boldsymbol{\theta})']\mathbf{F}(\mathbf{x}_i,\boldsymbol{\theta};\boldsymbol{\gamma}),$$

where $\mathbf{F}(\mathbf{x}_i,\boldsymbol{\theta};\boldsymbol{\gamma})$ is a $GP \times P$ matrix, where P is the total number of parameters, that involves Jacobians of the rows of $\boldsymbol{\Omega}^{-1}\nabla_\theta \mathbf{m}_i(\boldsymbol{\theta})$ with respect to $\boldsymbol{\theta}$. The key is that $\mathbf{F}(\mathbf{x}_i,\boldsymbol{\theta};\boldsymbol{\gamma})$ depends on $\mathbf{x}_i$, not on $\mathbf{y}_i$. So,

$$\begin{aligned}
\mathrm{E}[\mathbf{H}_i(\boldsymbol{\theta}_o;\boldsymbol{\gamma}_o)|\mathbf{x}_i] &= \nabla_\theta \mathbf{m}_i(\boldsymbol{\theta}_o)'\boldsymbol{\Omega}_o^{-1}\nabla_\theta \mathbf{m}_i(\boldsymbol{\theta}_o) + [\mathbf{I}_P \otimes \mathrm{E}(\mathbf{u}_i|\mathbf{x}_i)']\mathbf{F}(\mathbf{x}_i,\boldsymbol{\theta}_o;\boldsymbol{\gamma}_o) \\
&= \nabla_\theta \mathbf{m}_i(\boldsymbol{\theta}_o)'\boldsymbol{\Omega}_o^{-1}\nabla_\theta \mathbf{m}_i(\boldsymbol{\theta}_o).
\end{aligned}$$

Now iterated expectations gives $\mathbf{A}_o = \mathrm{E}[\nabla_\theta \mathbf{m}_i(\boldsymbol{\theta}_o)'\boldsymbol{\Omega}_o^{-1}\nabla_\theta \mathbf{m}_i(\boldsymbol{\theta}_o)]$. So, we have verified (12.37) and that $\mathbf{A}_o = \mathbf{B}_o$. Therefore, from Theorem 12.3, Avar $\sqrt{N}(\hat{\boldsymbol{\theta}} -$

$\boldsymbol{\theta}_o) = \mathbf{A}_o^{-1} = \{E[\nabla_\theta \mathbf{m}_i(\boldsymbol{\theta}_o)'\boldsymbol{\Omega}_o^{-1}\nabla_\theta \mathbf{m}_i(\boldsymbol{\theta}_o)]\}^{-1}$.

c. As usual, we replace expectations with sample averages and unknown parameters, and divide the result by N to get $\widehat{\text{Avar}}(\hat{\boldsymbol{\theta}})$:

$$\begin{aligned}\widehat{\text{Avar}}(\hat{\boldsymbol{\theta}}) &= \left(N^{-1}\sum_{i=1}^{N}\nabla_\theta \mathbf{m}_i(\hat{\boldsymbol{\theta}})'\hat{\boldsymbol{\Omega}}^{-1}\nabla_\theta \mathbf{m}_i(\hat{\boldsymbol{\theta}})\right)^{-1}/N \\ &= \left(\sum_{i=1}^{N}\nabla_\theta \mathbf{m}_i(\hat{\boldsymbol{\theta}})'\hat{\boldsymbol{\Omega}}^{-1}\nabla_\theta \mathbf{m}_i(\hat{\boldsymbol{\theta}})\right)^{-1}.\end{aligned}$$

The estimate $\hat{\boldsymbol{\Omega}}$ can be based on the multivariate NLS residuals or can be updated after the nonlinear SUR estimates have been obtained.

d. First, note that $\nabla_\theta \mathbf{m}_i(\boldsymbol{\theta}_o)$ is a block-diagonal matrix with blocks $\nabla_{\theta_g} m_{ig}(\boldsymbol{\theta}_{og})$, a $1 \times P_g$ matrix. (I implicityly assumed that there are no cross-equation restrictions imposed in the nonlinear SUR estimation.) If $\boldsymbol{\Omega}_o$ is block-diagonal, so is its inverse. Standard matrix multiplication shows that

$$\nabla_\theta \mathbf{m}_i(\boldsymbol{\theta}_o)'\boldsymbol{\Omega}_o^{-1}\nabla_\theta \mathbf{m}_i(\boldsymbol{\theta}_o) = \begin{pmatrix} \sigma_{o1}^{-2}\nabla_{\theta_1} m_{i1}^{o\prime}\nabla_{\theta_1} m_{i1}^{o} & \mathbf{0} & \cdots & \mathbf{0} \\ \mathbf{0} & & & \\ \vdots & & & \\ \mathbf{0} & \cdots & \mathbf{0} & \sigma_{oG}^{-2}\nabla_{\theta_G} m_{iG}^{o\prime}\nabla_{\theta_G} m_{iG}^{o} \end{pmatrix}.$$

Taking expectations and inverting the result shows that Avar $\sqrt{N}(\hat{\boldsymbol{\theta}}_g - \boldsymbol{\theta}_{og}) = \sigma_{og}^2[E(\nabla_{\theta_g} m_{ig}^{o\prime}\nabla_{\theta_g} m_{ig}^{o})]^{-1}$, $g = 1,\ldots,G$. (Note also that the nonlinear SUR estimators are asymptotically uncorrelated across equations.) These asymptotic variances are easily seen to be the same as those for nonlinear least squares on each equation; see p. 360.

e. I cannot see a nonlinear analogue of Theorem 7.7. The first hint given in Problem 7.5 does not extend readily to nonlinear models, even when the same regressors appear in each equation. The key is that $\mathbf{X}_i$ is replaced with $\nabla_\theta \mathbf{m}(\mathbf{x}_i,\boldsymbol{\theta}_o)$. While this $G \times P$ matrix has a block-diagonal form, as described in part d, the blocks are not the same even when the same regressors appear in each equation. In the linear case, $\nabla_{\theta_g} m_g(\mathbf{x}_i,\boldsymbol{\theta}_{og}) = \mathbf{x}_i$ for all g. But, unless $\boldsymbol{\theta}_{og}$ is the same in all equations -- a very restrictive assumption -- $\nabla_{\theta_g} m_g(\mathbf{x}_i,\boldsymbol{\theta}_{og})$ varies across g. For example, if $m_g(\mathbf{x}_i,\boldsymbol{\theta}_{og}) = \exp(\mathbf{x}_i\boldsymbol{\theta}_{og})$ then $\nabla_{\theta_g} m_g(\mathbf{x}_i,\boldsymbol{\theta}_{og}) = \exp(\mathbf{x}_i\boldsymbol{\theta}_{og})\mathbf{x}_i$, and the gradients differ across g.

12.9. a. We cannot say anything in general about $\text{Med}(y|\mathbf{x})$, since $\text{Med}(y|\mathbf{x}) = m(\mathbf{x},\boldsymbol{\beta}_o) + \text{Med}(u|\mathbf{x})$, and $\text{Med}(u|\mathbf{x})$ could be a general function of $\mathbf{x}$.

b. If u and $\mathbf{x}$ are independent, then $\text{E}(u|\mathbf{x})$ and $\text{Med}(u|\mathbf{x})$ are both constants, say α and δ. Then $\text{E}(y|\mathbf{x}) - \text{Med}(y|\mathbf{x}) = \alpha - \delta$, which does not depend on $\mathbf{x}$.

c. When u and $\mathbf{x}$ are independent, the partial effects of x_j on the conditional mean and conditional median are the same, and there is no ambiguity about what is "the effect of x_j on y," at least when only the mean and median are in the running. Then, we could interpret large differences between LAD and NLS as perhaps indicating an outlier problem. But it could just be that u and $\mathbf{x}$ are not independent.

12.11. a. For consistency of the MNLS estimator, we need -- in addition to the regularity conditions, which I will ignore -- the identification condition. That is, $\boldsymbol{\beta}_o$ must uniquely minimize $\text{E}[q(\mathbf{w}_i,\boldsymbol{\beta})] = \text{E}\{[\mathbf{y}_i - \mathbf{m}(\mathbf{x}_i,\boldsymbol{\beta})]'[\mathbf{y}_i - \mathbf{m}(\mathbf{x}_i,\boldsymbol{\beta})]\} = \text{E}(\{\mathbf{u}_i + [\mathbf{m}(\mathbf{x}_i,\boldsymbol{\beta}_o) - \mathbf{m}(\mathbf{x}_i,\boldsymbol{\beta})]\}'\{\mathbf{u}_i + [\mathbf{m}(\mathbf{x}_i,\boldsymbol{\beta}_o) - \mathbf{m}(\mathbf{x}_i,\boldsymbol{\beta})]\}) = \text{E}(\mathbf{u}_i'\mathbf{u}_i) + 2\text{E}\{[\mathbf{m}(\mathbf{x}_i,\boldsymbol{\beta}_o) - \mathbf{m}(\mathbf{x}_i,\boldsymbol{\beta})]'\mathbf{u}_i\} + \text{E}\{[\mathbf{m}(\mathbf{x}_i,\boldsymbol{\beta}_o) - \mathbf{m}(\mathbf{x}_i,\boldsymbol{\beta})]'[\mathbf{m}(\mathbf{x}_i,\boldsymbol{\beta}_o) - \mathbf{m}(\mathbf{x}_i,\boldsymbol{\beta})]\} = \text{E}(\mathbf{u}_i\mathbf{u}_i') + \text{E}\{[\mathbf{m}(\mathbf{x}_i,\boldsymbol{\beta}_o) - \mathbf{m}(\mathbf{x}_i,\boldsymbol{\beta})]'[\mathbf{m}(\mathbf{x}_i,\boldsymbol{\beta}_o) - \mathbf{m}(\mathbf{x}_i,\boldsymbol{\beta})]\}$ because $\text{E}(\mathbf{u}_i|\mathbf{x}_i) = \mathbf{0}$. Therefore, the identification assumption is that

$$E\{[\mathbf{m}(\mathbf{x}_i,\boldsymbol{\beta}_o) - \mathbf{m}(\mathbf{x}_i,\boldsymbol{\beta})]'[\mathbf{m}(\mathbf{x}_i,\boldsymbol{\beta}_o) - \mathbf{m}(\mathbf{x}_i,\boldsymbol{\beta})]\} > 0, \ \boldsymbol{\beta} \neq \boldsymbol{\beta}_o.$$

In a linear model, where $\mathbf{m}(\mathbf{x}_i,\boldsymbol{\beta}) = \mathbf{X}_i\boldsymbol{\beta}$ for $\mathbf{X}_i$ a $G \times K$ matrix, the condition is

$$(\boldsymbol{\beta}_o - \boldsymbol{\beta})'E(\mathbf{X}_i'\mathbf{X}_i)(\boldsymbol{\beta}_o - \boldsymbol{\beta}) > 0, \ \boldsymbol{\beta} \neq \boldsymbol{\beta}_o,$$

and this holds provided $E(\mathbf{X}_i'\mathbf{X}_i)$ is positive definite.

Provided $\mathbf{m}(\mathbf{x},\cdot)$ is twice continuously differentiable, there are no problems in applying Theorem 12.3. Generally, $\mathbf{B}_o = E[\nabla_\theta\mathbf{m}_i(\boldsymbol{\beta}_o)'\mathbf{u}_i\mathbf{u}_i'\nabla_\theta\mathbf{m}_i(\boldsymbol{\beta}_o)]$ and $\mathbf{A}_o = E[\nabla_\theta\mathbf{m}_i(\boldsymbol{\beta}_o)'\nabla_\theta\mathbf{m}_i(\boldsymbol{\beta}_o)]$. These can be consistently estimated in the obvious way after obtain the MNLS estimators.

b. We can apply the results on two-step M-estimation. The key is that, underl general regularity conditions,

$$N^{-1}\sum_{i=1}^{N}[\mathbf{y}_i - \mathbf{m}(\mathbf{x}_i,\boldsymbol{\beta})]'[\mathbf{W}_i(\hat{\boldsymbol{\delta}})]^{-1}[\mathbf{y}_i - \mathbf{m}(\mathbf{x}_i,\boldsymbol{\beta})]/2,$$

converges uniformly in probability to

$$E\{[\mathbf{y}_i - \mathbf{m}(\mathbf{x}_i,\boldsymbol{\beta})]'[\mathbf{W}(\mathbf{x}_i,\boldsymbol{\delta}_o)]^{-1}[\mathbf{y}_i - \mathbf{m}(\mathbf{x}_i,\boldsymbol{\beta})]\}/2,$$

which is just to say that the usual consistency proof can be used provided we verify identification. But we can use an argument very similar to the unweighted case to show

$$E\{[\mathbf{y}_i - \mathbf{m}(\mathbf{x}_i,\boldsymbol{\beta})]'[\mathbf{W}(\mathbf{x}_i,\boldsymbol{\delta}_o)]^{-1}[\mathbf{y}_i - \mathbf{m}(\mathbf{x}_i,\boldsymbol{\beta})]\} = E\{\mathbf{u}_i'[\mathbf{W}_i(\boldsymbol{\delta}_o)]^{-1}\mathbf{u}_i\}$$
$$+ E\{[\mathbf{m}(\mathbf{x}_i,\boldsymbol{\beta}_o) - \mathbf{m}(\mathbf{x}_i,\boldsymbol{\beta})]'[\mathbf{W}_i(\boldsymbol{\delta}_o)]^{-1}[\mathbf{m}(\mathbf{x}_i,\boldsymbol{\beta}_o) - \mathbf{m}(\mathbf{x}_i,\boldsymbol{\beta})]\},$$

where $E(\mathbf{u}_i|\mathbf{x}_i) = \mathbf{0}$ is used to show the cross-product term, $2E\{[\mathbf{m}(\mathbf{x}_i,\boldsymbol{\beta}_o) - \mathbf{m}(\mathbf{x}_i,\boldsymbol{\beta})]'[\mathbf{W}_i(\boldsymbol{\delta}_o)]^{-1}\mathbf{u}_i\}$, is zero (by iterated expectations, as always). As before, the first term does not depend on $\boldsymbol{\beta}$ and the second term is minimized at $\boldsymbol{\beta}_o$; we would have to assume it is uniquely minimized.

To get the asymptotic variance, we proceed as in Problem 12.7. First, it can be shown that condition (12.37) holds. In particular, we can write $\nabla_\delta\mathbf{s}_i(\boldsymbol{\beta}_o;\boldsymbol{\delta}_o) = (\mathbf{I}_P \otimes \mathbf{u}_i)'\mathbf{G}(\mathbf{x}_i,\boldsymbol{\beta}_o;\boldsymbol{\delta}_o)$ for some function $\mathbf{G}(\mathbf{x}_i,\boldsymbol{\beta}_o;\boldsymbol{\delta}_o)$. It follows easily that $E[\nabla_\delta \mathbf{s}_i(\boldsymbol{\beta}_o;\boldsymbol{\delta}_o)|\mathbf{x}_i] = \mathbf{0}$, which implies (12.37). This means that, under $E(\mathbf{y}_i|\mathbf{x}_i) = \mathbf{m}(\mathbf{x}_i,\boldsymbol{\beta}_o)$, we can ignore preliminary estimation of $\boldsymbol{\delta}_o$ provided we have a $\sqrt{N}$-consistent estimator.

To obtain the asymptotic variance when the conditional variance matrix is correctly specified, that is, when $\mathrm{Var}(\mathbf{y}_i|\mathbf{x}_i) = \mathrm{Var}(\mathbf{u}_i|\mathbf{x}_i) = \mathbf{W}(\mathbf{x}_i,\boldsymbol{\delta}_o)$, we can use an argument very similar to the nonlinear SUR case in Problem 12.7:

$$\begin{aligned}
E[\mathbf{s}_i(\boldsymbol{\beta}_o;\boldsymbol{\delta}_o)\mathbf{s}_i(\boldsymbol{\beta}_o;\boldsymbol{\delta}_o)'] &= E[\nabla_\beta \mathbf{m}_i(\boldsymbol{\beta}_o)'[\mathbf{W}_i(\boldsymbol{\delta}_o)]^{-1}\mathbf{u}_i\mathbf{u}_i'[\mathbf{W}_i(\boldsymbol{\delta}_o)]^{-1}\nabla_\beta \mathbf{m}_i(\boldsymbol{\beta}_o)] \\
&= E\{E[\nabla_\beta \mathbf{m}_i(\boldsymbol{\beta}_o)'[\mathbf{W}_i(\boldsymbol{\delta}_o)]^{-1}\mathbf{u}_i\mathbf{u}_i'[\mathbf{W}_i(\boldsymbol{\delta}_o)]^{-1}\nabla_\beta \mathbf{m}_i(\boldsymbol{\beta}_o)|\mathbf{x}_i]\} \\
&= E[\nabla_\beta \mathbf{m}_i(\boldsymbol{\beta}_o)'[\mathbf{W}_i(\boldsymbol{\delta}_o)]^{-1}E(\mathbf{u}_i\mathbf{u}_i'|\mathbf{x}_i)[\mathbf{W}_i(\boldsymbol{\delta}_o)]^{-1}\nabla_\beta \mathbf{m}_i(\boldsymbol{\beta}_o)] \\
&= E\{\nabla_\beta \mathbf{m}_i(\boldsymbol{\beta}_o)'[\mathbf{W}_i(\boldsymbol{\delta}_o)]^{-1}]\nabla_\beta \mathbf{m}_i(\boldsymbol{\beta}_o)\}.
\end{aligned}$$

Now, the Hessian (with respect to $\boldsymbol{\beta}$), evaluated at $(\boldsymbol{\beta}_o,\boldsymbol{\delta}_o)$, can be written as

$$\mathbf{H}_i(\boldsymbol{\beta}_o;\boldsymbol{\delta}_o) = \nabla_\beta \mathbf{m}(\mathbf{x}_i,\boldsymbol{\beta}_o)'[\mathbf{W}_i(\boldsymbol{\delta}_o)]^{-1}\nabla_\beta \mathbf{m}(\mathbf{x}_i,\boldsymbol{\beta}_o) + (\mathbf{I}_P \otimes \mathbf{u}_i)']\mathbf{F}(\mathbf{x}_i,\boldsymbol{\beta}_o;\boldsymbol{\delta}_o),$$

for some complicated function $\mathbf{F}(\mathbf{x}_i,\boldsymbol{\beta}_o;\boldsymbol{\delta}_o)$ that depends only on $\mathbf{x}_i$. Taking expectations gives

$$\mathbf{A}_o \equiv E[\mathbf{H}_i(\boldsymbol{\beta}_o;\boldsymbol{\delta}_o)] = E\{\nabla_\beta \mathbf{m}(\mathbf{x}_i,\boldsymbol{\beta}_o)'[\mathbf{W}_i(\boldsymbol{\delta}_o)]^{-1}\nabla_\beta \mathbf{m}(\mathbf{x}_i,\boldsymbol{\beta}_o)\} = \mathbf{B}_o.$$

Therefore, from the usual results on M-estimation, $\mathrm{Avar}\,\sqrt{N}(\hat{\boldsymbol{\beta}} - \boldsymbol{\beta}_o) = \mathbf{A}_o^{-1}$, and a consistent estimator of $\mathbf{A}_o$ is

$$\hat{\mathbf{A}} = N^{-1}\sum_{i=1}^{N}\nabla_\beta \mathbf{m}(\mathbf{x}_i,\hat{\boldsymbol{\beta}})'[\mathbf{W}_i(\hat{\boldsymbol{\delta}})]^{-1}\nabla_\beta \mathbf{m}(\mathbf{x}_i,\hat{\boldsymbol{\beta}}).$$

c. The consistency argument in part b did not use the fact that $\mathbf{W}(\mathbf{x},\boldsymbol{\delta})$ is correctly specified for $\mathrm{Var}(\mathbf{y}|\mathbf{x})$. Exactly the same derivation goes through. But, of course, the asymptotic variance is affected because $\mathbf{A}_o \neq \mathbf{B}_o$, and the expression for $\mathbf{B}_o$ no longer holds. The estimator of $\mathbf{A}_o$ in part b still works, of course. To consistently estimate $\mathbf{B}_o$ we use

$$\hat{\mathbf{B}} = N^{-1}\sum_{i=1}^{N}\nabla_\beta \mathbf{m}(\mathbf{x}_i,\hat{\boldsymbol{\beta}})'[\mathbf{W}_i(\hat{\boldsymbol{\delta}})]^{-1}\hat{\mathbf{u}}_i\hat{\mathbf{u}}_i'[\mathbf{W}_i(\hat{\boldsymbol{\delta}})]^{-1}\nabla_\beta \mathbf{m}(\mathbf{x}_i,\hat{\boldsymbol{\beta}}).$$

Now, we estimate $\mathrm{Avar}\,\sqrt{N}(\hat{\boldsymbol{\beta}} - \boldsymbol{\beta}_o)$ in the usual way: $\hat{\mathbf{A}}^{-1}\hat{\mathbf{B}}\hat{\mathbf{A}}^{-1}$.

12.12. (Bonus Question): Let $\hat{\boldsymbol{\theta}}$ be an M-estimator with score $\mathbf{s}_i(\boldsymbol{\theta}) \equiv \mathbf{s}(\mathbf{w}_i,\boldsymbol{\theta})$ and expected Hessian $\mathbf{A}_o$. Let $\mathbf{g}(\mathbf{w},\boldsymbol{\theta})$ be an $M \times 1$ vector function of the random vector $\mathbf{w}$ and the parameter vector, and suppose we wish to estimate $\boldsymbol{\delta}_o \equiv E[\mathbf{g}(\mathbf{w}_i,\boldsymbol{\theta}_o)]$. The natural estimator is $\hat{\boldsymbol{\delta}} = N^{-1}\sum_{i=1}^{N}\mathbf{g}(\mathbf{w}_i,\hat{\boldsymbol{\theta}})$.

a. Assuming that $\mathbf{g}(\mathbf{w},\cdot)$ is continuously differentiable on int(Θ), $\boldsymbol{\theta}_o \in$ int(Θ), and other standard regularity conditions, find Avar $\sqrt{N}(\hat{\boldsymbol{\delta}} - \boldsymbol{\delta}_o)$.

b. How would you estimate Avar $\sqrt{N}(\hat{\boldsymbol{\delta}} - \boldsymbol{\delta}_o)$?

c. Show that if $\mathbf{g}(\mathbf{w},\boldsymbol{\theta}) = \mathbf{g}(\mathbf{x},\boldsymbol{\theta})$, and $\mathbf{x}$ is exogenous in the estimation problem used to obtain $\hat{\boldsymbol{\theta}}$ -- more precisely, $E[\mathbf{s}(\mathbf{w}_i,\boldsymbol{\theta}_o)|\mathbf{x}_i] = \mathbf{0}$ -- then

$$\text{Avar } \sqrt{N}(\hat{\boldsymbol{\delta}} - \boldsymbol{\delta}_o) = \text{Var}[\mathbf{g}(\mathbf{x}_i,\boldsymbol{\theta}_o)] + \mathbf{G}_o[\text{Avar } \sqrt{N}(\hat{\boldsymbol{\delta}} - \boldsymbol{\delta}_o)]\mathbf{G}_o'.$$

Answer:

a. We use a mean value expansion, similar to the delta method from Chapter 3 but now allowing for the randomness of $\mathbf{w}_i$. By a mean value expansion, we can write

$$N^{-1/2}\sum_{i=1}^{N}\mathbf{g}(\mathbf{w}_i,\hat{\boldsymbol{\theta}}) = N^{-1/2}\sum_{i=1}^{N}\mathbf{g}(\mathbf{w}_i,\boldsymbol{\theta}_o) + \left(N^{-1}\sum_{i=1}^{N}\ddot{\mathbf{G}}_i\right)\sqrt{N}(\hat{\boldsymbol{\theta}} - \boldsymbol{\theta}_o),$$

where $\ddot{\mathbf{G}}_i$ is the $M \times P$ Jacobian of $\mathbf{g}(\mathbf{w}_i,\boldsymbol{\theta})$ evaluate at mean values between $\boldsymbol{\theta}_o$ and $\hat{\boldsymbol{\theta}}$. Now, since $\sqrt{N}(\hat{\boldsymbol{\theta}} - \boldsymbol{\theta}_o) \overset{a}{\sim} \text{Normal}(\mathbf{0},\mathbf{A}_o^{-1}\mathbf{B}_o\mathbf{A}_o^{-1})$, it follows that $\sqrt{N}(\hat{\boldsymbol{\theta}} - \boldsymbol{\theta}_o) = O_p(1)$. Further, by Lemma 12.1, $N^{-1}\sum_{i=1}^{N}\ddot{\mathbf{G}}_i \overset{p}{\to} E[\nabla_\theta\mathbf{g}(\mathbf{w},\boldsymbol{\theta}_o)] \equiv \mathbf{G}_o$, since the mean values converge in probability to $\boldsymbol{\theta}_o$. Therefore,

$$\left(N^{-1}\sum_{i=1}^{N}\ddot{\mathbf{G}}_i\right)\sqrt{N}(\hat{\boldsymbol{\theta}} - \boldsymbol{\theta}_o) = \mathbf{G}_o\sqrt{N}(\hat{\boldsymbol{\theta}} - \boldsymbol{\theta}_o) + o_p(1),$$

and so

$$N^{-1/2}\sum_{i=1}^{N}\mathbf{g}(\mathbf{w}_i,\hat{\boldsymbol{\theta}}) = N^{-1/2}\sum_{i=1}^{N}\mathbf{g}(\mathbf{w}_i,\boldsymbol{\theta}_o) + \mathbf{G}_o\sqrt{N}(\hat{\boldsymbol{\theta}} - \boldsymbol{\theta}_o) + o_p(1).$$

Since $\sqrt{N}(\hat{\boldsymbol{\theta}} - \boldsymbol{\theta}_o) = -N^{-1/2}\sum_{i=1}^{N}\mathbf{A}_o^{-1}\mathbf{s}_i(\boldsymbol{\theta}_o) + o_p(1)$, we can write

$$N^{-1/2}\sum_{i=1}^{N}\mathbf{g}(\mathbf{w}_i,\hat{\boldsymbol{\theta}}) = N^{-1/2}\sum_{i=1}^{N}[\mathbf{g}(\mathbf{w}_i,\boldsymbol{\theta}_o) - \mathbf{G}_o\mathbf{A}_o^{-1}\mathbf{s}_i(\boldsymbol{\theta}_o)] + o_p(1)$$

or, subtracting $\sqrt{N}\boldsymbol{\delta}_o$ from both sides,

$$\sqrt{N}(\hat{\boldsymbol{\delta}} - \boldsymbol{\delta}_o) = N^{-1/2}\sum_{i=1}^{N}[\mathbf{g}(\mathbf{w}_i,\boldsymbol{\theta}_o) - \boldsymbol{\delta}_o - \mathbf{G}_o\mathbf{A}_o^{-1}\mathbf{s}_i(\boldsymbol{\theta}_o)] + o_p(1).$$

Since the term in the summation has zero mean, it follows from the CLT that

$$\sqrt{N}(\hat{\boldsymbol{\delta}} - \boldsymbol{\delta}_o) \overset{a}{\sim} \text{Normal}(\mathbf{0},\mathbf{D}_o)$$

where $\mathbf{D}_o = \text{Var}[(\mathbf{g}_i - \boldsymbol{\delta}_o - \mathbf{G}_o\mathbf{A}_o^{-1}\mathbf{s}_i)]$, where hopefully the shorthand is clear. This differs from the usual delta method result by the presence of $\mathbf{g}_i = \mathbf{g}_i(\boldsymbol{\theta}_o)$.

b. We assume we have $\hat{\mathbf{A}}$ consistent for $\mathbf{A}_o$. By the usual arguments, $\hat{\mathbf{G}} = N^{-1}\sum_{i=1}^{N}\nabla_{\theta}\mathbf{g}(\mathbf{w}_i,\hat{\boldsymbol{\theta}})$ is consistent for $\mathbf{G}_o$. Then

$$\hat{\mathbf{D}} = N^{-1}\sum_{i=1}^{N}(\hat{\mathbf{g}}_i - \hat{\boldsymbol{\delta}} - \hat{\mathbf{G}}\hat{\mathbf{A}}^{-1}\hat{\mathbf{s}}_i)(\hat{\mathbf{g}}_i - \hat{\boldsymbol{\delta}} - \hat{\mathbf{G}}\hat{\mathbf{A}}^{-1}\hat{\mathbf{s}}_i)'$$

is consistent for $\mathbf{D}_o$, where the "^" denotes evaluation at $\hat{\boldsymbol{\theta}}$.

c. Using our shorthand notation, if $E(\mathbf{s}_i|\mathbf{x}_i) = \mathbf{0}$ then $\mathbf{g}_i$ is uncorrelated with $\mathbf{s}_i$ (since $\mathbf{g}_i$ is a function of $\mathbf{x}_i$), which means $(\mathbf{g}_i - \boldsymbol{\delta}_o)$ is uncorrelated with $\mathbf{G}_o\mathbf{A}_o^{-1}\mathbf{s}_i$. But then $\mathbf{D}_o = \text{Var}[(\mathbf{g}_i - \boldsymbol{\delta}_o - \mathbf{G}_o\mathbf{A}_o^{-1}\mathbf{s}_i)] = \text{Var}(\mathbf{g}_i) + \mathbf{G}_o\mathbf{A}_o^{-1}\mathbf{B}_o\mathbf{A}_o^{-1}\mathbf{G}_o'$, which is what we wanted to show.

SOLUTIONS TO CHAPTER 13 PROBLEMS

13.1. No. We know that $\boldsymbol{\theta}_o$ solves

$$\max_{\boldsymbol{\theta}\in\Theta} \mathrm{E}[\log f(\mathbf{y}_i|\mathbf{x}_i;\boldsymbol{\theta})],$$

where the expectation is over the joint distribution of $(\mathbf{x}_i,\mathbf{y}_i)$. Therefore, because $\exp(\cdot)$ is an increasing function, $\boldsymbol{\theta}_o$ also maximizes $\exp\{\mathrm{E}[\log f(\mathbf{y}_i|\mathbf{x}_i;\boldsymbol{\theta})]\}$ over Θ. The problem is that the expectation and the exponential function cannot be interchanged: $\mathrm{E}[f(\mathbf{y}_i|\mathbf{x}_i;\boldsymbol{\theta})] \neq \exp\{\mathrm{E}[\log f(\mathbf{y}_i|\mathbf{x}_i;\boldsymbol{\theta})]\}$. In fact, Jensen's inequality tells us that $\mathrm{E}[f(\mathbf{y}_i|\mathbf{x}_i;\boldsymbol{\theta})] > \exp\{\mathrm{E}[\log f(\mathbf{y}_i|\mathbf{x}_i;\boldsymbol{\theta})]\}$.

13.3. a. The conditional log-likelihood for observation i is

$$\ell_i(\boldsymbol{\theta}) = y_i\log[G(\mathbf{x}_i,\boldsymbol{\theta})] + (1 - y_i)\log[1 - G(\mathbf{x}_i,\boldsymbol{\theta})].$$

b. The derivation for the probit case in Example 13.1 extends immediately:

$$\begin{aligned}\mathbf{s}_i(\boldsymbol{\theta}) &= y_i\nabla_\theta G(\mathbf{x}_i,\boldsymbol{\theta})'/G(\mathbf{x}_i,\boldsymbol{\theta}) - (1 - y_i)\nabla_\theta G(\mathbf{x}_i,\boldsymbol{\theta})'/[1 - G(\mathbf{x}_i,\boldsymbol{\theta})] \\ &= \nabla_\theta G(\mathbf{x}_i,\boldsymbol{\theta})'[y_i - G(\mathbf{x}_i,\boldsymbol{\theta})]/\{G(\mathbf{x}_i,\boldsymbol{\theta})[1 - G(\mathbf{x}_i,\boldsymbol{\theta})]\}.\end{aligned}$$

If we plug in $\boldsymbol{\theta}_o$ for $\boldsymbol{\theta}$ and take the expectation conditional on $\mathbf{x}_i$ we get $\mathrm{E}[\mathbf{s}_i(\boldsymbol{\theta}_o)|\mathbf{x}_i] = \mathbf{0}$ because $\mathrm{E}[y_i - G(\mathbf{x}_i,\boldsymbol{\theta}_o)|\mathbf{x}_i] = \mathrm{E}(y_i|\mathbf{x}_i) - G(\mathbf{x}_i,\boldsymbol{\theta}_o) = 0$, and the functions multiplying $y_i - G(\mathbf{x}_i,\boldsymbol{\theta}_o)$ depend only on $\mathbf{x}_i$.

c. We need to evaluate the score and the expected Hessian with respect to the full set of parameters, but then evaluate these at the restricted estimates. Now,

$$\nabla_\theta G(\mathbf{x}_i,\boldsymbol{\beta},\mathbf{0}) = \phi(\mathbf{x}\boldsymbol{\beta})[\mathbf{x}, (\mathbf{x}\boldsymbol{\beta})^2, (\mathbf{x}\boldsymbol{\beta})^3],$$

a $1 \times (K + 2)$ vector. Let $\tilde{\boldsymbol{\beta}}$ denote the probit estimates of $\boldsymbol{\beta}$, obtained under the null. The score for observation i, evaluated under the null estimates, is the $(K + 2) \times 1$ vector

$$\mathbf{s}_i(\tilde{\boldsymbol{\theta}}) = \nabla_\theta G(\mathbf{x}_i,\tilde{\boldsymbol{\beta}},\mathbf{0})'[y_i - \Phi(\mathbf{x}_i\tilde{\boldsymbol{\beta}})]/\{\Phi(\mathbf{x}_i\tilde{\boldsymbol{\beta}})[1 - \Phi(\mathbf{x}_i\tilde{\boldsymbol{\beta}})]\}$$

$$= \phi(\mathbf{x}_i\tilde{\boldsymbol{\beta}})\tilde{\mathbf{z}}_i'[y_i - \Phi(\mathbf{x}_i\tilde{\boldsymbol{\beta}})]/\{\Phi(\mathbf{x}_i\tilde{\boldsymbol{\beta}})[1 - \Phi(\mathbf{x}_i\tilde{\boldsymbol{\beta}})]\},$$

where $\tilde{\mathbf{z}}_i \equiv [\mathbf{x}_i, (\mathbf{x}_i\tilde{\boldsymbol{\beta}})^2, (\mathbf{x}_i\tilde{\boldsymbol{\beta}})^3]$. The negative of the expected Hessian, evaluated under the null, is the $(K + 2) \times (K + 2)$ matrix

$$\mathbf{A}(\mathbf{x}_i,\tilde{\boldsymbol{\theta}}) = [\phi(\mathbf{x}_i\tilde{\boldsymbol{\beta}})]^2\tilde{\mathbf{z}}_i'\tilde{\mathbf{z}}_i/\{\Phi(\mathbf{x}_i\tilde{\boldsymbol{\beta}})[1 - \Phi(\mathbf{x}_i\tilde{\boldsymbol{\beta}})]\}.$$

These can be plugged into the second expression in equation (13.26) to obtain a nonnegative, well-behaved LM statistic. Simple algebra shows that the statistic can be computed as the explained sum of squares from the regression

$$\tilde{u}_i/[\tilde{\Phi}_i(1 - \tilde{\Phi}_i)]^{1/2} \text{ on } \tilde{\phi}_i\cdot\mathbf{x}_i/[\tilde{\Phi}_i(1 - \tilde{\Phi}_i)]^{1/2},$$

$$\tilde{\phi}_i\cdot(\mathbf{x}_i\tilde{\boldsymbol{\beta}})^2/[\tilde{\Phi}_i(1 - \tilde{\Phi}_i)]^{1/2},\ \tilde{\phi}_i\cdot(\mathbf{x}_i\tilde{\boldsymbol{\beta}})^3/[\tilde{\Phi}_i(1 - \tilde{\Phi}_i)]^{1/2},\ i = 1,\ldots,N,$$

where "~" denotes evaluation at $(\tilde{\boldsymbol{\beta}},\mathbf{0})$ and $\tilde{u}_i = y_i - \tilde{\Phi}_i$. Under H_0, LM is distributed asymptotically as χ^2_2.

13.5. a. Since $\mathbf{s}_i^g(\boldsymbol{\phi}_o) = [\mathbf{G}(\boldsymbol{\theta}_o)']^{-1}\mathbf{s}_i(\boldsymbol{\theta}_o)$,

$$\mathrm{E}[\mathbf{s}_i^g(\boldsymbol{\phi}_o)\mathbf{s}_i^g(\boldsymbol{\phi}_o)'|\mathbf{x}_i] = \mathrm{E}\{[\mathbf{G}(\boldsymbol{\theta}_o)']^{-1}\mathbf{s}_i(\boldsymbol{\theta}_o)\mathbf{s}_i(\boldsymbol{\theta}_o)'[\mathbf{G}(\boldsymbol{\theta}_o)]^{-1}|\mathbf{x}_i\}$$

$$= [\mathbf{G}(\boldsymbol{\theta}_o)']^{-1}\mathrm{E}[\mathbf{s}_i(\boldsymbol{\theta}_o)\mathbf{s}_i(\boldsymbol{\theta}_o)'|\mathbf{x}_i][\mathbf{G}(\boldsymbol{\theta}_o)]^{-1}$$

$$= [\mathbf{G}(\boldsymbol{\theta}_o)']^{-1}\mathbf{A}_i(\boldsymbol{\theta}_o)[\mathbf{G}(\boldsymbol{\theta}_o)]^{-1}.$$

b. In part b, we just replace $\boldsymbol{\theta}_o$ with $\tilde{\boldsymbol{\theta}}$ and $\boldsymbol{\phi}_o$ with $\tilde{\boldsymbol{\phi}}$:

$$\tilde{\mathbf{A}}_i^g = [\mathbf{G}(\tilde{\boldsymbol{\theta}})']^{-1}\mathbf{A}_i(\tilde{\boldsymbol{\theta}})[\mathbf{G}(\tilde{\boldsymbol{\theta}})]^{-1} \equiv \tilde{\mathbf{G}}'^{-1}\tilde{\mathbf{A}}_i\tilde{\mathbf{G}}^{-1}.$$

c. The expected Hessian form of the statistic is given in the second part of equation (13.36), but where it is based on $\tilde{\mathbf{s}}_i^g$ and $\tilde{\mathbf{A}}_i^g$:

$$LM_g = \left(\sum_{i=1}^N \tilde{\mathbf{s}}_i^g\right)'\left(\sum_{i=1}^N \tilde{\mathbf{A}}_i^g\right)^{-1}\left(\sum_{i=1}^N \tilde{\mathbf{s}}_i^g\right)$$

$$= \left(\sum_{i=1}^N \tilde{\mathbf{G}}'^{-1}\tilde{\mathbf{s}}_i\right)'\left(\sum_{i=1}^N \tilde{\mathbf{G}}'^{-1}\tilde{\mathbf{A}}_i\tilde{\mathbf{G}}^{-1}\right)^{-1}\left(\sum_{i=1}^N \tilde{\mathbf{G}}'^{-1}\tilde{\mathbf{s}}_i\right)$$

$$= \left(\sum_{i=1}^N \tilde{\mathbf{s}}_i\right)'\tilde{\mathbf{G}}^{-1}\tilde{\mathbf{G}}\left(\sum_{i=1}^N \tilde{\mathbf{A}}_i\right)^{-1}\tilde{\mathbf{G}}'\tilde{\mathbf{G}}'^{-1}\left(\sum_{i=1}^N \tilde{\mathbf{s}}_i\right)$$

$$= \left(\sum_{i=1}^{N} \tilde{\mathbf{s}}_i\right)' \left(\sum_{i=1}^{N} \tilde{\mathbf{A}}_i\right)^{-1} \left(\sum_{i=1}^{N} \tilde{\mathbf{s}}_i\right) = LM.$$

13.7. a. The joint density is simply $g(y_1|y_2,\mathbf{x};\boldsymbol{\theta}_o)\cdot h(y_2|\mathbf{x};\boldsymbol{\theta}_o)$. The log-likelihood for observation i is

$$\ell_i(\boldsymbol{\theta}) \equiv \log g(y_{i1}|y_{i2},\mathbf{x}_i;\boldsymbol{\theta}) + \log h(y_{i2}|\mathbf{x}_i;\boldsymbol{\theta}),$$

and we would use this in a standard MLE analysis (conditional on $\mathbf{x}_i$).

b. First, we know that, for all $(y_{i2},\mathbf{x}_i)$, $\boldsymbol{\theta}_o$ maximizes $\mathrm{E}[\ell_{i1}(\boldsymbol{\theta})|y_{i2},\mathbf{x}_i]$. Since r_{i2} is a function of $(y_{i2},\mathbf{x}_i)$,

$$\mathrm{E}[r_{i2}\ell_{i1}(\boldsymbol{\theta})|y_{i2},\mathbf{x}_i] = r_{i2}\mathrm{E}[\ell_{i1}(\boldsymbol{\theta})|y_{i2},\mathbf{x}_i];$$

since $r_{i2} \geq 1$, $\boldsymbol{\theta}_o$ maximizes $\mathrm{E}[r_{i2}\ell_{i1}(\boldsymbol{\theta})|y_{i2},\mathbf{x}_i]$ for all $(y_{i2},\mathbf{x}_i)$, and therefore $\boldsymbol{\theta}_o$ maximizes $\mathrm{E}[r_{i2}\ell_{i1}(\boldsymbol{\theta})]$. Similary, $\boldsymbol{\theta}_o$ maximizes $\mathrm{E}[\ell_{i2}(\boldsymbol{\theta})]$, and so it follows that $\boldsymbol{\theta}_o$ maximizes $r_{i2}\ell_{i1}(\boldsymbol{\theta}) + \ell_{i2}(\boldsymbol{\theta})$. For identification, we have to assume or verify uniqueness.

c. The score is

$$\mathbf{s}_i(\boldsymbol{\theta}) = r_{i2}\mathbf{s}_{i1}(\boldsymbol{\theta}) + \mathbf{s}_{i2}(\boldsymbol{\theta}),$$

where $\mathbf{s}_{i1}(\boldsymbol{\theta}) \equiv \nabla_{\theta}\ell_{i1}(\boldsymbol{\theta})'$ and $\mathbf{s}_{i2}(\boldsymbol{\theta}) \equiv \nabla_{\theta}\ell_{i2}(\boldsymbol{\theta})'$. Therefore,

$$\mathrm{E}[\mathbf{s}_i(\boldsymbol{\theta}_o)\mathbf{s}_i(\boldsymbol{\theta}_o)'] = \mathrm{E}[r_{i2}\mathbf{s}_{i1}(\boldsymbol{\theta}_o)\mathbf{s}_{i1}(\boldsymbol{\theta}_o)'] + \mathrm{E}[\mathbf{s}_{i2}(\boldsymbol{\theta}_o)\mathbf{s}_{i2}(\boldsymbol{\theta}_o)']$$
$$+ \mathrm{E}[r_{i2}\mathbf{s}_{i1}(\boldsymbol{\theta}_o)\mathbf{s}_{i2}(\boldsymbol{\theta}_o)'] + \mathrm{E}[r_{i2}\mathbf{s}_{i2}(\boldsymbol{\theta}_o)\mathbf{s}_{i1}(\boldsymbol{\theta}_o)'].$$

Now by the usual conditional MLE theory, $\mathrm{E}[\mathbf{s}_{i1}(\boldsymbol{\theta}_o)|y_{i2},\mathbf{x}_i] = \mathbf{0}$ and, since r_{i2} and $\mathbf{s}_{i2}(\boldsymbol{\theta})$ are functions of $(y_{i2},\mathbf{x}_i)$, it follows that $\mathrm{E}[r_{i2}\mathbf{s}_{i1}(\boldsymbol{\theta}_o)\mathbf{s}_{i2}(\boldsymbol{\theta}_o)'|y_{i2},\mathbf{x}_i] = \mathbf{0}$, and so its transpose also has zero conditional expectation. As usual, this implies zero unconditional expectation. We have shown

$$\mathrm{E}[\mathbf{s}_i(\boldsymbol{\theta}_o)\mathbf{s}_i(\boldsymbol{\theta}_o)'] = \mathrm{E}[r_{i2}\mathbf{s}_{i1}(\boldsymbol{\theta}_o)\mathbf{s}_{i1}(\boldsymbol{\theta}_o)'] + \mathrm{E}[\mathbf{s}_{i2}(\boldsymbol{\theta}_o)\mathbf{s}_{i2}(\boldsymbol{\theta}_o)'].$$

Now, by the unconditional information matrix equality for the density $h(y_2|\mathbf{x};\boldsymbol{\theta})$, $\mathrm{E}[\mathbf{s}_{i2}(\boldsymbol{\theta}_o)\mathbf{s}_{i2}(\boldsymbol{\theta}_o)'] = -\mathrm{E}[\mathbf{H}_{i2}(\boldsymbol{\theta}_o)]$, where $\mathbf{H}_{i2}(\boldsymbol{\theta}) = \nabla_{\theta}\mathbf{s}_{i2}(\boldsymbol{\theta})$.

Further, by the conditional IM equality for the density $g(y_1|y_2,\mathbf{x};\boldsymbol{\theta})$,

$$E[\mathbf{s}_{i1}(\boldsymbol{\theta}_o)\mathbf{s}_{i1}(\boldsymbol{\theta}_o)'|y_{i2},\mathbf{x}_i] = -E[\mathbf{H}_{i1}(\boldsymbol{\theta}_o)|y_{i2},\mathbf{x}_i], \qquad (13.70)$$

where $\mathbf{H}_{i1}(\boldsymbol{\theta}) = \nabla_\theta \mathbf{s}_{i1}(\boldsymbol{\theta})$. Since r_{i2} is a function of $(y_{i2},\mathbf{x}_i)$, we can put r_{i2} inside both expectations in (13.70). Then, by iterated expectatins,

$$E[r_{i2}\mathbf{s}_{i1}(\boldsymbol{\theta}_o)\mathbf{s}_{i1}(\boldsymbol{\theta}_o)'] = -E[r_{i2}\mathbf{H}_{i1}(\boldsymbol{\theta}_o)].$$

Combining all the pieces, we have shown that

$$\begin{aligned} E[\mathbf{s}_i(\boldsymbol{\theta}_o)\mathbf{s}_i(\boldsymbol{\theta}_o)'] &= -E[r_{i2}\mathbf{H}_{i1}(\boldsymbol{\theta}_o)] - E[\mathbf{H}_{i2}(\boldsymbol{\theta}_o)] \\ &= -\{E[r_{i2}\nabla_\theta \mathbf{s}_{i1}(\boldsymbol{\theta}) + \nabla_\theta \mathbf{s}_{i2}(\boldsymbol{\theta})] \\ &= -E[\nabla_\theta^2 \ell_i(\boldsymbol{\theta})] \equiv -E[\mathbf{H}_i(\boldsymbol{\theta})]. \end{aligned}$$

So we have verified that an unconditional IM equality holds, which means we can estimate the asymptotic variance of $\sqrt{N}(\hat{\boldsymbol{\theta}} - \boldsymbol{\theta}_o)$ by $\{-E[\mathbf{H}_i(\boldsymbol{\theta})]\}^{-1}$.

d. From part c, one consistent estimator of Avar $\sqrt{N}(\hat{\boldsymbol{\theta}} - \boldsymbol{\theta}_o)$ is

$$\left(-N^{-1}\sum_{i=1}^{N}(r_{i2}\hat{\mathbf{H}}_{i1} + \hat{\mathbf{H}}_{i2})\right)^{-1}$$

where the notation should be obvious. But, as we discussed in Chapters 12 and 13, this estimator need not be positive definite. Instead, we can break the problem into needed consistent estimators of $-E[r_{i2}\mathbf{H}_{i1}(\boldsymbol{\theta}_o)]$ and $-E[\mathbf{H}_{i2}(\boldsymbol{\theta}_o)]$, for which we can use iterated expectations. Since, by definition, $\mathbf{A}_{i2}(\boldsymbol{\theta}_o) \equiv -E[\mathbf{H}_{i2}(\boldsymbol{\theta}_o)|\mathbf{x}_i]$, $N^{-1}\sum_{i=1}^{N}\hat{\mathbf{A}}_{i2}$ is consistent for $-E[\mathbf{H}_{i2}(\boldsymbol{\theta}_o)]$ by the usual iterated expectations argument. Similarly, since $\mathbf{A}_{i1}(\boldsymbol{\theta}_o) \equiv -E[\mathbf{H}_{i1}(\boldsymbol{\theta}_o)|y_{i2},\mathbf{x}_i]$, and r_{i2} is a function of $(y_{i2},\mathbf{x}_i)$, it follows that $E[r_{i2}\mathbf{A}_{i1}(\boldsymbol{\theta}_o)] = -E[r_{i2}\mathbf{H}_{i1}(\boldsymbol{\theta}_o)]$. This implies that, under general regularity conditions, $N^{-1}\sum_{i=1}^{N} r_{i2}\hat{\mathbf{A}}_{i1}$ consistently estimates $-E[r_{i2}\mathbf{H}_{i1}(\boldsymbol{\theta}_o)]$. This completes what we needed to show. Interestingly, even though we do not have a true conditional maximum likelihood problem, we can still use the conditional expectations of the hessians -- but conditioned on different sets of variables, $(y_{i2},\mathbf{x}_i)$ in one case, and $\mathbf{x}_i$ in the other -- to consistently estimate the asymptotic variance of the partial MLE.

e. (Bonus Question): Show that if we were able to use the entire random sample, the result conditional MLE would be more efficient than the partial MLE based on the selected sample.

Answer: We use a basic fact about positive definite matrices that is used throughout the text, and often shows up in efficiency comparisons: if $\mathbf{A}$ and $\mathbf{B}$ are $P \times P$ positive definite matrices, then $\mathbf{A} - \mathbf{B}$ is p.s.d. if and only if $\mathbf{B}^{-1} - \mathbf{A}^{-1}$ is positive definite. Now, as we showed in part d, the asymptotic variance of the partial MLE is $\{E[r_{i2}\mathbf{A}_{i1}(\boldsymbol{\theta}_o) + \mathbf{A}_{i2}(\boldsymbol{\theta}_o)]\}^{-1}$. If we could use the entire random sample for both terms, the asymptotic variance would be $\{E[\mathbf{A}_{i1}(\boldsymbol{\theta}_o) + \mathbf{A}_{i2}(\boldsymbol{\theta}_o)]\}^{-1}$. But $\{E[r_{i2}\mathbf{A}_{i1}(\boldsymbol{\theta}_o) + \mathbf{A}_{i2}(\boldsymbol{\theta}_o)]\}^{-1} - \{E[\mathbf{A}_{i1}(\boldsymbol{\theta}_o) + \mathbf{A}_{i2}(\boldsymbol{\theta}_o)]\}^{-1}$ is p.s.d. because $E[\mathbf{A}_{i1}(\boldsymbol{\theta}_o) + \mathbf{A}_{i2}(\boldsymbol{\theta}_o)] - E[r_{i2}\mathbf{A}_{i1}(\boldsymbol{\theta}_o) + \mathbf{A}_{i2}(\boldsymbol{\theta}_o)]$ $= E[(1 - r_{i2})\mathbf{A}_{i1}(\boldsymbol{\theta}_o)]$ is p.s.d. [since $\mathbf{A}_{i1}(\boldsymbol{\theta}_o)$ is p.s.d. and $1 - r_{i2} \geq 0$.]

13.9. a. Under the Markov assumption, the joint density of $(y_{i0},\ldots,y_{iT})$ is given by

$$f_T(y_T|y_{T-1})\cdot f_{T-1}(y_{T-1}|y_{T-2})\cdots f_1(y_1|y_0)\cdot f_0(y_0),$$

so we would need to model $f_0(y_0)$ to obtain a model of the joint density.

b. The log-likelihood

$$\ell_i(\boldsymbol{\theta}) = \sum_{t=1}^{T}\log[f_t(y_{it}|y_{i,t-1};\boldsymbol{\theta})]$$

is the conditional log-likelihood for the density of $(y_{i1},\ldots,y_{iT})$ given y_{i0}, and so the usual theory of conditional maximum likelihood applies. In practice, this is MLE pooled across i and t.

c. Because we have the density of $(y_{i1},\ldots,y_{iT})$ given y_{i0}, we can use any of the three asymptotic variance estimators implied by the information matrix equality. However, we can also use the simplifications due to dynamice completeness of each conditional density. Let $\mathbf{s}_{it}(\boldsymbol{\theta}) = \nabla_{\theta}\log[f(y_{it}|y_{i,t-1};\boldsymbol{\theta})$, $\mathbf{H}_{it}(\boldsymbol{\theta}) = \nabla_{\theta}\mathbf{s}_{it}(\boldsymbol{\theta})$, and $\mathbf{A}_{it}(\boldsymbol{\theta}_o) = -E[\mathbf{H}_{it}(\boldsymbol{\theta})|y_{i,t-1}]$, $t = 1,\ldots,T$. Then Avar $\sqrt{N}(\hat{\boldsymbol{\theta}} - \boldsymbol{\theta}_o)$ is consistently estimated using the inverse of any of the three matrices in equation (13.50). If we have a canned package that computes a particular MLE, we can just use any of the usual asymptotic variance estimates obtained from the pooled MLE.

13.10. a. Because of conditional independence, by the usual product rule,

$$f(y_1,y_2,\ldots,y_G|\mathbf{x},c) = \prod_{g=1}^{G} f_g(y_g|\mathbf{x},c).$$

b. Let $g(y_1,\ldots,y_G|\mathbf{x})$ be the joint density of $\mathbf{y}_i$ given $\mathbf{x}_i = \mathbf{x}$. Then

$$g(y_1,\ldots,y_G|\mathbf{x}) = \int_{\mathbb{R}} f(y_1,y_2,\ldots,y_G|\mathbf{x},c)h(c|\mathbf{x})dc.$$

c. The density $g(y_1,\ldots,y_G|\mathbf{x})$ is now

$$g(y_1,\ldots,y_G|\mathbf{x};\boldsymbol{\gamma}_o,\boldsymbol{\delta}_o) = \int_{\mathbb{R}} f(y_1,y_2,\ldots,y_G|\mathbf{x},c;\boldsymbol{\gamma}_o)h(c|\mathbf{x};\boldsymbol{\delta}_o)dc$$

$$= \int_{\mathbb{R}} \prod_{g=1}^{G} f_g(y_g|\mathbf{x},c;\boldsymbol{\gamma}_o^g)h(c|\mathbf{x};\boldsymbol{\delta}_o)dc,$$

and so the log likelihood for observation i is

$$\log[g(y_{i1},\ldots,y_{iG}|\mathbf{x}_i;\boldsymbol{\gamma}_o,\boldsymbol{\delta}_o)]$$

$$= \log\left[\int_{\mathbb{R}} \prod_{g=1}^{G} f_g(y_{ig}|\mathbf{x}_i,c;\boldsymbol{\gamma}_o^g)h(c|\mathbf{x}_i;\boldsymbol{\delta}_o)dc\right].$$

d. This setup has some features in common with a linear SUR model, although here the correlation across equations is assumed to come through a single common component, c. Because of computational issues with general nonlinear models -- especially if G is large and some of the models are for qualitative response -- one probably needs to restrict the cross correlation somehow.

13.11. a. For each $t \geq 1$, the density of y_{it} given $y_{i,t-1} = y_{i,t-1}$, $y_{i,t-2} = y_{t-2}$, , ..., $y_{i0} = y_0$, and $c_i = c$ is

$$f_t(y_t | y_{t-1}, c) = (2\pi\sigma_e^2)^{-1/2}\exp[-(y_t - \rho y_{t-1} - c)^2/(2\sigma_e^2)].$$

Therfore, the density of $(y_{i1},\ldots,y_{iT})$ given $y_{i0} = y_0$ and $c_i = c$ is obtained by the product of these densities:

$$\prod_{t=1}^{T} (2\pi\sigma_e^2)^{-1/2}\exp[-(y_t - \rho y_{t-1} - c)^2/(2\sigma_e^2)].$$

If we plug in the data for observation i and take the log we get

$$\sum_{t=1}^{T} \{-(1/2)\log(\sigma_e^2) - (y_{it} - \rho y_{i,t-1} - c_i)^2/(2\sigma_e^2)\}$$

where we have dropped the term that does not depend on the parameters. It is not a good idea to "estimate" the c_i along with ρ and σ_e^2, as the incidental parameters problem causes inconsistency -- severe in some cases -- in the estimator of ρ.

b. If we write $c_i = \alpha_0 + \alpha_1 y_{i0} + a_i$, under the maintained assumption, then the density of $(y_{i1},\ldots,y_{iT})$ given $(y_{i0} = y_0, a_i = a)$ is

$$\prod_{t=1}^{T} (2\pi\sigma_e^2)^{-1/2}\exp[-(y_t - \rho y_{t-1} - \alpha_0 - \alpha_1 y_0 - a)^2/(2\sigma_e^2)].$$

Now, to get the density condition on $y_{i0} = y_0$ only, we integrate this density over the density of a_i given $y_{i0} = y_0$. But a_i and y_{i0} are independent, and $a_i \sim \text{Normal}(0,\sigma_a^2)$. So the density of $(y_{i1},\ldots,y_{iT})$ given $y_{i0} = y_0$ is

$$\int_{-\infty}^{\infty}\left(\prod_{t=1}^{T} (2\pi\sigma_e^2)^{-1/2}\exp[-(y_t - \rho y_{t-1} - \alpha_0 - \alpha_1 y_0 - a)^2/(2\sigma_e^2)]\right)\sigma_a^{-1}\phi(a/\sigma_a)da.$$

If we now plug in the data $(y_{i0},y_{i1},\ldots,y_{iT})$ for each i and take the log we get a conditional log-likelihood (conditional on y_{i0}) for each i. We can estimate the parameters by maximizing the sum of the log-likelihoods across i.

c. As before, we can replace c_i with $\alpha_0 + \alpha_1 y_{i0} + a_i$. Then, the density of y_{it} given $(y_{i,t-1},\ldots,y_{i1},y_{i0},a_i)$ is

$\text{Normal}[\rho y_{i,t-1} + \alpha_0 + \alpha_1 y_{i0} + a_i + \delta(\alpha_0 + \alpha_1 y_{i0} + a_i)y_{i,t-1}, \sigma_e^2]$,

$t = 1,\ldots,T$. Using the same argument as in part b, we just integrate out a_i to get the density of $(y_{i1},\ldots,y_{iT})$ given $y_{i0} = y_0$:

$$\int_{-\infty}^{\infty}\left(\prod_{t=1}^{T}(2\pi\sigma_e^2)^{-1/2}\exp[-(y_t - \rho y_{t-1} - \alpha_0 - \alpha_1 y_0 - a - \delta(\alpha_0 + \alpha_1 y_0 + a)y_{t-1})^2/(2\sigma_e^2)]\right)\sigma_a^{-1}\phi(a/\sigma_a)da.$$

Numerically, this could be a difficult MLE problem to solve. Assuming we can get the MLEs, we would estimate $\rho + \mathrm{E}(c_i)$ as $\hat{\rho} + \hat{\alpha}_0 + \hat{\alpha}_1\bar{y}_0$, where $\bar{y}_0$ is the cross-sectional average of the initial observation.

d. The log likelihood for observation i, now conditional on $(y_{i0},\mathbf{z}_i)$, is the log of

$$\int_{-\infty}^{\infty}\left(\prod_{t=1}^{T}(2\pi\sigma_e^2)^{-1/2}\exp[-(y_{it} - \rho y_{i,t-1} - \mathbf{z}_{it}\boldsymbol{\beta} - \alpha_0 - \alpha_1 y_0 - \bar{\mathbf{z}}_i\boldsymbol{\delta} - a)^2/(2\sigma_e^2)]\right)\sigma_a^{-1}\phi(a/\sigma_a)da.$$

The assumption that we can put in the time average, $\bar{\mathbf{z}}_i$, to account for correlation between c_i and $(y_{i0},\mathbf{z}_i)$, may be too strong. It would be better to put in the full vector $\mathbf{z}_i$, although this leads to many more parameters to estimate.

13.12 (Bonus Question): Let $\{f(y_t|\mathbf{x}_t;\boldsymbol{\theta}): t = 1,\ldots,T\}$ be a sequence of correctly specified densities for y_{it} given $\mathbf{x}_{it}$. That is, assume that there is $\boldsymbol{\theta}_o \in \mathrm{int}(\Theta)$ such that $f(y_t|\mathbf{x}_t;\boldsymbol{\theta}_o)$ is the density of y_{it} given $\mathbf{x}_{it} = \mathbf{x}_t$. Also assume that $\{\mathbf{x}_{it}: t=1,2,\ldots,T\}$ is strictly exogenous for each t: $\mathrm{D}(y_{it}|\mathbf{x}_{i1},\ldots,\mathbf{x}_{iT}) = \mathrm{D}(y_{it}|\mathbf{x}_{it})$.

a. Is it true that, under the standard regularity conditions for partial MLE, that $\mathrm{E}[\mathbf{s}_{it}(\boldsymbol{\theta}_o)|\mathbf{x}_{i1},\ldots,\mathbf{x}_{iT}] = \mathbf{0}$, where $\mathbf{s}_{it}(\boldsymbol{\theta}) = \nabla_\theta \log f_t(y_{it}|\mathbf{x}_{it};\boldsymbol{\theta})'$?

b. Under the assumptions given, is $\{\mathbf{s}_{it}(\boldsymbol{\theta}_o): t = 1,\ldots,T\}$ necessarily serially uncorrelated?

c. Let c_i be "unobserved heterogeneity" for cross section unit i, and assume that, for each t, $D(y_{it}|\mathbf{z}_{i1},\ldots,\mathbf{z}_{iT},c_i) = D(y_{it}|\mathbf{z}_{it},c_i)$. In other words, $\{\mathbf{z}_{it}: t = 1,\ldots,T\}$ is strictly exogenous conditional on c_i. Further, assume that $D(c_i|\mathbf{z}_{i1},\ldots,\mathbf{z}_{iT}) = D(c_i|\bar{\mathbf{z}}_i)$, where $\bar{\mathbf{z}}_i = T^{-1}(\mathbf{z}_{i1} + \ldots + \mathbf{z}_{iT})$ is the time average. Assuming that well-behaved, correctly-specifed conditional densities are available, how do we choose $\mathbf{x}_{it}$ to make part a applicable?

Answer:

a. This is true, because, by the general theory for partial MLE, we know that $E[\mathbf{s}_{it}(\boldsymbol{\theta}_o)|\mathbf{x}_{it}] = \mathbf{0}$, $t = 1,\ldots,T$. But if $D(y_{it}|\mathbf{x}_{i1},\ldots,\mathbf{x}_{iT}) = D(y_{it}|\mathbf{x}_{it})$ then, for any function $\mathbf{m}_t(y_{it},\mathbf{x}_{it})$, $E[\mathbf{m}_t(y_{it},\mathbf{x}_{it})|\mathbf{x}_{i1},\ldots,\mathbf{x}_{iT}] = E[\mathbf{m}_t(y_{it},\mathbf{x}_{it})|\mathbf{x}_{it}]$, including the score function.

b. No. Strict exogeneity and complete dynamic specification of the conditional density are entirely different. Saying that $D(y_{it}|\mathbf{x}_{i1},\ldots,\mathbf{x}_{iT})$ does not depend on $\mathbf{x}_{is}$, $s \neq t$, says nothing about whether y_{ir}, $r < t$, appears in $D(y_{it}|\mathbf{x}_{it},y_{i,t-1},\mathbf{x}_{i,t-1},\ldots)$.

c. We take $\mathbf{x}_{it} = (\mathbf{z}_{it},\bar{\mathbf{z}}_i)$, $t = 1,\ldots,T$. If $g_t(y_t|\mathbf{z}_t,c;\boldsymbol{\gamma})$ is correctly specified for the density of y_{it} given $(\mathbf{z}_{it} = \mathbf{z}_t, c_i = c)$, and $h(c|\bar{\mathbf{z}};\boldsymbol{\delta})$ is correctly specified for the density of c_i given $\bar{\mathbf{z}}_i = \bar{\mathbf{z}}$, then the density of y_{it} given $(\mathbf{z}_{it},\mathbf{z}_i)$ is obtained as

$$f_t(y_t|\mathbf{z}_{it},\mathbf{z}_i;\boldsymbol{\theta}_o) = \int_{\mathcal{C}} g_t(y_t|\mathbf{z}_{it},c;\boldsymbol{\gamma}_o)h(c|\bar{\mathbf{z}}_i;\boldsymbol{\delta}_o)\nu(dc).$$

Under the assumptions given, $D(y_{it}|\mathbf{z}_{i1},\ldots,\mathbf{z}_{iT},\bar{\mathbf{z}}_i) = D(y_{it}|\mathbf{z}_{it},\bar{\mathbf{z}}_i)$, $t = 1,\ldots,T$. However, we have not eliminated the serial dependence in $\{y_{it}\}$ after only conditioning on $(\mathbf{z}_{it},\bar{\mathbf{z}}_i)$: the part of c_i not explained by $\bar{\mathbf{z}}_i$ affects y_{it} in each time period.

SOLUTIONS TO CHAPTER 14 PROBLEMS

14.1. a. The simplest way to estimate (14.35) is by 2SLS, using instruments $(\mathbf{x}_1,\mathbf{x}_2)$. Nonlinear functions of these can be added to the instrument list -- these would generally improve efficiency if $\gamma_2 \neq 1$. If $E(u_2^2|\mathbf{x}) = \sigma_2^2$, 2SLS using the given list of instruments is the efficient, single equation GMM estimator. Otherwise, the optimal weighting matrix that allows heteroskedasticity of unknown form should be used. Finally, one could try to use the optimal instruments derived in section 14.5.3. Even under homoskedasticity, these are difficult, if not impossible, to find analytically if $\gamma_2 \neq 1$.

b. No. If $\gamma_1 = 0$, the parameter γ_2 does not appear in the model. Of course, if we knew $\gamma_1 = 0$, we would consistently estimate $\boldsymbol{\delta}_1$ by OLS.

c. We can see this by obtaining $E(y_1|\mathbf{x})$:

$$\begin{aligned} E(y_1|\mathbf{x}) &= \mathbf{x}_1\boldsymbol{\delta}_1 + \gamma_1 E(y_2^{\gamma_2}|\mathbf{x}) + E(u_1|\mathbf{x}) \\ &= \mathbf{x}_1\boldsymbol{\delta}_1 + \gamma_1 E(y_2^{\gamma_2}|\mathbf{x}). \end{aligned}$$

Now, when $\gamma_2 \neq 1$, $E(y_2^{\gamma_2}|\mathbf{x}) \neq [E(y_2|\mathbf{x})]^{\gamma_2}$, so we cannot write

$$E(y_1|\mathbf{x}) = \mathbf{x}_1\boldsymbol{\delta}_1 + \gamma_1(\mathbf{x}\boldsymbol{\delta}_2)^{\gamma_2};$$

in fact, we cannot find $E(y_1|\mathbf{x})$ without more assumptions. While the regression y_2 on $\mathbf{x}_2$ consistently estimates $\boldsymbol{\delta}_2$, the two-step NLS estimator of y_{i1} on $\mathbf{x}_{i1}$, $(\mathbf{x}_i\hat{\boldsymbol{\delta}}_2)^{\gamma_2}$ will not be consistent for $\boldsymbol{\delta}_1$ and γ_2. (This is an example of a "forbidden regression.") When $\gamma_2 = 1$, the plug-in method works: it is just the usual 2SLS estimator.

14.3. Let $\mathbf{Z}_i^*$ be the $G \times G$ matrix of optimal instruments in (14.63), where we suppress its dependence on $\mathbf{x}_i$. Let $\mathbf{Z}_i$ be a $G \times L$ matrix that is a function of $\mathbf{x}_i$ and let Ξ_o be the probability limit of the weighting matrix. Then the asymptotic variance of the GMM estimator has the form (14.10) with $\mathbf{G}_o = \mathrm{E}[\mathbf{Z}_i'\mathbf{R}_o(\mathbf{x}_i)]$. So, in (14.54), take $\mathbf{A} \equiv \mathbf{G}_o'\Xi_o\mathbf{G}_o$ and $\mathbf{s}(\mathbf{w}_i) \equiv \mathbf{G}_o'\Xi_o\mathbf{Z}_i'\mathbf{r}(\mathbf{w}_i,\boldsymbol{\theta}_o)$. The optimal score function is $\mathbf{s}^*(\mathbf{w}_i) \equiv \mathbf{R}_o(\mathbf{x}_i)'\Omega_o(\mathbf{x}_i)^{-1}\mathbf{r}(\mathbf{w}_i,\boldsymbol{\theta}_o)$. Now we can verify (14.57) with $\rho = 1$:

$$
\begin{aligned}
\mathrm{E}[\mathbf{s}(\mathbf{w}_i)\mathbf{s}^*(\mathbf{w}_i)'] &= \mathbf{G}_o'\Xi_o\mathrm{E}[\mathbf{Z}_i'\mathbf{r}(\mathbf{w}_i,\boldsymbol{\theta}_o)\mathbf{r}(\mathbf{w}_i,\boldsymbol{\theta}_o)'\Omega_o(\mathbf{x}_i)^{-1}\mathbf{R}_o(\mathbf{x}_i)] \\
&= \mathbf{G}_o'\Xi_o\mathrm{E}[\mathbf{Z}_i'\mathrm{E}\{\mathbf{r}(\mathbf{w}_i,\boldsymbol{\theta}_o)\mathbf{r}(\mathbf{w}_i,\boldsymbol{\theta}_o)'|\mathbf{x}_i\}\Omega_o(\mathbf{x}_i)^{-1}\mathbf{R}_o(\mathbf{x}_i)] \\
&= \mathbf{G}_o'\Xi_o\mathrm{E}[\mathbf{Z}_i'\Omega_o(\mathbf{x}_i)\Omega_o(\mathbf{x}_i)^{-1}\mathbf{R}_o(\mathbf{x}_i)] = \mathbf{G}_o'\Xi_o\mathbf{G}_o = \mathbf{A}.
\end{aligned}
$$

14.5. We can write the unrestricted linear projection as

$$y_{it} = \pi_{t0} + \mathbf{x}_i\boldsymbol{\pi}_t + v_{it}, \quad t = 1,2,3,$$

where $\boldsymbol{\pi}_t$ is $1 + 3K \times 1$, and then $\boldsymbol{\pi}$ is the $3 + 9K \times 1$ vector obtained by stacking the $\boldsymbol{\pi}_t$. Let $\boldsymbol{\theta} = (\psi,\boldsymbol{\lambda}_1',\boldsymbol{\lambda}_2',\boldsymbol{\lambda}_3',\boldsymbol{\beta}')'$. With the restrictions imposed on the $\boldsymbol{\pi}_t$ we have

$$
\begin{aligned}
&\pi_{t0} = \psi, \; t = 1,2,3, \; \boldsymbol{\pi}_1 = [(\boldsymbol{\lambda}_1 + \boldsymbol{\beta})',\boldsymbol{\lambda}_2',\boldsymbol{\lambda}_3']', \\
&\boldsymbol{\pi}_2 = [\boldsymbol{\lambda}_1',(\boldsymbol{\lambda}_2 + \boldsymbol{\beta})',\boldsymbol{\lambda}_3']', \; \boldsymbol{\pi}_3 = [\boldsymbol{\lambda}_1',\boldsymbol{\lambda}_2',(\boldsymbol{\lambda}_3 + \boldsymbol{\beta})']'.
\end{aligned}
$$

Therefore, we can write $\boldsymbol{\pi} = \mathbf{H}\boldsymbol{\theta}$ for the $(3 + 9K) \times (1 + 4K)$ matrix $\mathbf{H}$ defined by

$$
\mathbf{H} = \begin{pmatrix}
1 & \mathbf{0} & \mathbf{0} & \mathbf{0} & \mathbf{0} \\
0 & \mathbf{I}_K & \mathbf{0} & \mathbf{0} & \mathbf{I}_K \\
0 & \mathbf{0} & \mathbf{I}_K & \mathbf{0} & \mathbf{0} \\
0 & \mathbf{0} & \mathbf{0} & \mathbf{I}_K & \mathbf{0} \\
1 & \mathbf{0} & \mathbf{0} & \mathbf{0} & \mathbf{0} \\
0 & \mathbf{I}_K & \mathbf{0} & \mathbf{0} & \mathbf{0} \\
0 & \mathbf{0} & \mathbf{I}_K & \mathbf{0} & \mathbf{I}_K \\
0 & \mathbf{0} & \mathbf{0} & \mathbf{I}_K & \mathbf{0} \\
1 & \mathbf{0} & \mathbf{0} & \mathbf{0} & \mathbf{0} \\
0 & \mathbf{I}_K & \mathbf{0} & \mathbf{0} & \mathbf{0} \\
0 & \mathbf{0} & \mathbf{I}_K & \mathbf{0} & \mathbf{0} \\
0 & \mathbf{0} & \mathbf{0} & \mathbf{I}_K & \mathbf{I}_K
\end{pmatrix}.
$$

14.6. By the hint, it suffices to show that

$$[\text{Avar}\ \sqrt{N}(\hat{\boldsymbol{\theta}} - \boldsymbol{\theta}_o)]^{-1} - [\text{Avar}\ \sqrt{N}(\tilde{\boldsymbol{\theta}} - \boldsymbol{\theta}_o)]^{-1}$$

is p.s.d. This difference is $\mathbf{H}_o'\Xi_o^{-1}\mathbf{H}_o - \mathbf{H}_o'\boldsymbol{\Lambda}_o^{-1}\mathbf{H}_o = \mathbf{H}_o'(\Xi_o^{-1} - \boldsymbol{\Lambda}_o^{-1})\mathbf{H}_o$. This is positive semi-definite if $\Xi_o^{-1} - \boldsymbol{\Lambda}_o^{-1}$ is p.s.d., which again holds by the hint because $\boldsymbol{\Lambda}_o - \Xi_o$ is assumed to be p.s.d.

14.7. With $\mathbf{h}(\boldsymbol{\theta}) = \mathbf{H}\boldsymbol{\theta}$, the minimization problem becomes

$$\min_{\boldsymbol{\theta}\in\mathbb{R}^P} (\hat{\boldsymbol{\pi}} - \mathbf{H}\boldsymbol{\theta})'\hat{\Xi}^{-1}(\hat{\boldsymbol{\pi}} - \mathbf{H}\boldsymbol{\theta}),$$

where it is assumed that no restrictions are placed on $\boldsymbol{\theta}$. The first order condition is easily seen to be

$$-2\mathbf{H}'\hat{\Xi}^{-1}(\hat{\boldsymbol{\pi}} - \mathbf{H}\hat{\boldsymbol{\theta}}) = \mathbf{0} \quad \text{or} \quad (\mathbf{H}'\hat{\Xi}^{-1}\mathbf{H})\hat{\boldsymbol{\theta}} = \mathbf{H}'\hat{\Xi}^{-1}\hat{\boldsymbol{\pi}}.$$

Therefore, assuming $\mathbf{H}'\hat{\Xi}^{-1}\mathbf{H}$ is nonsingular -- which occurs w.p.a.1. when $\mathbf{H}'\Xi_o^{-1}\mathbf{H}$ -- is nonsingular -- we have $\hat{\boldsymbol{\theta}} = (\mathbf{H}'\hat{\Xi}^{-1}\mathbf{H})^{-1}\mathbf{H}'\hat{\Xi}^{-1}\hat{\boldsymbol{\pi}}$.

14.9. We have to verify equations (14.55) and (14.56) for the random effects and fixed effects estimators. The choices of $\mathbf{s}_{i1}$, $\mathbf{s}_{i2}$ (with added i subscripts for clarity), $\mathbf{A}_1$, and $\mathbf{A}_2$ are given in the hint. Now, from Chapter 10, we know that $\text{E}(\mathbf{r}_i\mathbf{r}_i'|\mathbf{x}_i) = \sigma_u^2\mathbf{I}_T$ under RE.1, RE.2, and RE.3, where $\mathbf{r}_i = \mathbf{v}_i - \lambda\mathbf{j}_T\bar{v}_i$. Therefore, $\text{E}(\mathbf{s}_{i1}\mathbf{s}_{i1}') = \text{E}(\check{\mathbf{X}}_i'\mathbf{r}_i\mathbf{r}_i'\check{\mathbf{X}}_i) = \sigma_u^2\text{E}(\check{\mathbf{X}}_i'\check{\mathbf{X}}_i) \equiv \sigma_u^2\mathbf{A}_1$ by the usual iterated expectations argument. This means that, in (14.55), $\rho \equiv \sigma_u^2$. Now, we just need to verify (14.56) for this choice of ρ. But $\mathbf{s}_{i2}\mathbf{s}_{i1}' = \ddot{\mathbf{X}}_i'\mathbf{u}_i\mathbf{r}_i'\check{\mathbf{X}}_i$. Now, as described in the hint, $\ddot{\mathbf{X}}_i'\mathbf{r}_i = \ddot{\mathbf{X}}_i'(\mathbf{v}_i - \lambda\mathbf{j}_T\bar{v}_i) = \ddot{\mathbf{X}}_i'\mathbf{v}_i = \ddot{\mathbf{X}}_i'(c_i\mathbf{j}_T + \mathbf{u}_i) = \ddot{\mathbf{X}}_i'\mathbf{u}_i$. So $\mathbf{s}_{i2}\mathbf{s}_{i1}' = \ddot{\mathbf{X}}_i'\mathbf{r}_i\mathbf{r}_i'\check{\mathbf{X}}_i$ and therefore $\text{E}(\mathbf{s}_{i2}\mathbf{s}_{i1}'|\mathbf{x}_i) = \ddot{\mathbf{X}}_i'\text{E}(\mathbf{r}_i\mathbf{r}_i'|\mathbf{x}_i)\check{\mathbf{X}}_i = \sigma_u^2\ddot{\mathbf{X}}_i'\check{\mathbf{X}}_i$. It follows that $\text{E}(\mathbf{s}_{i2}\mathbf{s}_{i1}') = \sigma_u^2\text{E}(\ddot{\mathbf{X}}_i'\check{\mathbf{X}}_i)$. To finish off the proof, note that $\ddot{\mathbf{X}}_i'\check{\mathbf{X}}_i = \ddot{\mathbf{X}}_i'(\mathbf{X}_i - \lambda \mathbf{j}_T \bar{\mathbf{x}}_i) = \ddot{\mathbf{X}}_i'\mathbf{X}_i = \ddot{\mathbf{X}}_i'\ddot{\mathbf{X}}_i$. This verifies (14.56) with $\rho = \sigma_u^2$.

SOLUTIONS TO CHAPTER 15 PROBLEMS

15.1. a. Since the regressors are all orthogonal by construction -- $dk_i \cdot dm_i = 0$ for $k \neq m$, and all i -- the coefficient on dm is obtained from the regression y_i on dm_i, $i = 1,\ldots,N$. But this is easily seen to be the fraction of y_i in the sample falling into category m. Therefore, the fitted values are just the cell frequencies, and these are necessarily in [0,1].

b. The fitted values for each category will be the same. If we drop $d1$ but add an overall intercept, the overall intercept is the cell frequency for the first category, and the coefficient on dm becomes the difference in cell frequency between category m and category one, $m = 2, \ldots, M$.

15.3. a. If $\mathrm{P}(y = 1|\mathbf{z}_1, z_2) = \Phi(\mathbf{z}_1\boldsymbol{\delta}_1 + \gamma_1 z_2 + \gamma_2 z_2^2)$ then

$$\frac{\partial \mathrm{P}(y = 1|\mathbf{z}_1, z_2)}{\partial z_2} = (\gamma_1 + 2\gamma_2 z_2)\cdot\phi(\mathbf{z}_1\boldsymbol{\delta}_1 + \gamma_1 z_2 + \gamma_2 z_2^2);$$

for given $\mathbf{z}$, this is estimated as

$$(\hat{\gamma}_1 + 2\hat{\gamma}_2 z_2)\cdot\phi(\mathbf{z}_1\hat{\boldsymbol{\delta}}_1 + \hat{\gamma}_1 z_2 + \hat{\gamma}_2 z_2^2),$$

where, of course, the estimates are the probit estimates.

b. In the model

$$\mathrm{P}(y = 1|\mathbf{z}_1, z_2, d_1) = \Phi(\mathbf{z}_1\boldsymbol{\delta}_1 + \gamma_1 z_2 + \gamma_2 d_1 + \gamma_3 z_2 d_1),$$

the partial effect of z_2 is

$$\frac{\partial \mathrm{P}(y = 1|\mathbf{z}_1, z_2, d_1)}{\partial z_2} = (\gamma_1 + \gamma_3 d_1)\cdot\phi(\mathbf{z}_1\boldsymbol{\delta}_1 + \gamma_1 z_2 + \gamma_2 d_1 + \gamma_3 z_2 d_1).$$

The effect of d_1 is measured as the difference in the probabilities at $d_1 = 1$ and $d_1 = 0$:

$$\mathrm{P}(y = 1|\mathbf{z}, d_1 = 1) - \mathrm{P}(y = 1|\mathbf{z}, d_1 = 0)$$

$$= \Phi[\mathbf{z}_1\boldsymbol{\delta}_1 + (\gamma_1 + \gamma_3)z_2 + \gamma_2] - \Phi(\mathbf{z}_1\boldsymbol{\delta}_1 + \gamma_1 z_2).$$

Again, to estimate these effects at given $\mathbf{z}$ and -- in the first case, d_1 -- we just replace the parameters with their probit estimates, and use average or other interesting values of $\mathbf{z}$.

c. We would apply the delta method from Chapter 3. Thus, we would require the full variance matrix of the probit estimates as well as the gradient of the expression of interest, such as $(\gamma_1 + 2\gamma_2 z_2)\cdot\phi(\mathbf{z}_1\boldsymbol{\delta}_1 + \gamma_1 z_2 + \gamma_2 z_2^2)$, with respect to all probit parameters. (Not with respect to the z_j.)

15.4. This is the kind of statement that arises out of failure to distinguish between the underlying latent variable model and the model for $P(y = 1|\mathbf{x})$. The linear probability model assumes $P(y = 1|\mathbf{x}) = \mathbf{x}\boldsymbol{\beta}$ while, for example, the probit model assumes that $P(y = 1|\mathbf{x}) = \Phi(\mathbf{x}\boldsymbol{\beta})$. Thus, both models make very particular functional form assumptions on the response probabilities. The fact that the probit model can be derived from a latent variable model with a normal, homoskedastic error does not make it less plausible than the LPM. In fact, we know that the probit functional form has some attractive properties that the linear model does not have: $\Phi(\mathbf{x}\boldsymbol{\beta})$ is always between zero and one, and the marginal effect of any x_j is diminishing after some point. Incidentally, the LPM can be obtained from a latent variable model by assuming that e has a uniform distribution over [-1,1] (actually, any symmetric, uniform interval will do).

15.5. a. If $P(y = 1|\mathbf{z},q) = \Phi(\mathbf{z}_1\boldsymbol{\delta}_1 + \gamma_1 z_2 q)$ then

$$\frac{\partial P(y = 1|\mathbf{z},q)}{\partial z_2} = \gamma_1 q\cdot\phi(\mathbf{z}_1\boldsymbol{\delta}_1 + \gamma_1 z_2 q),$$

assuming that z_2 is not functionally related to $\mathbf{z}_1$.

b. Write $y^* = \mathbf{z}_1\boldsymbol{\delta}_1 + r$, where $r = \gamma_1 z_2 q + e$, and e is independent of $(\mathbf{z},q)$ with a standard normal distribution. Because q is assumed independent of $\mathbf{z}$, $q|\mathbf{z} \sim \text{Normal}(0,\gamma_1^2 z_2^2 + 1)$; this follows because $E(r|\mathbf{z}) = \gamma_1 z_2 E(q|\mathbf{z}) + E(e|\mathbf{z}) = 0$. Also,

$$\text{Var}(r|\mathbf{z}) = \gamma_1^2 z_2^2 \text{Var}(q|\mathbf{z}) + \text{Var}(e|\mathbf{z}) + 2\gamma_1 z_2 \text{Cov}(q,e|\mathbf{z}) = \gamma_1^2 z_2^2 + 1$$

because $\text{Cov}(q,e|\mathbf{z}) = 0$ by independence between e and $(\mathbf{z},q)$. Thus, $r/\sqrt{\gamma_1^2 z_2^2 + 1}$ has a standard normal distribution independent of $\mathbf{z}$. It follows that

$$P(y = 1|\mathbf{z}) = \Phi\left(\mathbf{z}_1\boldsymbol{\delta}_1/\sqrt{\gamma_1^2 z_2^2 + 1}\right). \tag{15.90}$$

c. Because $P(y = 1|\mathbf{z})$ depends only on γ_1^2, this is what we can estimate along with $\boldsymbol{\delta}_1$. (For example, $\gamma_1 = -2$ and $\gamma_1 = 2$ give exactly the same model for $P(y = 1|\mathbf{z})$.) This is why we define $\rho_1 = \gamma_1^2$. Testing H_0: $\rho_1 = 0$ is most easily done using the score or LM test because, under H_0, we have a standard probit model. Let $\hat{\boldsymbol{\delta}}_1$ denote the probit estimates under the null that $\rho_1 = 0$. Define $\hat{\Phi}_i = \Phi(\mathbf{z}_{i1}\hat{\boldsymbol{\delta}}_1)$, $\hat{\phi}_i = \phi(\mathbf{z}_{i1}\hat{\boldsymbol{\delta}}_1)$, $\hat{u}_i = y_i - \hat{\Phi}_i$, and $\tilde{u}_i \equiv \hat{u}_i/\sqrt{\hat{\Phi}_i(1 - \hat{\Phi}_i)}$ (the standardized residuals). The gradient of the mean function in (15.90) with respect to $\boldsymbol{\delta}_1$, evaluated under the null estimates, is simply $\hat{\phi}_i\mathbf{z}_{i1}$. The only other quantity needed is the gradient with respect to ρ_1 evaluated at the null estimates. But the partial derivative of (15.90) with respect to ρ_1 is, for each i,

$$-(\mathbf{z}_{i1}\boldsymbol{\delta}_1)(z_{i2}^2/2)\left(\rho_1 z_{i2}^2 + 1\right)^{-3/2}\phi\left(\mathbf{z}_{i1}\boldsymbol{\delta}_1/\sqrt{\gamma_1^2 z_{i2}^2 + 1}\right).$$

When we evaluate this at $\rho_1 = 0$ and $\hat{\boldsymbol{\delta}}_1$ we get $-(\mathbf{z}_{i1}\hat{\boldsymbol{\delta}}_1)(z_{i2}^2/2)\hat{\phi}_i$. Then, the score statistic can be obtained as NR_u^2 from the regression

$$\tilde{u}_i \quad \text{on} \quad \hat{\phi}_i\mathbf{z}_{i1}/\sqrt{\hat{\Phi}_i(1 - \hat{\Phi}_i)},\ (\mathbf{z}_{i1}\hat{\boldsymbol{\delta}}_1)z_{i2}^2\hat{\phi}_i/\sqrt{\hat{\Phi}_i(1 - \hat{\Phi}_i)};$$

under H_0, $NR_u^2 \overset{a}{\sim} \chi_1^2$.

d. The model can be estimated by MLE using the formulation with ρ_1 in place of γ_1^2. But this is not a standard probit estimation.

15.7. a. The following Stata output is for part a:

```
. reg arr86 pcnv avgsen tottime ptime86 inc86 black hispan born60

      Source |       SS       df       MS              Number of obs =    2725
-------------+------------------------------           F(  8,  2716) =   30.48
       Model |  44.9720916     8  5.62151145           Prob > F      =  0.0000
    Residual |  500.844422  2716  .184405163           R-squared     =  0.0824
-------------+------------------------------           Adj R-squared =  0.0797
       Total |  545.816514  2724   .20037317           Root MSE      =  .42942

------------------------------------------------------------------------------
       arr86 |      Coef.   Std. Err.       t     P>|t|     [95% Conf. Interval]
-------------+----------------------------------------------------------------
        pcnv |  -.1543802   .0209336     -7.37   0.000     -.1954275   -.1133329
      avgsen |   .0035024   .0063417      0.55   0.581     -.0089326    .0159374
     tottime |  -.0020613   .0048884     -0.42   0.673     -.0116466     .007524
     ptime86 |  -.0215953   .0044679     -4.83   0.000     -.0303561   -.0128344
       inc86 |  -.0012248    .000127     -9.65   0.000     -.0014738   -.0009759
       black |   .1617183   .0235044      6.88   0.000      .1156299    .2078066
      hispan |   .0892586   .0205592      4.34   0.000      .0489454    .1295718
      born60 |   .0028698   .0171986      0.17   0.867     -.0308539    .0365936
       _cons |   .3609831   .0160927     22.43   0.000       .329428    .3925382
------------------------------------------------------------------------------

. reg arr86 pcnv avgsen tottime ptime86 inc86 black hispan born60, robust

Regression with robust standard errors                 Number of obs =    2725
                                                       F(  8,  2716) =   37.59
                                                       Prob > F      =  0.0000
                                                       R-squared     =  0.0824
                                                       Root MSE      =  .42942

------------------------------------------------------------------------------
             |               Robust
       arr86 |      Coef.   Std. Err.       t     P>|t|     [95% Conf. Interval]
-------------+----------------------------------------------------------------
        pcnv |  -.1543802    .018964     -8.14   0.000     -.1915656   -.1171948
      avgsen |   .0035024   .0058876      0.59   0.552     -.0080423    .0150471
     tottime |  -.0020613   .0042256     -0.49   0.626      -.010347    .0062244
     ptime86 |  -.0215953   .0027532     -7.84   0.000     -.0269938   -.0161967
       inc86 |  -.0012248   .0001141    -10.73   0.000     -.0014487    -.001001
       black |   .1617183   .0255279      6.33   0.000      .1116622    .2117743
      hispan |   .0892586   .0210689      4.24   0.000      .0479459    .1305714
      born60 |   .0028698   .0171596      0.17   0.867     -.0307774     .036517
       _cons |   .3609831   .0167081     21.61   0.000      .3282214    .3937449
```

The estimated effect from increasing *pcnv* from .25 to .75 is about -.154(.5) = -.077, so the probability of arrest falls by about 7.7 points. There are no important differences between the usual and robust standard errors. In fact, in a couple of cases the robust standard errors are notably smaller.

b. The robust statistic and its *p*-value are gotten by using the "test" command after appending "robust" to the regression command:

```
. test avgsen tottime

 ( 1)  avgsen = 0.0
 ( 2)  tottime = 0.0

       F(  2,  2716) =    0.18
            Prob > F =    0.8320


. qui reg arr86 pcnv avgsen tottime ptime86 inc86 black hispan born60

. test avgsen tottime

 ( 1)  avgsen = 0.0
 ( 2)  tottime = 0.0

       F(  2,  2716) =    0.18
            Prob > F =    0.8360
```

c. The probit model is estimated as follows:

```
. probit arr86 pcnv avgsen tottime ptime86 inc86 black hispan born60

Iteration 0:   log likelihood = -1608.1837
Iteration 1:   log likelihood = -1486.3157
Iteration 2:   log likelihood = -1483.6458
Iteration 3:   log likelihood = -1483.6406

Probit estimates                                  Number of obs   =       2725
                                                  LR chi2(8)      =     249.09
                                                  Prob > chi2     =     0.0000
Log likelihood = -1483.6406                       Pseudo R2       =     0.0774

------------------------------------------------------------------------------
       arr86 |      Coef.   Std. Err.       z     P>|z|     [95% Conf. Interval]
```

```
-------------+----------------------------------------------------------------
        pcnv |  -.5529248   .0720778    -7.67   0.000    -.6941947   -.4116549
      avgsen |   .0127395   .0212318     0.60   0.548     -.028874    .0543531
     tottime |  -.0076486   .0168844    -0.45   0.651    -.0407414    .0254442
     ptime86 |  -.0812017    .017963    -4.52   0.000    -.1164085   -.0459949
       inc86 |  -.0046346   .0004777    -9.70   0.000    -.0055709   -.0036983
       black |   .4666076   .0719687     6.48   0.000     .3255516    .6076635
      hispan |   .2911005   .0654027     4.45   0.000     .1629135    .4192875
      born60 |   .0112074   .0556843     0.20   0.840    -.0979318    .1203466
       _cons |  -.3138331   .0512999    -6.12   0.000    -.4143791    -.213287
------------------------------------------------------------------------------
```

Now, we must compute the difference in the normal cdf at the two different values of *pcnv*, *black* = 1, *hispan* = 0, *born60* = 1, and at the average values of the remaining variables:

```
. sum avgsen tottime ptime86 inc86

Variable |     Obs        Mean   Std. Dev.       Min        Max
---------+-----------------------------------------------------
  avgsen |    2725    .6322936   3.508031          0       59.2
 tottime |    2725    .8387523   4.607019          0       63.4
 ptime86 |    2725     .387156   1.950051          0         12
   inc86 |    2725    54.96705   66.62721          0        541


. di -.313 + .0127*.632 - .0076*.839 - .0812*.387 - .0046*54.97 + .467 + .0112
-.1174364

. di normprob(-.553*.75 - .117) - normprob(-.553*.25 - .117)
-.10181543
```

This last command shows that the probability falls by about .10, which is somewhat larger than the effect obtained from the LPM.

d. To obtain the percent correctly predicted for each outcome, we first generate the predicted values of *arr86* as described on page 465:

```
. predict phat
(option p assumed; Pr(arr86))

. gen arr86h = phat > .5

. tab arr86h arr86

           |         arr86
```

```
    arr86h |         0          1 |     Total
-----------+----------------------+----------
         0 |      1903        677 |      2580
         1 |        67         78 |       145
-----------+----------------------+----------
     Total |      1970        755 |      2725
```

```
. di 1903/1970
.96598985

. di 78/755
.10331126
```

For men who were not arrested, the probit predicts correctly about 96.6% of the time. Unfortunately, for the men who were arrested, the probit is correct only about 10.3% of the time. The overall percent correctly predicted is quite high, but we cannot very well predict the outcome we would most like to predict.

e. Adding the quadratic terms gives

```
. probit arr86 pcnv avgsen tottime ptime86 inc86 black hispan born60 pcnvsq
pt86sq inc86sq

Iteration 0:   log likelihood = -1608.1837
Iteration 1:   log likelihood = -1452.2089
Iteration 2:   log likelihood = -1444.3151
Iteration 3:   log likelihood = -1441.8535
Iteration 4:   log likelihood =  -1440.268
Iteration 5:   log likelihood = -1439.8166
Iteration 6:   log likelihood = -1439.8005
Iteration 7:   log likelihood = -1439.8005

Probit estimates                                  Number of obs   =       2725
                                                  LR chi2(11)     =     336.77
                                                  Prob > chi2     =     0.0000
Log likelihood = -1439.8005                       Pseudo R2       =     0.1047

------------------------------------------------------------------------------
       arr86 |      Coef.   Std. Err.       z     P>|z|      [95% Conf. Interval]
-------------+----------------------------------------------------------------
        pcnv |   .2167615   .2604937     0.83   0.405     -.2937968    .7273198
      avgsen |   .0139969   .0244972     0.57   0.568     -.0340166    .0620105
     tottime |  -.0178158   .0199703    -0.89   0.372      -.056957    .0213253
     ptime86 |   .7449712   .1438485     5.18   0.000      .4630333    1.026909
       inc86 |  -.0058786   .0009851    -5.97   0.000     -.0078094   -.0039478
```

```
      black |   .4368131   .0733798     5.95   0.000     .2929913     .580635
     hispan |   .2663945    .067082     3.97   0.000     .1349163    .3978727
     born60 |  -.0145223   .0566913    -0.26   0.798    -.1256351    .0965905
    pcnvsq |  -.8570512   .2714575    -3.16   0.002    -1.389098   -.3250042
     pt86sq |  -.1035031   .0224234    -4.62   0.000    -.1474522    -.059554
    inc86sq |   8.75e-06   4.28e-06     2.04   0.041     3.63e-07    .0000171
      _cons |   -.337362   .0562665    -6.00   0.000    -.4476423   -.2270817
------------------------------------------------------------------------------

note: 51 failures and 0 successes completely determined.

. test pcnvsq pt86sq inc86sq

 ( 1)  pcnvsq = 0.0
 ( 2)  pt86sq = 0.0
 ( 3)  inc86sq = 0.0

          chi2(  3) =   38.54
        Prob > chi2 =    0.0000
```

The quadratics are individually and jointly significant. The quadratic in *pcnv* means that, at low levels of *pcnv*, there is actually a positive relationship between probability of arrest and *pcnv*, which does not make much sense. The turning point is easily found as $.217/(2*.857) \approx .127$, which means that there is an estimated deterrent effect over most of the range of *pcnv*.

15.9. a. Let $P(y = 1|\mathbf{x}) = \mathbf{x}\boldsymbol{\beta}$, where $x_1 = 1$. Then, for each i,

$$\ell_i(\boldsymbol{\beta}) = y_i \log(\mathbf{x}_i\boldsymbol{\beta}) + (1 - y_i)\log(1 - \mathbf{x}_i\boldsymbol{\beta}),$$

which is only well-defined for $0 < \mathbf{x}_i\boldsymbol{\beta} < 1$.

b. For any possible estimate $\hat{\boldsymbol{\beta}}$, the log-likelihood function is well-defined only if $0 < \mathbf{x}_i\hat{\boldsymbol{\beta}} < 1$ for all $i = 1,\ldots,N$. Therefore, during the iterations to obtain the MLE, this condition must be checked. It may be impossible to find an estimate that satisfies these inequalities for every observation, especially if N is large.

c. This follows from the KLIC: the true density of y given $\mathbf{x}$ -- evaluated at the true values, of course -- maximizes the KLIC. Since the MLEs are consistent for the unknown parameters, asymptotically the true density will produce the highest average log likelihood function. So, just as we can use an R-squared to choose among different functional forms for $E(y|\mathbf{x})$, we can use values of the log-likelihood to choose among different models for $P(y = 1|\mathbf{x})$ when y is binary.

15.11. We really need to make two assumptions. The first is a conditional independence assumption: given $\mathbf{x}_i = (\mathbf{x}_{i1},\ldots,\mathbf{x}_{iT})$, $(y_{i1},\ldots,y_{iT})$ are independent. This allows us to write

$$f(y_1,\ldots,y_T|\mathbf{x}_i) = f_1(y_1|\mathbf{x}_i)\cdots f_T(y_T|\mathbf{x}_i),$$

that is, the joint density (conditional on $\mathbf{x}_i$) is the product of the marginal densities (each conditional on $\mathbf{x}_i$). The second assumption is a strict exogeneity assumption: $D(y_{it}|\mathbf{x}_i) = D(y_{it}|\mathbf{x}_{it})$, $t = 1,\ldots,T$. When we add the standard assumption for pooled probit -- that $D(y_{it}|\mathbf{x}_{it})$ follows a probit model -- then

$$f(y_1,\ldots,y_T|\mathbf{x}_i) = \prod_{t=1}^{T} [G(\mathbf{x}_{it}\boldsymbol{\beta})]^{y_t}[1 - G(\mathbf{x}_{it}\boldsymbol{\beta})]^{1-y_t},$$

and so pooled probit is conditional MLE.

15.13. a. If there are no covariates, there is no point in using any method other than a straight comparison of means. The estimated probabilities for the treatment and control groups, both before and after the policy change, will be identical across models.

b. Let $d2$ be a binary indicator for the second time period, and let dB be an indicator for the treatment group. Then a probit model to evaluate the treatment effect is

$$P(y = 1|\mathbf{x}) = \Phi(\delta_0 + \delta_1 d2 + \delta_2 dB + \delta_3 d2\cdot dB + \mathbf{x}\boldsymbol{\gamma}),$$

where **x** is a vector of covariates. We would estimate all parameters from a probit of y on 1, $d2$, dB, $d2 \cdot dB$, and **x** using all observations. Once we have the estimates, we need to compute the "difference-in-differences" estimate, which requires either plugging in a value for **x**, say $\bar{\mathbf{x}}$, or averaging the differences across $\mathbf{x}_i$. In the former case, we have

$$\hat{\theta} \equiv [\Phi(\hat{\delta}_0 + \hat{\delta}_1 + \hat{\delta}_2 + \hat{\delta}_3 + \bar{\mathbf{x}}\hat{\boldsymbol{\gamma}}) - \Phi(\hat{\delta}_0 + \hat{\delta}_2 + \bar{\mathbf{x}}\hat{\boldsymbol{\gamma}})] - [\Phi(\hat{\delta}_0 + \hat{\delta}_1 + \bar{\mathbf{x}}\hat{\boldsymbol{\gamma}}) - \Phi(\hat{\delta}_0 + \bar{\mathbf{x}}\hat{\boldsymbol{\gamma}})],$$

and in the latter we have

$$\tilde{\theta} \equiv N^{-1}\sum_{i=1}^{N}\{[\Phi(\hat{\delta}_0 + \hat{\delta}_1 + \hat{\delta}_2 + \hat{\delta}_3 + \mathbf{x}_i\hat{\boldsymbol{\gamma}}) - \Phi(\hat{\delta}_0 + \hat{\delta}_2 + \mathbf{x}_i\hat{\boldsymbol{\gamma}})] - [\Phi(\hat{\delta}_0 + \hat{\delta}_1 + \mathbf{x}_i\hat{\boldsymbol{\gamma}}) - \Phi(\hat{\delta}_0 + \mathbf{x}_i\hat{\boldsymbol{\gamma}})]\}.$$

Both are estimates of the difference, between groups B and A, of the change in the response probability over time.

c. We would have to use the delta method to obtain a valid standard error for either $\hat{\theta}$ or $\tilde{\theta}$.

15.14. a. The following Stata output contains the linear regression results. Since *pctstck* is discrete (taking on only 0, 50, 100), it seems likely that heteroskedasticity is present in a linear model. In fact, the robust standard errors are not very different from the usual ones (not reported).

```
. reg pctstck choice age educ female black married finc25-finc101 wealth89
prftshr, robust

Regression with robust standard errors                 Number of obs =     194
                                                       F( 14,   179) =    2.15
                                                       Prob > F      =  0.0113
                                                       R-squared     =  0.0998
                                                       Root MSE      =  39.134

------------------------------------------------------------------------------
             |               Robust
     pctstck |      Coef.   Std. Err.      t    P>|t|     [95% Conf. Interval]
```

choice	12.04773	5.994437	2.01	0.046	.2188715	23.87658
age	-1.625967	.8327895	-1.95	0.052	-3.269315	.0173813
educ	.7538685	1.172328	0.64	0.521	-1.559493	3.06723
female	1.302856	7.148595	0.18	0.856	-12.80351	15.40922
black	3.967391	8.974971	0.44	0.659	-13.74297	21.67775
married	3.303436	8.369616	0.39	0.694	-13.21237	19.81924
finc25	-18.18567	16.00485	-1.14	0.257	-49.76813	13.39679
finc35	-3.925374	15.86275	-0.25	0.805	-35.22742	27.37668
finc50	-8.128784	15.3762	-0.53	0.598	-38.47072	22.21315
finc75	-17.57921	16.6797	-1.05	0.293	-50.49335	15.33493
finc100	-6.74559	16.7482	-0.40	0.688	-39.7949	26.30372
finc101	-28.34407	16.57814	-1.71	0.089	-61.05781	4.369671
wealth89	-.0026918	.0114136	-0.24	0.814	-.0252142	.0198307
prftshr	15.80791	8.107663	1.95	0.053	-.190984	31.80681
_cons	134.1161	58.87288	2.28	0.024	17.9419	250.2902

b. With relatively few husband-wife pairs -- 23 in this application -- we do not expect big differences in standard errors, and we do not see them:

```
. reg pctstck choice age educ female black married finc25-finc101 wealth89
prftshr, robust cluster(id)

Regression with robust standard errors                 Number of obs =     194
                                                       F( 14,    170) =   2.12
                                                       Prob > F      =  0.0128
                                                       R-squared     =  0.0998
Number of clusters (id) = 171                          Root MSE      =  39.134
```

pctstck	Coef.	Robust Std. Err.	t	P>|t|	[95% Conf.	Interval]
choice	12.04773	6.184085	1.95	0.053	-.1597615	24.25521
age	-1.625967	.8192942	-1.98	0.049	-3.243267	-.0086663
educ	.7538685	1.1803	0.64	0.524	-1.576064	3.083801
female	1.302856	7.000538	0.19	0.853	-12.51632	15.12203
black	3.967391	8.711611	0.46	0.649	-13.22948	21.16426
married	3.303436	8.624168	0.38	0.702	-13.72082	20.32769
finc25	-18.18567	16.82939	-1.08	0.281	-51.40716	15.03583
finc35	-3.925374	16.17574	-0.24	0.809	-35.85656	28.00581
finc50	-8.128784	15.91447	-0.51	0.610	-39.54421	23.28665
finc75	-17.57921	17.2789	-1.02	0.310	-51.68804	16.52963
finc100	-6.74559	17.24617	-0.39	0.696	-40.78983	27.29865
finc101	-28.34407	17.10783	-1.66	0.099	-62.1152	5.427069
wealth89	-.0026918	.0119309	-0.23	0.822	-.0262435	.02086
prftshr	15.80791	8.356266	1.89	0.060	-.6874976	32.30332
_cons	134.1161	58.1316	2.31	0.022	19.36333	248.8688

For later use, the predicted *pctstck* for the person described in the problem, with *choice* = 0, is about 38.37. With choice, it is roughly 50.42.

c. The ordered probit estimates follow, including commands that provide the predictions for *pctstck* with and without choice:

```
. oprobit pctstck choice age educ female black married finc25-finc101 wealth89
 prftshr

Iteration 0:   log likelihood = -212.37031
Iteration 1:   log likelihood =  -202.0094
Iteration 2:   log likelihood =  -201.9865
Iteration 3:   log likelihood =  -201.9865

Ordered probit estimates                          Number of obs   =        194
                                                  LR chi2(14)     =      20.77
                                                  Prob > chi2     =     0.1077
Log likelihood =  -201.9865                       Pseudo R2       =     0.0489

------------------------------------------------------------------------------
     pctstck |      Coef.   Std. Err.      z     P>|z|     [95% Conf. Interval]
-------------+----------------------------------------------------------------
      choice |    .371171   .1841121     2.02   0.044      .010318    .7320241
         age |  -.0500516   .0226063    -2.21   0.027    -.0943591   -.005744
        educ |   .0261382   .0352561     0.74   0.458    -.0429626    .0952389
      female |   .0455642    .206004     0.22   0.825    -.3581963    .4493246
       black |   .0933923   .2820403     0.33   0.741    -.4593965    .6461811
     married |   .0935981   .2332114     0.40   0.688    -.3634878     .550684
      finc25 |  -.5784299    .423162    -1.37   0.172    -1.407812    .2509524
      finc35 |  -.1346721   .4305242    -0.31   0.754    -.9784841    .7091399
      finc50 |  -.2620401   .4265936    -0.61   0.539    -1.098148    .5740681
      finc75 |  -.5662312   .4780035    -1.18   0.236    -1.503101    .3706385
     finc100 |  -.2278963   .4685942    -0.49   0.627    -1.146324    .6905316
     finc101 |  -.8641109   .5291111    -1.63   0.102     -1.90115    .1729279
    wealth89 |  -.0000956   .0003737    -0.26   0.798    -.0008279    .0006368
     prftshr |   .4817182   .2161233     2.23   0.026     .0581243     .905312
-------------+----------------------------------------------------------------
       _cut1 |  -3.087373   1.623765          (Ancillary parameters)
       _cut2 |  -2.053553   1.618611
------------------------------------------------------------------------------

. * The estimated cut points are -3.087 and -2.053.

. * Now compute index to obtain prediction for the person described.
. * First, without choice.
. di  - .050*60 + .026*12 + .046  - .262  - .000096*150
```

```
-2.9184

. * Now, with choice:
. di -2.918 + .371
-2.547

. * Now, compute probabilities.
. * First, P(pctstck = 50):

. di normprob(-2.054 + 2.918) - normprob(-3.087 + 2.918)
.37330773

. * Now, P(pctstck = 100)

. di 1 - normprob(-2.054 + 2.918)
.19379395

. * Now estimate the expected value:

. di 50*.373 + 100*.194
38.05

. * With choice:

. di normprob(-2.054 + 2.547) - normprob(-3.087 + 2.547)
.39439519

. di 1 - normprob(-2.054 + 2.547)
.31100629

. di 50*.394 + 100*.311
50.8

. di 50.8 - 38.05
12.75

. * So, using the ordered probit, the effect of choice for this person is
. * about 12.8 percentage points more in stock, which is not far from the
. * 12.1 points obtained with the linear model.
```

d. We can compute an *R*-squared for the ordered probit model by using the squared correlation between the predicted $pctstck_i$ and the actual. The following Stata session does this, after using the "oprobit" command:

```
. predict p1 p2 p3
(option p assumed; predicted probabilities)
(32 missing values generated)
```

```
. sum p1 p2 p3

    Variable |       Obs        Mean    Std. Dev.       Min        Max
-------------+-----------------------------------------------------
          p1 |       194     .331408    .1327901   .0685269   .8053644
          p2 |       194    .3701685    .0321855   .1655734   .3947809
          p3 |       194    .2984236    .1245914   .0290621   .6747374

. gen pctstcko = 50*p2 + 100*p3
(32 missing values generated)

. corr pctstck pctstcko
(obs=194)

             | pctstck pctstcko
-------------+------------------
     pctstck |   1.0000
    pctstcko |   0.3119   1.0000


. di .321^2
.103041
```

The R-squared for the linear regression was about .100, so the R-squared is only slightly higher for ordered probit. In fact, the correlation between the fitted values for the linear regression and ordered probit is .998, so the fitted values are very similar.

15.15. We should use an interval regression model, that is, ordered probit with known cut points. We would be assuming that the underlying GPA is normally distributed conditional on $\mathbf{x}$, but we only observe interval coded data. (Clearly a conditional normal distribution for the GPAs is at best an approximation.) Along with the β_j -- including an intercept -- we estimate σ^2. The estimated coefficients are interpreted as if we had done a linear regression with actual GPAs.

15.17. a. We obtain the joint density by the product rule, since we have independence conditional on $(\mathbf{x}, c)$:

$$f(y_1,\ldots,y_G|\mathbf{x},c;\boldsymbol{\gamma}_o) = f_1(y_1|\mathbf{x},c;\boldsymbol{\gamma}_o^1)f_2(y_1|\mathbf{x},c;\boldsymbol{\gamma}_o^2)\cdots f_G(y_G|\mathbf{x},c;\boldsymbol{\gamma}_o^G).$$

b. The density of $(y_1,\ldots,y_G)$ given $\mathbf{x}$ is obtained by integrating out with respect to the distribution of c given $\mathbf{x}$:

$$g(y_1,\ldots,y_G|\mathbf{x};\boldsymbol{\gamma}_o) = \int_{-\infty}^{\infty}\left[\prod_{g=1}^{G} f_g(y_g|\mathbf{x},c;\boldsymbol{\gamma}_o^g)\right]h(c|\mathbf{x};\boldsymbol{\delta}_o)dc,$$

where c is a dummy argument of integration. Because c appears in each $\mathrm{D}(y_g|\mathbf{x},c)$, $y_1,\ldots,y_G$ are dependent without conditioning on c.

c. The log likelihood for each i is

$$\log\left[\int_{-\infty}^{\infty}\left(\prod_{g=1}^{G} f_g(y_{ig}|\mathbf{x}_i,c;\boldsymbol{\gamma}^g)\right)h(c|\mathbf{x}_i;\boldsymbol{\delta})dc\right].$$

As expected, this depends only on the observed data, $(\mathbf{x}_i,y_{i1},\ldots,y_{iG})$, and the unknown parameters.

15.19. a, b. Here is the Stata output for black men. I have balanced the panel, so that only men in the sample from 1981 through 1987 appear.

```
. probit employ employ_1 if black

Iteration 0:   log likelihood = -2793.6715
Iteration 1:   log likelihood = -2251.6435
Iteration 2:   log likelihood = -2248.0357
Iteration 3:   log likelihood = -2248.0349

Probit estimates                                  Number of obs   =       4038
                                                  LR chi2(1)      =    1091.27
                                                  Prob > chi2     =     0.0000
Log likelihood = -2248.0349                       Pseudo R2       =     0.1953

------------------------------------------------------------------------------
      employ |      Coef.   Std. Err.       z     P>|z|     [95% Conf. Interval]
-------------+----------------------------------------------------------------
    employ_1 |   1.389433   .0437182     31.78   0.000     1.303747    1.475119
       _cons |  -.5396127   .0281709    -19.15   0.000    -.5948268   -.4843987
------------------------------------------------------------------------------

. di normprob(-.540)
.29459852
```

```
. di normprob(-.540 + 1.389)
.80205935

. di .802 - .295
.507
```

The difference in employment probabilities this year, based on employment status last year, is .507.

c. With year dummies, the story is very similar:

```
. probit employ employ_1 y83-y87 if black

Iteration 0:   log likelihood = -2793.6715
Iteration 1:   log likelihood = -2220.9214
Iteration 2:   log likelihood = -2215.1822
Iteration 3:   log likelihood = -2215.1795

Probit estimates                                  Number of obs   =       4038
                                                  LR chi2(6)      =    1156.98
                                                  Prob > chi2     =     0.0000
Log likelihood = -2215.1795                       Pseudo R2       =     0.2071

------------------------------------------------------------------------------
      employ |      Coef.   Std. Err.       z     P>|z|     [95% Conf. Interval]
-------------+----------------------------------------------------------------
    employ_1 |   1.321349   .0453568    29.13   0.000      1.232452    1.410247
         y83 |   .3427664   .0749844     4.57   0.000      .1957997    .4897331
         y84 |   .4586078   .0755742     6.07   0.000      .3104852    .6067304
         y85 |   .5200576   .0767271     6.78   0.000      .3696753    .6704399
         y86 |   .3936516   .0774703     5.08   0.000      .2418125    .5454907
         y87 |   .5292136   .0773031     6.85   0.000      .3777023    .6807249
       _cons |  -.8850412   .0556041   -15.92   0.000     -.9940233   -.7760591
------------------------------------------------------------------------------

. di normprob(-.885 + .529)
.36092028

. di normprob(-.885 + .529 + 1.321)
.83272759
```

The estimated state dependence in 1987 is about .472. Employment probabilties are generally rising over this period.

d. Here is one way to estimate the unobserved effects model:

```
. gen employ81 = employ if y81
(10428 missing values generated)

. replace employ81 = employ[_n-1] if y82
(1738 real changes made)

. replace employ81 = employ[_n-2] if y83
(1738 real changes made)

. replace employ81 = employ[_n-3] if y84
(1738 real changes made)

. replace employ81 = employ[_n-4] if y85
(1738 real changes made)

. replace employ81 = employ[_n-5] if y86
(1738 real changes made)

. replace employ81 = employ[_n-6] if y87
(1738 real changes made)

. xtprobit employ employ_1 employ81 y83-y87 if black, re

Fitting comparison model:

Iteration 0:   log likelihood = -2793.6715
Iteration 1:   log likelihood = -2207.2397
Iteration 2:   log likelihood = -2200.3265
Iteration 3:   log likelihood = -2200.3214

Fitting full model:

rho =  0.0     log likelihood = -2200.3214
rho =  0.1     log likelihood =  -2189.493
rho =  0.2     log likelihood = -2194.3834
Iteration 0:   log likelihood =  -2189.493
Iteration 1:   log likelihood = -2179.9725
Iteration 2:   log likelihood = -2176.3849
Iteration 3:   log likelihood = -2176.3738
Iteration 4:   log likelihood = -2176.3738

Random-effects probit                           Number of obs      =      4038
Group variable (i) : id                         Number of groups   =       673

Random effects u_i ~ Gaussian                   Obs per group: min =         6
                                                               avg =       6.0
                                                               max =         6

                                                Wald chi2(7)       =    677.59
Log likelihood  = -2176.3738                    Prob > chi2        =    0.0000
```

employ	Coef.	Std. Err.	z	P>|z|	[95% Conf.	Interval]
employ_1	.8987858	.0677035	13.28	0.000	.7660893	1.031482
employ81	.5662849	.088493	6.40	0.000	.3928418	.739728
y83	.4339896	.0804062	5.40	0.000	.2763964	.5915828
y84	.6563064	.0841192	7.80	0.000	.4914358	.821177
y85	.7919761	.0887153	8.93	0.000	.6180972	.9658549
y86	.6896298	.0901566	7.65	0.000	.5129262	.8663335
y87	.8381973	.0910525	9.21	0.000	.6597376	1.016657
_cons	-1.0051	.0660937	-15.21	0.000	-1.134641	-.8755586
/lnsig2u	-1.178755	.1995222			-1.569811	-.7876984
sigma_u	.5546726	.0553347			.4561628	.6744557
rho	.2352762	.0358983			.1722434	.3126631

Likelihood ratio test of rho=0: chibar2(01) = 47.90 Prob >= chibar2 = 0.000

e. There is strong evidence of state dependence conditional on c_i because the coefficient on lagged employment is very significant with t statistic = 13.3. As yet, we do not know how the coefficient .899 into the estimated state dependence. Note that $employ_{81}$ is also very significant, showing that c_i and $employ_{i,81}$ are positively correlated. The estimate of σ_a^2 is $(.555)^2$, or $\hat{\sigma}_a^2 \approx .308$.

f. The average state dependence, where we average out the distribution of c_i, is gotten as follows:

```
. gen prbdif87 = normprob((-1.005 + .838 + .899 + .566*employ81)/sqrt(1 +
.555^2)) - normprob((-1.005 + .838 + .566*employ81)/sqrt(1 + .555^2)) if y87
& black
(11493 missing values generated)

. sum prbdif87 if y87 & black
```

Variable	Obs	Mean	Std. Dev.	Min	Max
prbdif87	673	.2831544	.025709	.2353894	.2969714

The estimated state dependence, averaged across the distribution of c_i, is

.283. More precisely, this is our estimate of $\mathrm{E}[\Phi(\delta_{87} + \rho + c_i)] - \mathrm{E}[\Phi(\delta_{87} + c_i)]$, where the expectation is with respect to the distribution of c_i. The estimate is based on $\mathrm{E}\{\Phi[(\psi + \delta_{87} + \rho + \xi y_{i0})/(1 + \sigma_a^2)^{1/2}]\} - \mathrm{E}\{\Phi[(\psi + \delta_{87} + \xi y_{i0})/(1 + \sigma_a^2)^{1/2}]\}$ (by iterated expectations):

$$N^{-1}\sum_{i=1}^{N}\{\Phi[(\hat{\psi} + \hat{\delta}_{87} + \hat{\rho} + \hat{\xi} y_{i0})/(1 + \hat{\sigma}_a^2)^{1/2}] - \Phi[(\hat{\psi} + \hat{\delta}_{87} + \hat{\xi} y_{i0})/(1 + \hat{\sigma}_a^2)^{1/2}]\};$$

see page 495 in the text. Interestingly, .283 is just over half if the estimated state dependence if we ignore c_i.

15.20. Since $y_1^* = \mathbf{z}_1\boldsymbol{\delta}_1 + \mathbf{g}(y_2)\boldsymbol{\alpha}_1 + u_1$, and we can write, just as before, $u_1 = \theta_1 v_2 + e_1$, where $e_1|\mathbf{z},v_2 \sim \mathrm{Normal}(0,1 - \rho_1^2)$, we have

$$\mathrm{P}(y_1 = 1|\mathbf{z},y_2,v_2) = \Phi\{[\mathbf{z}_1\boldsymbol{\delta}_1 + \mathbf{g}(y_2)\boldsymbol{\alpha}_1 + \theta_1 v_2]/(1 - \rho_1^2)^{1/2}\}.$$

Therefore, in Procedure 15.1, we will consistently estimate $\boldsymbol{\delta}_1/(1 - \rho_1^2)^{1/2}$, $\boldsymbol{\alpha}_1/(1 - \rho_1^2)^{1/2}$, and $\theta_1/(1 - \rho_1^2)^{1/2}$, where recall that $\boldsymbol{\alpha}_1$ is now a vector of parameters. The discussion for computing average partial effects is identical to that on page 475.

It should also be clear that allowing for a $1 \times G_1$ vector of endogenous explanatory variables, $\mathbf{y}_2$, which appear as $\mathbf{g}_1(y_{21})$, ..., $\mathbf{g}_{G_1}(y_{2,G_1})$, is not difficult. The key restriction is that the vector of reduced form errors, $\mathbf{v}_2$, would have to be jointly normally distributed (along with u_1). But the endogeneity is solved by including in the vector of reduced form residuals in the probit. For details, see J.M. Wooldridge, "Unobserved Heterogeneity and Estimation of Average Partial Effects," mimeo, Michigan State University Department of Economics, 2002.

SOLUTIONS TO CHAPTER 16 PROBLEMS

16.1. a. $P[\log(t_i) = \log(c)|\mathbf{x}_i] = P[\log(t_i^*) > \log(c)|\mathbf{x}_i]$

$$= P[u_i > \log(c) - \mathbf{x}_i\boldsymbol{\beta}|\mathbf{x}_i] = 1 - \Phi\{[\log(c) - \mathbf{x}_i\boldsymbol{\beta}]/\sigma\}.$$

As $c \to \infty$, $\Phi\{[\log(c) - \mathbf{x}_i\boldsymbol{\beta}]/\sigma\} \to 1$, and so $P[\log(t_i) = \log(c)|\mathbf{x}_i] \to 0$ as $c \to \infty$. This simply says that, the longer we wait to censor, the less likely it is that we observe a censored observation.

b. The density of $y_i \equiv \log(t_i)$ (given $\mathbf{x}_i$) when $t_i < c$ is the same as the density of $y_i^* \equiv \log(t_i^*)$, which is just $\text{Normal}(\mathbf{x}_i\boldsymbol{\beta},\sigma^2)$. This is because, for $y < \log(c)$, $P(y_i \le y|\mathbf{x}_i) = P(y_i^* \le y|\mathbf{x}_i)$. Thus, the density for $y_i = \log(t_i)$ is

$$f(y|\mathbf{x}_i) = 1 - \Phi\{[\log(c) - \mathbf{x}_i\boldsymbol{\beta}]/\sigma\}, \quad y = \log(c)$$

$$f(y|\mathbf{x}_i) = \frac{1}{\sigma}\phi[(y - \mathbf{x}_i\boldsymbol{\beta})/\sigma], \quad y < \log(c).$$

c. $$\ell_i(\boldsymbol{\beta},\sigma^2) = 1[y_i = \log(c)]\cdot\log(1 - \Phi\{[\log(c) - \mathbf{x}_i\boldsymbol{\beta}]/\sigma\}) + 1[y_i < \log(c)]\cdot\log\{\sigma^{-1}\phi[(y_i - \mathbf{x}_i\boldsymbol{\beta})/\sigma]\}.$$

d. To test H_0: $\boldsymbol{\beta}_2 = \mathbf{0}$, I would probably use the likelihood ratio statistic. This requires estimating the model with all variables, and then the model without $\mathbf{x}_2$. The LR statistic is $\mathcal{LR} = 2(\mathcal{L}_{ur} - \mathcal{L}_r)$. Under H_0, $\mathcal{LR}$ is distributed asymptotically as $\chi^2_{K_2}$.

e. Since u_i is independent of $(\mathbf{x}_i,c_i)$, the density of y_i given $(\mathbf{x}_i,c_i)$ has the same form as the density of y_i given $\mathbf{x}_i$ above, except that c_i replaces c. The assumption that u_i is independent of c_i means that the decision to censor an individual (or other economic unit) is not related to unobservables affecting t_i^*. Thus, in something like an unemployment duration equation, where u_i might contain unobserved ability, we do not wait longer to censor people of lower ability. Note that c_i can be related to $\mathbf{x}_i$. Thus, if $\mathbf{x}_i$ contains something like education, which is treated as exogenous, then the censoring time can depend on education.

16.3. a. $P(y_i = a_1|\mathbf{x}_i) = P(y_i^* \le a_1|\mathbf{x}_i) = P[(u_i/\sigma) \le (a_1 - \mathbf{x}_i\boldsymbol{\beta})/\sigma]$

$$= \Phi[(a_1 - \mathbf{x}_i\boldsymbol{\beta})/\sigma].$$

Similarly,

$$P(y_i = a_2|\mathbf{x}_i) = P(y_i^* \ge a_2|\mathbf{x}_i) = P(\mathbf{x}_i\boldsymbol{\beta} + u_i \ge a_2|\mathbf{x}_i)$$

$$= P[(u_i/\sigma) \ge (a_2 - \mathbf{x}_i\boldsymbol{\beta})/\sigma] = 1 - \Phi[(a_2 - \mathbf{x}_i\boldsymbol{\beta})/\sigma]$$

$$= \Phi[-(a_2 - \mathbf{x}_i\boldsymbol{\beta})/\sigma].$$

Next, for $a_1 < y < a_2$, $P(y_i \le y|\mathbf{x}_i) = P(y_i^* \le y|\mathbf{x}_i) = \Phi[(y - \mathbf{x}_i\boldsymbol{\beta})/\sigma]$. Taking the derivative of this cdf with respect to y gives the pdf of y_i conditional on $\mathbf{x}_i$ for values of y strictly between a_1 and a_2: $(1/\sigma)\phi[(y - \mathbf{x}_i\boldsymbol{\beta})/\sigma]$.

b. Since $y = y^*$ when $a_1 < y^* < a_2$, $E(y|\mathbf{x},a_1 < y < a_2) = E(y^*|\mathbf{x},a_1 < y^* < a_2)$. But $y^* = \mathbf{x}\boldsymbol{\beta} + u$, and $a_1 < y^* < a_2$ if and only if $a_1 - \mathbf{x}\boldsymbol{\beta} < u < a_2 - \mathbf{x}\boldsymbol{\beta}$. Therefore, using the hint,

$$E(y^*|\mathbf{x},a_1 < y^* < a_2) = \mathbf{x}\boldsymbol{\beta} + E(u|\mathbf{x},a_1 - \mathbf{x}\boldsymbol{\beta} < u < a_2 - \mathbf{x}\boldsymbol{\beta})$$

$$= \mathbf{x}\boldsymbol{\beta} + \sigma E[(u/\sigma)|\mathbf{x},(a_1 - \mathbf{x}\boldsymbol{\beta})/\sigma < u/\sigma < (a_2 - \mathbf{x}\boldsymbol{\beta})/\sigma]$$

$$= \mathbf{x}\boldsymbol{\beta} + \sigma\{\phi[(a_1 - \mathbf{x}\boldsymbol{\beta})/\sigma]$$

$$- \phi[(a_2 - \mathbf{x}\boldsymbol{\beta})/\sigma]\}/\{\Phi[(a_2 - \mathbf{x}\boldsymbol{\beta})/\sigma] - \Phi[(a_1 - \mathbf{x}\boldsymbol{\beta})/\sigma]\}$$

$$= E(y|\mathbf{x},a_1 < y < a_2).$$

Now, we can easily get $E(y|\mathbf{x})$ by using the following:

$$E(y|\mathbf{x}) = a_1P(y = a_1|\mathbf{x}) + E(y|\mathbf{x},a_1 < y < a_2)\cdot P(a_1 < y < a_2|\mathbf{x})$$

$$+ a_2P(y_2 = a_2|\mathbf{x})$$

$$= a_1\Phi[(a_1 - \mathbf{x}\boldsymbol{\beta})/\sigma]$$

$$+ E(y|\mathbf{x},a_1 < y < a_2)\cdot\{\Phi[(a_2 - \mathbf{x}\boldsymbol{\beta})/\sigma] - \Phi[(a_1 - \mathbf{x}\boldsymbol{\beta})/\sigma]\}$$

$$+ a_2\Phi[(\mathbf{x}\boldsymbol{\beta} - a_2)/\sigma]$$

$$= a_1\Phi[(a_1 - \mathbf{x}\boldsymbol{\beta})/\sigma]$$

$$+ \ (\mathbf{x}\boldsymbol{\beta})\cdot\{\Phi[(a_2 - \mathbf{x}\boldsymbol{\beta})/\sigma] - \Phi[(a_1 - \mathbf{x}\boldsymbol{\beta})/\sigma]\} \qquad (16.57)$$

$$+ \ \sigma\{\phi[(a_1 - \mathbf{x}\boldsymbol{\beta})/\sigma] - \phi[(a_2 - \mathbf{x}\boldsymbol{\beta})/\sigma]\}$$

$$+ \ a_2\Phi[(\mathbf{x}\boldsymbol{\beta} - a_2)/\sigma].$$

c. From part b it is clear that $E(y^*|\mathbf{x}, a_1 < y^* < a_2) \neq \mathbf{x}\boldsymbol{\beta}$, and so it would be a fluke if OLS on the restricted sample consistently estimated $\boldsymbol{\beta}$. The linear regression of y_i on $\mathbf{x}_i$ using only those y_i such that $a_1 < y_i < a_2$ consistently estimates the linear projection of y^* on $\mathbf{x}$ in the subpopulation for which $a_1 < y^* < a_2$. Generally, there is no reason to think that this will have any simple relationship to the parameter vector $\boldsymbol{\beta}$. [In some restrictive cases, the regression on the restricted subsample could consistently estimate $\boldsymbol{\beta}$ up to a common scale coefficient.]

d. We get the log-likelihood immediately from part a:

$$\ell_i(\theta) = 1[y_i = a_1]\log\{\Phi[(a_1 - \mathbf{x}_i\boldsymbol{\beta})/\sigma]\}$$

$$+ \ 1[y_i = a_2]\log\{\Phi[(\mathbf{x}_i\boldsymbol{\beta} - a_2)/\sigma]\}$$

$$+ \ 1[a_1 < y_i < a_2]\log\{(1/\sigma)\phi[(y_i - \mathbf{x}_i\boldsymbol{\beta})/\sigma]\}.$$

Note how the indicator function selects out the appropriate density for each of the three possible cases: at the left endpoint, at the right endpoint, or strictly between the endpoints.

e. After obtaining the maximum likelihood estimates $\hat{\boldsymbol{\beta}}$ and $\hat{\sigma}^2$, just plug these into the formulas in part b. The expressions can be evaluated at interesting values of $\mathbf{x}$.

f. We can show this by brute-force differentiation of equation (16.57). As a shorthand, write $\phi_1 \equiv \phi[(a_1 - \mathbf{x}\boldsymbol{\beta})/\sigma]$, $\phi_2 \equiv \phi[(a_2 - \mathbf{x}\boldsymbol{\beta})/\sigma] = \phi[(\mathbf{x}\boldsymbol{\beta} - a_2)/\sigma]$, $\Phi_1 \equiv \Phi[(a_1 - \mathbf{x}_i\boldsymbol{\beta})/\sigma]$, and $\Phi_2 \equiv \Phi[(a_2 - \mathbf{x}\boldsymbol{\beta})/\sigma]$. Then

$$\frac{\partial E(y|\mathbf{x})}{\partial x_j} = -(a_1/\sigma)\phi_1\beta_j + (a_2/\sigma)\phi_2\beta_j$$

$$+ \ (\Phi_2 - \Phi_1)\beta_j + [(\mathbf{x}\boldsymbol{\beta}/\sigma)(\phi_1 - \phi_2)]\beta_j$$

$$+ \{[(a_1 - \mathbf{x}\boldsymbol{\beta})/\sigma]\phi_1\}\beta_j - \{[(a_2 - \mathbf{x}\boldsymbol{\beta})/\sigma]\phi_2\}\beta_j,$$

where the first two parts are the derivatives of the first and third terms, respectively, in (16.57), and the last two lines are obtained from differentiating the second term in $E(y|\mathbf{x})$. Careful inspection shows that all terms cancel except $(\Phi_2 - \Phi_1)\beta_j$, which is the expression we wanted to be left with.

The scale factor is simply the probability that a standard normal random variable falls in the interval $[(a_1 - \mathbf{x}\boldsymbol{\beta})/\sigma, (a_2 - \mathbf{x}\boldsymbol{\beta})/\sigma]$, which is necessarily between zero and one.

g. The partial effects on $E(y|\mathbf{x})$ are given in part f. These are estimated as

$$\{\Phi[(a_2 - \mathbf{x}\hat{\boldsymbol{\beta}})/\hat{\sigma}] - \Phi[(a_1 - \mathbf{x}\hat{\boldsymbol{\beta}})/\hat{\sigma}]\}\hat{\beta}_j, \tag{16.58}$$

where the estimates are the MLEs. We could evaluate these partial effects at, say, $\bar{\mathbf{x}}$. Or, we could average $\{\Phi[(a_2 - \mathbf{x}_i\hat{\boldsymbol{\beta}})/\hat{\sigma}] - \Phi[(a_1 - \mathbf{x}_i\hat{\boldsymbol{\beta}})/\hat{\sigma}]\}$ across all i to obtain the average partial effect. In either case, the scaled $\hat{\beta}_j$ can be compared to the $\hat{\gamma}_j$. Generally, we expect

$$\hat{\gamma}_j \approx \hat{\rho}\cdot\hat{\beta}_j,$$

where $0 < \hat{\rho} < 1$ is the scale factor. Of course, this approximation need not be very good in a partiular application, but it is often roughly true. It does not make sense to directly compare the magnitude of $\hat{\beta}_j$ with that of $\hat{\gamma}_j$. By the way, note that $\hat{\sigma}$ appears in the partial effects along with the $\hat{\beta}_j$; there is no sense in which $\hat{\sigma}$ is "ancillary."

h. For data censoring where the censoring points might change with i, the analysis is essentially the same but a_1 and a_2 are replaced with a_{i1} and a_{i2}. Interpretating the results is even easier, since we act as if we were able to do OLS on an uncensored sample.

16.5. a. The results from OLS estimation of the linear model are

```
. reg hrbens exper age educ tenure married male white nrtheast nrthcen south
union

  Source |       SS       df       MS                  Number of obs =     616
---------+------------------------------               F( 11,   604) =   32.50
   Model |  101.132288    11  9.19384436               Prob > F      =  0.0000
Residual |  170.839786   604  .282847328               R-squared     =  0.3718
---------+------------------------------               Adj R-squared =  0.3604
   Total |  271.972074   615  .442231015               Root MSE      =  .53183

------------------------------------------------------------------------------
  hrbens |      Coef.   Std. Err.       t     P>|t|       [95% Conf. Interval]
---------+--------------------------------------------------------------------
   exper |   .0029862   .0043435      0.688   0.492       -.005544    .0115164
     age |  -.0022495   .0041162     -0.547   0.585      -.0103333    .0058343
    educ |    .082204   .0083783      9.812   0.000       .0657498    .0986582
  tenure |   .0281931   .0035481      7.946   0.000        .021225    .0351612
 married |   .0899016   .0510187      1.762   0.079       -.010294    .1900971
    male |    .251898   .0523598      4.811   0.000       .1490686    .3547274
   white |    .098923   .0746602      1.325   0.186      -.0477021    .2455481
nrtheast |  -.0834306   .0737578     -1.131   0.258      -.2282836    .0614223
 nrthcen |  -.0492621   .0678666     -0.726   0.468      -.1825451     .084021
   south |  -.0284978   .0673714     -0.423   0.672      -.1608084    .1038129
   union |   .3768401   .0499022      7.552   0.000       .2788372    .4748429
   _cons |  -.6999244   .1772515     -3.949   0.000      -1.048028   -.3518203
------------------------------------------------------------------------------
```

b. The Tobit estimates are

```
. tobit hrbens exper age educ tenure married male white nrtheast nrthcen south
union, ll(0)

Tobit Estimates                                         Number of obs =    616
                                                        chi2(11)      = 283.86
                                                        Prob > chi2   = 0.0000
Log Likelihood = -519.66616                             Pseudo R2     = 0.2145

------------------------------------------------------------------------------
  hrbens |      Coef.   Std. Err.       t     P>|t|       [95% Conf. Interval]
---------+--------------------------------------------------------------------
   exper |   .0040631   .0046627      0.871   0.384      -.0050939    .0132201
     age |  -.0025859   .0044362     -0.583   0.560      -.0112981    .0061263
    educ |   .0869168   .0088168      9.858   0.000       .0696015    .1042321
  tenure |   .0287099   .0037237      7.710   0.000        .021397    .0360227
 married |   .1027574   .0538339      1.909   0.057      -.0029666    .2084814
    male |   .2556765   .0551672      4.635   0.000       .1473341     .364019
   white |   .0994408    .078604      1.265   0.206       -.054929    .2538105
```

```
nrtheast |  -.0778461   .0775035     -1.004   0.316     -.2300547    .0743625
 nrthcen |  -.0489422   .0713965     -0.685   0.493     -.1891572    .0912729
   south |  -.0246854   .0709243     -0.348   0.728     -.1639731    .1146022
   union |   .4033519   .0522697      7.717   0.000      .3006999    .5060039
   _cons |  -.8137158   .1880725     -4.327   0.000      -1.18307   -.4443616
---------+--------------------------------------------------------------------
     _se |   .5551027   .0165773               (Ancillary parameter)
------------------------------------------------------------------------------

Obs. summary:         41 left-censored observations at hrbens<=0
                     575 uncensored observations
```

The Tobit and OLS estimates are similar because only 41 of 616 observations, or about 6.7% of the sample, have *hrbens* = 0. As expected, the Tobit estimates are all slightly larger in magnitude; this reflects that the scale factor is always less than unity. Again, the parameter "_se" is $\hat{\sigma}$. You should ignore the phrase "Ancillary parameter" (which essentially means "subordinate") associated with "_se" as it is misleading for corner solution applications: as we know, $\hat{\sigma}^2$ appears directly in $\hat{E}(y|\mathbf{x})$ and $\hat{E}(y|\mathbf{x},y > 0)$.

c. Here is what happens when $exper^2$ and $tenure^2$ are included:

```
. tobit hrbens exper age educ tenure married male white nrtheast nrthcen south
union expersq tenuresq, ll(0)

Tobit Estimates                                   Number of obs =      616
                                                  chi2(13)      =   315.95
                                                  Prob > chi2   =   0.0000
Log Likelihood = -503.62108                       Pseudo R2     =   0.2388

------------------------------------------------------------------------------
  hrbens |      Coef.   Std. Err.        t     P>|t|      [95% Conf. Interval]
---------+--------------------------------------------------------------------
   exper |   .0306652   .0085253      3.597   0.000      .0139224     .047408
     age |  -.0040294   .0043428     -0.928   0.354     -.0125583    .0044995
    educ |   .0802587   .0086957      9.230   0.000      .0631812    .0973362
  tenure |   .0581357   .0104947      5.540   0.000       .037525    .0787463
 married |   .0714831   .0528969      1.351   0.177     -.0324014    .1753675
    male |   .2562597   .0539178      4.753   0.000      .1503703    .3621491
   white |   .0906783   .0768576      1.180   0.239     -.0602628    .2416193
nrtheast |  -.0480194   .0760238     -0.632   0.528      -.197323    .1012841
 nrthcen |   -.033717   .0698213     -0.483   0.629     -.1708394    .1034053
   south |   -.017479   .0693418     -0.252   0.801     -.1536597    .1187017
   union |   .3874497    .051105      7.581   0.000      .2870843    .4878151
 expersq |  -.0005524   .0001487     -3.715   0.000     -.0008445   -.0002604
```

tenuresq	-.0013291	.0004098	-3.243	0.001	-.002134	-.0005242
_cons	-.9436572	.1853532	-5.091	0.000	-1.307673	-.5796409
_se	.5418171	.0161572	(Ancillary parameter)			

```
Obs. summary:         41 left-censored observations at hrbens<=0
                     575 uncensored observations
```

Both squared terms are very signficant, so they should be included in the model.

d. There are nine industries, and we use *ind1* as the base industry:

```
. tobit hrbens exper age educ tenure married male white nrtheast nrthcen south
union expersq tenuresq ind2-ind9, ll(0)

Tobit Estimates                                   Number of obs =    616
                                                  chi2(21)      = 388.99
                                                  Prob > chi2   = 0.0000
Log Likelihood = -467.09766                       Pseudo R2     = 0.2940
```

hrbens	Coef.	Std. Err.	t	P>|t|	[95% Conf.	Interval]
exper	.0267869	.0081297	3.295	0.001	.0108205	.0427534
age	-.0034182	.0041306	-0.828	0.408	-.0115306	.0046942
educ	.0789402	.0088598	8.910	0.000	.06154	.0963403
tenure	.053115	.0099413	5.343	0.000	.0335907	.0726393
married	.0547462	.0501776	1.091	0.276	-.0438005	.1532928
male	.2411059	.0556864	4.330	0.000	.1317401	.3504717
white	.1188029	.0735678	1.615	0.107	-.0256812	.2632871
nrtheast	-.1016799	.0721422	-1.409	0.159	-.2433643	.0400045
nrthcen	-.0724782	.0667174	-1.086	0.278	-.2035085	.0585521
south	-.0379854	.0655859	-0.579	0.563	-.1667934	.0908226
union	.3143174	.0506381	6.207	0.000	.2148662	.4137686
expersq	-.0004405	.0001417	-3.109	0.002	-.0007188	-.0001623
tenuresq	-.0013026	.0003863	-3.372	0.000	-.0020613	-.000544
ind2	-.3731778	.3742017	-0.997	0.319	-1.108095	.3617389
ind3	-.0963657	.368639	-0.261	0.794	-.8203574	.6276261
ind4	-.2351539	.3716415	-0.633	0.527	-.9650425	.4947348
ind5	.0209362	.373072	0.056	0.955	-.7117618	.7536342
ind6	-.5083107	.3682535	-1.380	0.168	-1.231545	.214924
ind7	.0033643	.3739442	0.009	0.993	-.7310468	.7377754
ind8	-.6107854	.376006	-1.624	0.105	-1.349246	.127675
ind9	-.3257878	.3669437	-0.888	0.375	-1.04645	.3948746
_cons	-.5750527	.4137824	-1.390	0.165	-1.387704	.2375989
_se	.5099298	.0151907	(Ancillary parameter)			

```
Obs. summary:         41 left-censored observations at hrbens<=0
                     575 uncensored observations

. test ind2 ind3 ind4 ind5 ind6 ind7 ind8 ind9

 ( 1)  ind2 = 0.0
 ( 2)  ind3 = 0.0
 ( 3)  ind4 = 0.0
 ( 4)  ind5 = 0.0
 ( 5)  ind6 = 0.0
 ( 6)  ind7 = 0.0
 ( 7)  ind8 = 0.0
 ( 8)  ind9 = 0.0

       F(  8,   595) =    9.66
            Prob > F =    0.0000
```

Each industry dummy variable is individually insignificant at even the 10% level, but the joint Wald test says that they are jointly very significant. This is somewhat unusual for dummy variables that are necessarily orthogonal (so that there is not a multicollinearity problem among them). The likelihood ratio statistic is 2(503.621 - 467.098) = 73.046; notice that this is roughly 8 (= number of restrictions) times the F statistic; the p-value for the LR statistic is also essentially zero. Certainly several estimates on the industry dummies are economically significant, with a worker in, say, industry eight earning about 61 cents less per hour in benefits than comparable worker in industry one. [Remember, in this example, with so few observations at zero, it is roughly legitimate to use the parameter estimates as the partial effects.]

16.6. a. The hint for this problem is basically fouled up. First, since y_1 is a corner solution response, its density is not normal, no matter what we condition on. Let $g(y|\mu,\sigma^2)$ denote the density of a standard Tobit response, where μ is the mean of the underlying latent normal random variable and σ^2 is its variance. Then, the distribution of y_1 given $(\mathbf{z}, v_2)$ can be written as $g(y_1|\mathbf{z}_1\boldsymbol{\delta}_1 + \alpha_1 y_2 + \rho_1 v_2, \sigma_1^2 - \rho_1^2)$. Next, we need the density of v_2 given $(\mathbf{z}, y_2)$, which is given on page 478. To obtain the density of y_1 given $(\mathbf{z}, y_2)$, we can apply Property CD.3 on page 420. The density of $v_2|(\mathbf{z}, y_2 = 1)$ is $\phi(v_2)/\Phi(\mathbf{z}\boldsymbol{\delta}_2)$ for $v_2 > -\mathbf{z}\boldsymbol{\delta}_2$. So the density of y_1 given $(\mathbf{z}, y_2 = 1)$ is

$$\frac{1}{\Phi(\mathbf{z}\boldsymbol{\delta}_2)} \int_{-\mathbf{z}\boldsymbol{\delta}_2}^{\infty} g(y_1|\mathbf{z}_1\boldsymbol{\delta}_1 + \alpha_1 y_2 + \rho_1 v_2, \sigma_1^2 - \rho_1^2)\phi(v_2)dv_2$$

and the density given $(\mathbf{z}, y_2 = 0)$ is

$$\frac{1}{[1 - \Phi(\mathbf{z}\boldsymbol{\delta}_2)]} \int_{-\infty}^{-\mathbf{z}\boldsymbol{\delta}_2} g(y_1|\mathbf{z}_1\boldsymbol{\delta}_1 + \alpha_1 y_2 + \rho_1 v_2, \sigma_1^2 - \rho_1^2)\phi(v_2)dv_2.$$

b. We need to combine the density obtained from part a -- called it $f(y_1|y_2, \mathbf{z}; \boldsymbol{\delta}_1, \alpha_1, \rho_1, \sigma_1^2)$, and let $h(y_2|\mathbf{z}; \boldsymbol{\delta}_2)$ be the probit density for y_2 given $\mathbf{z}$. Then the log likelihood for observation i is

$$\log[f(y_{i1}|y_{i2}, \mathbf{z}_i; \boldsymbol{\delta}_1, \alpha_1, \rho_1, \sigma_1^2, \boldsymbol{\delta}_2)] + \log[h(y_{i2}|\mathbf{z}_i; \boldsymbol{\delta}_2)],$$

which simplifies to

$$y_{i2}\log\left(\int_{-\mathbf{z}_i\boldsymbol{\delta}_2}^{\infty} g(y_{i1}|\mathbf{z}_{i1}\boldsymbol{\delta}_1 + \alpha_1 + \rho_1 v_2, \sigma_1^2 - \rho_1^2)\phi(v_2)dv_2\right)$$
$$+ (1 - y_{i2})\log\left(\int_{-\infty}^{-\mathbf{z}_i\boldsymbol{\delta}_2} g(y_{i1}|\mathbf{z}_{i1}\boldsymbol{\delta}_1 + \rho_1 v_2, \sigma_1^2 - \rho_1^2)\phi(v_2)dv_2\right).$$

If $\rho_1 = 0$, this simplifies into two separate log likelihoods, one the standard Tobit for y_{i1} given $(\mathbf{z}_{i1}, y_{i2})$ and the second for probit of y_{i2} given $\mathbf{z}_i$.

c. (Bonus Question): Discuss the properties of the following two step method for estimating $(\boldsymbol{\delta}_1, \alpha_1)$: (1) Run probit of y_{i2} on $\mathbf{z}_i$ and obtain the fitted probabilities, $\Phi(\mathbf{z}_i\hat{\boldsymbol{\delta}}_2)$, $i = 1, ..., N$. (2) Run Tobit of y_{i1} on $\mathbf{z}_{i1}$, $\Phi(\mathbf{z}_i\hat{\boldsymbol{\delta}}_2)$ to obtain $\hat{\boldsymbol{\delta}}_1$, $\hat{\alpha}_1$, and some variance estimator.

Answer: As in the probit case (page 478), this is another example of a forbidden regression. There is no way that $E(y_1|\mathbf{z})$ has the Tobit form with $\mathbf{z}_1$ and $\Phi(\mathbf{z}\boldsymbol{\delta}_2) = E(y_2|\mathbf{z})$ as the explanatory variables. Indeed, since $y_1 = \max(0, \mathbf{z}_1\boldsymbol{\delta}_1 + \alpha_1 y_2 + u_1)$, $E(y_1|\mathbf{z})$ has no simple form, although it could be computed.

16.7. a. This follows because the densities conditional on $y > 0$ are identical for the Tobit model and Cragg's model. A more general case is done in Section 17.3. Briefly, if $f(\cdot|\mathbf{x})$ is the continuous density of y given $\mathbf{x}$, then the density of y given $\mathbf{x}$ and $y > 0$ is $f(\cdot|\mathbf{x})/[1 - F(0|\mathbf{x})]$, where $F(\cdot|\mathbf{x})$ is the cdf of y given $\mathbf{x}$. When f is the normal pdf with mean $\mathbf{x}\boldsymbol{\beta}$ and variance σ^2, we get that $f(y|\mathbf{x}, y > 0) = \{\Phi(\mathbf{x}\boldsymbol{\beta}/\sigma)\}^{-1}\{\phi[(y - \mathbf{x}\boldsymbol{\beta})/\sigma]/\sigma\}$ for the Tobit model, and this is exactly the density specified for Cragg's model given $y > 0$.

b. From (6.8) we have

$$E(y|\mathbf{x}) = \Phi(\mathbf{x}\boldsymbol{\gamma})\cdot E(y|\mathbf{x}, y > 0) = \Phi(\mathbf{x}\boldsymbol{\gamma})[\mathbf{x}\boldsymbol{\beta} + \sigma\lambda(\mathbf{x}\boldsymbol{\beta}/\sigma)].$$

c. This follows very generally -- not just for Cragg's model or the Tobit model -- from (16.8):

$$\log[E(y|\mathbf{x})] = \log[P(y > 0|\mathbf{x})] + \log[E(y|\mathbf{x}, y > 0)].$$

If we take the partial derivative with respect to $\log(x_1)$ we clearly get the sum of the elasticities.

16.9. a. A two-limit Tobit model, of the kind analyzed in Problem 16.3, is appropriate, with $a_1 = 0$, $a_2 = 10$.

b. The lower limit at zero is logically necessary considering the kind of response: the smallest percentage of one's income that can be invested in a pension plan is zero. On the other hand, the upper limit of 10 is an arbitrary corner imposed by law. One can imagine that some people at the corner $y = 10$ would choose $y > 10$ if they could. So, we can think of an underlying variable, which would be the percentage invested in the absense of any restrictions. Then, there would be no upper bound required (since we would not have to worry about 100 percent of income being invested in a pension plan).

c. From Problem 16.3(b), with $a_1 = 0$, we have

$$\begin{aligned} E(y|\mathbf{x}) &= (\mathbf{x}\boldsymbol{\beta})\cdot\{\Phi[(a_2 - \mathbf{x}\boldsymbol{\beta})/\sigma] - \Phi(-\mathbf{x}\boldsymbol{\beta}/\sigma)\} \\ &\quad + \sigma\{\phi(\mathbf{x}\boldsymbol{\beta}/\sigma) - \phi[(a_2 - \mathbf{x}\boldsymbol{\beta})/\sigma]\} + a_2\Phi[(\mathbf{x}\boldsymbol{\beta} - a_2)/\sigma]. \end{aligned}$$

Taking the derivative of this function with respect to a_2 gives

$$\begin{aligned} \partial E(y|\mathbf{x})/\partial a_2 &= (\mathbf{x}\boldsymbol{\beta}/\sigma)\cdot\phi[(a_2 - \mathbf{x}\boldsymbol{\beta})/\sigma] + [(a_2 - \mathbf{x}\boldsymbol{\beta})/\sigma]\cdot\phi[(a_2 - \mathbf{x}\boldsymbol{\beta})/\sigma] \\ &\quad + \Phi[(\mathbf{x}\boldsymbol{\beta} - a_2)/\sigma] - (a_2/\sigma)\phi[(\mathbf{x}\boldsymbol{\beta} - a_2)/\sigma] \\ &= \Phi[(\mathbf{x}\boldsymbol{\beta} - a_2)/\sigma]. \end{aligned} \quad (16.59)$$

We can plug in $a_2 = 10$ to obtain the approximate effect of increasing the cap from 10 to 11. For a given value of $\mathbf{x}$, we would compute $\Phi[(\mathbf{x}\hat{\boldsymbol{\beta}} - 10)/\hat{\sigma}]$, where $\hat{\boldsymbol{\beta}}$ and $\hat{\sigma}$ are the MLEs. We might evaluate this expression at the sample average of $\mathbf{x}$ or at other interesting values (such as across gender or race).

d. If $y_i < 10$ for $i = 1,...,N$, $\hat{\boldsymbol{\beta}}$ and $\hat{\sigma}$ are just the usual Tobit estimates with the "censoring" at zero.

16.11. No. OLS always consistently estimates the parameters of a linear projection -- provided the second moments of y and the x_j are finite, and $\text{Var}(\mathbf{x})$ has full rank K -- regardless of the nature of y or $\mathbf{x}$. That is why a linear regression analysis is always a reasonable first step for binary outcomes, corner solution outcomes, and count outcomes, provided there is not true data censoring.

16.13. This extension has no practical effect on how we estimate an unobserved effects Tobit or probit model, or how we estimate a variety of unobserved effects panel data models with conditional normal heterogeneity. We simply have

$$c_i = -\left(T^{-1}\sum_{t=1}^{T}\boldsymbol{\pi}_t\right)\xi + \bar{\mathbf{x}}_i\xi + a_i \equiv \psi + \bar{\mathbf{x}}_i\xi + a_i,$$

where $\psi \equiv -\left(T^{-1}\sum_{t=1}^{T}\boldsymbol{\pi}_t\right)\xi$. Of course, any aggregate time dummies explicitly get swept out of $\bar{\mathbf{x}}_i$ in this case but would usually be included in $\mathbf{x}_{it}$.

An interesting follow-up question would have been: What if we standardize each $\mathbf{x}_{it}$ by its cross-sectional mean *and* variance at time t, and assume c_i is related to the mean and variance of the standardized vectors. In other words, let $\mathbf{z}_{it} \equiv (\mathbf{x}_{it} - \boldsymbol{\pi}_t)\Omega_t^{-1/2}$, $t = 1,\ldots,T$, for each random draw i from the population. Then, we might assume $c_i|\mathbf{x}_i \sim \text{Normal}(\psi + \bar{\mathbf{z}}_i\xi,\sigma_a^2)$ (where, again, $\mathbf{z}_{it}$ would not contain aggregate time dummies). This is the kind of scenario that is handled by Chamberlain's more general assumption concerning the relationship between c_i and $\mathbf{x}_i$: $c_i = \psi + \sum_{r=1}^{T}\mathbf{x}_{ir}\boldsymbol{\lambda}_r + a_i$, where $\boldsymbol{\lambda}_r = \Omega_r^{-1/2}\xi/T$, $t = 1,2,\ldots,T$. Alternatively, one could estimate estimate $\boldsymbol{\pi}_t$ and Ω_t for each t using the cross section observations $\{\mathbf{x}_{it}: i = 1,2,\ldots,N\}$. The usual sample means and sample variance matrices, say $\hat{\boldsymbol{\pi}}_t$ and $\hat{\Omega}_t$, are consistent and $\sqrt{N}$-asymptotically normal. Then, form $\hat{\mathbf{z}}_{it} \equiv \hat{\Omega}_t^{-1/2}(\mathbf{x}_{it} - \hat{\boldsymbol{\pi}}_t)$, and proceed with the usual Tobit (or probit) unobserved effects analysis that includes the time averages $\hat{\bar{\mathbf{z}}}_i = T^{-1}\sum_{t=1}^{T}\hat{\mathbf{z}}_{it}$. This is a rather simple two-step estimation method, but accounting for the sample variation in $\hat{\boldsymbol{\pi}}_t$ and $\hat{\Omega}_t$ would be cumbersome. It may be possible to use a much larger to obtain $\hat{\boldsymbol{\pi}}_t$ and $\hat{\Omega}_t$, in which case one might ignore the sampling error in the first-stage estimates.

SOLUTIONS TO CHAPTER 17 PROBLEMS

17.1. If you are interested in the effects of things like age of the building and neighborhood demographics on fire damage, given that a fire has occured, then there is no problem. We simply need a random sample of buildings that actually caught on fire. You might want to supplement this with an analysis of the probability that buildings catch fire, given building and neighborhood characteristics. But then a two-stage analysis is appropriate.

17.3. This is essentially given in equation (17.14). Let y_i given $\mathbf{x}_i$ have density $f(y|\mathbf{x}_i,\boldsymbol{\beta},\boldsymbol{\gamma})$, where $\boldsymbol{\beta}$ is the vector indexing $\mathrm{E}(y_i|\mathbf{x}_i)$ and $\boldsymbol{\gamma}$ is another set of parameters (usually a single variance parameter). Then the density of y_i given $\mathbf{x}_i$, $s_i = 1$, when $s_i = 1[a_1(\mathbf{x}_i) < y_i < a_2(\mathbf{x}_i)]$, is

$$p(y|\mathbf{x}_i,s_i=1) = \frac{f(y|\mathbf{x}_i;\boldsymbol{\beta},\boldsymbol{\gamma})}{F(a_2(\mathbf{x}_i)|\mathbf{x}_i;\boldsymbol{\beta},\boldsymbol{\gamma}) - F(a_1(\mathbf{x}_i)|\mathbf{x}_i;\boldsymbol{\beta},\boldsymbol{\gamma})},\ a_1(\mathbf{x}_i) < y < a_2(\mathbf{x}_i).$$

In the Hausman and Wise (1977) study, $y_i = \log(income_i)$, $a_1(\mathbf{x}_i) = -\infty$, and $a_2(\mathbf{x}_i)$ was a function of family size (which determines the official poverty level).

17.5. If we replace y_2 with $\hat{y}_2$, we need to see what happens when $y_2 = \mathbf{z}\boldsymbol{\delta}_2 + v_2$ is plugged into the structural mode:

$$\begin{aligned} y_1 &= \mathbf{z}_1\boldsymbol{\delta}_1 + \alpha_1\cdot(\mathbf{z}\boldsymbol{\delta}_2 + v_2) + u_1 \\ &= \mathbf{z}_1\boldsymbol{\delta}_1 + \alpha_1\cdot(\mathbf{z}\boldsymbol{\delta}_2) + (u_1 + \alpha_1 v_2). \end{aligned} \tag{17.81}$$

So, the procedure is to replace $\boldsymbol{\delta}_2$ in (17.81) its $\sqrt{N}$-consistent estimator, $\hat{\boldsymbol{\delta}}_2$. The key is to note how the error term in (17.81) is $u_1 + \alpha_1 v_2$. If the selection correction is going to work, we need the expected value of $u_1 + \alpha_1 v_2$

given $(\mathbf{z}, v_3)$ to be linear in v_3 (in particular, it cannot depend on $\mathbf{z}$). Then we can write

$$E(y_1|\mathbf{z}, v_3) = \mathbf{z}_1\boldsymbol{\delta}_1 + \alpha_1\cdot(\mathbf{z}\boldsymbol{\delta}_2) + \gamma_1 v_3,$$

where $E[(u_1 + \alpha_1 v_2)|v_3] = \gamma_1 v_3$ by normality. Conditioning on $y_3 = 1$ gives

$$E(y_1|\mathbf{z}, y_3 = 1) = \mathbf{z}_1\boldsymbol{\delta}_1 + \alpha_1\cdot(\mathbf{z}\boldsymbol{\delta}_2) + \gamma_1\lambda(\mathbf{z}\boldsymbol{\delta}_3). \quad (17.82)$$

A sufficient condition for (17.82) is that (u_1, v_2, v_3) is independent of $\mathbf{z}$ with a trivariate normal distribution. We can get by with less than this, but the nature of v_2 is restricted. If we use an IV approach, we need assume nothing about v_2 except for the usual linear projection assumption.

As a practical matter, if we cannot write $y_2 = \mathbf{z}\boldsymbol{\delta}_2 + v_2$, where v_2 is independent of $\mathbf{z}$ and approximately normal, then the OLS alternative will not be consistent. Thus, equations where y_2 is binary, or is some other variable that exhibits nonnormality, cannot be consistently estimated using the OLS procedure. This is why 2SLS is generally preferred.

17.7. a. Substitute the reduced forms for y_1 and y_2 into the third equation:

$$y_3 = \max(0, \alpha_1(\mathbf{z}\boldsymbol{\delta}_1) + \alpha_2(\mathbf{z}\boldsymbol{\delta}_2) + \mathbf{z}_3\boldsymbol{\delta}_3 + v_3)$$
$$\equiv \max(0, \mathbf{z}\boldsymbol{\pi}_3 + v_3),$$

where $v_3 \equiv u_3 + \alpha_1 v_1 + \alpha_2 v_2$. Under the assumptions given, v_3 is indepdent of $\mathbf{z}$ and normally distributed. Thus, if we knew $\boldsymbol{\delta}_1$ and $\boldsymbol{\delta}_2$, we could consistently estimate α_1, α_2, and $\boldsymbol{\delta}_3$ from a Tobit of y_3 on $\mathbf{z}\boldsymbol{\delta}_1$, $\mathbf{z}\boldsymbol{\delta}_2$, and $\mathbf{z}_3$. >From the usual argument, consistent estimators are obtained by using initial consistent estimators of $\boldsymbol{\delta}_1$ and $\boldsymbol{\delta}_2$. Estimation of $\boldsymbol{\delta}_2$ is simple: just use OLS using the entire sample. Estimation of $\boldsymbol{\delta}_1$ follows exactly as in Procedure 17.3 using the system

$$y_1 = \mathbf{z}\boldsymbol{\delta}_1 + v_1 \quad (17.83)$$

$$y_3 = \max(0, \mathbf{z}\boldsymbol{\pi}_3 + v_3), \tag{17.84}$$

where y_1 is observed only when $y_3 > 0$.

Given $\hat{\boldsymbol{\delta}}_1$ and $\hat{\boldsymbol{\delta}}_2$, form $\mathbf{z}_i\hat{\boldsymbol{\delta}}_1$ and $\mathbf{z}_i\hat{\boldsymbol{\delta}}_2$ for each observation i in the sample. Then, obtain $\hat{\alpha}_1$, $\hat{\alpha}_2$, and $\hat{\boldsymbol{\delta}}_3$ from the Tobit

$$y_{i3} \text{ on } (\mathbf{z}_i\hat{\boldsymbol{\delta}}_1),\ (\mathbf{z}_i\hat{\boldsymbol{\delta}}_2),\ \mathbf{z}_{i3}$$

using all observations.

For identification, $(\mathbf{z}\boldsymbol{\delta}_1, \mathbf{z}\boldsymbol{\delta}_2, \mathbf{z}_3)$ can contain no exact linear dependencies. Necessary is that there must be at least two elements in $\mathbf{z}$ not also in $\mathbf{z}_3$.

Obtaining the correct asymptotic variance matrix is complicated. It is most easily done in a generalized method of moments framework.

b. This is not very different from part a. The only difference is that $\boldsymbol{\delta}_2$ must be estimated using Procedure 17.3. Then follow the steps from part a.

c. We need to estimate the variance of u_3, σ_3^2.

17.9. First, we can write the unweighted objective function as

$$N^{-1}\sum_{j=1}^{J}\sum_{i=1}^{N_j} q(\mathbf{w}_{ij}, \boldsymbol{\theta}) = \sum_{j=1}^{J}(N_j/N)N_j^{-1}\sum_{i=1}^{N_j} q(\mathbf{w}_{ij}, \boldsymbol{\theta})$$
$$= \sum_{j=1}^{J} H_j\left(N_j^{-1}\sum_{i=1}^{N_j} q(\mathbf{w}_{ij}, \boldsymbol{\theta})\right),$$

as suggested in the hint. Further, by the same argument as on page 595, $N_j^{-1}\sum_{i=1}^{N_j} q(\mathbf{w}_{ij}, \boldsymbol{\theta})$ converges uniformly to $\mathrm{E}[q(\mathbf{w},\boldsymbol{\theta})|\mathbf{w} \in \mathcal{W}_j] = \mathrm{E}[q(\mathbf{w},\boldsymbol{\theta})|\mathbf{x} \in \mathcal{X}_j]$, we we use the fact that the strata are $\mathcal{X}_1, \ldots, \mathcal{X}_J$. If $H_j \to \bar{H}_j$ then the unweighted objective function converges uniformly to the expression given in (17.82). Given that $\boldsymbol{\theta}_o$ solves (17.78) for each $\mathbf{x}$, $\boldsymbol{\theta}_o$ also minimizes $\mathrm{E}[q(\mathbf{w},\boldsymbol{\theta})|\mathbf{x} \in \mathcal{X}_j]$ over $\boldsymbol{\Theta}$ for each j: by iterated expectations (since the indicator $1[\mathbf{x} \in \mathcal{X}_j]$ is a function of $\mathbf{x}$),

$$E[q(\mathbf{w},\boldsymbol{\theta})|\mathbf{x} \in \mathcal{X}_j] = E\{E[q(\mathbf{w},\boldsymbol{\theta})|\mathbf{x}]|\mathbf{x} \in \mathcal{X}_j\}.$$

and if $\boldsymbol{\theta}_o$ minimizes $E[q(\mathbf{w},\boldsymbol{\theta})|\mathbf{x}]$, it must also minimize $E\{E[q(\mathbf{w},\boldsymbol{\theta})|\mathbf{x}]|\mathbf{x} \in \mathcal{X}_j\}$. Therefore, $\boldsymbol{\theta}_o$ is one minimizer of (17.82) over $\boldsymbol{\Theta}$. We now just have to show it is unique if $\boldsymbol{\theta}_o$ uniquely minimizes $E[q(\mathbf{w},\boldsymbol{\theta})]$. Without the assumption $\bar{H}_j > 0$, $\boldsymbol{\theta}_o$ need not be the unique minimizer of (17.82). But, letting $s_j = 1[\mathbf{x} \in \mathcal{X}_j]$, we can write, for $\boldsymbol{\theta} \neq \boldsymbol{\theta}_o$,

$$E[q(\mathbf{w},\boldsymbol{\theta})] - E[q(\mathbf{w},\boldsymbol{\theta}_o)] = \sum_{j=1}^{J} Q_j\{E[q(\mathbf{x},\boldsymbol{\theta})|s_j] - E[q(\mathbf{x},\boldsymbol{\theta}_o)|s_j]\},$$

where the Q_j are the population frequencies. By assumption, the left hand side is strictly positive which means, because $Q_j > 0$ for all j, $E[q(\mathbf{x},\boldsymbol{\theta})|s_j] - E[q(\mathbf{x},\boldsymbol{\theta}_o)|s_j]$ must be strictly positive for at least one j. This, along with the fact that $\bar{H}_j > 0$, $j = 1,\ldots,J$, implies that (17.82) is uniquely minimized at $\boldsymbol{\theta}_o$.

17.11. a. There is no sample selection problem because, by definition, you have specified the distribution of y given $\mathbf{x}$ and $y > 0$. We only need to obtain a random sample from the subpopulation with $y > 0$.

b. Again, there is no sample selection bias because we have specified the conditional expectation for the population of interest. If we have a random sample from that population, NLS is generally consistent and $\sqrt{N}$-asymptotically normal.

c. We would use a standard probit model. Let $w = 1[y > 0]$. Then w given $\mathbf{x}$ follows a probit model with $P(w = 1|\mathbf{x}) = \Phi(\mathbf{x}\boldsymbol{\gamma})$.

d. $E(y|\mathbf{x}) = P(y > 0|\mathbf{x})\cdot E(y|\mathbf{x},y > 0) = \Phi(\mathbf{x}\boldsymbol{\gamma})\cdot\exp(\mathbf{x}\boldsymbol{\beta})$. So we would plug in the NLS estimator of $\boldsymbol{\beta}$ and the probit estimator of $\boldsymbol{\gamma}$.

e. Not when you specify the conditional distributions, or conditional means, for the two parts. By definition, there is no sample selection problem. Confusion arises, I think, when two part models are specified with unobservables that may be correlated. For example, we could write

$$y = w \cdot \exp(\mathbf{x}\boldsymbol{\beta} + u),$$

$$w = 1[\mathbf{x}\boldsymbol{\gamma} + v > 0],$$

so that $w = 0 \Rightarrow y = 0$. Assume that (u,v) is independent of $\mathbf{x}$. Then, if u and v are independent -- so that u is independent of $(\mathbf{x},w)$ -- we have

$$\mathrm{E}(y|\mathbf{x},w) = w \cdot \exp(\mathbf{x}\boldsymbol{\beta})\mathrm{E}[\exp(u)|\mathbf{x},w] = w \cdot \exp(\mathbf{x}\boldsymbol{\beta})\mathrm{E}[\exp(u)],$$

which implies the specification in part b (by setting $w = 1$, once we absorb $\mathrm{E}[\exp(u)]$ into the intercept). The interesting twist here is if u and v are correlated. Given $w = 1$, we can write $\log(y) = \mathbf{x}\boldsymbol{\beta} + u$. So

$$\mathrm{E}[\log(y)|\mathbf{x},w = 1] = \mathbf{x}\boldsymbol{\beta} + \mathrm{E}(u|\mathbf{x},w = 1).$$

If we make the usual linearity assumption, $\mathrm{E}(u|v) = \rho v$ and assume a standard normal distribution for v then we have the usual inverse Mills ratio added to the linear model:

$$\mathrm{E}[\log(y)|\mathbf{x},w = 1] = \mathbf{x}\boldsymbol{\beta} + \rho\lambda(\mathbf{x}\boldsymbol{\gamma}).$$

A two-step strategy for estimating $\boldsymbol{\gamma}$ and $\boldsymbol{\beta}$ is pretty clear. First, estimate a probit of w_i on $\mathbf{x}_i$ to get $\hat{\boldsymbol{\gamma}}$ and $\lambda(\mathbf{x}_i\hat{\boldsymbol{\gamma}})$. Then, using the $y_i > 0$ observations, run the regression $\log(y_i)$ on $\mathbf{x}_i$, $\lambda(\mathbf{x}_i\hat{\boldsymbol{\gamma}})$ to obtain $\hat{\boldsymbol{\beta}}$, $\hat{\rho}$. A standard t statistic on $\hat{\rho}$ is a simple test of $\mathrm{Cov}(u,v) = 0$.

This two-step procedure reveals a potential problem with the model that allows u and v to be correlated: adding the inverse Mills ratio means that we are adding a nonlinear function of $\mathbf{x}$. In other words, identification of $\boldsymbol{\beta}$ comes entirely from the nonlinearity of the IMR, which we warned about in this chapter. Ideally, we would have a variable that affects $\mathrm{P}(w = 1|\mathbf{x})$ that can be excluded from $\mathbf{x}\boldsymbol{\beta}$. In labor economics, where two-part models are used to allow for fixed costs of entering the labor market, one would try to find a variable that affects the fixed costs of being employed that does not affect the choice of hours.

If we assume (u,v) is multivariate normal, with mean zero, then we can use a full maximum likelihood procedure. While this would be a little less robust, making full distributional assumptions has a subtle advantage: we can then compute partial effects on $E(y|\mathbf{x})$ and $E(y|\mathbf{x},y > 0)$. Even with a full set of assumptions, the partial effects are not straightforward to obtain. For one,

$$E(y|\mathbf{x},y > 0) = \exp(\mathbf{x},\boldsymbol{\beta})\cdot E[\exp(u)|\mathbf{x},w = 1)],$$

where $E[\exp(u)|\mathbf{x},w = 1)]$ can be obtained under joint normality. A similar example is given in Section 19.5.2; see, particularly, equation (19.44). Then, we can multiply this expectation by $P(w = 1|\mathbf{x}) = \Phi(\mathbf{x}\boldsymbol{\gamma})$. The point is that we cannot simply look at $\boldsymbol{\beta}$ to obtain partial effects of interest. This is very different from the sample selection model.

17.13. a. We cannot use censored Tobit because that requires observing $\mathbf{x}$ when whatever the value of y. Instead, we can use truncated Tobit: we use the distribution of y given $\mathbf{x}$ and $y > 0$. Notice that our reason for using truncated Tobit differs from the usual application. Usually, the underlying variable y of interest has a conditional normal distribution in the population. Here, y given $\mathbf{x}$ follows a standard Tobit model in the population (for a corner solution outcome). But, conditional on $y > 0$, the truncated normal distribution is appropriate.

b. Because we have assumed y given $\mathbf{x}$ follows a standard Tobit, $E(y|\mathbf{x})$ is the parametric function $E(y|\mathbf{x}) = \Phi(\mathbf{x}\boldsymbol{\beta}/\sigma)\mathbf{x}\boldsymbol{\beta} + \sigma\phi(\mathbf{x}\boldsymbol{\beta}/\sigma)$. Therefore, even though we never observe some elements of $\mathbf{x}$ when $y = 0$, we can still estimate $E(y|\mathbf{x})$

because we can estimate $\boldsymbol{\beta}$ and σ. We do have to assume that $\mathbf{x}$ varies enough in the subpopulation where $y > 0$, namely, rank $\mathrm{E}(\mathbf{x}'\mathbf{x} | y > 0) = K$. In the case where an element of $\mathbf{x}$ is a derived price, we need sufficient price variation for the population that consumes some of the good.

SOLUTIONS TO CHAPTER 18 PROBLEMS

18.1. a. This follows from equation (18.5). First, $\mathrm{E}(\bar{y}_1) = \mathrm{E}(y|w = 1)$ and $\mathrm{E}(\bar{y}_0) = \mathrm{E}(y|w = 1)$. Therefore, by (18.5),

$$\mathrm{E}(\bar{y}_1 - \bar{y}_0) = [\mathrm{E}(y_0|w = 1) - \mathrm{E}(y_0|w = 0)] + ATE_1,$$

and so the bias is given by the first term.

b. If $\mathrm{E}(y_0|w = 1) < \mathrm{E}(y_0|w = 0)$, those who participate in the program would have had lower average earnings without training than those who chose not to participate. This is a form of sample selection, and, on average, leads to an underestimate of the impact of the program.

18.3. The following Stata session estimates α using the three different regression approaches. It would have made sense to add *unem74* and *unem75* to the vector **x**, but I did not do so:

```
. probit train re74 re75 age agesq nodegree married black hisp

Iteration 0:   log likelihood =     -302.1
Iteration 1:   log likelihood = -294.07642
Iteration 2:   log likelihood = -294.06748
Iteration 3:   log likelihood = -294.06748

Probit estimates                                  Number of obs   =        445
                                                  LR chi2(8)      =      16.07
                                                  Prob > chi2     =     0.0415
Log likelihood = -294.06748                       Pseudo R2       =     0.0266

------------------------------------------------------------------------------
       train |      Coef.   Std. Err.      z    P>|z|     [95% Conf. Interval]
-------------+----------------------------------------------------------------
        re74 |  -.0189577   .0159392    -1.19   0.234    -.0501979    .0122825
        re75 |   .0371871   .0271086     1.37   0.170    -.0159447     .090319
         age |  -.0005467   .0534045    -0.01   0.992    -.1052176    .1041242
       agesq |   .0000719   .0008734     0.08   0.934    -.0016399    .0017837
    nodegree |    -.44195   .1515457    -2.92   0.004    -.7389742   -.1449258
     married |    .091519   .1726192     0.53   0.596    -.2468083    .4298464
       black |  -.1446253   .2271609    -0.64   0.524    -.5898524    .3006019
```

```
        hisp |  -.5004545   .3079227    -1.63   0.104    -1.103972    .1030629
       _cons |   .2284561   .8154273     0.28   0.779    -1.369752    1.826664
------------------------------------------------------------------------------

. predict phat
(option p assumed; Pr(train))

. sum phat

    Variable |     Obs        Mean   Std. Dev.       Min        Max
-------------+-----------------------------------------------------
        phat |     445    .4155321   .0934459   .1638736   .6738951

. gen traphat0 = train*(phat - .416)

. reg unem78 train phat

      Source |       SS       df       MS              Number of obs =     445
-------------+------------------------------           F(  2,   442) =    3.13
       Model |  1.3226496     2  .661324802            Prob > F      =  0.0449
    Residual | 93.4998223   442   .21153806            R-squared     =  0.0139
-------------+------------------------------           Adj R-squared =  0.0095
       Total | 94.8224719   444  .213564126            Root MSE      =  .45993

------------------------------------------------------------------------------
      unem78 |      Coef.   Std. Err.      t    P>|t|     [95% Conf. Interval]
-------------+----------------------------------------------------------------
       train |   -.110242    .045039    -2.45   0.015    -.1987593   -.0217247
        phat |  -.0101531   .2378099    -0.04   0.966    -.4775317    .4572254
       _cons |   .3579151   .0994803     3.60   0.000     .1624018    .5534283
------------------------------------------------------------------------------

. reg unem78 train phat traphat0

      Source |       SS       df       MS              Number of obs =     445
-------------+------------------------------           F(  3,   441) =    2.84
       Model | 1.79802041     3  .599340137            Prob > F      =  0.0375
    Residual | 93.0244515   441  .210939799            R-squared     =  0.0190
-------------+------------------------------           Adj R-squared =  0.0123
       Total | 94.8224719   444  .213564126            Root MSE      =  .45928

------------------------------------------------------------------------------
      unem78 |      Coef.   Std. Err.      t    P>|t|     [95% Conf. Interval]
-------------+----------------------------------------------------------------
       train |  -.1066934   .0450374    -2.37   0.018     -.195208   -.0181789
        phat |   .3009852   .3151992     0.95   0.340    -.3184939    .9204644
    traphat0 |   -.719599   .4793509    -1.50   0.134    -1.661695     .222497
       _cons |    .233225    .129489     1.80   0.072    -.0212673    .4877173
------------------------------------------------------------------------------

. reg unem78 train re74 re75 age agesq nodegree married black hisp
```

```
      Source |       SS       df       MS              Number of obs =     445
-------------+------------------------------           F(  9,   435) =    2.75
       Model |  5.09784844     9  .566427604           Prob > F      =  0.0040
    Residual |  89.7246235   435  .206263502           R-squared     =  0.0538
-------------+------------------------------           Adj R-squared =  0.0342
       Total |  94.8224719   444  .213564126           Root MSE      =  .45416

------------------------------------------------------------------------------
      unem78 |      Coef.   Std. Err.      t    P>|t|     [95% Conf. Interval]
-------------+----------------------------------------------------------------
       train |  -.1105582   .0444832    -2.49   0.013    -.1979868   -.0231295
        re74 |  -.0025525   .0053889    -0.47   0.636    -.0131441    .0080391
        re75 |   -.007121   .0094371    -0.75   0.451     -.025669    .0114269
         age |   .0304127   .0189565     1.60   0.109    -.0068449    .0676704
       agesq |  -.0004949   .0003098    -1.60   0.111    -.0011038    .0001139
    nodegree |   .0421444   .0550176     0.77   0.444    -.0659889    .1502777
     married |  -.0296401   .0620734    -0.48   0.633    -.1516412    .0923609
       black |    .180637   .0815002     2.22   0.027     .0204538    .3408202
        hisp |  -.0392887   .1078464    -0.36   0.716    -.2512535    .1726761
       _cons |  -.2342579   .2905718    -0.81   0.421    -.8053572    .3368413
------------------------------------------------------------------------------
```

In all three cases, the average treatment effect is estimated to be right around -.11: participating in job training is estimated to reduce the unemployment probability by about .11. Of course, in this example, training status was randomly assigned, so we are not surprised that different methods lead to roughly the same estimate. An alternative, of course, is to use a probit model for *unem78* on *train* and **x**.

18.5. a. I used the following Stata session to answer all parts:

```
. probit train re74 re75 age agesq nodegree married black hisp

Iteration 0:   log likelihood =     -302.1
Iteration 1:   log likelihood = -294.07642
Iteration 2:   log likelihood = -294.06748
Iteration 3:   log likelihood = -294.06748

Probit estimates                                  Number of obs   =        445
                                                  LR chi2(8)      =      16.07
                                                  Prob > chi2     =     0.0415
Log likelihood = -294.06748                       Pseudo R2       =     0.0266

------------------------------------------------------------------------------
```

```
       train |      Coef.   Std. Err.      z    P>|z|     [95% Conf. Interval]
-------------+----------------------------------------------------------------
        re74 |  -.0189577   .0159392    -1.19   0.234    -.0501979    .0122825
        re75 |   .0371871   .0271086     1.37   0.170    -.0159447     .090319
         age |  -.0005467   .0534045    -0.01   0.992    -.1052176    .1041242
       agesq |   .0000719   .0008734     0.08   0.934    -.0016399    .0017837
    nodegree |    -.44195   .1515457    -2.92   0.004    -.7389742   -.1449258
     married |    .091519   .1726192     0.53   0.596    -.2468083    .4298464
       black |  -.1446253   .2271609    -0.64   0.524    -.5898524    .3006019
        hisp |  -.5004545   .3079227    -1.63   0.104    -1.103972    .1030629
       _cons |   .2284561   .8154273     0.28   0.779    -1.369752    1.826664
------------------------------------------------------------------------------

. predict phat
(option p assumed; Pr(train))


. reg re78 train re74 re75 age agesq nodegree married black hisp (phat re74
re75 age agesq nodegree married black hisp)

Instrumental variables (2SLS) regression

      Source |       SS       df       MS              Number of obs =     445
-------------+------------------------------           F(  9,   435) =    1.75
       Model |  703.776258     9  78.197362            Prob > F      =  0.0763
    Residual |  18821.8804   435  43.2686905           R-squared     =  0.0360
-------------+------------------------------           Adj R-squared =  0.0161
       Total |  19525.6566   444  43.9767041           Root MSE      =  6.5779

------------------------------------------------------------------------------
        re78 |      Coef.   Std. Err.      t    P>|t|     [95% Conf. Interval]
-------------+----------------------------------------------------------------
       train |   .0699177   18.00172     0.00   0.997    -35.31125    35.45109
        re74 |   .0624611   .1453799     0.43   0.668    -.2232733    .3481955
        re75 |   .0863775   .2814839     0.31   0.759    -.4668602    .6396151
         age |   .1998802   .2746971     0.73   0.467    -.3400184    .7397788
       agesq |  -.0024826   .0045238    -0.55   0.583    -.0113738    .0064086
    nodegree |  -1.367622   3.203039    -0.43   0.670    -7.662979    4.927734
     married |   -.050672   1.098774    -0.05   0.963    -2.210237    2.108893
       black |  -2.203087   1.554259    -1.42   0.157    -5.257878    .8517046
        hisp |  -.2953534   3.656719    -0.08   0.936    -7.482387     6.89168
       _cons |   4.613857   11.47144     0.40   0.688    -17.93248     27.1602
------------------------------------------------------------------------------

. reg phat re74 re75 age agesq nodegree married black hisp

      Source |       SS       df       MS              Number of obs =     445
-------------+------------------------------           F(  8,   436) =69767.44
       Model |  3.87404126     8  .484255158           Prob > F      =  0.0000
    Residual |  .003026272   436  6.9410e-06           R-squared     =  0.9992
-------------+------------------------------           Adj R-squared =  0.9992
       Total |  3.87706754   444  .008732134           Root MSE      =  .00263
```

phat	Coef.	Std. Err.	t	P>|t|	[95% Conf.	Interval]
re74	-.0069301	.0000312	-222.04	0.000	-.0069914	-.0068687
re75	.0139209	.0000546	254.82	0.000	.0138135	.0140283
age	-.0003207	.00011	-2.92	0.004	-.0005368	-.0001046
agesq	.0000293	1.80e-06	16.31	0.000	.0000258	.0000328
nodegree	-.1726018	.000316	-546.14	0.000	-.1732229	-.1719806
married	.0352802	.00036	98.01	0.000	.0345727	.0359877
black	-.0562315	.0004726	-118.99	0.000	-.0571603	-.0553027
hisp	-.1838453	.0006238	-294.71	0.000	-.1850713	-.1826192
_cons	.5907578	.0016786	351.93	0.000	.5874586	.594057

b. The IV estimate of α is very small -- .070, much smaller than when we used either linear regression or the propensity score in a regression in Example 18.2. (When we do not instrument for *train*, $\hat{\alpha}$ = 1.625, se = .640.) The very large standard error (18.00) suggests severe collinearity among the instruments.

c. The collinearity suspected in part b is confirmed by regressing $\hat{\Phi}_i$ on the $\mathbf{x}_i$: the *R*-squared is .9992, which means there is virtually no separate variation in $\hat{\Phi}_i$ that cannot be explained by $\mathbf{x}_i$.

d. This example illustrates why trying to achieve identification off of a nonlinearity can be fraught with problems. Generally, it is not a good idea

18.7. a. In Stata, nonlinear regression with an exponential mean function is easily carried out using the "glm" command, specifying a log link function and Gaussian distribution. The usual nonlinear least squares standard errors are reported as the default. (The heteroskedasticity-robust ones turn out not to be very different.)

```
. glm mostrn re74 re75 age agesq nodegree married black hisp, link(log)
family(gaussian)
```

```
Iteration 0:   log likelihood = -1752.6455
Iteration 1:   log likelihood =   -1660.14
Iteration 2:   log likelihood = -1631.4361
Iteration 3:   log likelihood =  -1631.423
Iteration 4:   log likelihood =  -1631.423

Generalized linear models                          No. of obs      =       445
Optimization     : ML: Newton-Raphson              Residual df     =       436
                                                   Scale param     =  91.35866
Deviance         =  39832.37492                    (1/df) Deviance =  91.35866
Pearson          =  39832.37492                    (1/df) Pearson  =  91.35866

Variance function: V(u) = 1                        [Gaussian]
Link function    : g(u) = ln(u)                    [Log]
Standard errors  : OIM

Log likelihood   = -1631.422974                    AIC             =  7.372688
BIC              =  39777.49225

------------------------------------------------------------------------------
      mostrn |      Coef.   Std. Err.      z    P>|z|     [95% Conf. Interval]
-------------+----------------------------------------------------------------
        re74 |   -.006513   .0132386    -0.49   0.623    -.0324602    .0194341
        re75 |   .0395582   .0196727     2.01   0.044     .0010005     .078116
         age |   .0048675   .0513727     0.09   0.925    -.0958211    .1055561
       agesq |  -.0000426   .0008297    -0.05   0.959    -.0016687    .0015835
    nodegree |  -.3744698    .127725    -2.93   0.003    -.6248062   -.1241335
     married |   .0489132   .1620591     0.30   0.763    -.2687167    .3665432
       black |  -.0936286   .1858126    -0.50   0.614    -.4578145    .2705574
        hisp |  -.3773443   .3162523    -1.19   0.233    -.9971873    .2424987
       _cons |   2.278041   .7857691     2.90   0.004     .7379621     3.81812
------------------------------------------------------------------------------
```

Real earnings in 1975 is positively related to months spent in training, while not having a high school degree is negatively related. No other variable is very close to significance.

b. Here is the Stata session that estimates the δ_j. These commands were entered after the previous "glm" command:

```
. predict mostrnh
(option mu assumed; predicted mean mostrn)

. * Obtain the NLS residuals:

. gen uhat = mostrn - mostrnh
```

```
. gen uhatsq = uhat^2

. gen moshsq = mostrnh^2

. reg uhatsq mostrnh moshsq

      Source |       SS       df       MS              Number of obs =     445
-------------+------------------------------           F(  2,   442) =    5.89
       Model |  64344.9572     2  32172.4786           Prob > F      =  0.0030
    Residual |  2416316.84   442  5466.78018           R-squared     =  0.0259
-------------+------------------------------           Adj R-squared =  0.0215
       Total |  2480661.80   444  5587.07612           Root MSE      =  73.938

------------------------------------------------------------------------------
      uhatsq |      Coef.   Std. Err.       t     P>|t|     [95% Conf. Interval]
-------------+----------------------------------------------------------------
     mostrnh |   24.60161   11.33658      2.17   0.031      2.321317    46.88191
      moshsq |  -1.048248   .6217775     -1.69   0.093     -2.270256    .1737593
       _cons |  -34.33536    49.5212     -0.69   0.488     -131.6616    62.99091
------------------------------------------------------------------------------
```

. * The above table contains the $\hat{\delta}_j$.

```
. predict hhat
(option xb assumed; fitted values)

. sum hhat

    Variable |     Obs        Mean    Std. Dev.       Min        Max
-------------+-----------------------------------------------------
        hhat |     445    89.51095    12.03832   61.56561     110.01
```

None of the $\hat{h}_i$ is negative. They range from 61.57 to 110.01.

c. I meant the response variable to be *re78*, just as in Problem 18.5. The following Stata output gives the IV estimates, using the $\hat{r}_i$ as an instrument for w_i, and the OLS estimates. The estimated treatment effect is very similar:

```
. gen rhat = uhat/hhat

. reg re78 mostrn re74 re75 age agesq nodegree married black hisp

      Source |       SS       df       MS              Number of obs =     445
-------------+------------------------------           F(  9,   435) =    2.84
       Model |  1081.87106     9  120.207896           Prob > F      =  0.0030
    Residual |  18443.7856   435   42.399507           R-squared     =  0.0554
-------------+------------------------------           Adj R-squared =  0.0359
```

```
       Total |  19525.6566   444  43.9767041           Root MSE      =  6.5115

------------------------------------------------------------------------------
        re78 |      Coef.   Std. Err.      t    P>|t|     [95% Conf. Interval]
-------------+----------------------------------------------------------------
      mostrn |   .1005424    .032682     3.08   0.002      .0363081    .1647767
        re74 |   .0696775   .0771811     0.90   0.367     -.0820168    .2213718
        re75 |   .0439601   .1357556     0.32   0.746     -.2228583    .3107785
         age |   .1924248    .271796     0.71   0.479     -.3417719    .7266216
       agesq |  -.0023713   .0044415    -0.53   0.594     -.0111007    .0063581
    nodegree |  -1.061765    .787908    -1.35   0.178     -2.610345    .4868153
     married |  -.1163739   .8899627    -0.13   0.896     -1.865535    1.632787
       black |  -2.101363   1.168453    -1.80   0.073     -4.397879    .1951526
        hisp |    .002569   1.545089     0.00   0.999     -3.034199    3.039337
       _cons |    3.68608   4.160766     0.89   0.376     -4.491624    11.86378
------------------------------------------------------------------------------

. reg re78 mostrn re74 re75 age agesq nodegree married black hisp (rhat re74
re75 age agesq nodegree married black hisp)

Instrumental variables (2SLS) regression

      Source |       SS       df       MS              Number of obs =     445
-------------+------------------------------           F(  9,   435) =    2.77
       Model |  1081.66423     9  120.184915           Prob > F      =  0.0037
    Residual |  18443.9924   435  42.3999825           R-squared     =  0.0554
-------------+------------------------------           Adj R-squared =  0.0359
       Total |  19525.6566   444  43.9767041           Root MSE      =  6.5115

------------------------------------------------------------------------------
        re78 |      Coef.   Std. Err.      t    P>|t|     [95% Conf. Interval]
-------------+----------------------------------------------------------------
      mostrn |   .0982597   .0329802     2.98   0.003      .0334393    .1630801
        re74 |   .0695028   .0771823     0.90   0.368     -.0821938    .2211994
        re75 |   .0449449   .1357697     0.33   0.741     -.2219014    .3117911
         age |   .1925933   .2717978     0.71   0.479     -.3416068    .7267934
       agesq |  -.0023737   .0044415    -0.53   0.593     -.0111032    .0063557
    nodegree |  -1.068982   .7880366    -1.36   0.176     -2.617815    .4798502
     married |  -.1148266   .8899727    -0.13   0.897     -1.864008    1.634355
       black |  -2.103762   1.168469    -1.80   0.072     -4.400309     .192785
        hisp |  -.0044866   1.545158    -0.00   0.998     -3.041391    3.032418
       _cons |   3.708085   4.161007     0.89   0.373     -4.470094    11.88626
------------------------------------------------------------------------------
```

18.9. a. We can start with equation (18.66),

$$y = \eta_0 + \mathbf{x}\boldsymbol{\gamma} + \beta w + w\cdot(\mathbf{x} - \boldsymbol{\psi})\boldsymbol{\delta} + u + w\cdot v + e,$$

and, again, we will replace $w\cdot v$ with its expectation given $(\mathbf{x},\mathbf{z})$ and an error.

But $\mathrm{E}(w\cdot v|\mathbf{x},\mathbf{z}) = \mathrm{E}[\mathrm{E}(w\cdot v|\mathbf{x},\mathbf{z},v)|\mathbf{x},\mathbf{z}] = \mathrm{E}[\mathrm{E}(w|\mathbf{x},\mathbf{z},v)\cdot v|\mathbf{x},\mathbf{z}] = \mathrm{E}[\exp(\pi_0 + \mathbf{x}\boldsymbol{\pi}_1 + \mathbf{z}\boldsymbol{\pi}_2 + \pi_3 v)\cdot v|\mathbf{x},\mathbf{z}] = \xi\cdot\exp(\pi_0 + \mathbf{x}\boldsymbol{\pi}_1 + \mathbf{z}\boldsymbol{\pi}_2)$ where $\xi = \mathrm{E}[\exp(\pi_3 v)\cdot v]$, and we have used the assumption that v is independent of $(\mathbf{x},\mathbf{z})$. Now, define $r = u + [w - \mathrm{E}(w\cdot v|\mathbf{x},\mathbf{z})] + e$. Given the assumptions, $\mathrm{E}(r|\mathbf{x},\mathbf{z}) = 0$. [Note that we do not need to replace π_0 with a different constant, as is implied in the statement of the problem.] So we can write

$$y = \eta_0 + \mathbf{x}\boldsymbol{\gamma} + \beta w + w\cdot(\mathbf{x} - \boldsymbol{\psi})\boldsymbol{\delta} + \xi\mathrm{E}(w|\mathbf{x},\mathbf{z}) + r,\ \mathrm{E}(r|\mathbf{x},\mathbf{z}) = 0.$$

b. The ATE β is not identified by the IV estimator applied to the extended equation. If $h \equiv h(\mathbf{x},\mathbf{z})$ is any function of $(\mathbf{x},\mathbf{z})$, $\mathrm{L}(w|1,\mathbf{x},q,h) = \mathrm{L}(w|q) = q$ because $q = \mathrm{E}(w|\mathbf{x},\mathbf{z})$. In effect, becaue we need to include $\mathrm{E}(w|\mathbf{x},\mathbf{z})$ in the estimating equation, no other functions of $(\mathbf{x},\mathbf{z})$ are valid as instruments. This is a clear weakness of the approach.

c. This is not what I intended to ask. What I should have said is, assume we can write $w = \exp(\pi_0 + \mathbf{x}\boldsymbol{\pi}_1 + \mathbf{z}\boldsymbol{\pi}_2 + g)$, where $\mathrm{E}(u|g,\mathbf{x},\mathbf{z}) = \rho\cdot g$ and $\mathrm{E}(v|g,\mathbf{x},\mathbf{z}) = \theta\cdot g$. These are standard linearity assumptions under independence of (u,v,g) and $(\mathbf{x},\mathbf{z})$. Then we take the expected value of (18.66) conditional on $(g,\mathbf{x},\mathbf{z})$:

$$\begin{aligned}\mathrm{E}(y|v,\mathbf{x},\mathbf{z}) &= \eta_0 + \mathbf{x}\boldsymbol{\gamma} + \beta w + w\cdot(\mathbf{x} - \boldsymbol{\psi})\boldsymbol{\delta} + \mathrm{E}(u|g,\mathbf{x},\mathbf{z}) + w\mathrm{E}(v|g\mathbf{x},\mathbf{z}) \\ &\quad + \mathrm{E}(e|g,\mathbf{x},\mathbf{z}) \\ &= \eta_0 + \mathbf{x}\boldsymbol{\gamma} + \beta w + w\cdot(\mathbf{x} - \boldsymbol{\psi})\boldsymbol{\delta} + \rho\cdot g + \theta w\cdot g,\end{aligned}$$

where we have used the fact that w is a function of $(g,\mathbf{x},\mathbf{z})$ and $\mathrm{E}(e|g,\mathbf{x},\mathbf{z}) = 0$. The last equation suggests a two-step procedure. First, since $\log(w_i) = \pi_0 + \mathbf{x}_i\boldsymbol{\pi}_1 + \mathbf{z}_i\boldsymbol{\pi}_2 + g_i$, we can consistently estimate π_0, $\boldsymbol{\pi}_1$, and $\boldsymbol{\pi}_2$ from the OLS regression $\log(w_i)$ on 1, $\mathbf{x}_i$, $\mathbf{z}_i$, $i = 1,\ldots,N$. From this regression, we need the residuals, $\hat{g}_i$, $i = 1,\ldots,N$. In the second step, run the regression

$$y_i \text{ on } 1,\ \mathbf{x}_i,\ w_i,\ w_i(\mathbf{x}_i - \bar{\mathbf{x}}),\ \hat{g}_i,\ w_i\hat{g}_i,\ i = 1,\ldots,N.$$

As usual, the coefficient on w_i is the consistent estimator of β, the average treatment effect. A standard joint significant test -- for example, an F-type test -- on the last two terms effectively tests the null hypothesis that w is exogenous.

SOLUTIONS TO CHAPTER 19 PROBLEMS

19.1. a. This is a simple problem in univariate calculus. Write $q(\mu) \equiv \mu_o \log(\mu) - \mu$ for $\mu > 0$. Then $dq(\mu)/d\mu = \mu_o/\mu - 1$, so $\mu = \mu_o$ uniquely sets the derivative to zero. The second derivative of $q(\mu)$ is $-\mu_o\mu^{-2} > 0$ for all $\mu > 0$, so the sufficient second order condition is satisfied.

b. For the exponential case, $q(\mu) \equiv E[\ell_i(\mu)] = -\mu_o/\mu - \log(\mu)$. The first order condition is $\mu_o\mu^{-2} - \mu^{-1} = 0$, which is uniquely solved by $\mu = \mu_o$. The second derivative is $-2\mu_o\mu^{-3} + \mu^{-2}$, which, when evaluated at μ_o, gives $-2\mu_o^{-2} + \mu_o^{-2} = -\mu_o^{-2} < 0$.

19.3. The following is Stata output used to answer parts a through f. The answers are given below.

```
. reg cigs lcigpric lincome restaurn white educ age agesq

      Source |       SS       df       MS              Number of obs =     807
-------------+------------------------------           F(  7,   799) =    6.38
       Model |  8029.43631     7  1147.06233           Prob > F      =  0.0000
    Residual |  143724.246   799  179.880158           R-squared     =  0.0529
-------------+------------------------------           Adj R-squared =  0.0446
       Total |  151753.683   806  188.280003           Root MSE      =  13.412

------------------------------------------------------------------------------
        cigs |      Coef.   Std. Err.      t    P>|t|     [95% Conf. Interval]
-------------+----------------------------------------------------------------
    lcigpric |  -.8509044   5.782321    -0.15   0.883    -12.20124    10.49943
     lincome |   .8690144   .7287636     1.19   0.233     -.561503    2.299532
    restaurn |  -2.865621   1.117406    -2.56   0.011    -5.059019   -.6722235
       white |  -.5592363   1.459461    -0.38   0.702    -3.424067    2.305594
        educ |  -.5017533   .1671677    -3.00   0.003     -.829893   -.1736136
         age |   .7745021   .1605158     4.83   0.000     .4594197    1.089585
       agesq |  -.0090686   .0017481    -5.19   0.000    -.0124999   -.0056373
       _cons |  -2.682435   24.22073    -0.11   0.912    -50.22621    44.86134
------------------------------------------------------------------------------
```

```
. test lcigpric lincome

 ( 1)  lcigpric = 0.0
 ( 2)  lincome = 0.0

       F(  2,   799) =    0.71
            Prob > F =    0.4899


. reg cigs lcigpric lincome restaurn white educ age agesq, robust

Regression with robust standard errors                 Number of obs =     807
                                                       F(  7,   799) =    9.38
                                                       Prob > F      =  0.0000
                                                       R-squared     =  0.0529
                                                       Root MSE      =  13.412

------------------------------------------------------------------------------
             |               Robust
        cigs |      Coef.   Std. Err.      t    P>|t|     [95% Conf. Interval]
-------------+----------------------------------------------------------------
    lcigpric |  -.8509044   6.054396    -0.14   0.888     -12.7353     11.0335
     lincome |   .8690144    .597972     1.45   0.147    -.3047671    2.042796
    restaurn |  -2.865621   1.017275    -2.82   0.005    -4.862469   -.8687741
       white |  -.5592363   1.378283    -0.41   0.685     -3.26472    2.146247
        educ |  -.5017533   .1624097    -3.09   0.002    -.8205533   -.1829532
         age |   .7745021   .1380317     5.61   0.000     .5035545     1.04545
       agesq |  -.0090686   .0014589    -6.22   0.000    -.0119324   -.0062048
       _cons |  -2.682435   25.90194    -0.10   0.918    -53.52632    48.16145
------------------------------------------------------------------------------

. test lcigpric lincome

 ( 1)  lcigpric = 0.0
 ( 2)  lincome = 0.0

       F(  2,   799) =    1.07
            Prob > F =    0.3441


. poisson cigs lcigpric lincome restaurn white educ age agesq

Iteration 0:   log likelihood = -8111.8346
Iteration 1:   log likelihood = -8111.5191
Iteration 2:   log likelihood =  -8111.519

Poisson regression                                Number of obs   =        807
                                                  LR chi2(7)      =    1068.70
                                                  Prob > chi2     =     0.0000
Log likelihood =  -8111.519                       Pseudo R2       =     0.0618

------------------------------------------------------------------------------
```

```
        cigs |      Coef.   Std. Err.      z    P>|z|     [95% Conf. Interval]
-------------+----------------------------------------------------------------
    lcigpric |  -.1059607   .1433932    -0.74   0.460    -.3870061    .1750847
     lincome |   .1037275   .0202811     5.11   0.000     .0639772    .1434779
    restaurn |  -.3636059   .0312231   -11.65   0.000    -.4248021   -.3024098
       white |  -.0552012   .0374207    -1.48   0.140    -.1285444    .0181421
        educ |  -.0594225   .0042564   -13.96   0.000    -.0677648   -.0510802
         age |   .1142571   .0049694    22.99   0.000     .1045172    .1239969
       agesq |  -.0013708    .000057   -24.07   0.000    -.0014825   -.0012592
       _cons |   .3964494   .6139626     0.65   0.518    -.8068952    1.599794
------------------------------------------------------------------------------

. glm cigs lcigpric lincome restaurn white educ age agesq, family(poisson)
sca(x2)

Iteration 0:   log likelihood = -8380.1083
Iteration 1:   log likelihood = -8111.6454
Iteration 2:   log likelihood =  -8111.519
Iteration 3:   log likelihood =  -8111.519

Generalized linear models                          No. of obs      =       807
Optimization     : ML: Newton-Raphson              Residual df     =       799
                                                   Scale param     =         1
Deviance         =  14752.46933                    (1/df) Deviance =  18.46367
Pearson          =  16232.70987                    (1/df) Pearson  =  20.31628

Variance function: V(u) = u                        [Poisson]
Link function    : g(u) = ln(u)                    [Log]
Standard errors  : OIM

Log likelihood   = -8111.519022                    AIC             =  20.12272
BIC              =  14698.92274

------------------------------------------------------------------------------
        cigs |      Coef.   Std. Err.      z    P>|z|     [95% Conf. Interval]
-------------+----------------------------------------------------------------
    lcigpric |  -.1059607   .6463244    -0.16   0.870    -1.372733    1.160812
     lincome |   .1037275   .0914144     1.13   0.257    -.0754414    .2828965
    restaurn |  -.3636059   .1407338    -2.58   0.010    -.6394391   -.0877728
       white |  -.0552011   .1686685    -0.33   0.743    -.3857854    .2753831
        educ |  -.0594225   .0191849    -3.10   0.002    -.0970243   -.0218208
         age |   .1142571   .0223989     5.10   0.000     .0703561     .158158
       agesq |  -.0013708   .0002567    -5.34   0.000     -.001874   -.0008677
       _cons |   .3964493    2.76735     0.14   0.886    -5.027457    5.820355
------------------------------------------------------------------------------
(Standard errors scaled using square root of Pearson X2-based dispersion)

* The estimate of sigma is

. di sqrt(20.32)
4.5077711
```

```
. poisson cigs restaurn white educ age agesq

Iteration 0:   log likelihood =  -8125.618
Iteration 1:   log likelihood = -8125.2907
Iteration 2:   log likelihood = -8125.2906

Poisson regression                                Number of obs   =        807
                                                  LR chi2(5)      =    1041.16
                                                  Prob > chi2     =     0.0000
Log likelihood = -8125.2906                       Pseudo R2       =     0.0602

------------------------------------------------------------------------------
        cigs |      Coef.   Std. Err.      z    P>|z|     [95% Conf. Interval]
-------------+----------------------------------------------------------------
    restaurn |  -.3545336   .0308796   -11.48   0.000    -.4150564   -.2940107
       white |  -.0618025    .037371    -1.65   0.098    -.1350483    .0114433
        educ |  -.0532166   .0040652   -13.09   0.000    -.0611842   -.0452489
         age |   .1211174   .0048175    25.14   0.000     .1116754    .1305594
       agesq |  -.0014458   .0000553   -26.14   0.000    -.0015543   -.0013374
       _cons |   .7617484   .1095991     6.95   0.000     .5469381    .9765587
------------------------------------------------------------------------------

. di 2*(8125.291 - 8111.519)
27.544

. * This is the usual LR statistic.  The GLM version is obtained by
. * dividing by 20.32:

. di 2*(8125.291 - 8111.519)/(20.32)
1.3555118

. glm cigs lcigpric lincome restaurn white educ age agesq, family(poisson)
robust

Iteration 0:   log likelihood = -8380.1083
Iteration 1:   log likelihood = -8111.6454
Iteration 2:   log likelihood =  -8111.519
Iteration 3:   log likelihood =  -8111.519

Generalized linear models                          No. of obs      =       807
Optimization     : ML: Newton-Raphson              Residual df     =       799
                                                   Scale param     =         1
Deviance         =  14752.46933                    (1/df) Deviance =  18.46367
Pearson          =  16232.70987                    (1/df) Pearson  =  20.31628

Variance function: V(u) = u                        [Poisson]
Link function    : g(u) = ln(u)                    [Log]
Standard errors  : Sandwich

Log likelihood   = -8111.519022                    AIC             =  20.12272
BIC              =  14698.92274
```

cigs	Coef.	Robust Std. Err.	z	P>|z|	[95% Conf. Interval]	
lcigpric	-.1059607	.6681827	-0.16	0.874	-1.415575	1.203653
lincome	.1037275	.083299	1.25	0.213	-.0595355	.2669906
restaurn	-.3636059	.140366	-2.59	0.010	-.6387182	-.0884937
white	-.0552011	.1632959	-0.34	0.735	-.3752553	.264853
educ	-.0594225	.0192058	-3.09	0.002	-.0970653	-.0217798
age	.1142571	.0212322	5.38	0.000	.0726427	.1558715
agesq	-.0013708	.0002446	-5.60	0.000	-.0018503	-.0008914
_cons	.3964493	2.97704	0.13	0.894	-5.438442	6.23134

```
. di .1143/(2*.00137)
41.715328
```

a. Neither the price nor income variable is significant at any reasonable significance level, although the coefficient estimates are the expected sign. It does not matter whether we use the usual or robust standard errors. The two variables are jointly insignificant, too, using the usual and heteroskedasticity-robust tests (*p*-values = .490, .344, respectively).

b. While the price variable is still very insignificant (*p*-value = .46), the income variable, based on the usual Poisson standard errors, is very significant: *t* = 5.11. Both estimates are elasticities: the estimate price elasticity is -.106 and the estimated income elasticity is .104. Incidentally, if you drop *restaurn* -- a binary indicator for restaurant smoking restrictions at the state level -- then log(*cigpric*) becomes much more significant (but using the incorrect standard errors). In this data set, both *cigpric* and *restaurn* vary only at the state level, and, not surprisingly, they are significantly correlated. (States that have restaurant smoking restrictions also have higher average prices, on the order of 2.9%.)

c. The GLM estimate of σ is $\hat{\sigma} = 4.51$. This means all of the Poisson standard errors should be multiplied by this factor, as is done using the "glm" command in Stata, with the option "sca(x2)." The t statistic on *lcigpric* is now very small (-.16), and that on *lincome* falls to 1.13 -- much more in line with the linear model t statistic (1.19 with the usual standard errors). Clearly, using the maximum likelihood standard errors is very misleading in this example. With the GLM standard errors, the restaurant restriction variable, education, and the age variables are still significant. (Interestingly, there is no race effect, conditional on the other covariates.)

d. The usual LR statistic is 2(8125.291 - 8111.519) = 27.54, which is a very large value in a χ_2^2 distribution (p-value $\approx$ 0). The QLR statistic divides the usual LR statistic by $\hat{\sigma}^2$ = 20.32, so QLR = 1.36 (p-value $\approx$ .51). As expected, the QLR statistic shows that the variables are jointly insignificant, while the LR statistic shows strong significance.

e. Using the robust standard errors does not significantly change any conclusions; in fact, most explanatory variables become slightly more significant than when we use the GLM standard errors. In this example, it is the adjustment by $\hat{\sigma}$ > 1 that makes the most difference. Having fully robust standard errors has no additional effect.

f. We simply compute the turning point for the quadratic: $\hat{\beta}_{age}/(-2\hat{\beta}_{age^2})$ = 1143/(2*.00137) $\approx$ 41.72.

g. A double hurdle model -- which separates the initial decision to smoke at all from the decision of how much to smoke -- seems like a good idea. It is certainly worth investigating. One approach is to model $D(y|\mathbf{x}, y \geq 1)$ as a truncated Poisson distribution, and then to model $P(y = 0|\mathbf{x})$ as a logit or probit.

19.5. a. We just use iterated expectations:

$$E(y_{it}|\mathbf{x}_i) = E[E(y_{it}|\mathbf{x}_i,c_i)|\mathbf{x}_i] = E(c_i|\mathbf{x}_i)\exp(\mathbf{x}_{it}\boldsymbol{\beta})$$

$$= \exp(\alpha + \bar{\mathbf{x}}_i\boldsymbol{\gamma})\exp(\mathbf{x}_{it}\boldsymbol{\beta}) = \exp(\alpha + \mathbf{x}_{it}\boldsymbol{\beta} + \bar{\mathbf{x}}_i\boldsymbol{\gamma}).$$

b. We are explicitly testing H_0: $\boldsymbol{\gamma} = \mathbf{0}$, but we are maintaining full independence of c_i and $\mathbf{x}_i$ under H_0. We have enough assumptions to derive $\text{Var}(\mathbf{y}_i|\mathbf{x}_i)$, the $T \times T$ conditional variance matrix of $\mathbf{y}_i$ given $\mathbf{x}_i$ under H_0. First,

$$\text{Var}(y_{it}|\mathbf{x}_i) = E[\text{Var}(y_{it}|\mathbf{x}_i,c_i)|\mathbf{x}_i] + \text{Var}[E(y_{it}|\mathbf{x}_i,c_i)|\mathbf{x}_i]$$

$$= E[c_i\exp(\mathbf{x}_{it}\boldsymbol{\beta})|\mathbf{x}_i] + \text{Var}[c_i\exp(\mathbf{x}_{it}\boldsymbol{\beta})|\mathbf{x}_i]$$

$$= \exp(\alpha + \mathbf{x}_{it}\boldsymbol{\beta}) + \tau^2[\exp(\mathbf{x}_{it}\boldsymbol{\beta})]^2,$$

where $\tau^2 \equiv \text{Var}(c_i)$ and we have used $E(c_i|\mathbf{x}_i) = \exp(\alpha)$ under H_0. A similar, general expression holds for conditional covariances:

$$\text{Cov}(y_{it},y_{ir}|\mathbf{x}_i) = E[\text{Cov}(y_{it},y_{ir}|\mathbf{x}_i,c_i)|\mathbf{x}_i]$$

$$+ \text{Cov}[E(y_{it}|\mathbf{x}_i,c_i),E(y_{ir}|\mathbf{x}_i,c_i)|\mathbf{x}_i]$$

$$= 0 + \text{Cov}[c_i\exp(\mathbf{x}_{it}\boldsymbol{\beta}),c_i\exp(\mathbf{x}_{ir}\boldsymbol{\beta})|\mathbf{x}_i]$$

$$= \tau^2\exp(\mathbf{x}_{it}\boldsymbol{\beta})\exp(\mathbf{x}_{ir}\boldsymbol{\beta}).$$

So, under H_0, $\text{Var}(\mathbf{y}_i|\mathbf{x}_i)$ depends on α, $\boldsymbol{\beta}$, and τ^2, all of which we can estimate. It is natural to use a score test of H_0: $\boldsymbol{\gamma} = \mathbf{0}$. First, obtain consistent estimators $\tilde{\tilde{\alpha}}$, $\tilde{\tilde{\boldsymbol{\beta}}}$ by, say, pooled Poisson QMLE. Let $\tilde{\tilde{y}}_{it} = \exp(\tilde{\tilde{\alpha}} + \mathbf{x}_{it}\tilde{\tilde{\boldsymbol{\beta}}})$ and $\tilde{\tilde{u}}_{it} = y_{it} - \tilde{\tilde{y}}_{it}$. A consistent estimator of τ^2 can be obtained from a simple pooled regression, through the origin, of

$$\tilde{\tilde{u}}_{it}^2 - \tilde{\tilde{y}}_{it} \text{ on } [\exp(\mathbf{x}_{it}\tilde{\tilde{\boldsymbol{\beta}}})]^2, \; t = 1,\ldots,T; \; i = 1,\ldots,N.$$

Call this estimator $\tilde{\tau}^2$. This works because, under H_0, $E(u_{it}^2|\mathbf{x}_i) = E(u_{it}^2|\mathbf{x}_{it}) = \exp(\alpha + \mathbf{x}_{it}\boldsymbol{\beta}) + \tau^2[\exp(\mathbf{x}_{it}\boldsymbol{\beta})]^2$, where $u_{it} \equiv y_{it} - E(y_{it}|\mathbf{x}_{it})$. [We could also use the many covariance terms in estimating τ^2 because $\tau^2 = E\{[u_{it}^2/\exp(\mathbf{x}_{it}\boldsymbol{\beta})][u_{ir}^2/\exp(\mathbf{x}_{ir}\boldsymbol{\beta})]\}$, all $t \neq r$.

Next, we construct the $T \times T$ weighting matrix for observation i, as in

Section 19.6.3; see also Problem 12.11. The matrix $\mathbf{W}_i(\tilde{\boldsymbol{\delta}}) = \mathbf{W}(\mathbf{x}_i,\tilde{\boldsymbol{\delta}})$ has diagonal elements $\tilde{\tilde{y}}_{it} + \tilde{\tau}^2[\exp(\mathbf{x}_{it}\tilde{\tilde{\boldsymbol{\beta}}})]^2$, $t = 1,\ldots,T$ and off-diagonal elements $\tilde{\tau}^2\exp(\mathbf{x}_{it}\tilde{\tilde{\boldsymbol{\beta}}})\exp(\mathbf{x}_{ir}\tilde{\tilde{\boldsymbol{\beta}}})$, $t \neq r$. Let $\tilde{\alpha}$, $\tilde{\boldsymbol{\beta}}$ be the solutions to

$$\min_{\alpha,\boldsymbol{\beta}} (1/2)\sum_{i=1}^{N}[\mathbf{y}_i - \mathbf{m}(\mathbf{x}_i,\alpha,\boldsymbol{\beta})]'[\mathbf{W}_i(\tilde{\boldsymbol{\delta}})]^{-1}[\mathbf{y}_i - \mathbf{m}(\mathbf{x}_i,\alpha,\boldsymbol{\beta})],$$

where $\mathbf{m}(\mathbf{x}_i,\alpha,\boldsymbol{\beta})$ has t^{th} element $\exp(\alpha + \mathbf{x}_{it}\boldsymbol{\beta})$. Since $\text{Var}(\mathbf{y}_i|\mathbf{x}_i) = \mathbf{W}(\mathbf{x}_i,\boldsymbol{\delta})$, this is a MWNLS estimation problem with a correctly specified conditional variance matrix. Therefore, as shown in Problem 12.1, the conditional information matrix equality holds. To obtain the score test in the context of MWNLS, we need the score of the comditional mean function, with respect to all parameters, evaluated under H_0. Then, we can apply equation (12.69).

Let $\boldsymbol{\theta} \equiv (\alpha,\boldsymbol{\beta}',\boldsymbol{\gamma}')'$ denote the full vector of conditional mean parameters, where we want to test H_0: $\boldsymbol{\gamma} = \mathbf{0}$. The unrestricted conditional mean function, for each t, is

$$\mu_t(\mathbf{x}_i,\boldsymbol{\theta}) = \exp(\alpha + \mathbf{x}_{it}\boldsymbol{\beta} + \bar{\mathbf{x}}_i\boldsymbol{\gamma}).$$

Taking the gradient and evaluating it under H_0 gives

$$\nabla_\theta\mu_t(\mathbf{x}_i,\tilde{\boldsymbol{\theta}}) = \exp(\tilde{\alpha} + \mathbf{x}_{it}\tilde{\boldsymbol{\beta}})[1,\mathbf{x}_{it},\bar{\mathbf{x}}_i],$$

which would be $1 \times (1 + 2K)$ without any redundancies in $\bar{\mathbf{x}}_i$. Usually, $\mathbf{x}_{it}$ would contain year dummies or other aggregate effects, and these would be dropped from $\bar{\mathbf{x}}_i$; we do not make that explicit here. Let $\nabla_\theta\boldsymbol{\mu}(\mathbf{x}_i,\tilde{\boldsymbol{\theta}})$ denote the $T \times (1 + 2K)$ matrix obtained from stacking the $\nabla_\theta\mu_t(\mathbf{x}_i,\tilde{\boldsymbol{\theta}})$ from $t = 1,\ldots,T$. Then the score function, evaluate at the null estimates $\tilde{\boldsymbol{\theta}} \equiv (\tilde{\alpha},\tilde{\boldsymbol{\beta}}',\tilde{\boldsymbol{\gamma}}')'$, is

$$\mathbf{s}_i(\tilde{\boldsymbol{\theta}}) = -\nabla_\theta\boldsymbol{\mu}(\mathbf{x}_i,\tilde{\boldsymbol{\theta}})'[\mathbf{W}_i(\tilde{\boldsymbol{\delta}})]^{-1}\tilde{\mathbf{u}}_i,$$

where $\tilde{\mathbf{u}}_i$ is the $T \times 1$ vector with elements $\tilde{u}_{it} \equiv y_{it} - \exp(\tilde{\alpha} + \mathbf{x}_{it}\tilde{\boldsymbol{\beta}})$. The estimated conditional Hessian, under H_0, is

$$\tilde{\mathbf{A}} = N^{-1}\sum_{i=1}^{N}\nabla_\theta\boldsymbol{\mu}(\mathbf{x}_i,\tilde{\boldsymbol{\theta}})'[\mathbf{W}_i(\tilde{\boldsymbol{\delta}})]^{-1}\nabla_\theta\boldsymbol{\mu}(\mathbf{x}_i,\tilde{\boldsymbol{\theta}}),$$

a $(1 + 2K) \times (1 + 2K)$ matrix. The score or LM statistic is therefore

$$LM = \left(\sum_{i=1}^{N} \nabla_\theta \boldsymbol{\mu}(\mathbf{x}_i,\tilde{\boldsymbol{\theta}})'[\mathbf{W}_i(\tilde{\boldsymbol{\delta}})]^{-1}\tilde{\mathbf{u}}_i\right)' \left(\sum_{i=1}^{N} \nabla_\theta \boldsymbol{\mu}(\mathbf{x}_i,\tilde{\boldsymbol{\theta}})'[\mathbf{W}_i(\tilde{\boldsymbol{\delta}})]^{-1}\nabla_\theta \boldsymbol{\mu}(\mathbf{x}_i,\tilde{\boldsymbol{\theta}})\right)^{-1} \cdot \left(\sum_{i=1}^{N} \nabla_\theta \boldsymbol{\mu}(\mathbf{x}_i,\tilde{\boldsymbol{\theta}})'[\mathbf{W}_i(\tilde{\boldsymbol{\delta}})]^{-1}\tilde{\mathbf{u}}_i\right).$$

Under H_0, and the full set of maintained assumptions, $LM \overset{a}{\sim} \chi^2_K$. If only $J < K$ elements of $\bar{\mathbf{x}}_i$ are included, then the degrees of freedom gets reduced to J.

In practice, we might want a robust form of the test that does not require $\text{Var}(\mathbf{y}_i|\mathbf{x}_i) = \mathbf{W}(\mathbf{x}_i,\boldsymbol{\delta})$ under H_0, where $\mathbf{W}(\mathbf{x}_i,\boldsymbol{\delta})$ is the matrix described above. This variance matrix was derived under pretty restrictive assumptions. A fully robust form is given in equation (12.68), where $\mathbf{s}_i(\tilde{\boldsymbol{\theta}})$ and $\tilde{\mathbf{A}}$ are as given above, and $\tilde{\mathbf{B}} = N^{-1}\sum_{i=1}^{N} \mathbf{s}_i(\tilde{\boldsymbol{\theta}})\mathbf{s}_i(\tilde{\boldsymbol{\theta}})'$. Since the restrictions are written as $\boldsymbol{\gamma} = \mathbf{0}$, we take $\mathbf{c}(\boldsymbol{\theta}) = \boldsymbol{\gamma}$, and so $\tilde{\mathbf{C}} = [\mathbf{0}|\mathbf{I}_K]$, where the zero matrix is $K \times (1 + K)$.

c. If we assume (19.60), (19.61) and $c_i = a_i\exp(\alpha + \bar{\mathbf{x}}_i\boldsymbol{\gamma})$ where $a_i|\mathbf{x}_i \sim \text{Gamma}(\delta,\delta)$, then things are even easier -- at least if we have software that estimates random effects Poisson models. Under these assumptions, we have

$$y_{it}|\mathbf{x}_i,a_i \sim \text{Poisson}[a_i\exp(\alpha + \mathbf{x}_{it}\boldsymbol{\beta} + \bar{\mathbf{x}}_i\boldsymbol{\gamma})]$$

y_{it}, y_{ir} are independent conditional on $(\mathbf{x}_i,a_i)$, $t \neq r$

$a_i|\mathbf{x}_i \sim \text{Gamma}(\delta,\delta)$.

In other words, the full set of random effects Poisson assumptions holds, but where the mean function in the Poisson distribution is $a_i\exp(\alpha + \mathbf{x}_{it}\boldsymbol{\beta} + \bar{\mathbf{x}}_i\boldsymbol{\gamma})$. In practice, we just add the (nonredundant elements of) $\bar{\mathbf{x}}_i$ in each time period, along with a constant and $\mathbf{x}_{it}$, and carry out a random effects Poisson analysis. We can test H_0: $\boldsymbol{\gamma} = \mathbf{0}$ using the LR, Wald, or score approaches. Any of these wouldbe asymptotically efficient. But none is robust because we have used a full distribution for $\mathbf{y}_i$ given $\mathbf{x}_i$.

19.7. a. First, for each t, the density of y_{it} given $(\mathbf{x}_i = \mathbf{x},\ c_i = c)$ is

$$f(y_t|\mathbf{x},c;\boldsymbol{\beta}_o) = \exp[-c\cdot m(\mathbf{x}_t,\boldsymbol{\beta}_o)][c\cdot m(\mathbf{x}_t,\boldsymbol{\beta}_o)]^{y_t}/y_t!,\quad y_t = 0,1,2,\ldots.$$

Multiplying these together gives the joint density of $(y_{i1},\ldots,y_{iT})$ given $(\mathbf{x}_i = \mathbf{x},\ c_i = c)$. Taking the log, plugging in the observed data for observation i, and dropping the factorial term gives

$$\sum_{t=1}^{T}\{-c_i m(\mathbf{x}_{it},\boldsymbol{\beta}) + y_{it}[\log(c_i) + \log(m(\mathbf{x}_{it},\boldsymbol{\beta}))]\}.$$

b. Taking the derivative of $\ell_i(c_i,\boldsymbol{\beta})$ with respect to c_i, setting the result to zero, and rerranging gives

$$(n_i/c_i) = \sum_{t=1}^{T} m(\mathbf{x}_{it},\boldsymbol{\beta}).$$

Letting $c_i(\boldsymbol{\beta})$ denote the solution as a function of $\boldsymbol{\beta}$, we have $c_i(\boldsymbol{\beta}) = n_i/M_i(\boldsymbol{\beta})$, where $M_i(\boldsymbol{\beta}) \equiv \sum_{t=1}^{T} m(\mathbf{x}_{it},\boldsymbol{\beta})$. The second order sufficient condition for a maximum is easily seen to hold.

c. Plugging the solution from part b into $\ell_i(c_i,\boldsymbol{\beta})$ gives

$$\begin{aligned}\ell_i[c_i(\boldsymbol{\beta}),\boldsymbol{\beta}] &= -[n_i/M_i(\boldsymbol{\beta})]M_i(\boldsymbol{\beta}) + \sum_{t=1}^{T} y_{it}\{\log[n_i/M_i(\boldsymbol{\beta})] + \log[m(\mathbf{x}_{it},\boldsymbol{\beta})]\\ &= -n_i + n_i\log(n_i) + \sum_{t=1}^{T} y_{it}\{\log[m(\mathbf{x}_{it},\boldsymbol{\beta})/M_i(\boldsymbol{\beta})]\\ &= \sum_{t=1}^{T} y_{it}\log[p_t(\mathbf{x}_i,\boldsymbol{\beta})] + (n_i - 1)\log(n_i),\end{aligned}$$

because $p_t(\mathbf{x}_i,\boldsymbol{\beta}) = m(\mathbf{x}_{it},\boldsymbol{\beta})/M_i(\boldsymbol{\beta})$ [see equation (19.66)].

d. From part c it follows that if we maximize $\sum_{i=1}^{N}\ell_i(c_i,\boldsymbol{\beta})$ with respect to $(c_1,\ldots,c_N)$ -- that is, we concentrate out these parameters -- we get exactly $\sum_{i=1}^{N}\ell_i[c_i(\boldsymbol{\beta}),\boldsymbol{\beta}]$. But, except for the term $\sum_{i=1}^{N}(n_i - 1)\log(n_i)$ -- which does not depend on $\boldsymbol{\beta}$ -- this is exactly the conditional log likelihood for the conditional multinomial distribution obtained in Section 19.6.4. Therefore, this is another case where treating the c_i as parameters to be estimated leads us to a $\sqrt{N}$-consistent, asymptotically normal estimator of $\boldsymbol{\beta}_o$.

19.9. I will use the following Stata output. I first converted the dependent variable to be in [0,1], rather than [0,100]. This is required to easily use the "glm" command in Stata.

```
. replace atndrte = atndrte/100
(680 real changes made)

. reg atndrte ACT priGPA frosh soph

      Source |       SS       df       MS              Number of obs =     680
-------------+------------------------------           F(  4,   675) =   72.92
       Model |  5.95396289     4  1.48849072           Prob > F      =  0.0000
    Residual |  13.7777696   675  .020411511           R-squared     =  0.3017
-------------+------------------------------           Adj R-squared =  0.2976
       Total |  19.7317325   679  .029059989           Root MSE      =  .14287

------------------------------------------------------------------------------
     atndrte |      Coef.   Std. Err.      t    P>|t|     [95% Conf. Interval]
-------------+----------------------------------------------------------------
         ACT |  -.0169202    .001681   -10.07   0.000    -.0202207   -.0136196
      priGPA |   .1820163   .0112156    16.23   0.000     .1599947    .2040379
       frosh |   .0517097   .0173019     2.99   0.003     .0177377    .0856818
        soph |   .0110085    .014485     0.76   0.448    -.0174327    .0394496
       _cons |   .7087769   .0417257    16.99   0.000     .6268492    .7907046
------------------------------------------------------------------------------

. predict atndrteh
(option xb assumed; fitted values)

. sum atndrteh

    Variable |     Obs        Mean    Std. Dev.       Min        Max
-------------+-----------------------------------------------------
    atndrteh |     680    .8170956    .0936415   .4846666   1.086443

. count if atndrteh > 1
  12

. glm atndrte ACT priGPA frosh soph, family(binomial) sca(x2)
note: atndrte has non-integer values

Iteration 0:   log likelihood = -226.64509
Iteration 1:   log likelihood = -223.64983
Iteration 2:   log likelihood = -223.64937
Iteration 3:   log likelihood = -223.64937

Generalized linear models                          No. of obs      =       680
Optimization     : ML: Newton-Raphson              Residual df     =       675
                                                   Scale param     =         1
```

```
Deviance         =  285.7371358                   (1/df) Deviance =  .4233143
Pearson          =  85.57283238                   (1/df) Pearson  =  .1267746

Variance function: V(u) = u*(1-u)                 [Bernoulli]
Link function    : g(u) = ln(u/(1-u))             [Logit]
Standard errors  : OIM

Log likelihood   = -223.6493665                   AIC             =  .6724981
BIC              =  253.1266718

------------------------------------------------------------------------------
     atndrte |      Coef.   Std. Err.      z    P>|z|     [95% Conf. Interval]
-------------+----------------------------------------------------------------
         ACT |  -.1113802   .0113217    -9.84   0.000    -.1335703   -.0891901
      priGPA |   1.244375   .0771321    16.13   0.000     1.093199    1.395552
       frosh |   .3899318    .113436     3.44   0.001     .1676013    .6122622
        soph |   .0928127   .0944066     0.98   0.326    -.0922209    .2778463
       _cons |   .7621699   .2859966     2.66   0.008      .201627    1.322713
------------------------------------------------------------------------------
(Standard errors scaled using square root of Pearson X2-based dispersion)

. di (.1268)^2
.01607824

. di exp(.7622 - .1114*30 + 1.244*3)/(1 + exp(.7622 - .1114*30 + 1.244*3))
.75991253

. di exp(.7622 - .1114*25 + 1.244*3)/(1 + exp(.7622 - .1114*25 + 1.244*3))
.84673249

. di .760 - .847
-.087

. predict atndh
(option mu assumed; predicted mean atndrte)

. sum atndh

    Variable |     Obs        Mean    Std. Dev.       Min        Max
-------------+-----------------------------------------------------
       atndh |     680    .8170956    .0965356   .3499525   .9697185

. corr atndrte atndh
(obs=680)

             | atndrte   atndh
-------------+------------------
     atndrte |   1.0000
       atndh |   0.5725   1.0000


. di (.5725)^2
```

.32775625

a. The coefficient on *ACT* means that if the ACT score increases by 5 points -- more than a one standard deviation increase -- then the attendance rate is estimated to fall by about .017(5) = .085, or 8.5 percentage points. The coefficient on *priGPA* means that if prior GPA is one point higher, the attendance rate is predicted to be about .182 higher, or 18.2 percentage points. Naturally, these changes do not always make sense when starting at extreme values of *atndrte*. There are 12 fitted values greater than one; none less than zero.

b. The GLM standard errors are given in the output. Note that $\hat{\sigma} \approx .0161$. In other words, the usual MLE standard errors, obtained, say, from the expected Hessian of the quasi-log likelihood, are much too *large*. The standard errors that account for $\sigma^2 < 1$ are given by the GLM output. (If you omit the "sca(x2)" option in the "glm" command, you will get the usual MLE standard errors.)

c. Since the coefficient on *ACT* is negative, we know that an increase in ACT score, holding year and prior GPA fixed, actually reduces predicted attendance rate. The calculation shows that when *ACT* increases from 25 to 30, the estimated fall in *atndrte* is about .087, or about 8.7 percentage points. This is very similar to that found using the linear model.

d. The *R*-squared for the linear model is about .302. For the logistic functional form, I computed the squared correlation between $atndrte_i$ and $\hat{E}(atndrte_i|\mathbf{x}_i)$. This *R*-squared is about .328, and so the logistic functional form does fit better than the linear model. And, remember that the parameters in the logistic functional form are not chosen to maximize an *R*-squared.

19.11. a. For each t, the density is

$$f_t(y_t|\mathbf{x}_i,c_i) = \exp(-c_i m_{it}) m_{it}^{y_t}/y_t!, \quad y_t = 0,1,2,\ldots.$$

Under the conditional independence assumption, the joint density of $(y_{i1},\ldots,y_{iT})$ given $(\mathbf{x}_i,c_i)$ is

$$f(y_1,\ldots,y_T|\mathbf{x}_i,c_i) = \prod_{t=1}^{T} [\exp(-c_i m_{it})(c_i m_{it})^{y_t}/y_t!]$$

$$= \left(\prod_{t=1}^{T} m_{it}^{y_t}/y_t!\right) c_i^s \exp(-c_i M_i),$$

where $M_i \equiv m_{i1} + \ldots + m_{iT}$ and $s = y_1 + \ldots + y_T$, for all nonnegative integers $\{y_t: t = 1,\ldots,T\}$.

b. To obtain the density of $(y_{i1},\ldots,y_{iT})$ given $\mathbf{x}_i$, say $g(y_1,\ldots,y_T|\mathbf{x}_i)$, we integrate out with respect to the distribution of c_i (since c_i is independent of $\mathbf{x}_i$). Therefore,

$$g(y_1,\ldots,y_T|\mathbf{x}_i) = \left(\prod_{t=1}^{T} m_{it}^{y_t}/y_t!\right) \int_0^\infty c^s \exp(-cM_i)[\delta^\delta/\Gamma(\delta)]c^{\delta-1}\exp(-\delta c)dc.$$

Next, we follow the hint, noting that the general Gamma(α,β) density has the form $h(c) = [\beta^\alpha/\Gamma(\alpha)]c^{\alpha-1}\exp(-\beta c)$. Now 1

$$\int_0^\infty \exp(-cM_i)[\delta^\delta/\Gamma(\delta)]c^{\delta-1}\exp(-\delta c)dc = \int_0^\infty [\delta^\delta/\Gamma(\delta)]c^{(s+\delta-1)}\exp[-(M_i + \delta)c]dc$$

$$= [\delta^\delta/\Gamma(\delta)][\Gamma(s + \delta)/(M_i + \delta)^{(s+\delta)}]$$

$$\cdot\int_0^\infty [(M_i + \delta)^{(s+\delta)}/\Gamma(s + \delta)]c^{(s+\delta-1)}\exp[-(M_i + \delta)c]dc,$$

and the integrand is easily seen to be the Gamma$(s + \delta, M_i + \delta)$ density, and so it integrates to unity. Therefore, we have shown

$$g(y_1,\ldots,y_T|\mathbf{x}_i) = \left(\prod_{t=1}^{T} m_{it}^{y_t}/y_t!\right)[\delta^\delta/\Gamma(\delta)][\Gamma(s + \delta)/(M_i + \delta)^{(s+\delta)}]$$

for all nonnegative integers $\{y_t: t = 1,\ldots,T\}$.

SOLUTIONS TO CHAPTER 20 PROBLEMS

20.1. a. In Stata, there are two possibilities for estimating a lognormal duration model: the "cnreg" command (where we use the log of the duration as the response), and the "streg" command (where we specify "lognormal" as the distribution). The streg command is more flexible (and I use it in the next problem), but here I give the cnreg output. The value of the log likelihood is indeed -1,597.06.

```
. cnreg ldurat workprg priors tserved felon alcohol drugs black married educ
age, censored(cens)

Censored normal regression                        Number of obs   =       1445
                                                  LR chi2(10)     =     166.74
                                                  Prob > chi2     =     0.0000
Log likelihood =  -1597.059                       Pseudo R2       =     0.0496

------------------------------------------------------------------------------
      ldurat |      Coef.   Std. Err.       t    P>|t|     [95% Conf. Interval]
-------------+----------------------------------------------------------------
     workprg |  -.0625715   .1200369     -0.52   0.602    -.2980382    .1728951
      priors |  -.1372529   .0214587     -6.40   0.000    -.1793466   -.0951592
     tserved |  -.0193305   .0029779     -6.49   0.000    -.0251721    -.013489
       felon |   .4439947   .1450865      3.06   0.002     .1593903    .7285991
     alcohol |  -.6349092   .1442166     -4.40   0.000    -.9178072   -.3520113
       drugs |  -.2981602   .1327355     -2.25   0.025    -.5585367   -.0377837
       black |  -.5427179   .1174428     -4.62   0.000    -.7730958     -.31234
     married |   .3406837   .1398431      2.44   0.015      .066365    .6150024
        educ |   .0229196   .0253974      0.90   0.367    -.0269004    .0727395
         age |   .0039103   .0006062      6.45   0.000     .0027211    .0050994
       _cons |   4.099386    .347535     11.80   0.000     3.417655    4.781117
-------------+----------------------------------------------------------------
         _se |    1.81047   .0623022           (Ancillary parameter)
------------------------------------------------------------------------------

  Obs. summary:         552     uncensored observations
                        893 right-censored observations

. di 4.10 - .137*1.43 - .019*19.18 + .444 - .635 - .298 + .023*9.70 +
.0039*345.44
4.620986
```

So $\bar{\mathbf{x}}\hat{\beta}$ = 4.62, and this is where the hazard is evaluated for part b.

b. I graphed the hazard using the following Stata commands, and I also looked at the estimated hazard to determine the maximum value:

```
. range t .1 81 1000
obs was 0, now 1000

. * Evaluate the hazard at the specified values of the covariates:

. gen haz = (normden((log(t) - 4.62)/1.81)/(1 - normprob((log(t) -
4.62)/1.81)))/(1.81*t)

. sum haz

    Variable |     Obs        Mean    Std. Dev.       Min         Max
-------------+-----------------------------------------------------
         haz |    1000     .007394    .0020272    .0014685    .011625

. graph haz t, s(.) c(l) ylabel xlabel(5,10,20,30,50,80)

. * This graph gives the "big" picture.  A command such as

. graph haz t if t < 12, s(.) c(l) ylabel xlabel(1,2,3,4,5,6,9,12)

. * gives a better picture of the hazard for the first 12 months.

. * Listing the hazard values, maximum is at about t = 4.5, with a
. * hazard of about .01162

. * The hazard then falls to about .005 at t = 81.
```

The estimated hazard initially increases, until about t^* = 4.5, where it reaches the value .0016 (roughly). It then falls, until in levels off at about .005 at t = 81. It may make sense that there are startup costs to becoming involved in crime upon release, so that the instantaneous probility of recidivism initially increases (for about four and one-half months). After that, the hazard falls monotonically, although it does not become zero at the largest observed duration, 81 months.

c. Using the uncensored observations gives:

```
. reg ldurat workprg priors tserved felon alcohol drugs black married educ age
if ~cens

      Source |       SS       df       MS              Number of obs =     552
-------------+------------------------------           F( 10,   541) =    4.13
       Model |  33.7647818    10  3.37647818           Prob > F      =  0.0000
    Residual |  442.796158   541  .818477187           R-squared     =  0.0709
-------------+------------------------------           Adj R-squared =  0.0537
       Total |   476.56094   551  .864901888           Root MSE      =   .9047

------------------------------------------------------------------------------
      ldurat |      Coef.   Std. Err.      t    P>|t|     [95% Conf. Interval]
-------------+----------------------------------------------------------------
     workprg |   .0923415   .0827407     1.12   0.265    -.0701909     .254874
      priors |  -.0483627   .0140418    -3.44   0.001    -.0759459   -.0207795
     tserved |  -.0067761    .001938    -3.50   0.001     -.010583   -.0029692
       felon |   .1187173    .103206     1.15   0.251    -.0840163    .3214508
     alcohol |  -.2180496   .0970583    -2.25   0.025     -.408707   -.0273923
       drugs |   .0177737   .0891098     0.20   0.842    -.1572699    .1928172
       black |  -.0008505   .0822071    -0.01   0.992    -.1623348    .1606338
     married |   .2388998   .0987305     2.42   0.016     .0449577    .4328419
        educ |  -.0194548   .0189254    -1.03   0.304    -.0566312    .0177215
         age |   .0005345   .0004228     1.26   0.207     -.000296    .0013651
       _cons |   3.001025   .2438418    12.31   0.000     2.522032    3.480017
------------------------------------------------------------------------------
```

The *alcohol* and *drugs* coefficients are much smaller in magnitude, with the latter actually changing signs and becoming very insignificant.

d. Treating the censored durations as if they are uncensored gives:

```
. reg ldurat workprg priors tserved felon alcohol drugs black married educ age

      Source |       SS       df       MS              Number of obs =    1445
-------------+------------------------------           F( 10,  1434) =   17.49
       Model |  134.350088    10  13.4350088           Prob > F      =  0.0000
    Residual |  1101.29155  1434  .767985737           R-squared     =  0.1087
-------------+------------------------------           Adj R-squared =  0.1025
       Total |  1235.64163  1444  .855707503           Root MSE      =  .87635

------------------------------------------------------------------------------
      ldurat |      Coef.   Std. Err.      t    P>|t|     [95% Conf. Interval]
-------------+----------------------------------------------------------------
     workprg |    .008758   .0489457     0.18   0.858    -.0872548    .1047709
      priors |  -.0590636   .0091717    -6.44   0.000     -.077055   -.0410722
     tserved |  -.0094002   .0013006    -7.23   0.000    -.0119516   -.0068488
       felon |   .1785428   .0584077     3.06   0.002     .0639691    .2931165
```

```
     alcohol |  -.2628009   .0598092    -4.39   0.000    -.3801238   -.1454779
       drugs |  -.0907441   .0549372    -1.65   0.099      -.19851    .0170217
       black |  -.1791014   .0474354    -3.78   0.000    -.2721516   -.0860511
     married |   .1344326   .0554341     2.43   0.015      .025692    .2431732
        educ |   .0053914   .0099256     0.54   0.587    -.0140789    .0248618
         age |   .0013258   .0002249     5.90   0.000     .0008847    .0017669
       _cons |   3.569168    .137962    25.87   0.000     3.298539    3.839797
------------------------------------------------------------------------------
```

Again, the estimated alcohol and drug effects are attenuated toward zero, although not as much as when we drop all of the censored observations. In any case, we should use censored regression analysis.

20.2. a. For this question, I use the "streg" command. The "nohr" option means that the $\hat{\beta}_j$ in (20.25) are reported, rather than $\exp(\hat{\beta}_j)$.

```
. gen failed = ~cens

. stset durat, failure(failed)

. streg super rules workprg priors tserved felon alcohol drugs black married
educ age, dist(weibull) nohr

         failure _d:  failed
   analysis time _t:  durat


Fitting constant-only model:

Iteration 0:   log likelihood = -1739.8944
Iteration 1:   log likelihood = -1716.1367
Iteration 2:   log likelihood = -1715.7712
Iteration 3:   log likelihood = -1715.7711

Fitting full model:

Iteration 0:   log likelihood = -1715.7711
Iteration 1:   log likelihood = -1663.4495
Iteration 2:   log likelihood = -1631.2451
Iteration 3:   log likelihood = -1630.5206
Iteration 4:   log likelihood =  -1630.517
Iteration 5:   log likelihood =  -1630.517

Weibull regression -- log relative-hazard form

No. of subjects =         1445                  Number of obs   =       1445
```

```
No. of failures =          552
Time at risk    =        80013
                                                   LR chi2(12)      =     170.51
Log likelihood  =    -1630.517                     Prob > chi2      =     0.0000

------------------------------------------------------------------------------
          _t |      Coef.   Std. Err.      z    P>|z|     [95% Conf. Interval]
-------------+----------------------------------------------------------------
       super |  -.0078523   .0979703    -0.08   0.936    -.1998705     .184166
       rules |   .0386963   .0166936     2.32   0.020     .0059774    .0714151
     workprg |   .1039345   .0914158     1.14   0.256    -.0752371    .2831061
      priors |    .086349   .0136871     6.31   0.000     .0595227    .1131752
     tserved |   .0116506    .001933     6.03   0.000     .0078621    .0154392
       felon |  -.3111997   .1074569    -2.90   0.004    -.5218114   -.1005879
     alcohol |   .4510744   .1059953     4.26   0.000     .2433275    .6588214
       drugs |   .2623752   .0982732     2.67   0.008     .0697632    .4549872
       black |    .458454   .0884443     5.18   0.000     .2851063    .6318016
     married |  -.1563693     .10941    -1.43   0.153    -.3708088    .0580703
        educ |  -.0246717    .019442    -1.27   0.204    -.0627772    .0134339
         age |  -.0035167   .0005306    -6.63   0.000    -.0045567   -.0024767
       _cons |  -3.466394   .3105515   -11.16   0.000    -4.075064   -2.857724
-------------+----------------------------------------------------------------
       /ln_p |  -.2142514    .038881    -5.51   0.000    -.2904567   -.1380461
-------------+----------------------------------------------------------------
           p |   .8071455   .0313826                      .7479219    .8710585
         1/p |   1.238934   .0481709                      1.148028    1.337038
------------------------------------------------------------------------------
```

Whether or not a release was "supervised" has no effect on the hazard, whereas, not surprisingly, a history of rules violation while in prison does increase the recidivism hazard.

b. The lognormal estimates are

```
. streg super rules workprg priors tserved felon alcohol drugs black married
educ age, dist(lognormal)

         failure _d:  failed
   analysis time _t:  durat

Fitting constant-only model:

Iteration 0:   log likelihood =   -1999.58
Iteration 1:   log likelihood =  -1695.747
Iteration 2:   log likelihood = -1681.0153
Iteration 3:   log likelihood = -1680.4273
Iteration 4:   log likelihood =  -1680.427
```

```
Iteration 5:   log likelihood =  -1680.427

Fitting full model:

Iteration 0:   log likelihood =  -1680.427
Iteration 1:   log likelihood = -1606.6507
Iteration 2:   log likelihood = -1594.3174
Iteration 3:   log likelihood = -1594.1684
Iteration 4:   log likelihood = -1594.1683

Log-normal regression -- accelerated failure-time form

No. of subjects =         1445                     Number of obs   =      1445
No. of failures =          552
Time at risk    =        80013
                                                   LR chi2(12)     =    172.52
Log likelihood  =   -1594.1683                     Prob > chi2     =    0.0000

------------------------------------------------------------------------------
          _t |      Coef.   Std. Err.      z    P>|z|     [95% Conf. Interval]
-------------+----------------------------------------------------------------
       super |   .0328411   .1280452     0.26   0.798    -.2181229    .2838052
       rules |  -.0644316   .0276338    -2.33   0.020    -.1185929   -.0102703
     workprg |  -.0883445   .1208173    -0.73   0.465     -.325142     .148453
      priors |  -.1341294   .0215358    -6.23   0.000    -.1763388   -.0919199
     tserved |  -.0156015   .0033872    -4.61   0.000    -.0222403   -.0089628
       felon |   .4345115   .1460924     2.97   0.003     .1481757    .7208473
     alcohol |  -.6415683   .1439736    -4.46   0.000    -.9237515   -.3593851
       drugs |  -.2785464   .1326321    -2.10   0.036    -.5385007   -.0185922
       black |   -.549173   .1172236    -4.68   0.000    -.7789271   -.3194189
     married |   .3308228   .1399244     2.36   0.018      .056576    .6050695
        educ |   .0234116   .0253302     0.92   0.355    -.0262347     .073058
         age |   .0036626   .0006117     5.99   0.000     .0024637    .0048614
       _cons |   4.173851   .3580214    11.66   0.000     3.472142     4.87556
-------------+----------------------------------------------------------------
     /ln_sig |   .5904906    .034399    17.17   0.000     .5230698    .6579114
-------------+----------------------------------------------------------------
       sigma |   1.804874   .0620858                      1.687199    1.930755
------------------------------------------------------------------------------
```

The estimated coefficients on *super* and *rules* are consistent with the Weibull results, since a decrease in $\mathbf{x}\boldsymbol{\delta}$ tends to shift up the hazard in the lognormal case.

c. The coefficient from the lognormal model directly estimates the proportional effect of rules violations on the duration. So, one more rules violation reduces the duration by about 6.4%. To obtain the comparable Weibull estimate, we need $-\hat{\beta}_{rules}/\hat{\alpha} = -.0387/.807 \approx -.048$, or about a 4.8% reduction for each rules violation. This is a bit smaller than the lognormal estimate.

20.3. a. If all durations in the sample are censored, $d_i = 0$ for all i, and so the log-likelihood is $\sum_{i=1}^{N} \log[1 - F(t_i|\mathbf{x}_i;\boldsymbol{\theta})] = \sum_{i=1}^{N} \log[1 - F(c_i|\mathbf{x}_i;\boldsymbol{\theta})]$

b. For the Weibull case, $F(t|\mathbf{x}_i;\boldsymbol{\theta}) = 1 - \exp[-\exp(\mathbf{x}_i\boldsymbol{\beta})t^{\alpha}]$, and so the log-likelihood is $-\sum_{i=1}^{N} \exp(\mathbf{x}_i\boldsymbol{\beta})c_i^{\alpha}$.

c. Without covariates, the Weibull log-likelihood with complete censoring is $-\exp(\beta)\sum_{i=1}^{N} c_i^{\alpha}$. Since $c_i > 0$, we can choose any $\alpha > 0$ so that $\sum_{i=1}^{N} c_i^{\alpha} > 0$. But then, for any $\alpha > 0$, the log-likelihood is maximized by minimizing $\exp(\beta)$ across β. But as $\beta \to -\infty$, $\exp(\beta) \to 0$. So plugging any value α into the log-likelihood will lead to β getting more and more negative without bound. So no two real numbers for α and β maximize the log likelihood.

d. It is not possible to estimate duration models from flow data when all durations are right censored.

20.5. a. $P(t_i^* \le t|\mathbf{x}_i,a_i,c_i,s_i = 1) = P(t_i^* \le t|\mathbf{x}_i,t_i^* > b - a_i) = P(t_i^* \le t,t_i^* > b - a_i|\mathbf{x}_i)/P(t_i^* > b - a_i|\mathbf{x}_i) = P(t_i^* \le t|\mathbf{x}_i)/P(t_i^* > b - a_i|\mathbf{x}_i)$ (because $t < b - a_i$) $= [F(t|\mathbf{x}_i) - F(b - a_i|\mathbf{x}_i)]/[1 - F(b - a_i|\mathbf{x}_i)]$.

b. The derivative of the cdf in part a, with respect to t, is simply $f(t|\mathbf{x}_i)/[1 - F(b - a_i|\mathbf{x}_i)]$.

c. $P(t_i = c_i|\mathbf{x}_i,a_i,c_i,s_i = 1) = P(t_i^* \ge c_i|\mathbf{x}_i,t_i^* > b - a_i) = P(t_i^* \ge c_i|\mathbf{x}_i)/P(t_i^* \ge b - a_i|\mathbf{x}_i)$ (because $c_i > b - a_i$) $= [1 - F(c_i|\mathbf{x}_i)]/[1 - F(b - a_i|\mathbf{x}_i)]$.

20.7. a. We suppress the parameters in the densities. First, by (20.22) and

$D(a_i|c_i,\mathbf{x}_i) = D(a_i|\mathbf{x}_i)$, the density of (a_i,t_i^*) given $(c_i,\mathbf{x}_i)$ does not depend on c_i and is given by $k(a|\mathbf{x}_i)f(t|\mathbf{x}_i)$ for $0 < a < b$ and $0 < t < \infty$. This is also the conditional density of (a_i,t_i) given $(c_i,\mathbf{x}_i)$ when $t < c_i$, that is, the observation is uncensored. For $t = c_i$, the density is $k(a|\mathbf{x}_i)[1 - F(c_i|\mathbf{x}_i)]$, by the usual right censoring argument. Now, the probability of observing the random draw $(a_i,c_i,\mathbf{x}_i,t_i)$, conditional on $\mathbf{x}_i$, is $P(t_i^* \geq b - a_i,\mathbf{x}_i)$, which is exactly (20.32). From the standard result for densities for truncated distributions, the density of (a_i,t_i) given $(c_i,d_i,\mathbf{x}_i)$ and $s_i = 1$ is

$$k(a|\mathbf{x}_i)[f(t|\mathbf{x}_i)]^{d_i}[1 - F(c_i|\mathbf{x}_i)]^{(1 - d_i)}/P(s_i = 1|\mathbf{x}_i),$$

for all combinations (a,t) such that $s_i = 1$. Putting in the parameters and taking the log gives (20.56).

b. We have the usual tradeoff between robustness and efficiency. Using the log likelihood (20.56) results in more efficient estimators provided we have the two densities correctly specified; (20.30) requires us to only specify $f(\cdot|\mathbf{x}_i)$.

20.9. As written, this question is not interesting because the heterogeneity is allowed to take on the value zero. From (20.33), when $v_i = 0$, the hazard is everywhere zero. A better question is to let $0 < \eta < 1$ denote the value of v_i for type A people, and $P(v_i = \eta) = \rho$. Then, if we want $E(v_i) = 1$, the value of v_i for type B people would have to be $(1 - \rho\eta)/(1 - \rho)$. Now, the cdf conditional on $(\mathbf{x},v)$ is $F(t|\mathbf{x},v;\alpha,\boldsymbol{\beta}) = 1 - \exp[-v\exp(\mathbf{x}\boldsymbol{\beta})t^{\alpha}]$. The density conditional on $\mathbf{x}$ is $G(t|\mathbf{x};\alpha,\boldsymbol{\beta},\eta,\rho) = \rho\{1 - \exp[-\eta\exp(\mathbf{x}\boldsymbol{\beta})t^{\alpha}]\} + (1 - \rho)\{1 - \exp[-((1 - \rho\eta)/(1 - \rho))\exp(\mathbf{x}\boldsymbol{\beta})t^{\alpha}]\}$. The density function is

$$g(t|\mathbf{x};\alpha,\boldsymbol{\beta},\eta,\rho) = \rho\eta\exp(\mathbf{x}\boldsymbol{\beta})\alpha t^{\alpha-1}\exp[-\eta\exp(\mathbf{x}\boldsymbol{\beta})t^{\alpha}] +$$
$$(1 - \rho\eta)\exp(\mathbf{x}\boldsymbol{\beta})\alpha t^{\alpha-1}\exp[-((1 - \rho\eta)/(1 - \rho))\exp(\mathbf{x}\boldsymbol{\beta})t^{\alpha}]\}$$

The log-likelihood for each observation i is obtained by taking the log of this density in plugging in $(\mathbf{x}_i, t_i)$.